D1327989

THE PLACE

PLACE

WE CALL HOME

THE PLACE

WE CALL HOME

A History of Fort McMurray,
as its people remember

1778 - 1980

by
IRWIN HUBERMAN

Published by
Historical Book Society of Fort McMurray

Dedication

*To my family who lived
this experience with me.*

Copyright © 2001
by Irwin Huberman
All rights reserved
Printed and bound in Edmonton, Alberta Canada
2nd Printing August 2004
ISBN 0-9689339-1-2

Contents

Acknowledgments

I am deeply grateful to the following who helped make this book possible:

Bert MacKay, a dedicated and passionate McMurrayite, who initiated this dream and brought together a committee to make it a reality.

Frances Jean, a kindred soul, whose love for facts, people, history and weekly newspapers helped sustain my enthusiasm during this long journey.

Bernard Jean, whose decency, courage and love of things spiritual provided me with inspiration.

Anne Young, a former employee, who extracted her revenge by enforcing deadlines. Anne was key in the editing and production process.

Sarah Kelly for her steady editing, footnoting and indexing.

Patte Jordan Huberman for her invaluable editing input and support. Her unsung efforts keeping our lives afloat made this all possible.

Jessica Huberman for her transcribing work.

Art Avery, for his flawless memory and his attention to the project budget.

David and Fern Brooks, Jerry and Elva Bussieres, Diane and Ken Hill whose razor sharp proofreading and questions regarding content helped ensure the credibility of this work.

Ken Hill and Jerry Bussieres for their fact checking and referencing.

Additional thanks are due to Roy Hawkins for sharing almost seventy years of memories.

Thanks as well go to the other members of the Fort McMurray Historical Book Society. They include: Alice Haxton, Bev Ewashko, Ron Morgan

My special thanks to those who granted me interviews and provided anecdotes and memories.

Foreward
By Alex Mair

T. S. Elliot said it best. "We shall not cease from exploration, and the end of all our exploring will be to arrive where we started, and know the place for the first time."

Just how true that statement is becomes apparent as you work your way through this work on Fort McMurray, Alberta.

So much local history writing jolts us into the story with the arrival of railroads, the coming of the first homesteader, or the opening of the first post office.

In this work we begin at the beginning. What were the forces of nature that shaped the land? What happened with the passage of time? All of which unfolds naturally, as we move from page to page. There is nothing pedantic about it; it just sets the stage for what follows.

All too often, authors, when compiling a local history will dwell on the resources of a community above all else. In telling the story of Fort McMurray, this would have been easy and tempting, but the author, with great skill, weaves that part of the history of Fort McMurray into the stories of the people who made things happen over the decades.

This is a story of a geographic location, true, but it's also a story about people. You may never have had the chance to visit Fort McMurray, but before long, as you move from page to page, you realize that you're reading about old friends you've just not had the chance to meet.

Someone once made the point that northerners were often given credit for pushing back the frontier. Then the writer went on to say that in many case, northerners were really people who were so fiercely independent they retreated **behind** the frontier and carried on with their lives until the frontier caught up with them. You may very well meet a few people who fit that description as you enjoy this book.

Let it never be said that in Alberta we don't have a colourful history, or that our history lacks excitement. We have an incredible story to tell, and this work captures it and preserves it for our enjoyment.

Fort McMurray and its natural resources are an international treasure. Many people around the world have read about Fort McMurray, talked about it, and perhaps spent some time there. But no matter what your degree of familiarity may be, read this book, and you will indeed "Know the place for the first time."

Alex Mair was one of Alberta's foremost historian. The author of five books, Mr. Mair narrated local history on CBC. He died just before the first edition was launched.

Preface

This is the story of Fort McMurray. And like any good story, its content is made up of layers, time periods, personalities and interpretations. For most, the story begins with their own arrival in the community. Who knew? From their towns or cities of origin, Fort McMurray or Waterways existed as an obscure dot in the top right corner of a better than average map.

The name itself did not inspire confidence. A fort? Many of us came from bigger places like Edmonton, Calgary, Toronto, Montreal, Vancouver and St. John's. What were we giving up, and what were we getting into?

The story of Fort McMurray has many beginnings. Numerous books written during the 1900s refer to Fort McMurray's history beginning in 1778 with the arrival of the famous rascal and explorer Peter Pond. However, archaeologists and aboriginal elders tell us that life existed long before. Elders speak of a life not found in maps or diaries, but rather in the rich traditions and stories that passed between generations, or were held quietly in the earth's custody until the heavy machinery of Syncrude and Suncor dug them up during the latter part of the 20th century.

Newcomers of today and those of centuries ago share many common threads. They came to Fort McMurray in search of something better. They left family, friends and established communities and chose to pursue opportunity in a place most knew little about. They often shared unexpected results. While for many, it was an economic advantage that attracted them to Fort McMurray, in the end, the earnings they reaped were more personal in nature. Relationships, friendships, stability.

For each of us, life in Fort McMurray began with first impressions. Perhaps it was the weather, or the bumpy trip north, or the first day on the job, or that first night's lodging. If you are like most who lived here at one time, you will read some of these stories and recall a bit of yourself. For others who have never lived or visited Fort McMurray, these stories will speak volumes about the strength and tenacity of the human spirit.

While Fort McMurray's official census graph shows a population rising steadily through the 1900s to about forty-two thousand in 2001, it is believed that during the last third of the century more than three hundred thousand people from Alberta, Canada and beyond passed through. Each of these former and current residents carries a unique story or memory. After all, history is more than a series of places and dates; it is a collection of human experience.

There is much territory for this book to cover. We begin in prehistoric times and end in 1980 with the incorporation of the City of Fort McMurray. The book does not claim to provide an all-inclusive history. Rather, through a series of stories, accounts, gleanings and anecdotes, it pieces together a history focused on people. The book attempts to chronicle the development of the oil sands while following the rise of the community itself.

Information for this volume has been gathered from a variety of sources including books, logs and journals. Exhaustive work was completed during the 1970s by Darlene Comfort who during the 1970s immersed herself in materials obtained from museums, libraries and archives. The thoroughness of her research earns Comfort an unsung place within this history. Her research served as "ground zero" for much historical work which has been completed since. The reader is encouraged to pursue the works of Comfort, J. Joseph Fitzgerald, Barry Ferguson, J.G. MacGregor and others who have delved into specific subjects in considerably more detail than this space allows. A reading list is included at the end of this book.

Many of the stories and memories which occurred after 1920 were gathered through a series of first hand interviews with more than two hundred current and former residents. This book also utilizes excerpts from historical interviews conducted by the *Fort McMurray Express*, a weekly newspaper which I co-founded, and published between 1979-91. During the early 1980s, many residents and colleagues questioned the "newsworthiness" of publishing these "old timer" stories. A decade later, in the preparation of this book, these interviews proved invaluable.

Many of these "old timers" have passed on, but their memories serve as a lesson to us all that while a community's economy may undergo peaks and valleys, the human spirit is precious and eternal. Additional material was gleaned from the pages of the *McMurray Courier*, a spirited weekly newspaper published in the early 1970s by Bernard and Frances Jean. Together, these patches of human experience form the historical quilt that forms the basis for this book.

The circular and often untamed nature of Fort McMurray history touched me one weekend in October 2000, while in Fort McMurray to conduct additional interviews. I noticed "help wanted" signs dotting stores throughout the community. There were lineups at banks and at supermarket checkouts. Newcomers complained about the lack of accommodation and high rents. And it reminded me of my own first days in October 1976 as I began my time in Fort McMurray, living in a back yard holiday trailer, working as a junior reporter with the *Fort McMurray Today*.

As with any history which relies partially on oral traditions, some of these recollections may fall slightly short of absolute accuracy. Every attempt has been made to cross check and verify these stories. These personal recollections have been combined with written records and accounts which together form *The Place We Call Home*.

I would like to acknowledge the efforts by the Fort McMurray Historical Book Society whose ongoing dedication in identifying sources, checking facts, promoting, editing and fund raising helped make this book possible. I also appreciate the fact that without their encouragement and prodding, perhaps this book would have never been written. These are close friends whose encouragement and commitment to Fort McMurray I greatly respect. I would also like to thank the hundreds of Fort McMurrayites whose input and participation continuously added new layers and stories to this history. This book does not claim to be perfect. Many stories and events may have been overlooked, in particular those which occurred during the frantic 1960s and 70s. These stories will provide the foundation for future books.

It is hoped that this work will help all residents find their own place in the history of Fort McMurray. Wherever I travelled in North America during the last two years, I was constantly moved by the strong attachment so many still feel towards the community. Whether their time in McMurray consisted of a few years in the 1930s or 1940s, or whether they were born and raised here, and recently chose to retire elsewhere, I found common themes which will quickly become evident to you, the reader. In many ways, I felt like a maker of necklaces. Scattered throughout North America were beads each representing a disjointed period in time. My role was to run a thread through them.

Fort McMurray has never been good at holding on to its residents. Its graveyard is tiny compared to the numbers of people who have passed through. It is said that a Great Spirit lives within Fort McMurray which directs the same drama. Although the number of actors seems to increase which each performance, the basic plot remains the same. From calm to growth, from growth to calm. Through thousands of years, that has been the circular script which has guided Fort McMurray. For most of us, our incredible experiences in Fort McMurray are unique and frozen in time. Forever, Fort McMurray is *The Place We Call Home*.

And so it begins.

Chapter One:
Simple beginnings

Genesis and the Great Flood:

In the beginning, a Great Flood created the land, rivers and valleys that formed modern day Fort McMurray. About nine thousand nine hundred years ago, a catastrophic surge of water washed across the Clearwater River from the east, sending gravel, minerals and other debris through Fort McMurray to points north.

The fierce flow lasted an estimated seventy-eight days and carved valleys and cliffs along the Clearwater and Athabasca rivers, forming a natural cradle for Fort McMurray's lower townsite and Waterways area. So intense was the flood, that Clearwater River waters submerged large portions of present day Thickwood Heights. The rush was part of a continent wide flush which originated with the glacial Lake Agassiz and extended northwest through present-day Saskatchewan and Alberta, and south along the Mississippi River. Lake Winnipeg is a remnant of the ancient lake which used to flow into Lake Superior. When the link to Lake Superior sealed, huge volumes of water began to surge in all directions.

The "Great Flood" provides an explanation as to why so much gravel exists in and around Fort McMurray, and through the Poplar Creek and Bitumont sites. It also explains why the landscape takes such a dramatic dip from the current suburbs of Beacon Hill and Gregoire Park into the Lower Townsite, and why cuts and cliffs hang over the Athabasca River as it heads north. Recent studies also show a genetic connection between fish which swim through Fort McMurray and many of those inhabiting the Mississippi River.

Archeologists believe that heavy waters continued within the Fort McMurray area for at least another four hundred years. When the waters subsided, a valley emerged which would later provide prime hunting grounds for the region's first pre-historic transients. A series of beaches, coves, bays and inlets were formed along the Athabasca River north of Fort McMurray which would become nesting and hunting grounds for waterfowl and riparian animals. One of the richest areas for birds and animals was located about fifty-five miles north of Fort McMurray in an area now referred to as Aurora. The site is currently being developed by Syncrude Canada Ltd.

Archaeologists tell us that the Aurora area provided an excellent launch point for hunters in pursuit of caribou. It is estimated that the glacial ice sheet ended between fifty-five to ninety-five miles northwest of the Aurora site placing the caribou and other prized prey within striking distance. The Aurora area and the Fort McMurray River junction became a popular summer campground for hunters, fishers and other travellers from the south.

The Great Flood also shaped future oil development and explains why deposits north of Fort McMurray sit so close to the surface, while those south of the community lie substantially deeper. The waters of the Great Flood washed away tons of overburden exposing rich oil deposits to the north. The difference in depth between north and south deposits would stump scientists and entrepreneurs for decades, fuelling a belief that a mother pool of petroleum existed underground between Athabasca Landing and Fort McMurray.

Ancient communities:

So...who were the first McMurrayites?

Based on tens of thousands of artifacts uncovered at the Aurora site, we now know that the area's first part-time residents travelled north along the bulging rivers which had been produced by the Great Flood.

A recent paper released by Nancy Saxberg and Brian Reeves on behalf of Syncrude Canada Ltd. points to results of excavations at thirty archaeological sites in four clusters just northeast of Mildred Lake, and shows that almost ten thousand years ago, the oil sands region was a hotbed of human activity. In 1978-79, excavations conducted in the Cree Burn Lake site determined that a large, complex workshop and campsite existed, which served as a manufacturing centre for hunting and carving tools.

Throughout the 1970s, '80s and '90s, developers such as Northwestern Utilities, Alberta Transportation, Alsands, Oslo, Solvex, Syncrude and Suncor completed limited archaeological excavations. Results, though sporadic, unearthed similar types of carving and hunting tools dating back thousands of years.

The groundbreaking research conducted in 1998 by Saxberg and Reeves on behalf of Syncrude uncovered remnants of active peoples on the Nezu site within the Aurora oil sands lease. Artifacts point to the Nezu site as having been used for camping, hunting and the manufacture of tools. The Saxberg and Reeves report states that:

"The site contained a high percentage of diagnostic tool types which point to an early occupation. The projectile point types represented include Scottbluff, Jimmy Allen and laceolate Plano types commonly dating to around 9,000 years ago. Lanceolate knives, hafted and unhafted scrapers, backed bifaces, and a variety of retouched and utilized flakes...illustrates a variety of activities which occurred on this campsite....Blood residue analysis performed on a sample of the formed tools indicate that a variety of animal species were exploited during the occupation of the site. They include bison, caribou, moose, beaver, bear, canids (wolf) and other cervids (deer, elk)."[1]

Results at other sites were similar. Digs completed near Mildred Lake show the evolution of native tools, as hunters learned to adapt to northern conditions and local animal species. The way that tools and other materials were laid out also provides evidence of family and community structure. "The sites are the results of encampments of small hunter/gatherer bands or a smaller grouping of related families," says the report. "The large sites along the Athabasca were also quarry/workshop locations resulting in the deposition of vast waste materials from the production of cores, preforms and formed tools."[2]

The Saxberg and Reeve report trumpets the significance of these findings.

"Five years ago we knew that early plains hunters occasionally penetrated the boreal forest, but now we have learned that the occupation was much larger. The history of intensive resource use in the oil sands region must now be counted in millennia. We are also now able to accept a higher level of resourcefulness on the part of the early people of the Northern Plains. There are indications that they frequently hunted game other than bison and perhaps they also fished and traveled great distances on the water. Starting over nine thousand years ago and lasting for two thousand years, the oil sands region was not a hinterland, but a hub of human settlement and interaction with an environment rich in game and other resources."[3]

Who were they?

Archaeologists are not yet ready to state conclusively who the first inhabitants of the area were, but we do have clues. We know that a grouping of hunters were known as the Clovis. Men roamed the area about ten thousand years ago. Clovis were traditionally big game hunters who survived on hunting giant bison, woodland caribou and large mammoths similar to the types whose remains were unearthed by Suncor during the early 1970s. Artifacts linked to the Clovis have been found as close as Grande Prairie. When mammoths and bison disappeared due to weather changes, so did the Clovis. They were replaced by the Agate Basin culture, whose stone tools have been found at Syncrude's Beaver Creek lease.

Artifacts found within the current Syncrude lease, and at the Aurora site, point to a variety of spearheads and points. Differences in the types of points reflect the fact that the area was an active and adaptable community, capable of changing with local hunting conditions. Saxberg and Reeves also uncovered spearheads identical to those used by hunters in Montana, but manufactured near Fort McMurray with local sandstone.

Another culture, the Oxbow people, likely inhabited the area about five thousand years ago. Their spearheads and tools have been dug out of sites near Gregoire Lake, Lake Athabasca and along the Athabasca River. Eventually, those who possessed the bow and arrow, an important technological breakthrough, replaced spear-throwing hunters. The Avonlea roamed the Fort McMurray area about eighteen hundred years ago. Syncrude's Beaver Creek site has produced tools and shavings from the Avonlea along with items from the Besant who hunted locally about three thousand years ago.

The Dene, forerunners of the Chipewyan and Beaver, came to the region from the north and were cousins to the Navajo and Apache in the south. Later, names were changed to reflect new hunting patterns. For example, the Chipewyan were named "caribou eaters" because their hunting and living habits closely followed the migration of the caribou. While signs of the Dene begin appearing about five thousand years ago, it is believed that they only began inhabiting the area on a permanent basis about three thousand years ago.

The Woodland Cree came to the Athabasca region from the east. A five hundred-year-old piece of Cree pottery was taken in the late 1970s from an archaeological dig near Fort McMurray. While the Dene people tended to fish the southern rivers and then bear down in the north during winter, the Cree developed a new technology which enabled them to expand their territory year round.

About one thousand years ago, the Cree developed the ability to string nets below the frozen rivers, and this adaptive technology enabled them to remain mobile during winter months and to expand their territory. About four hundred years ago, the Cree are believed to have squeezed the Chipewyan and Beaver north, assuming increased control over the rivers and forests around Fort McMurray and area. By the early 1700s, the Cree had already traded with European explorers and had learned to use guns to further their territorial claims.

First oil sands sample

In 1719, "newcomers" from Europe would receive their first glimpse of the "natural tar" which oozed from the Athabasca. A party of three Cree trappers arrived in York Factory, Hudson's Bay on June 19 carrying an odd-looking black lump. A man identified as Wa Pa Su placed a sample of oil-laden sand in explorer Henry Kelsey's hand. Kelsey recorded in his York Fort Journal that a sample "of that Gum or pitch that flows out of the Banks of the River" had been received. Although the Europeans had heard of this material from the native people of the Athabasca, this was the first time they had seen it first hand.

The Athabasca visitors also spoke about the amazing properties of this oily material. When mixed with spruce tree sap, oil sand could serve as sealant to repair ripped birch canoes. And during long and bright summer months, the sand could produce smudge fires to ward off mosquitoes, no *see-ums* and other insect swarms.

Long before the invention of the combustible engine, oil heaters or asphalt roads, the oil sands sample merely served as a novelty. But the oddity which Wa Pa Su brought to York Factory moved Kelsey to record the event.

By 1777, the Cree had explored the Peace and Athabasca rivers to their sources and claimed the land around Lake Athabasca. The Cree were curious explorers as well as exceptional hunters. By the late 1700s, the Cree had established themselves as the main band at Fort Chipewyan, and had also established their main camp in Fort McMurray near the mouth of the Clearwater River. An uneasy peace took effect between the Cree and Chipewyan people in 1790.

In 1835, native people of the area were ravaged by a smallpox epidemic, and following two severe winters, both groups agreed to share the territory. A second peace treaty was signed at Peace Point. In 1883, a large group of Cree migrated to the Peace River area and founded the Fox Creek band. Others moved up the Clearwater River and formed the native population now at Anzac. Those remaining north of Fort McMurray became the Fort Chipewyan and Fort McKay bands.

Coming of the fur trade

It is often said that recorded history is past imperfect. While history presents itself as a direct reflection of the past, in truth it is often incomplete, based on the written accounts of those influenced by the present.

As such, the written history of North America almost always begins with "first contact," or accounts of the journeys of European explorers and their interactions with aboriginal people. The Athabasca region is no different. Although a rich oral tradition exists, guarded and passed on by Cree and Chipewyan elders, written accounts available to us today originate from diaries and journals of Europeans.

The written history of the Fort McMurray region begins in the late 1770s with the arrival of explorers and adventurers such as Peter Pond, Alexander Mackenzie and Alexander Henry. Their interest in the region was motivated by goals similar to those which fuelled Fort McMurray's oil exploration during the twentieth century: they were driven by a desire to develop new markets for coveted products of the day.

Remarkably, the fur trade began as a new fashion trend. The pelts and beaver robes which native people wore provided explorers with inspiration for a new kind of gentleman's hat. The appeal of these new fur hats quickly spread throughout England, and before long, demand for animal pelts began to grow across North America. Two companies invested in the fur trade, and eventually came into direct competition.

The first of these was the Hudson's Bay Company, established in 1670 under a charter granted by England's King Charles II (1660-1688), to "The Governor and Company of Adventurers of England trading into Hudson's Bay."[4] The corporation's shareholders included London merchants and English nobility, and were spearheaded by the adventurous brothers-in-law, Pierre Esprit Radisson and Medard Chouart des Groseilliers, nicknamed "Caesars of the Wilderness."[5]

The company's charter, establishing the Hudson's Bay region as an English colony, handed the corporation "the sole trade and commerce of all these seas, straits, bays, rivers, lakes, creeks, and sounds in whatsoever latitude they shall be, that lie within the entrance of the straits, commonly called Hudson's Straits, together with all the lands and territories upon the countries, coasts and confines of the seas, bays, lakes, river, creeks and sounds aforesaid."[6]

For many years, English explorers and merchants traded in the interior regions, and relied on native peoples' skill to bring import furs from the west and coastal areas. With the signing of the Peace of Paris in 1763, Canada became a British colony, and it was shortly thereafter that the threat of competition forced the Hudson's Bay Company to expand into the western plains.

The North West Company was created around 1780 based on a loose collection of private investors and entrepreneurs, and without a charter. Although the North West Company was smaller than the Hudson's Bay Company, as a private operation, it proved far more aggressive and ambitious. For several years, North West Company partners were wary of investing money further west than the Lake Superior and Saskatchewan River regions where the Hudson's Bay Company was already entrenched. They needed a gutsy adventurer who would establish their presence within the new frontier.

The arrival of Peter Pond

In his early years, Peter Pond would have seemed an unlikely candidate to spearhead the North West Company's expansion into the Lake Athabasca area. He was born in Milford, Connecticut in 1740, the son of a shoemaker. He apprenticed in his father's trade, but in 1756 enlisted in the Connecticut regiment of the British army. Pond was a restless soul who felt constrained in a small New England town and felt a burning urge to explore. As he later reflected in his journal, "I found [tarrying] at home was too inactive a life for me…"[7]

Pond served in the British army and participated in battles against the French and Indians at Ticonderoga, Fort Niagara and Montreal. He became a sergeant and gained his own commission. At age twenty, Pond retired from the army, and travelled to the West Indies. Upon his return three years later, he settled back in Milford, married and had at least two children. Pond later reflected in his journal, that the three years spent raising a family were (sic) "the ondley three years of my life I was three years in one place since I was sixteen years old to sixty."[8] He later joined his father in the fur trade near Detroit.

During his decade working in the Detroit and Albany areas, Pond developed a love for the independent and free-enterprising nature of the fur trade. However, after six years trapping in the region, Pond shot a man in a duel and although no prosecution took place, Pond thought it wise to return to the West Indies until his notoriety cooled. This shooting would not be the first time Pond would face scandal for a hot temper and an allegedly fast pistol.

Pond returned to the region at age thirty, and entered into a partnership with Felix Graham, a trader working in the upper Mississippi region. Pond became remarkably adept at trading with native people, shipping enormous cargoes of material goods in exchange for furs. His success with Graham allowed Pond some degree of financial independence, and helped to fund his travels to the Lake Winnipeg area in 1775.

As he passed through the area he met Alexander Henry the Elder, a fellow New Englander who had in his earlier years peddled furs from Albany to Montreal through Detroit. Henry, along with the brothers Thomas and Joseph Frobisher, had previously opened western trails into present-day Manitoba and Saskatchewan.

During the winters of 1776-78, Pond wintered in Hudson House, not far from present day Prince Albert. Pond used this time to ply his trade and to establish important personal and professional points of contact.

In spring 1778, a number of independent fur traders in the area agreed to combine forces and form a "joint stock venture,"[9] of which Pond was put in charge. He set sail with four canoes for an area known as the Athabasca. Although no European had visited the area, native people spoke of it. The new business provided "free traders" with an opportunity to pool capital, share risk, and avoid feuds and competition which no doubt lessened profits.

Fort McMurray's first "newcomer"

In late 1778, Pond entered the Athabasca River through the lakes and rivers of Saskatchewan. Using travelled trails and directions provided by native people, Pond and his entourage discovered the twelve-mile Methye (La Loche) Portage, from Methye Lake to the Clearwater River. The portage culminated with a breath-taking six hundred and seventy foot drop. Pond's group paddled along the Clearwater River to its juncture with the Athabasca River at the site of current day Fort McMurray.

The Athabasca River north from Fort McMurray would open vast new frontiers, and would allow Pond to exchange goods with enthusiastic Cree and Chipewyan trappers. During the winter of 1778-79, Pond established a fort known as Pond's House on the Elk River, located about thirty-eight miles south of Lake Athabasca. While Peter Pond's journals after 1775 have been destroyed, some of his primitive maps remain. On some, Pond records locations where he observes "tar" oozing from the banks of Lake Athabasca[10].

Vast numbers of Cree and Chipewyan trappers passed by Pond's House that winter, and were only too eager to trade with Pond on the spot, rather than continue on the long journey to Fort Churchill on Hudson's Bay. In effect, Pond cut off the Hudson's Bay Company's fur supply at the source. Native people were also willing to accept fewer goods in return. Pond's foray into the Athabasca region produced immediate profit and devastating results for the Hudson's Bay Company.

While Pond's party wintered north of Fort McMurray, his partners and rivals in Saskatchewan held their breath, waiting for any news of the expedition. In June 1779 Pond's continued silence caused a rash of rumours to circulate. Surveyor Philip

Turnor reported. "Some think he has starved for want of provisions...others think he is gone too far into the Country for them to receive any intelligence of him."[11]

On July 2, 1779, Pond's entourage arrived at Cumberland House with one hundred and forty packs of the finest furs that had yet been seen. It was spitefully recorded by one envious Hudson's Bay employee that native people were so eager to trade furs for European goods that Pond had literally traded the shirt off his own back.

Alexander Henry realized the "larger" significance of Pond's foray. He impressed upon Sir Joseph Banks of the Royal Society of London the scientific and economic potential which awaited the British Empire by following Pond's steps. Henry's argument fell on deaf ears, but was later revived by Alexander Mackenzie, Pond's successor.

Pond arrived in Montreal in mid-1779, loaded with furs from the new frontier. Entrepreneurs clamored to support Pond, inaugurating a sixteen-share company which would later form the basis of the NorthWest Company. Pond returned to the Athabasca in 1779-80, engaging in additional trade with the Cree and Chipewyan. He returned to Montreal with new furs, and those which his overloaded canoes could not carry the previous year.

The suddenly invincible Pond left Montreal in 1781, destined for further glory in the Athabasca region. But Pond's luck was about to change. A dark event one evening in March 1882 would change Pond's fortunes forever.

Peter Pond and the murders

While Pond's fiery disposition and adventurous spirit produced benefits for his trading partners, it also brought with it notoriety. Historian Barry Gough writes:

"Even this early Pond had acquired a reputation, as Alexander Henry the Elder observed, that had given him some "celebrity" in the Northwest. Pond's aggressive trading practices had earned him a reputation as someone not to be antagonized, as he had a tendency to take the law into his own hands."[12]

Historians to this day disagree over whether Pond was a hero or a scoundrel. Although he was never convicted, history has indicted Pond for two murders. The first allegedly occurred during a journey to Lake Athabasca in early 1782. Pond was travelling with Swiss born Jean-Etienne Waddens, founder of Waddens & Co., one of the Montreal partners which originally formed the North West Company. An outbreak of smallpox among native people in the early 1780s had dramatically decreased the amount of fur being shipped to the east. This had significantly decreased profits and Waddens was one of many disenchanted investors who had recently withdrawn from the company.

In many ways, Waddens was Pond's perfect foil, and was described by Alexander Mackenzie as a "Swiss gentleman of strict probity and known sobriety...two men of more opposite characters could not perhaps have been found."[13]

Pond's journey was stalled by an early freeze up of the North Saskatchewan

River, and his party was forced to spend the winter in Lac La Ronge. Pond had carried only enough supplies for the journey; the rest of his winter provisions were located at his final destination, Lake Athabasca. Historians speculate that these troubles helped ignite personal differences between the two travellers. One winter night, Wadden was shot in the upper leg and bled to death in his cabin. There were two suspects: Pond, and one of Waddens' clerks.

One member of Waddens' entourage, Joseph Faignant, stated that he had heard Pond and Waddens arguing the night of the murder. Faignant claimed he saw Pond and a "voyageur" leaving Waddens' cabin[14]. Waddens died without naming his attacker, and was buried the next morning. Pond was eventually cleared of the murder, but suspicions regarding his guilt remained. After all, Pond made for an extremely likely suspect. He had previously been involved in the Detroit duel, and had over time developed a reputation as a hot headed maverick whom often exercised his anger outside the law.

It is said that Pond earned the reputation of an imperious and arrogant trader who tried to earn the fear, not the friendship, of native people. On one occasion a witness saw him strike a Chipewyan man with the flat of a sword and when his victim complained at such rough treatment Pond told him that "the country and the Indians belonged to him and he would do with them as he pleased ..."[15]

However, the pelts Pond brought from the Athabasca region were of such high quality that in spite of speculation regarding Waddens' murder, tolerance of Pond's conduct continued.

In the winter of 1786-87, the competitive nature of the industry again played itself out at Pond's post. North West Company rival John Ross was stationed in the region, and during one of Pond's trade negotiations with a Chipewyan band, an argument ensued between Ross and one of Pond's men. Ross was fatally shot. Pond's employee, who was later described as "a little crack-brained and variable as the wind"[16] ran off into the "bush," and was not heard from for three years.

Although Pond's whereabouts at the time of the shooting were never determined, and he was never charged, Pond was implicated by many of his colleagues. With the North West Company now established in the Athabasca, Pond had become a liability. The Company revised its shareholding schedule in 1787 and in spite of Pond's substantial contribution, he was awarded only one share of twenty. The share structure reflected a growing wariness of Pond and his temper.

Pond became bitter of his pariah status. In his journal, which is punctuated by miserable spelling, he speaks of those who sought to "abuse me in a Shamfull manner."[17] He proclaimed his innocence and reminded his accusers of his vast contribution to the North West Company.

Pond's dream and demise

While Peter Pond continued to profit from the fur trade, he soon turned his sights to a greater treasure: the elusive passage through Canada to the Pacific Ocean. Through his contacts with native people, Pond gained vital information about the flow of the Peace and Mackenzie rivers. In 1785, Pond and a group of Montreal investors began lobbying the governor to support an expedition to locate the lucrative passage.

Pond used information gleaned from the Cree and Chipewyan, along with observations from explorers such as Captain James Cook, to produce a map of the west. In an effort to hide some of the details, Pond altered some of his maps. Because Pond appeared ready to sell his knowledge to the Americans, his activities troubled British authorities.

While the colonial governor discussed who should lead a western expedition proposed both by Pond and Alexander Henry, news reached Montreal in fall 1790 that Pond's successor with the North West Company, Alexander Mackenzie, had explored what would later be known as the Mackenzie River. Mackenzie found that the actual route of the great northern river differed significantly from that described in Pond's maps.

Mackenzie's discovery proved to be the final blow to Pond's already wounded reputation. Pond left the Athabasca region in the spring of 1788, and sold his share to William McGillvray for eight hundred pounds. McGillvray would later name a child after Pond to acknowledge the man who provided him with a start in the fur trade.

Pond moved to the United States and was commissioned into the army in January 1792. He served as a special agent in charge of Indian affairs for Secretary of War, Henry Knox.

In his later years, Pond became increasingly suspicious and vindictive. One night while dining with friends, he was approached by an old acquaintance from Montreal. Pond allegedly picked up a carving knife and threatened his old friend, ordering him to leave.

It was Pond who advised the United States government on how to align the Great Lakes border with Canada to best suit American interests. Although Pond was hired from time to time to assist the American government, Pond did not fare well removed from his beloved fur trade. Pond died penniless in his hometown of Milford, Connecticut, at the age of sixty-seven.

In his defense, it can be argued that faced with a hostile environment, cut throat competition, and brutal economic realities, an aggressive leader of Pond's caliber was necessary to achieve success. Pond also blazed a trail which other traders and adventurers were quick to follow.

Surveyor David Thompson would later write of Peter Pond: "He was a person of industrious habits, a good common education, but of violent temper and unprincipled character."[18]

Pond's successor, Alexander Mackenzie, is credited with establishing the North West Company's permanent presence. However, it is generally held that much of Mackenzie's progress can be attributed to Peter Pond. Historian Barry Gough writes:

Mackenzie dissociated himself, indeed rapidly distanced himself, from Pond, whose hands were bloodied and whose cartography was flawed. ... But Pond opened what Mackenzie and others called the "new el dorado" of the North West Company[19].

Sir Alexander Mackenzie

It is Sir Alexander Mackenzie who is ultimately credited with establishing the North West Company's financial success. Born in 1762, Mackenzie emigrated from Scotland at the age of twelve. Mackenzie arrived in New York in 1775 and was almost immediately enlisted as a soldier in the American Revolution.

However, soldiering was not Mackenzie's passion, and in 1778, with the help of his two aunts, he escaped north to Montreal, where he began his education. MacKenzie embodied the rare balance of qualities which was necessary for success. He possessed youth and experience, along with a zeal for adventure and exploration. At the time of the North West Company's launch, Mackenzie was twenty-one years old. The fur trade was a young man's game.

In 1787, Mackenzie was given one of twenty shares in the newly restructured North West Company, and was sent to replace Pond at the posts of Lake Athabasca and Great Slave Lake. During the winter of 1787, Mackenzie and Pond remained together at the Great Slave Lake post. Despite promised possibilities, and the belief that the region was the future of the fur trade, Mackenzie was aware that his work was perilous. On the heels of Ross' shooting, Peter Pond's reputation for violence heightened. Cold weather, ice, and consistent scarcity of food dominated conditions. The atmosphere was similar to that previously experienced by Alexander Henry the Elder, who wrote in 1775:

[The Indians] tell [the trader], that the Indians are happy in seeing him return to their country; that they have been long in expectation of his arrival; that their wives have deprived themselves of their provisions, in order to afford him a supply; that they are in great want, being destitute of every thing, and particularly of ammunition and clothing; and that what they most long for, is a taste of his rum... [20].

Competition again became an increasing factor in trade at the Athabasca and Slave Lake posts. In particular, trading with Cree and Chipewyan nations was coveted both by the North West Company and the Hudson's Bay Company.

By 1788, Pond had left the Athabasca region. Mackenzie was eager to step into his shoes, and along with his cousin Roderick Mackenzie, established a new depot on the Lake Athabasca site, calling it Chipewyan, after the local band whose business he coveted. Although it was Peter Pond who first established a settlement in the area in 1778, on February 14, 1789, the North West Company proudly announced the building of a new fort to serve as a base to trade with the Chipewyan, and to launch further northwest expeditions.

In his journal, Mackenzie proudly marked the founding of Fort Chipewyan.

About forty miles from the lake is the Old Establishment as formed by Mr. Pond in the year 1778-9, and which was the only one in this part of the world till the year 1785. In the year 1788 it was transferred to the Lake of the Hills on a point on its southern side at about eight miles from the discharge of the river. It was named Fort Chipewyan[21].

Mackenzie's relations with the Cree were less successful than those with the Chipewyan. Fewer in number than the Chipewyan, the Cree proved more hostile towards the traders, and a resentful Mackenzie commented that they had "done little or nothing ... they are always in the same place close by the fort and they have ruined it."[22]

As the fur trade continued to grow, the NorthWest Company discovered a competitive edge: alcohol. While native tribes were growing increasingly dependent on guns, pots and cloth supplied by both the North West Company and the Hudson's Bay Company, as historian Darlene Comfort observes "these reaped nothing like the profit got by firewater."[23] The "Nor'Westers" offerings, particularly of rum, produced two results.

Alcohol helped swing the attention of Cree and Chipewyan trappers closer to the North West Company. As well, while native people in the Lake Athabasca region had always been respectful of the balance between humans and the environment, their growing addiction to alcohol caused them to harvest more pelts than what the region could sustain. In the past, native people had been selective with regard to the animals they trapped. Mothers were left behind to create offspring for the next year. However, this changed with the arrival of alcohol. It is recorded that furs in increasing quantities passed to the traders, and neither they nor the Cree or Chipewyan, appeared to be committed to maintaining the animal population.

Mackenzie's pole experiment

While furs and northwest exploration were Mackenzie's priorities, there is no question that the surrounding oil sands aroused Mackenzie's curiosity. In 1789, Mackenzie stopped by the Athabasca River and conducted an experiment to determine the depth of the mysterious bitumen deposits. He observed in his journal:

At about twenty-four miles from the fork, are some bituminous fountains into which a pole of twenty feet long may be inserted without the least resistance. The bitumen is in a fluid state and when mixed with gum or the resinous substance collected from the spruce fir serves to gum the canoes. In its heated state it emits a smell like that of seacoal. The banks of the river which are there very elevated over veins of the same bituminous quality[24].

Mackenzie may have unknowingly provided the first reference to an area which nearly two centuries later would host large-scale oil sands development.

Fort McMurray's first house

While the attention of the fur trade during the late 1780s focused on Fort Chipewyan, the strategic value of Fort McMurray was not completely overlooked.

In 1979, a team of University of Alberta archaeologists excavated a site near the junction of the Athabasca and Clearwater rivers, and returned to Edmonton with hundreds of artifacts including buttons, tools, cutlery and other signs of civilization. They had unearthed McLeod's House, also know as Fort of the Forks.

No accounts exist of how or why McLeod's House was built, or why it was abandoned soon after. It is likely that traders travelled north to the Birch Hills, where a second fort was built. The earliest mention of Fort of the Forks occurs in 1791, when surveyor Philip Turnor passed through en route to Lake Athabasca on behalf of the Hudson's Bay Company. Turnor remarked on approaching the junction of the Clearwater and Athabasca rivers, that he came to a "Canadian House" devoid of any people who may have occupied it.

In June 1791, Peter Fidler, Turnor's assistant, referred to the abandoned fort as McLeod's House. Fidler speculates that McLeod's House was built "three or four" years back.

Explorer David Thompson made mention of a new post at the mouth of the Clearwater River as he arrived in May 10, 1799. Thompson remained at the new post for a few days before resuming his expedition. Thompson returned to the fort in May 1804. The Hudson's Bay Company took over the site in 1821 and sporadically operated from the area until 1870, when Henry Moberly established a permanent presence there.

Philip Turnor

Fired by their declining success, the Hudson's Bay Company launched a campaign in the early 1790s to restore their market share in the region. In 1790, Philip Turnor was dispatched to the area as the leader of an expedition to map the Athabasca region and return to the company the information necessary to re-establish its monopoly.

Competition from the North West Company was only one factor in the Hudson's Bay Company's rededication to the area. The United States posed a threat from Canada's southern borders, forcing both Canadian and British commercial interests to focus as far north as possible.

Turnor surveyed the areas around Swan Lake, and the Clearwater and Athabasca rivers near Fort McMurray, determining central trading regions, empty houses and fortifications. His conclusions in 1792 identified Lake Athabasca as the key area for dominance of northern trade. After presenting these conclusions, Turnor returned to England.

David Thompson the mapmaker

Turnor had trained David Thompson, who accompanied him on his survey of the Athabasca region. Born in 1770 in London, Thompson aspired early on to join the English Navy, but because peace had prompted the English government to cut back recruitment, he travelled to North America to apprentice with the Hudson's Bay Company.

In the winter of 1788, Thompson literally fell under Turnor's tutelage. While serving with the Hudson's Bay Company on the Saskatchewan River, Thompson fell and broke his leg. While he recovered at Cumberland House near York Fort, Thompson became acquainted with Turnor, who taught him mathematics, and engaged him in rigorous study of astronomy. During this time, Thompson learned how to use the telescope and the chronometer, and in time became versed in the tactics of surveying. Thompson himself called his fractured leg and its resultant complications "the best thing that ever happened to me."[25]

Soon after his recovery, Thompson defected to the North West Company. Thompson proved valuable to both companies, successively, in the Athabasca region. Strict religious beliefs opposed him to the use of alcohol to ply the Indian tribes in trading; it was mapmaking where Thompson excelled. The ultimate result of his journeys was the completion of a map of the west, which he produced in 1813.

The arrival of the XY Company

In early 1799, a new player emerged to challenge the Athabasca's traditional rivals. It called itself the XY Company, and its first recruit was Alexander Mackenzie, who quickly defected from the North West Company. The firm of Forsyth and Ogilvie acted for a group of independent traders and set up a post on the shores of Lake Athabasca at Fort Chipewyan. The Hudson's Bay Company finally erected Nottingham House in 1802 on an island opposite Fort Chipewyan.

The Hudson's Bay Company, the North West Company, and the XY Company were now posted in close proximity along Lake Athabasca. The North West Company had two posts, at Fort Chipewyan and Fond du Lac. Hudson's Bay was established at Nottingham House under the direction of surveyor and explorer Peter Fidler. The XY Company worked from its position near Fort Chipewyan.

Emergence of a third trading company heightened tensions along Lake Athabasca. During 1802-04, Fidler's Hudson's Bay post gained a narrow advantage. The North West Company had become more concerned with XY defections than with maintaining its business position in the area. Furthermore, the Chipewyan had begun to rebel against the hostile, often abusive dominance of the Nor'Westers. In the winter of 1804, the Chipewyan raided the Fond du Lac post along Lake Athabasca, killing two men and their families. Soon after, four others were killed in a similar ambush at the Fort Chipewyan site.

The following winter, in 1805-06, the North West traders waged a campaign of severe harassment on Nottingham House, building a house nearby and using it as headquarters for the physical abuse of Fidler's entourage, and stealing provisions. Finally, Fidler approached the North West Company and truce was agreed upon.

Despite the union of the North West Company and the XY Company soon after these incidents, a period of wartime enveloped the entire Canadian fur trade until 1821, when the Hudson's Bay Company and the North West Company finally amalgamated, ending an era of intense rivalry and competition.

Richardson's near perfect observations

Three times during the 1800s, English explorer Sir John Franklin passed through northern Canada in search of the "Frozen Ocean" which Alexander Mackenzie had earlier described in his attempt to locate the Pacific Ocean.

Franklin's initial journey took place in 1819, and he was accompanied by Sir John Richardson, an expert in the combined study of geology, biology, botany, and zoology. During the 1819 expedition, Richardson provided the first "scientific" account of the oil sands:

"... there is a peaty bog whose crevices are filled with petroleum. This mineral exists in great abundance in this district. We never observed it flowing from the limestone, but always above it and generally agglutinating the beds of sand into a kind of pitchy sandstone. Sometimes fragments of this stone contain so much petroleum as to float down the stream."[26]

In 1848, Sir John Franklin's third expedition to the polar sea ended in disaster. Franklin and his party disappeared, and Richardson was assigned to the search party.

As he passed through Fort McMurray, Richardson recorded a series of observations which would prove amazingly accurate in describing the oil sands' composition. While future scientists and entrepreneurs obsessed over locating a central underground oil source, Richardson observed that this was largely a surface phenomenon. Richardson asserted that the oil he identified was not chemically intermeshed with the sand and puzzled over the fact that oil sands seemed to combine oil with water and sand.

"The limestone is immediately covered by a thin stratum of a yellowish-white earth which from the fineness of its grain appears at first sight to be a marl or clay. It does not however effervesce with acids is harsh and meager and when examined under a microscope it seems to be chiefly composed of minute fragments of translucent quartz with a grayish basis in form of an impalpable powder."[27]

Simply stated, Richardson realized the probability that the oil sands phenomenon was likely not caused by the drenching of oil from subterranean pools. Perhaps had Richardson been assigned to further examining the oil sands samples, rather than searching for Sir John Franklin, he may have uncovered the secret of the oil sands seventy years before Karl Clark.

Moberly names McMurray

During the mid-1800s, Fort Chipewyan thrived as the economic centre of the Athabasca District. From its perch overlooking Lake Athabasca, it was perfect launching ground for economic activity north to Fort Smith, west to Peace River and south to the Clearwater River.

Prior to 1870, the junction of the Athabasca and Clearwater rivers had only a local name, "The Forks." It served as a natural resting ground for travellers, and although some attempts were made to establish a permanent outpost, these efforts were unsuccessful until the arrival of a reluctant Henry "John" Moberly.

Moberly, who joined the Hudson's Bay Company in 1853 at age eighteen, was known as an ardent explorer and adventurer. At age sixteen, he worked for Lloyd's in St. Petersburg, Russia. Upon his return to Canada, he joined the Hudson's Bay Company and ventured out west. During the early 1860s, Moberly quit the Hudson's Bay Company to launch a number of private ventures, but in the summer of 1869, he found himself in Fort Chipewyan, again drawn to the Company. While the Hudson's Bay agent at Fort Chipewyan was away on business, his wife became "very unwell, with no one to look after her."[28] Moberly remained in Fort Chipewyan and tended to her until the factor's return. With winter approaching, Moberly opted to remain in the community, accepting an unofficial job with the Hudson's Bay Company to "oversee the work of the post and of the other employees about the place."[29]

After the winter of 1869-70, the restless John Moberly set his sights south. William McMurray, the Hudson's Bay Company factor at Fort Chipewyan, persuaded Moberly to rejoin the company's service, and to establish a southern terminus at the forks for future steamboat travel. On May 11, 1870, Moberly left Fort Chipewyan with two boats and their crews, and set course for the junction of the Athabasca and Clearwater rivers.

Moberly's crew paddled for a day, but soon ran into a local phenomenon, the May snow storm. In his autobiography, Moberly describes the tempest and the official founding of Fort McMurray.

"A blizzard for the last three days of the trip made travelling anything but pleasant, but as the wind was fair we carried on and landed, in a foot of snow, at the mouth of the Clearwater River. I chose a site for the fort in a thick poplar wood and the weather having turned fine we began clearing the ground."[30]

Moberly soon discovered he wasn't the first to land at the site. He found the remains of a previous post and after making contact with local natives learned that: "Eighty-six years before, this forgotten post had been abandoned in consequence of the death from smallpox of almost all of the Indians in the locality."[31]

Naming of Fort McMurray

Moberly and crew went to work establishing a permanent settlement. Moberly felt moved to name the new fort after William McMurray. "This is named Fort McMurray after a chief factor who was one of my oldest friends,"[32] Moberly wrote in his autobiography.

The first buildings established were Moberly's residence, a store, a men's house and a carpenter's shop. Logs were also squared and boards were sawed for an officer's house, which would be erected the following spring.

Who was William McMurray, anyway?

William McMurray was a true son of the northwest who was born with Hudson's Bay Company blood running through his veins. His father was Chief Trader Thomas McMurray who spent the early 1800s working between the X Y Company, the North West Company and the Hudson's Bay Company. Following the amalgamation of the North West Company and the Hudson's Bay Company in 1821, Thomas McMurray became Chief Trader.

At age eighteen, William McMurray joined the Hudson's Bay Company and was dispatched to various isolated locations in the Northwest Territories. McMurray became an excellent marksman and an astute trader, and also became skilled in the Chipewyan language. At twenty-eight McMurray became Chief Trader and began to yield substantial personal profit from the Hudson's Bay Company's local ventures.

If nothing else, years of isolation in the north taught McMurray to be a survivor. In his journal, Sir Henry Lefroy recounts how one night he and McMurray struggled to stay warm while travelling near Great Slave Lake:

"Again and again, I woke half frozen to find that McMurray in his sleep, by persistent wriggling, had got all my blanket from me and wrapped around himself. Then came a tug and a struggle until I repossessed myself of it, only to repeat the same process after an hour or two."[33]

In 1867, McMurray was transferred from Fort Alexander to Fort Chipewyan, a substantially more developed community which overlooked Lake Athabasca near the convergence of the Peace and Athabasca rivers. The Peace/Athabasca Delta included the nearby Slave River which flowed north to the Great Slave Lake and to the Arctic. It was McMurray who encouraged John Moberly to establish a Hudson's Bay presence at "the forks." In return, Moberly named the post Fort McMurray.

Road goes nowhere

In the early 1870s, a number of technological advances would turn the sights of the government, investors and entrepreneurs to the north and its vast resource potential. Rumours existed of gold deposits. As well, technologies were being developed to use oil for heating and for fuel. The potential was also being assessed for settlement and mineral exploration of the arctic.

Based on news of Fort McMurray's economic potential, attention began to mount from the south. In 1871, Catholic missionaries based in Lac La Biche began cutting a cart road through the muskeg to Fort McMurray, but after spending eleven hundred dollars the project was abandoned.

In 1872, a Hudson's Bay officer followed the trail from Lac La Biche to assess whether the half-built road could become operational. The officer arrived in Fort McMurray after losing most of his horses and declared the south to north route a lost cause. Moberly was asked by the Hudson's Bay Company to investigate completing the road, or at least to develop an alternative land route to Cold Lake.

The plan was thwarted by monopoly-minded Hudson's Bay officials, who feared that improved access would open the door for more freelance fur buyers to set up business in the north.

Dutch Henry and the fire

John Moberly and crew were not alone for long. Trappers and explorers had for decades paused at the fork of the Athabasca and Clearwater rivers, and one day in the spring of 1871, a man known as Dutch Henry appeared. Henry was a trapper and labourer who had landed in the Peace Country in 1869 and who had completed some work for the Roman Catholic Mission.

Moberly described Henry as "a short stumpy man with a small pug nose in a round pink face, down the sides of which straggled a thin growth of sandy hair."[34] Henry insisted at one time he had been a head coachman and personal friend of both the King of Bavaria, and the Crown Prince.

Henry had come to Fort McMurray due to the spring flooding of the Athabasca and Clearwater rivers. The flood did not affect Moberly's fort, but it did make travel out of the area impossible. Henry agreed to stay until the waters subsided. He stored a small packet of furs under the counter of the Hudson's Bay store and ventured out to find a place to rest.

It was a hot afternoon and according to Moberly's account, the mosquitoes and other insects were "ferocious."[35] The Hudson's Bay crew was on its way to Fort Chipewyan to stock up with supplies, so Moberly and Henry were alone. Moberly lit a coal smudge to keep the insects away from the horses and then paddled over to his garden which was likely located on present day MacDonald Island.

Suddenly, Moberly felt a blast of heat and heard an ear-shattering explosion. Moberly turned to find a column of black smoke rising from the Hudson's Bay post. As he landed back on shore, Moberly saw two things. First, he saw his store in flames. He also noticed the darting figure of Dutch Henry dashing by with his precious packet of furs under his arm. For hours, Henry could not be found. Moberly cursed as he tried on his own to douse the fire.

Parched with thirst, Moberly walked to the shore of the river to fill a pail of water but was distracted by moaning sounds coming from a clump of willows. There was Dutch Henry, his hair, eyebrows and whiskers gone. His singed face was swollen, highlighted only by his bright red nose. Despite Henry's discomfort, Moberly howled with laughter. As Moberly described it, "it would have made a mummy laugh."[36]

It took ten days before Henry could use his eyes or walk. Finally, he disclosed what had happened. While Moberly was gone, a whirlwind had kicked up, tossing hot coals from the nearby smudge on to the Hudson's Bay store roof. This ignited a fire, and Henry dashed to the river banks, filled a pail of water and climbed up to put out the blaze.

Unbeknownst to Henry, a few days earlier, Moberly had stored a keg of gunpowder in a loft under the roof. The idea was to keep the explosives out of the way of tobacco smoking trappers and traders. Just as Henry had climbed to the top of the building, one of the coals dropped through the roof into the loft and landed directly on the keg of gunpowder. Henry was sent hurling into space amidst a sea of fire, smoke and wood. When Henry landed, he dashed into the store, rescued his furs and raced to the river to cool his face. That is where Moberly found him.

Within a few weeks, Henry's face healed and he continued on his journey. Moberly spent the next nine months rebuilding the post. "By next spring all was completed and we had a comfortable post."[37]

The case of the two wives

Like any good boss, Moberly was required to manage his employees' personal problems.

The Roman Catholic Church had been interested in the area since 1847 when Father Alexander Tache, the future Archbishop of St. Boniface, Manitoba came to Fort Chipewyan, passing through Fort McMurray *en route*. In 1853, visiting missionaries began serving Fort McMurray, accessing the community by dogsled and snowshoes.

In 1873, when Bishop Monseigneur Clut visited Fort McMurray, he was faced with a unique case. One of Moberly's hunters appeared at the fort with two wives. The Bishop was concerned about this, and told the man he must marry one woman and leave the other. Since the hunter had two children by the older of the two women, he remained with her, and they were married by the Bishop.

Two months later, the hunter appeared at the fort again and asked Moberly to write the Bishop asking him to exchange the marriage of his current wife for the one he had dismissed earlier. Moberly declined, but advised the hunter to consult with the Bishop next time he visited Fort McMurray. As Moberly wrote:

"The attempt to explain to his lordship must have been amusing if ineffectual, for he had promptly to take back his first wife."[38]

Anglican Diocese established:

The Roman Catholic Church was not alone within the Athabasca region. In

1858, Archdeacon James Hunter became the first Anglican missionary to travel to the Athabasca region. In 1865, William Bompas arrived and in 1874 became the Bishop of the Diocese of Athabasca.

Services were offered in Fort McMurray beginning in 1880. Bompas lived and travelled throughout the north until his death in 1906.

The flood of 1875

Moberly's post faced a number of economic challenges during the 1870s. The number of trappers living in the area was not substantial, and it was a struggle for Moberly to keep the fort economically viable.

But in the spring of 1875, Moberly faced an additional challenge, which would stretch his resources to the limit. The winter of 1874-75 was particularly harsh. On April 2, 1875, the area was blanketed in heavy snow. One day later, temperatures began to rise dramatically. In a matter of hours, the Athabasca River broke with tremendous force, hurling huge ice shards skyward. The volume of ice and snow entering the Athabasca/Clearwater river junction was too large to pass through, and soon waters began backing into the lower townsite.

The waters curled two miles up the Clearwater River, squeezing piles of ice forty to fifty feet high. In under an hour, parts of the Clearwater rose seventy-five feet flooding the entire lower plain. John Moberly recorded that trees three feet in diameter were "mowed down like grass."[39]

Moberly sent his workers to high ground to avoid the rising tide. Most of the fort's houses and facilities were out of the river's reach, but one house and its contents lay in the Clearwater's path. Moberly rushed into the house in an attempt to rescue its contents, but soon found himself up to the knees in water. Moberly waded and swam through five to ten feet of cold water and ice before reaching safe ground.

While the flood only damaged one house, it drowned thirty-six oxen, leaving only one surviving animal. This created considerable difficulty for the Hudson's Bay post which was now incapable of moving freight. Moberly and his men immediately set foot for Lac La Biche, where they secured new horses and oxen. The trip to and from Lac La Biche took twenty days.

While the flood had catastrophic effects for the Hudson's Bay post, Moberly did not come out of it empty-handed; he was handed a double promotion by the Hudson's Bay Company.

Moberly discovers salt

Moberly was extremely taken with the area's natural beauty. His belief in the economic potential of the settlement is expressed in his autobiography. "Fort McMurray occupies a flat about a mile long and in place a quarter wide, the upper part prairie, the rest covered with poplar and a few jackpine. The soil is a rich loose loam on solid limestone. Almost any vegetable that grows along the Saskatchewan can be raised, but apart from this flat, the country is not adapted for farming. The hills surround the flat are seven to eight hundred feet high and at the top muskegs stretch for miles."[40]

One day, during a side expedition about fifteen miles southeast of Fort McMurray, Moberly noticed a bed of white lying in an open area. He had discovered one of the many salt deposits which existed within the region. Moberly excitedly reported his find to Hudson's Bay officials, but without any economical way to transport the salt, company officials ignored his discovery. During the next century at least two commercial salt operations would be established near Fort McMurray. But as in Moberly's time, both ventures were abandoned due to the distance and cost required to ship the product to market.

Moberly remained in the community until March 1, 1878. Until his death in 1931 Moberly remained a booster of Fort McMurray. He would later boast that despite the fact that the Fort McMurray post served only eighteen local trappers, he could always secure forty to forty-five ninety-pound packs of fine furs each winter.

Moberly realized in the 1870s that Fort McMurray would one day become a hotbed of economic activity. He would transfer his enthusiasm to botanist John Macoun, who came to Fort McMurray in 1875 under extremely unexpected circumstances.

John Macoun: Survival and prophesy

Prior to 1875, the Canadian government's energy in the west was focused primarily on British Columbia. As part of the new province's terms of entry into Confederation, John A. Macdonald's federal government had committed to building a railway through the Rockies. The government's interest was clearly based on an east to west axis.

The Geological Survey of Canada — a group of geologists, botanists and engineers — was dispatched westward from Ontario during the early 1870s to identify an economical and reliable rail path through the Rockies. As news of the impending rail link spread within the eastern provinces, the government also began to receive a flurry of inquiries regarding the viability of the west to support crops and permanent settlements.

In 1872, John Macoun, a botanist from Ottawa, joined the geological survey team and conducted two years of research in British Columbia. The survey team returned to Ottawa in 1874 to publish its very promising findings. It concluded that a western rail route was possible, and that fertile soil in the west could support a variety of crops, including grain. Soon after the release of the initial report, Macoun returned to the west with a new geological team. But this time, the Geological Survey of Canada would pursue a new direction. Macoun and Dr. Alfred Selwyn, the Director of the Geological Survey of Canada, decided to explore the western territories on a south to north axis. The team had a particular interest in investigating the viability of a railway route which would follow the Peace River.

In the spring of 1875, a party of eight landed in Fort St. John, in northeastern British Columbia. Determined to locate a railway pass along the Pine River, Selwyn built a poplar canoe, which could not support the entire delegation. While Selwyn proceeded on the primary route, Macoun and a Hudson's Bay Company employee, Mr. King, were sent on light expedition to meet up with Hudson's Bay boats carrying provisions.

When they arrived in Dunvegan in early August, the Hudson's Bay boats had yet to arrive. Macoun and King continued northeast along the Peace River convinced they would soon meet up with the supply boats. With limited provisions, Macoun and King proceeded into uncharted waters. Living on berries and water and dogged endlessly by mosquitoes, the two became seriously ill. Exhausted and barely conscious, Macoun and King beached their canoe southwest of Fort Chipewyan.

Macoun's autobiography recalled the moment:

"A review of the situation brought me to myself and I rose up, determined to struggle on as long as I could hold a paddle."[41]

The next day, near Fort Chipewyan, Macoun and King collapsed in their canoe, weak to the point of exhaustion. Through blurred eyes, they looked up to see a group of concerned natives, who offered food and medicine to revive the strangers. The natives were incredulous that two men in a little canoe with few provisions had survived the seven hundred and twenty miles from Fort St. John to Fort Chipewyan, since, as Macoun's diary recounts, "such a thing had never been done before by two men."[42]

Macoun soon regained his strength. He joined a brigade of boats which was returning south after delivering supplies to Fort Chipewyan. The boats, led by voyageurs and adventurers, proceeded south along the Athabasca River taking advantage of geese passing overhead to snare much needed food. The flotilla arrived at the junction of the Athabasca and Clearwater rivers on September 8, 1875. Macoun marked his arrival in Fort McMurray in his journal, making special note of the abundance of oil in the area.

"When we landed, the ooze from the bank had flowed down the slope into the water and formed a tarred surface extending along the beach over one hundred yards, as hard as iron but in the bright sunshine the surface is quite soft and the men tracking along shore often sink into it up to their ankles."[43]

Macoun also wrote:

"I noticed a little stream of water flowing into the pool which was coated with an oil scum and under the stream was an abundance of tar…That there must be enormous quantities I am quite satisfied, on account of having seen that tar along the bank for over one hundred miles."[44]

John Moberly met Macoun at the shore. Macoun, Moberly and the Hudson's Bay post men spent that night talking about the Athabasca oil sands, the McMurray region and its economic potential. Moberly also had a plan to develop steamship travel along the Athabasca River and eventually, when Macoun left the Hudson's Bay post, he would carry those plans to Winnipeg. Soon after, the Hudson's Bay Company approved plans to build an Athabasca River steamboat, which it would send on commercial explorations north to Fort Chipewyan and beyond. Moberly also had visions of building a one hundred mile road from Fort McMurray to Cold Lake, thus connecting "the forks" with Fort Pitt, located in Saskatchewan.

Oil and bitumen deposits were not the only things Macoun observed during his unexpected trip to Fort McMurray. He noted that on September 8, 1875, the first frost of the season coated the settlement and that cucumber vines, pole beans, potatoes and a series of other vegetables had been affected. Macoun also noted:

"Mr. Moberly told me his wheat and barley were superb and that the country around the fork was well suited for farming purposes...The Hudson's Bay Company if so minded could raise enough wheat here to supply the demands of the whole north instead of bringing it all the way from Manitoba."[45]

In his Geological Survey of Canada report, Macoun reflected on Fort McMurray's potential. As he lay under the stars that night, listening to the loud chatter and laughter of men who manned the Hudson's Bay post, Macoun wrote prophetically:

"I lay and thought of the not far-distant future when other noises than those would take up the silent forest: when white man would be busy with his ready instrument, steam, raising the untold wealth which lies buried beneath the surface and converting the present desolation into a bustling mart of trade."[46]

Macoun arrived in Winnipeg on November 3, 1875 armed with samples of Fort McMurray wheat and barley, along with bottles containing bitumen and fossils. Upon his return to the east, Macoun was invited to recount the details of his adventures to Prime Minister Alexander Mackenzie, who, according to Macoun's journal "would not believe one word I told him about the Northwest."[47]

Macoun's accidental landing in Fort McMurray helped bring the oil sands to the attention of the Geological Survey of Canada and to the Canadian government. Following the release of Macoun's 1875-76 journals, the Geological Survey of Canada began to focus attention on investigating Macoun's amazing accounts. Macoun's observations aroused the interest of Dr. George M. Dawson, the newly appointed director of the Geological Survey of Canada. Intrigued by the samples contained in Macoun's bottles, Dawson began organizing an excursion to the northwest.

Dawson and the Canadian government were about to get serious about Fort McMurray and the Athabasca Oil Sands.

Dr. Bell tracks the mystery

Soon after the Geological Survey of Canada digested Macoun's accounts of the Athabasca oil sands, a scientific team was assembled to explore his observations in more detail. After all, Macoun was a botanist and had little expertise in geology.

Despite Macoun's scientific limitations, excitement surrounding his accounts was considerable. In his 1878 annual report, Dawson devotes considerable attention to the tar sands. A number of theories were advanced to explain how it was that oil could mesh so completely with sand without any evidence of a "mother" source.

Speculation mounted that a massive pool lay trapped below the earth's surface south of Fort McMurray. Scientists hypothesized that the oil had been carried north by a network of streams and had washed into the soil as it surfaced north of Fort McMurray. Dr. Robert Bell, a distinguished geologist, speculated in 1882 that due to the abundance of gas which lay on top of many oil pools, there must exist a stream of oil leading from a large central source. Bell also noted that the type of rock found south of Fort McMurray was of the kind typically associated with oil deposits.

Bell told an 1888 Senate Committee hearing which was examining the resources of the Mackenzie Basin that, " the pitch found along the Athabasca may probably be of considerable value in the future. The quantity appeared to be practically inexhaustible."[18]

Another attendee at the hearing was Father Emile Petitot, an oblate missionary who travelled the Canadian northwest between 1862 and 1882. In a letter to Bell in the early 1870s, Petitot described the oil sands phenomenon and offered first hand accounts to the Senate Committee concerning the richness of resources within the Region. Reports from a person of such religious integrity added credibility to accounts from geologists, botanists and adventurers.

What was in the sand?

The idea of oil and sand existing together was not a new concept. During the early 1800s, scientists had identified oil sands in areas of France, Spain, Italy, Russia, Romania and Albania. Shale deposits were noted in the United States and parts of Africa.

In Europe, great thinkers had already been assigned to extract oil from these mysterious deposits. In Russia, experiments were conducted using oil sands mined from the Gigulev deposits. Material was first crushed and then placed in large kettles and boiling water was added. This process caused sand to settle at the bottom of the kettle and oil to rise to the top where it was skimmed. A purity level of sixty per cent oil was achieved, and hopes were high that the process could be refined either to produce petroleum or some type of asphalt.

In the early 1880s, Bell brought oil sand samples to Dr. G. Christian Hoffman, a chemist with the Geological Survey of Canada. Hoffman exposed the oil sand to European techniques and published his findings in 1883. Although Hoffman held out hope that the source of oil in the region could be found, he did focus scientists' attention on the potential for oil to be extracted from existing deposits. Hoffman wrote:

Should it be more expedient to separate the bitumen, this may be effected by simply boiling or macerating the material with hot water, when the bituminous matter entering into fusion will rise as a scum to the surface and may be removed by skimmers whilst the sand falls to the bottom of the vessel[19].

Of the eight-two per cent sand in his sample, Hoffman was able to remove about eighty-five per cent through hot water treatment. Aside from confirming that some type of separation process was possible, the experiment also confirmed the high oil content contained in Bell's samples.

Although results were promising, they did conclude that substantial scientific resources were required to extract a relatively small amount of oil. Efforts continued to find the motherlode.

McConnell's shift in theory

Based on first hand reports from such highly credible individuals such as Selwyn, Dawson, Bell, Petitot and Macoun, the east flushed with unbridled optimism. The potential seemed endless for the development of agriculture and petroleum, and for exploration north of Fort McMurray, into the arctic.

The commitment of eastern investment dollars hinged on verification by the Geological Survey of Canada that oil deposits in and around Fort McMurray could be economically produced and brought to market. Eastern and American oil and banking interests were reluctant to commit to the Athabasca oil deposits until the federal government, through the Geological Survey, provided its assessment.

In 1882, an explorer and geologist of considerable reputation, Robert McConnell, came west to investigate the phenomenon. One of his major tasks was to quantify the actual petroleum content of the deposit and to assess how difficult it would be to develop a viable production technology. McConnell applied some basic math. He estimated that about one thousand square miles of oil sands existed within the major deposit and that the thickness varied between one hundred fifty and two hundred twenty-five feet. With an average bitumen content of twelve per cent, he estimated that there were six and a half cubic miles of bitumen or thirty million tons in the sand.

This approach allowed for a slight variation from Bell's theories about a central oil source. McConnell set realistic sights on assessing oil sands *in situ*, that is, where they lay. McConnell speculated that some geological answers could be found by drilling under the oil sands. While McConnell did not completely discard Bell's theory, he did turn the attention of scientists and investors towards extracting the oil which existed within surface deposits.

Although most of Bell's theories proved incorrect, his accounts in Ottawa and during his lectures in eastern Canada stirred excitement among officials, investors and potential settlers. Bell also advocated development of rail and water links, in order to help bring Athabasca oil and other minerals to market.

His comments were eagerly quoted by the *Edmonton Bulletin* and buoyed Edmonton business interests eager to expand north to the arctic. While development of a rail link from Edmonton to Fort McMurray would have to wait another 40 years, his dreams of commercial river travel would soon be realized.

Bell raised economic hopes within Edmonton by publicly heralding the potential of the northern territory in his "Report on Part of the Basin of the Athabasca River." He writes:

"Independent of railway construction, an outlet for the oil to foreign markets might be found by conveying it by steamers for which there is uninterrupted navigation from the Athabasca River to Lake Athabasca and by pipe to Churchill Harbour on Hudson Bay."[50]

Edmonton's bid to host the Canadian national railway had failed, but Bell's comments placed the issue of a south-north transportation network on the table.

Birth of the Athabasca district

The early 1880s were highlighted by enthusiastic national attention towards the west. As rail workers cobbled a steel ribbon across Winnipeg to Calgary, settlers followed behind, establishing loosely knit communities of shacks and shanties which would later become villages, towns and cities. By 1883, the rail had arrived in Calgary, and the Canadian government grappled with more efficient ways to administer and manage the new west.

Under the Hudson's Bay Company's original mandate, Canada was divided into four districts, Northern, Southern, Montreal and Columbia. Smaller areas were subdivided according to natural river boundaries. In 1882, an Order of Council was passed establishing the districts of Athabasca, Alberta, Assiniboine and Saskatchewan. The District of Alberta was named by the Governor General after his wife, the daughter of Queen Victoria. While taxes and representation were to be established for Alberta, Assiniboine and Saskatchewan, The District of Athabasca was still considered untamed, and therefore exempt. The Athabasca district, which largely consisted of the MacKenzie river basin, including the Peace and Athabasca rivers, were ignored due to its lack of significant population.

By boat to McMurray

In 1882, construction of a new type of transportation began which would revolutionize travel in the area. During the winter of 1882-83, work was launched in Fort Chipewyan on the SS Grahame, a huge sternwheel steamer that would serve as the "steam locomotive of the Athabasca River."[51]

The Grahame was built from Fort Chipewyan timber and was crafted under the strict supervision of Captain John McKenzie Smith, an American who had earned his rivers stripes battling the moody Mississippi River. The Grahame was a sturdy freighter built with no frills, and designed to haul freight to and from Fort McMurray to the south, and along the Slave River to the north.

The boat was one hundred thirty feet long and twenty-four feet wide, and while it was primarily designed to haul freight, it did provide spartan passenger transportation. During the evening, the boat docked at shore rather than risk running aground on sandbars in the often-shallow Athabasca and Clearwater rivers. Passengers who did not have a cabin fought mosquitoes and blackflies, and often slept under tables, or in the middle of bags of bacon or dried fruit. Those who were fortunate to rent a small cabin slept on pink bags of hay. During the daytime the SS Grahame moved at a brisk clip of eight miles per hour.

The Grahame also had an insatiable appetite for wood. It could consume a bundle of wood the width of a small room in half an hour. This created a new industry. Because it took the Grahame one-day to consume two days of cut wood, scores of men were employed to chop wood in the forests around Fort McMurray and Fort Chipewyan.

The Graham ran from Fort Chipewyan through Fort McMurray and up the Clearwater River where it linked up with freight and passengers coming from the east through Lake Winnipeg, and the Churchill and Saskatchewan rivers.

Everything from oxen, to food, tobacco and baby grand pianos was shipped up and down the river. Fort McMurray and Fort Chipewyan were now linked by a lifeline which would establish Fort McMurray as a terminal, and a storage area for goods heading to and from the arctic.

North from Edmonton

In 1889, the SS Athabasca was launched at Athabasca Landing. The occasion was momentous because it enabled Fort McMurray to link with Edmonton through a shorter but much more turbulent route. Passengers could travel by sternwheel steamer from Athabasca to a point about a mile from Grand Rapids, located about eighty miles south of Fort McMurray.

Rapids began at Grand Island where passengers disembarked, and freight was transported to the other side of the rapids.

Large flat bottom boats, known as scows, were loaded and freight was maneuvered through the rapids. Some cargo was also moved across the island by a small manual railroad. The boats were taken through the rapids one at a time and then reloaded. Between Grand Rapids and Fort McMurray there were still about ninety miles of rapids to negotiate. The journey required considerable skill.

The challenge of moving valuable cargo through the rapids launched a tradition of aboriginal captains and pilots whose skill and knowledge of the deadly Athabasca rapids would be instrumental in moving people and cargo north.

One of the most famous of these captains was Captain Louis "Shott" Fosseneuve.

The legendary "Shott" Fosseneuve

Louis "Shott" Fosseneuve was a strapping six foot three inch Metis who was born in 1841 in St. Boniface, Manitoba.

At a very early age, Fosseneuve gained a reputation as an excellent fisherman, and a superb hunter. His "sure shot" skills earned him the nickname "Shott", a handle which in his later years would also describe his ability to "shoot" the Athabasca Rapids.

While northern river travel was initiated during the early 1880s, it took some time before it gained credibility. Fort Edmonton's Chief Factor Richard Hardisty, was not yet certain that the Grand Rapids option was safe and instead sent materials north via a longer but more established Lesser Slave Lake/Peace River route. Aside from the time considerations, boatmen had to haul materials upstream through Mirror Landing and then to Lesser Slave Lake. It was long and difficult work.

The idea of "shooting" the Grand Rapids appealed to the boatmen, not only for practical purposes, but also for its excitement. A new breed of river captains emerged who gained legendary status for their ability to run the white water rapids. One of them was Captain Shott, who set out to prove that even packed flatbottom scows could "shoot" the Grand Rapids with the right man at the helm.

Years of navigating the rapids had provided Fosseneuve with a "feel" for the white water. Years earlier, the Catholic Mission serving the region had grown weary of long overland hauls between Lac La Biche and Fort McMurray, so it entrusted Fosseneuve to help navigate priests, nuns, and their cargo across the rapids.

Between 1883 and 1885, Captain Shott compiled an almost flawless record moving materials across the dangerous waters. Many other captains would attempt to emulate, and though most were successful, there were occasions when cargo would be washed overboard, sprayed or drenched.

Shooting the rapids became a matter of pride and profit for captains like Shott whose reputation spread throughout the Region. To this day, the reputation of Louis "Shott" Fosseneuve remains through stories still told by "oldtimers" who routinely observed Fosseneuve's skill.

Harsh land link to Edmonton

Development of a river link north from Athabasca Landing served as a boon to the freight business, eager to take advantage of the stream of materials and supplies earmarked for Fort McMurray, Fort Chipewyan and the arctic.

In 1891, the rail arrived in Edmonton from Calgary and the east, making it possible to ship and receive goods from anywhere in Canada to and from Fort McMurray. Freighters would carry goods through the Grand Rapids linking up with Edmonton by horse and cart. The History of Athabasca Landing notes that:

"Freighting provided a solid and reasonably secure livelihood in the 1890s

and 1900s to anyone with both sufficient capital to purchase a cart, sleigh and horses, and sufficient determination to ensure the hardships of the freighter's life. It was an all-season, all weather activity."[52]

Freighter Laurence Rye, who began his business in 1892 recalled that, "a good two-horse team could haul two tons twenty-two miles a day. A yoke of oxen would haul about one third more but would take two or three hours longer to travel the same distance. The roads and trails would be occupied by scores of teams going and coming..."[53]

The dirt roads from Edmonton to Athabasca were jammed with carts hauling freight and passengers. During the dry times, mosquitoes and horseflies relentlessly attacked passengers and the horses, which pulled the carts. During wet months, the journey was sloppy and arduous. Often, passengers were forced to leap from their seating to push carts and freight through boggy roads.

However, most passengers, trappers and northern adventurers appeared ready to endure the harsh travel. Compared to the previous alternatives, the Edmonton to Fort McMurray route was a blessing.

Ottawa funds initial drilling

In 1894, the Canadian government funded a specific project to help solve the oil sands mystery. Its commitment to finance a further investigation of the oil sands was based largely on R.G. McConnell's 1890-91 report which recommended digging "under" the oil sands mystery. McConnell writes:

"The question of the continuity of the Tar Sands and their petroliferous character under cover can, however, only be settled in a decided manner by boring and it is highly desirable that drilling operations should be undertaken for that purpose."[54]

In 1894, Ottawa allocated seven thousand dollars to A.W. Fraser, an Ontario oil driller, who set up a boring operation north of where the Town of Athabasca stands today. Cable rigs wormed to a depth of eleven hundred feet where natural gas was discovered, but there was little or no evidence of a massive oil pool streaming north.

Fraser's work, however, did stimulate increased economic interest in the region. A number of other drilling projects conducted in the Wabasca and Pelican Rapids areas produced some natural gas finds and identified some tar sand deposits, but again no major underground source was found.

The Wonderful Light of Pelican Portage

The 1893-94 explorations did produce one bright result. It was known as the Wonderful Light of Pelican Portage.

In July 1893, four geologists set out from Edmonton in an attempt to drill deep into the core of an Athabasca River site about one hundred miles south of Fort

---

McMurray. It didn't take long for the crew to produce major results. In their first attempt, the team struck gas at the depth of about six hundred twenty-five feet and unleashed a natural gas blast estimated at six hundred pounds per square inch. The earth rocked as the gas exploded. Exuberant about their amazing find, a team member scrambled to Edmonton to report to Ottawa by telegraph that a substantial gas source had been tapped. The team asked, "what should we do?"

Ottawa replied in two words, "do nothing." In a subsequent letter, the Pelican Rapids geologists were told that since their gas was located far from any viable transportation link, their mission had come to an end. Efforts now turned to containing the well. The geologists developed a concrete seal, but were unable to cap the well's intense force. Finally, to prevent the well from further fouling the air, the team ignited the gas causing a bright and blinding light which could be seen for miles.

In her book *Tales of the Tarsands*, author Dorothy Dahlgren notes that "the Wonderful Light of Pelican Portage was born to be a beacon and a boon to lonely explorers, freighters and trappers – a high beckoning finger of flame which later promised untold undiscovered riches still hidden underground on the banks of the Athabasca River."[55]

The bright light acquired mystical significance in local culture, and even aroused the curiosity of a group of scientific experts and journalists in October 1912 — nearly thirty years after it originally was lit.

During the early 1900s, entrepreneurs developed a number of schemes to tap the well and bring its free flowing product to market. Debates raged in Edmonton concerning the safety of natural gas. While the discussions ensued, gas was discovered in Viking, located only forty miles from Edmonton, effectively ending talk of developing the Pelican Rapids site. The light was finally extinguished in 1918, but from time to time, it would re-ignite and would remain lit for years.

Pelican Rapids would later become the site of a trading post and a sawmill. Its natural flowing gas made it an oasis for trappers and travellers *en route* to Fort McMurray. The heat generated enabled crops to be grown virtually year-round. The energy also fuelled a sawmill which would later provide wood for the building of Fort McMurray homes.

Pelican Rapids also boasted one final claim to fame. Gas from the well was routed to a small cubicle at the outskirts of the trading post, providing the passersby with the area's only heated outhouse.

Oil development wanes

As the 1880s drew to a close, Dr. George M. Dawson, director of the Geological Survey of Canada, refused to waver from the Bell's theory of underground oil pools. It was his view that the Fraser's crew had either not drilled deep enough, or had not accurately located the central oil source.

In 1895, Dawson personally visited the drilling site and insisted in his 1890-91 report that layers of shale were likely blocking access to the region's oil pool. He recommended drilling as deep as two thousand feet. Dawson urged the government to carry on. He wrote:

"It is also necessary to bear in mind that even in the more productive oil fields, the occurrence of valuable accumulations of petroleum is confined to certain limited areas of "pools" and although there can scarcely be any reasonable doubt of the existence of an important oil field in northern Alberta and Athabasca, the first experimental sinking in an entirely new region may not prove to be successful as a source of oil."[56]

While the Canadian government remained optimistic about natural gas deposits and various mineral finds within the Athabasca district, its enthusiasm about finding the elusive petroleum pool was sinking fast.

After 1898, no further drilling by the Canadian government was undertaken. It had become apparent to federal officials that unlocking the secret source of Athabasca oil would require additional cash, expertise and technology. At a time when the county's energies were focusing on more conventional oil sources, interest in the Athabasca oil sands began to fade.

During the early part of the 1900s it would be up to a series of adventurers, explorers and opportunists to keep the flame alive. As the decade closed, Fort McMurray's local attention returned to the fur trade. Unbeknownst to the handful of local residents, Fort McMurray was about to endure another mini-boom. Events were transpiring in the Yukon which would soon flood the region with northbound transients and gold diggers.

Gold and the first RCMP patrol

In 1895, the imagination of the Edmonton media, speculators and investors was briefly captured by rumours of a gold discovery along the Athabasca River. Two prospectors returned to Edmonton following a profitable visit to an Athabasca River tributary. Hundreds of prospectors rushed north following the Athabasca in hopes of duplicating the reported strike. The June 6, 1895 *Edmonton Bulletin* heralded the excitement with a banner story headlined "Gold on the Athabasca." The details of this supposed gold find were vague, but the news spurred considerable interest in Edmonton as gold seekers streamed north in search of their fortune.

Excitement surrounding a Yukon gold strike in 1897 inspired thousands of speculators to pack their bags and wind their way north to the Klondike by boat, sled, cart, rail or foot.

Up to eight routes were being touted to reach the Yukon and one of these involved overland and river travel through Fort McMurray. In the face of a huge human push to the Yukon a Northwest Mounted Police detachment was established in 1892 at Athabasca Landing. Although sporadic patrols had previously ventured north in an attempt to keep peace and thwart liquor smuggling, the first regular patrol was launched to Fort McMurray in 1897. A trio of NWMP officers left Athabasca and travelled by sled to the House River.

The NWMP's priority remained to stem the tide of illegal liquor to the north, and stopped at a cabin occupied by a trapper about thirty miles south of the Grand Rapids. On December 27, the group purchased additional provisions and continued their journey to Fort McMurray. Along the way, they met a number of Klondike-bound speculators.

On January 5, 1898, the three officers entered Fort McMurray, the first time an organized police presence had visited the community. In his patrol report, Inspector Routledge, head of the detachment, describes the Fort McMurray settlement.

"At Fort McMurray, I found Mr. R. Flett the Hudson's Bay Company clerk in charge. The so called Fort consists of five small log shacks situated at the junction of the Clearwater and Athabasca Rivers put up in 1885. During the summer months McMurray is a fairly busy place owing to the transshipment of the freight brought down the rapids in scows to the steamer Grahame....I was informed by Mr. Flett that two families of Crees living a short distance in a south easterly direction from that post were in fair circumstances. He stated to me that the fur in the district was very scarce due principally to the frequent forest fires of late years. A short distance from the fort, there is a small section of country from which a fair supply of hay is obtained for the company's stock...I was informed by a man named John McDonald a servant of the Hudson's Bay Company who has resided at McMurray for some years (26) that the bench between that place and the Grand Rapids is fairly level and that there is a summer horse trail between these points." [57]

By 1898, Flett had complained to a second NWMP patrol that more than two hundred boats had passed through en route to the Klondike, and that parties had shot three of his dogs. One of the members of the second RCMP detachment, D. M. Howard, described Fort McMurray in 1898. "The Hudson's Bay's Company have a small trading post here. There is no settlement outside of the company's houses." [58]

Bill and Christine Gordon

There existed a handful of entrepreneurs who, in the late 1890s recognized Fort McMurray's potential. One of them was William "Bill" Gordon.

In 1898, Gordon, a trader from La Loche, Saskatchewan sold his business and established a trading post and general store next to the Hudson's Bay post on the east banks of the Athabasca River. The site is roughly where the Grant MacEwan Bridge stands today.

His sister, Christine, had been running a store in Athabasca, and joined her brother in Fort McMurray, becoming the community's first fulltime "white" female resident. During Bill Gordon's frequent absences from Fort McMurray, Christine was left to operate the store and restaurant. She was known as a compassionate and kind individual, who quickly won the respect of local aboriginal residents. In his book *Paddle*

Wheels to Bucketwheels, J.G. MacGregor refers to Christine Gordon as follows:

"Throughout all the decades till her death during the 1940s, she was in many ways the town's most esteemed citizen."[59]

The presence of the Gordons in the Fort McMurray area came to be marked in the names of water bodies. Gordon Lake, located northeast of Fort McMurray would be named after Bill Gordon. The Christina River, formerly known as Pembina or Summerberry River, would carry the name (misspelled) of Christine.

Christine Gordon: Honoured above all

Picture a woman arriving in the wild north with a phonograph, a museum oil painting and two panes of imported glass. Picture a half dozen fur traders and adventurers sharing tobacco and frontier stories with the strains of Beethoven's Moonlight Sonata wafting from Christine Gordon's cabin.

For a half century, Christine Gordon was a diamond in the Fort McMurray rough as she brought Scottish charm and the luxuries of the old country to the untamed frontier. With her bare hands, it is said, she built her own log cabin. Her shack offered a clear view of the Athabasca River, thanks to two panes of glass which she painstakingly packed in her steamer trunk before leaving the "old country."

She was a proud and cultured person. Gordon brought with her from England an oil painting which had once hung in London's Royal Academy of Arts Gallery. It hung in her cabin. Her grandfather was known as the man who had discovered a cure for scurvy. She was both tough and compassionate. Local legend has it that on one occasion she travelled one hundred miles to personally deliver food and clothing to a needy family. Christine Gordon made sure that no one was ever denied food.

Her glass-paned shack became a gathering place for native people. At the rear, she would offer a rack for local folks to dry their furs. Aside from being the friendly thing to do, it was also good business. Gordon would serve home made bread with jam produced from locally picked berries. She'd also offer tea and trade stories. Gordon also became a gardener, taking packs of seeds which had been shipped from Scotland, turning them into potatoes, carrots, peas and beans which grew to huge sizes thanks to Fort McMurray's long summer days.

Gordon was also a protector of animals. While hunting for food or skin, local people would often kill mother bears or wolves. Gordon's house was frequently filled with bear and wolf cubs which she raised until they could be released in the wild.

It was legendary Chief Paul Cree who afforded Gordon one of the region's highest honours. Paul Cree and Christine Gordon had been close friends for years. Gordon had, shortly after her arrival, bought a book on home nursing and began applying her new skills to an assortment of local ailments. Local elders returned the favour by sharing lessons about herb and local medicines.

In her book, *Tales of the Tarsands*, author and raconteur Dorothy Dahlgren notes, "she could dose a fever as well as she could put splints on a broken arm. There was never a time she was unwilling to go out in any kind of weather to perform acts of mercy."[60]

In his waning years, ailing and blind, Chief Paul Cree lay in his tent outside Fort McMurray, and Gordon would come daily to bring food and to help maintain his fire. Even though his faculties were fading, Gordon continued to accord Cree the respect of a Chief. On his deathbed, Chief Paul Cree made one final request.

He asked that his people find the tallest spruce tree on the Athabasca River and erect a lobstick in honour of Christine Gordon, a sign to all that Gordon was a person of substance and stature. A lobstick is a living totem pole cut with all branches removed except for two at the top which appear as wings.

As late as the 1940s the Christine Gordon lobstick continued to tower above the Athabasca River in tribute to a woman of substance who was never too busy to care.

Closure of Hudson's Bay

Faced with competition from the Gordons and other free traders, the Hudson's Bay Company assessed its McMurray operation and concluded that it was not profitable to retain its trading post. Severe winters and recent forest fires had caused an overall decline in fur trade revenues. While the fort maintained a post office and served as a steamboat transfer point, it was not enough to support a full Hudson's Bay operation.

In 1898, a communiqué was received from Winnipeg, ordering closure of the trading post. It would maintain a presence in the community as a transportation terminus. At the close of the century, the post that John Moberly built and named Fort McMurray was no more.

As long as the sun shines...

Not only did Klondike-bound adventurers cause trouble for the RCMP in the north, they also threatened aboriginal people. Sacred lands which had been used for hunting and fishing now became the staging point for hundreds of fortune seekers. Traplines were trampled and natural habitats destroyed.

Routes within the Athabasca District became byways for the smuggling of liquor to the north. The newcomers also harmed sled dogs through their use of poison bait. Native people sought protection from the federal government, which at the same time was looking for a way to assume control of natural resources within the north.

In 1899, the Canadian government sent a negotiating party to the Athabasca region, aimed at developing a pact to secure lands for oil and agricultural development. This would enable new European immigrants to populate the west, and for private investors to begin exploring petroleum resources. During the summer of 1899, Woodland Cree in the region signed Treaty 8 with the Crown. Missionaries, police and others touted the advantages of signing the Treaty, which would set aside reserve land for native people to hunt, fish, trap and maintain a traditional lifestyle.

Signees included the Cree, Beaver, Chipewyan and Slavey. Under the agreement the aboriginal peoples promised to "conduct and behave themselves as good and loyal subjects of Her Majesty the Queen." In addition they would maintain Canadian laws and assist "in bringing to justice and punishment any Indian offending against the stipulations of this treaty."[61]

In turn, the Crown agreed to set aside lands for hunting, trapping and fishing and to provide education, medical assistance and a variety of other services. On an annual basis native people covered by the treaty would receive a payment of no less than five dollars. The deal looked good at the time, but inflation had not been considered. To this day, the RCMP dress in ceremonial red coats once a year and appear in Fort McKay and other settlements on Treaty Days to hand out money to native people.

On August 4, 1899, the Chipewyan and Cree Indians of Fort McMurray met and signed Treaty 8. The Treaty was read and explained to the "headmen" by Rev. Father Lacombe and T.M. Clarke.

Representing the Crown were A. Lacombe, Arthur Warwick, T.M. Clarke, F.J. Fitzgerald, W.G.H. Vernon and Treaty Commissioner J.A.J. McKenna. Signing for Fort McMurray's native people were Headman Seapotakinum Cree and Chipewyan Chief Adam Boucher. Similar signings were held in communities throughout the north.

The Canadian government was satisfied that the Treaty zoned native people into reserves and opened the door for widespread farming, trade, mining, logging and homesteading. The Treaty covered the northern half of Alberta, the northwest corner of Saskatchewan, the east corner of British Columbia and the southern tip of the Northwest Territories.

While the elders who signed the Treaty did not fully comprehend the legal wording of the document, they were clear that the treaty guaranteed their people a number of benefits. Oral tradition, recently recorded, indicates that Treaty 8 included: schools and education; doctors, hospitals and medicines; retention of hunting and fishing rights; land acquired by the Queen had only six-inch surface rights; exempt from taxation; policing; cattle and horses provided as well as farming and harvesting equipment; and in case of hunger, all gates would be opened.

Over time, as the federal government forgot many of its oral promises, the full clout of the written word took precedence. During the latter half of the twentieth century, differences in written and oral understandings led to lengthy court battles over control of natural resources and land settlements.

While the written version of Treaty 8 does not include a closing date for the Treaty, native tradition is quite specific. Native tradition holds that Treaty 8 will hold: "As long as the sun shines, the grass grows, and the water flows…"[62]

Raphael Cree remembers

More than a century after the signing of Treaty 8, Raphael Cree remembers the day and the place. Born in 1893, Cree recalled the signing in a 1999 interview "I was six years old at the time and remembers it was a nice day . The signing was at the Snye because it was the only place you could beach canoes. Father Lacombe was there. He did a lot of interpreting and that. It was a big change but you had to live with it."[63]

Throughout the twentieth century, Raphael and wife Louise, who died in 1996, were fixtures in Fort McMurray. Raphael Cree will be recorded in local history as one of the area's best runners.

He and Joe Cheecham were known as excellent hunters, but it was Cree who was known for his strong legs. In 1910, the world's champion runner was reported to have covered twenty-five miles in two hours and forty-five minutes. But Raphael Cree had his own personal best. He was known as a strong man who, in the early years, could outrun anyone. One day, Cree left the Christina at about six in the morning to buy a gun at Bill Gordon's store in Fort McMurray. The distance was twenty-one miles. By noon, Cree had returned. When you consider the time it took for Cree to try out the gun, stop for some food and run back with the rifle, his feat was truly incredible.

Cree has a simple formula for living a long life. He talks about staying fit by chopping wood and hauling water. He also refers to the native emphasis on living purely, and on the importance of sharing.

"A lot of times you come back from hunting you would see people who had a family with hungry kids," he said. "I'd say there's a moose there, go help yourself."[64]

As the century turns

With the signing of Treaty 8, the gates were opened for those with sharp entrepreneurial skills to develop the plentiful natural resources that had been identified in and around Fort McMurray. The community stood at a crossroads. Its feet were planted in a rich native tradition which for generations had supported families through hunting, fishing and trapping.

Its future, however, would be linked to a scientific mystery which had yet to be solved. Its untapped oil reserves would serve as a lure for thousands to come and would produce growth and prosperity which few could have ever imagined.

Chapter Two:
1900-1919

As the twentieth century progressed, words such as boom and mega were used to measure Fort McMurray's growth. But in the beginning, the words were much simpler - trapping, fishing, survival and promise. The fledgling community of Fort McMurray was held together by a handful of native residents and entrepreneurs, attracted by the isolation, the adventure and the call of opportunity.

In 1901, Fort McMurray's population stood at twenty-eight. There were a number of explorers and opportunists who passed through the community, but few remained.

However, the destiny of the community was about to change. Just prior to Alberta's incorporation as a province, longstanding rumours about pools of untapped oil began to reach a fever pitch. Aboriginal people and local traders had known about the Athabasca oil sands for generations. By using a mixture of tar and spruce tree gum, a highly effective sealant was produced, which could plug holes in canoes and other river craft. With the advent of the combustible engine and the automobile, increasing attention was focused on the mysterious substance oozing from the ground north of Fort McMurray.

Dreamers and innovators had no lack of ideas and applications for the "tarsands." Entrepreneur Robert Fitzsimmons would boast in the early 1920s that tarsands had potential for the production of road-paving material, ink, explosives, roofing, varnishes, kerosene, rust proofing, fence post preservatives, and skin disease medicine.

In 1897, an Ontario-born traveller and adventurist, James Cornwall, began exploring the north and in particular the Peace and Athabasca river basins. In his travels as a labourer, trapper, trader and steamboat builder, he became Fort McMurray's informal ambassador, expounding in political and social circles on the region's vast economic potential. Cornwall was a visionary, but his motives weren't completely selfless. He quickly realized that improved transportation links and economic development would improve his own financial standing.

"He was quite a promoter," recalled pharmacist Walter Hill in a 1985 interview. "He was full of BS, and even though a lot of his own ventures failed, he was very responsible for the development of our part of the country."[1]

Cornwall's timing was perfect. As yet, Fort McMurray's potential was untapped. In July 1905, Prime Minister Wilfred Laurier's Liberal government passed a series of autonomy bills which set the stage for the establishment of the provinces of Alberta and Saskatchewan. Laurier appointed George Bulyea, a prominent Liberal, as the Province's first Lieutenant Governor. It was Bulyea's responsibility to choose a premier until elections could be held. At the time, the Liberal party was the strongest political force in Alberta, and when Liberal Member of Parliament and *Edmonton Bulletin* publisher Frank Oliver declined Bulyea's offer to serve as premier, the opportunity was handed to Alexander Rutherford, a Strathcona lawyer and member of the Alberta Territorial Legislature.

The first election was fiercely fought between Rutherford's Liberals and the Conservatives of R.B. Bennett, but one factor was a "given." Both parties believed that economic expansion through modern science and technology held the key to the province's future growth. It would be observed later in the century that "Albertans don't vote, they stampede,"[2] and the 1905 election was no exception. Rutherford carried the 1905 vote with twenty-three of twenty-five seats.

A total of 25,163 votes were cast province-wide, but none of them came from Fort McMurray. Peace River businessman William Fletcher Bredin became the first Member of the Legislative Assembly (MLA) to serve the huge Athabasca constituency. He was elected by acclamation.

Rutherford's government quickly looked for ways to assure the province's economic health and prosperity. As the Liberals looked north, there was a strong sense of history in the air. Surveys from the Canadian government, reports from scientists and travellers, and centuries of anecdotal information, clearly focused the provincial government's attention on the northern Athabasca river basin.

James Cornwall's advocacy efforts in Edmonton, coupled with promising scientific studies began to produce results. In 1905, Cornwall and Edmonton-based business interests began promoting the development of a railway that would connect the capital city with Fort McMurray. Cornwall also launched his own drilling campaign, in an attempt to tap the elusive oil source that bubbled so seductively in and around Fort McMurray.

By the late 1910s, it was time to officially place Fort McMurray on the map. Around 1909, Cornwall began informally subdividing the Clearwater flatlands, in order to create a townsite. The need to identify some general lots and homesteads was spurred by Fort McMurray's first major boom. From 1901-1906, the number of confirmed residents in the community had increased almost tenfold. In 1906, Fort McMurray had an official population of two hundred thirty-six.

The Count: Charisma and phony claims

As news of the oilsands' vast potential spread across the country, Fort McMurray served as a magnet for explorers, entrepreneurs and speculators. Many could be termed "characters," and none was more flamboyant or self-promoting than Count Alfred Von Hammerstein, son of a German army colonel. Von Hammerstein quit his military career in the 1890s, travelled to New York, and then began drifting towards northern Alberta.

He became a Canadian citizen in 1903 and soon after began spending summers in the Fort McMurray area where he brought in drilling machinery and began searching for oil near Bitumont, about fifty-five miles north. Von Hammerstein promoted his efforts so aggressively that he was invited to Ottawa in 1907 to report to a Parliamentary Committee studying natural resources in the Mackenzie River basin.

Von Hammerstein parlayed his eastern trip into a successful investment campaign. During a trip to Montreal, he snared the interest of Canadian businessmen and some American investors. In 1910, The Athabasca Oil and Asphalt Company was organized at a founding meeting in Montreal, which included a United States senator, representatives of two American banks and an official from the Marshall Oil Company. By 1910, Von Hammerstein announced to the federal Department of the Interior that he had struck oil. In 1911, based largely on his reported results, he sold 11,404 acres of land to investors for twenty-one thousand nine hundred thirteen dollars.

However, rumours circulating within Fort McMurray placed a different spin on Von Hammerstein's oil strike. An informant told the Royal Canadian Mounted Police that Von Hammerstein had actually poured tar into one of his wells prior to an investor's arrival. Charges of falsely reporting drilling results were never laid, but the rumours served to sully Von Hammerstein's already dubious reputation.

For starters, Von Hammerstein was not the most popular person in town. Soon after his arrival in Fort McMurray, Von Hammerstein acquired some Athabasca River shore land where the Hudson's Bay chose to beach its boats during winter. Until the settlement was officially subdivided, Von Hammerstein arranged for the Hudson's Bay Company to pay his taxes in return for shore rent.

In 1905, while leading a barge through the Grand Rapids, just south of Fort McMurray, his boat overturned, killing those on board. Von Hammerstein swam ashore, walked back to town, and quickly secured another rig to continue his explorations.

In a letter to a government official in Calgary in February 1909, J. Keele of the federal Department of Mines in Ottawa writes with tongue in cheek, "please try to drown Hammerstein as he is trying to make trouble for us in the west."[3]

Von Hammerstein remained fixed on Bell's theory of a "mother" pool of oil with a series of streams which fed the oil sands. But while Von Hammerstein was unsuccessful in his quest for oil, he did tap into a motherlode of a different kind. Between 1907 and 1912, his company, Northern Alberta Exploration, drilled a number of wells at the mouth of the Horse River. While the company failed to find oil, it did locate huge quantities of salt. Hammerstein and his partner Alban Burnetta wrestled briefly with how to mine the salt, and how to bring it to market. When Von Hammerstein and Burnetta dissolved their unsuccessful oil partnership in 1912, Von Hammerstein pounced on a new opportunity. He filed a claim for salt. The lease would lay dormant until the mid-1920s when Von Hammerstein returned to launch a commercial salt operation.

Von Hammerstein also gained the rights to mine salt on two Fort McKay River lots. Looking for oil in 1909, Von Hammerstein hit a pool of brine and laid claim to the lease under the title "Salt of the Earth."

Von Hammerstein was not completely a man of business. He was also an accomplished flautist, and in 1929-30 spent some time at the University of Alberta, where he played in the University Orchestra alongside Dr. Karl Clark, another oil sands pioneer. Clark played the clarinet.

Although Von Hammerstein never made large profits with his oil operations, he did focus national attention on the emerging Athabasca Oil Sands. As well, he did identify large quantities of buried salt, which he would later attempt to mine commercially. Von Hammerstein died in St. Albert in 1941, at the age of seventy-four.

George Golosky: twelve- year old runaway

In 1909, William "Bill" Gordon was named Fort McMurray's first postmaster. The town post office was located in his general store that also served as the commercial hub for the area. Bill Gordon had come to Fort McMurray a decade earlier with his sister Christine, and in 1903, they were joined by a lost and lonely pre-teenager named George.

George had come to Canada in the late 1800s from Romania with his father, Ivan Yurejckuk. When George's dad remarried and relations with his new step-mother became strained, the twelve-year-old ran away from home, finding shelter in a livery stable. In the Beverly area of Edmonton, he became a type of "Oliver" character, living on the street, earning a few cents at odd jobs. While on the street, George heard about the opportunities in Fort McMurray that awaited hard working young men.

In 1903, George presented himself at Bill Gordon's store. At the time, there were barely three dozen inhabitants of the settlement, and there existed an unwritten rule etched in aboriginal tradition that no one should go without food or shelter. The Gordons took George under their wings, informally adopting him. George assumed Bill and Christine's surname, and initially raised his own children as Gordons. In 1915, George launched a sawmill with Gordon and Nick Moore. The sawmill, which produced lumber and siding, was located at the east end of Franklin Avenue near the current location of Marshall Street.

A few years after the sawmill's opening, George and Bill Gordon had a "falling out" and their relationship was severed. It was a painful breakup for George, who dropped Gordon and assumed the name Golosky. To his death, George Golosky refused to disclose where the name Golosky came from, although it's suspected by some family members that Golosky was the maiden name of George's mother in Romania.

Plan of the McMurray Settlement

During the first decade of the 1900s, surveyors began mapping Fort McMurray and dividing the townsite into river lots. The lots were divided in parcels up to ninety-four acres in a grid that ran from the Clearwater River, across the lower townsite, and up the hill to Abasand.

On July 9, 1910, surveyor H.W. Selby completed his mapping and submitted his "Plan of the McMurray Settlement," which was ratified in Ottawa by the federal Department of the Interior on Feb. 13, 1911.

Twenty-seven river lots were assigned to a number of businessmen, investors and speculators, who in turn could subdivide the area into farms and housing lots. In the first municipal map of 1911, the Gordon family commanded the vast majority of land, under a variety of names. Bill controlled space near the Athabasca River. Christine was granted land on the east end of Franklin Avenue.

George is listed as owning two large tracts of land under two names. The plan shows that George Golosky owned the forty-four acres in and around where the Grant MacEwan Bridge stands today. George Gordon, the same person, is listed as owning thirty-eight acres along the Clearwater River in the Riedel Street area. Through a number of names, the Gordons controlled about twenty-five per cent of the townsite.

Other names of landowners identified in the first McMurray plan include William Biggs, Alex McDonald, John McDonald, D.S. MacKenzie, Wallis Hungenberg, Robert Armick and Robert Dewar.

While some landowners readily subdivided their property, some speculators preferred to speculate, and let their land remain undeveloped. During Fort McMurray's early days, free land to develop dwellings was hard to find. Reports from 1914 indicate some residential lots went on the block for as high as fourteen hundred dollars.

The natural attraction

In the early 1900s, Fort McMurray's rivers teemed with walleye, pickerel, burbot, goldeye, whitefish, northern pike and more. In the forests and wetlands, there was an abundance of animals for food and trapping, including moose, deer, muskrat, beaver, fisher, fox, lynx, marten and mink.

In many ways, Fort McMurray was a self-contained environment. The land provided meat and fish year round, and during the long summer days, backyard gardens yielded potatoes, carrots, tomatoes, lettuce and more. The nearby forests burst with raspberries, blueberries, cranberries, saskatoons and strawberries. These naturally grown foods, along with moose and deer were canned to sustain families during the long cold winters. It was a hard life, but no one starved. The land provided if you were prepared to work.

As word began to spread about the development of Waterways and McMurray, native and Metis families began migrating north from the Lac La Biche and Athabasca areas. The crush of new immigrants seeking homesteads in the area just north of Edmonton had caused some settlers and aboriginal people to feel claustrophobic. With a lack of economic activity other than farming, many families began to focus their attention on the open spaces and the rumoured economic potential in and around Fort McMurray.

Birth in the muskeg

In 1911, Caroline Desjarlais was pregnant and expecting her fifth child when her husband, Michel, announced that the family would soon move from Lac La Biche to Fort McMurray. Although Caroline's family had set the couple up with a house, a cow and with some household possessions, due to Michel's freewheeling lifestyle, it didn't take long before the family was penniless.

The family had few options as it prepared to travel north. The rail link to Waterways had yet to be built. There were no roads. But there was a series of traplines and paths that extended north to the House River and then to Fort McMurray.

While Michel carefully packed the family's possessions into a canoe, Caroline prepared her four daughters for the journey. The two older girls, Philomena and Mary, carried their two younger sisters through the muskeg. When conditions allowed, Caroline pulled the canoe along the river, while Michel rode with the children and the provisions.

But there was a complication along the way. Somewhere in the muskeg between Lac La Biche and the House River, Caroline went into labour and gave birth to her fifth daughter, Eva. After a short rest, the family picked up and continued their walk to Fort McMurray.

Soon after the family's arrival in Fort McMurray, Caroline left her husband and sustained her family by taking in sewing and laundry. But her major contribution to the community came as a birthing attendant. Before Fort McMurray's first physician and surgeon, Dr. George Ings came north in 1921; Caroline served as a midwife, and as a lay nurse.

During the winter of 1917-18, Fort McMurray fell victim to the pandemic flu, which tore across the world claiming millions of lives. The men living at the Hudson's Bay outpost were the hardest hit. Caroline agreed to care for the Hudson's Bay men, putting herself at risk in the process. It is said that due to her tough disposition, Caroline never came down with the flu. Treating the Hudson's Bay men reaped one benefit. She met Fred Newsam, who after regaining his health, proposed marriage. The two launched a family.

Even after a fulltime doctor arrived in town, the midnight knocks at Caroline's door did not subside. "It was nothing for me to hear those voices in the middle of the night '*Caroline, Caroline somebody needs you*',"[4] recalls daughter Sarah Finch. It was often a young native woman in labour. Caroline would comfort them in Cree and help them through childbirth. No money ever changed hands. Most of the women she helped were poor and couldn't afford to pay the doctor's twenty-five dollar fee. Payment was made with moose meat or a rabbit. In her later years, Caroline's generosity paid off. During the 1940s and 1950s Caroline made a habit of frequenting the Oilsands Hotel. She'd slap down 20 cents for her first two beers, but never had to pay after that. Invariably, the beer hall was full of McMurrayites who she had either delivered, or had nursed in sickness. The beer was always free. She would wander home each night around ten, check in on her mother, and come up the steps of her home singing *You Are My Sunshine*.

"There was not a lazy bone in her body," recalls daughter Sarah. "She would chop wood, sew, do laundry and care for others. She looked at the faces of the people of Waterways and McMurray, and smiled because she knew that they were all her's."[5] Caroline Desjarlais died in 1958 at the age of seventy-six.

Psychic powers and the first "newcomer" birth

In 1911, Charlie Eymundson, an Icelandic immigrant and his bride Sophia arrived in Fort McMurray and immersed themselves in the trapping business. Eymundson became a skilled bushman, and eventually became a free fur trader in competition with the Hudson's Bay Company.

While a small aboriginal community already existed in the area, Sophia earned the distinction of giving birth to Fort McMurray's first "newcomer baby."

In 1911, Romeo Eymundson was born, followed two years later by sister Iona. When Romeo was thirteen, his father Charles bought a run-down single phone line system and connected houses by running wire through trees. Romeo took over the telephone business and ran it until 1958. Iona was Fort McMurray's first born "newcomer" girl and was brought up within a household that spoke three languages, Icelandic, Cree and English. Charlie Eymundson was a hard-working local character who believed strongly in the value of reading and education. On a regular basis, the McMurray post office received bundles of the Chicago Herald, London Mirror and Toronto Star Weekly addressed to Eymundson.

It was also said that Eymundson possessed psychic powers. At age four in Iceland, he once woke up screaming claiming that he had dreamt about a schooner crashing just outside the bay where the family lived. His father carried Charlie to the window to convince him that his vision was merely a dream. Exactly two weeks later, a schooner was caught in a gale and crashed into the rocks, killing a number of sailors.

But it was Eymundson's amazing vision regarding his son Romeo that raised local eyebrows. One day Eymundson was chopping wood when he felt a sudden chill and stopped in his tracks. Dropping his axe, Eymundson declared "there's something wrong with Romeo."[6] Eymundson knew that Romeo was alone on the trapline. Charlie hitched up his dogs and raced to the family cabin. Eymundson could not locate his son. When Charlie saw odd tracks at the top of a hill, he immediately understood what had happened.

Romeo had shot a moose, but while trying to negotiate a steep slope, his toboggan had tipped over sending, the moose and the provisions tumbling. Romeo was pinned for hours at minus twenty-five degrees, but was kept alive by the warmth of the freshly killed moose.

Charlie Eymundson freed Romeo, reloaded the moose, untangled the dogs and brought the whole party home safely.

Romeo Eymundson lived most of his life in Waterways, and through the years, gained a reputation as both an early riser and hard worker. It was not uncommon for residents to awaken as early as four-thirty a.m., and see Eymundson shoveling his Bulyea Avenue sidewalk.

Birth of a community

In 1911-12, a number of events occurred which provided evidence within Fort McMurray that a human migration was underway.

In previous years, the existence of forest fires was not seen as a risk to human life. Traditional culture held that naturally caused fire was a way for the earth to replenish its trees and vegetation. But in 1911, with Fort McMurray's population bulging at three hundred and twelve concern over human safety and the potential for property loss sparked the Department of the Interior to establish the Fort McMurray Fire District. The district covered almost twenty thousand square miles.

Catholic Church services had been provided in the area on and off since the mid-1850s. In 1904, Father Lucien Croise began serving Fort McMurray from the church's larger base in Fort McKay, located about thirty-five miles to the north. On May 29, 1911, Bishop Emile Grouard, Father Lucien Croise and Brother Guillaume Leroux set sail from Fort Chipewyan aboard the SS St. Joseph headed for Fort McMurray to build a mission chapel.

Until he landed on June 3, 1911, the Bishop had not fully understood Fort McMurray's potential. Father Adophe Laffont, Fort McMurray's local priest, wrote in his journal:

"Up until this time the Bishop had never believed the rumours that Fort McMurray might become an important place. He could have taken some land and had it registered. Now it's too late; every piece of land is already claimed by others –Metis, English and Americans. So the Catholic mission is forced to buy some land."[7]

The Bishop met with Alex McDonald, a local Metis, and received a land donation of one acre. Because none of McMurray's new landowners had received patent letters from Ottawa, land could not officially be exchanged. Based on a handshake between Grouard and McDonald, plans began for construction of the Saint Jean-Baptiste Mission, known locally as the "Old Log Mission." The mission was located just south of the current River Park Glen "Syncrude Towers." Father Croisé, Father Laffont, Brother Hermon and Brother LeRoux built the mission over three years. Living quarters were located in the attic.

Father Laffront's journal reports:

"Logs had been cut and squared seven or eight years previous. They are carried to the site, but the quantity falls short of our requirement. More have to be cut in the bush and then squared into construction timbers. This takes time and men...Brother Leroux made a contraption to haul the logs to the construction site and so the building is started."[8]

Through their busy building schedule Father Croise took time to hear confessions of aboriginal people, who came to Fort McMurray twice during the church's construction period. The first was in mid-June, as natives arrived to receive their Treaty 8 money and to purchase tea, flour and lard. The second time was at the end of July, to buy additional supplies.

Building supplies were hard to find and while the shell of the mission was soon complete, more luxurious features such as floors and windows had not been installed. Father Laffont's journal recalls:

"The summer (1913) goes by in the same way as last year, except for the fact that Father is alone and acts as a carpenter. He was in a hurry to keep the Blessed Sacrament and to this end he improvises an altar with some discarded boards, as there was nothing else available. In spite of this deficiency, the altar was made ready; not very rich neither very beautiful, but Our Lord was there present to keep company with Father Laffont."[9]

Aside from his skills as a priest and carpenter, Laffont was a sturdy man who loved to swim. Before Fort McMurray's recreational facilities were in place, Laffont, in later years with the assistance of pharmacist Walter Hill, would teach swimming to many young people. Their outdoor pool was the Syne.

In 1912, D.C. McTavish, Fort McMurray's first Presbyterian Minister, petitioned for the establishment of "McMurray School District No. 2833 of the Province of Alberta." A carpenter by trade, McTavish and wife Cassia launched classes in a log cabin located on the north side of Franklin Avenue between Fr. Mercredi Street and Alberta Drive. They began with thirteen students and it was only after the school swelled to sixty-two grades one to nine students in one classroom that the Fort McMurray school board brought in an additional teacher.

McTavish built Fort McMurray's first Presbyterian Church and school house in 1914. For his efforts, McTavish earned about six hundred dollars per year. McTavish and his wife remained in Fort McMurray until 1927. The church that McTavish built is currently in Heritage Park and during the 1980s served as the headquarters for the Fort McMurray Golden Years Society.

In 1912, the Hudson's Bay Company returned to Fort McMurray setting up a large freight storage warehouse on the eastern banks of the Athabasca River, just below where the Grant MacEwan Bridge stands today. Although the fur trade remained poor, increased trading buoyed business as Fort McMurray began serving as a launching point for travel and exploration to the Northwest Territories.

As the decade turned, the area along the Athabasca River served as an economic hub. Hudson's Bay Company and William Gordon's store served as clearing houses and bartering ground for furs, food, firearms and other provisions. The area today has been abandoned, used only during summer months as a go-kart track and miniature golf course.

With land for churches, housing, and businesses becoming a priority, Fort McMurray began to expand east from the Athabasca River. At first, the Clearwater River served as the settlement's main downtown thoroughfare. In 1913, tree clearing began to allow the development of a "road allowance," which would be named Franklin Avenue after Sir John Franklin who, in 1845, led the ill-fated expedition to find the NorthWest Passage to the Pacific Ocean. Franklin often camped in Fort McMurray in early spring waiting for his mail to arrive from England.

That year, William Biggs and Roy Field set up timber stands along the Clearwater River to supply lumber down river and to points north. The year 1913 also marked the establishment of the first Fort McMurray North West Mounted Police (NWMP) detachment. Corporal Denny LaNauze, a staunch Irishman, led the detachment. LaNauze would eventually rise within the NWMP ranks to become an inspector.

Four years later, the NWMP pulled out of McMurray, and was replaced by a provincial police detachment led by Sergeant Jack MacDonald. MacDonald served the community until 1935.

Fort McMurray's first lawyer

It was no great wonder that after the establishment of Fort McMurray's first police detachment that a lawyer would soon take up residence in town.

Cecil Potts arrived in 1913, and would soon become one of the community's leading citizens. His culture and refinement earned him a special status. Potts' floral arrangements were known throughout the north. He was also well read, but it was his unique outhouse calendar that earned him status as a bona-fide local "character."

Potts felt that developing an outdoor toilet/outhouse would be out of step with his primitive surroundings. Author J.D. MacGregor recounts how Potts dug seven shallow pits one for each day of the week. Each morning after completing his personal business, Potts would shovel some clay into the pit, and then move the shovel ahead in preparation for his next day's activity. On Saturday he would return the shovel to the first pit for the start of the new week.

Potts was soon named Justice of the Peace and worked closely with Corporal LaNauze and his successor Constable Hubert "Nitchie" Thorne. In a 1985 interview, longtime pharmacist Walter Hill recalled Potts as "an English barrister who travelled around the world and ended up in Fort McMurray where he stayed the rest of his life. He was a very fine wonderful old English gentleman."[10]

Murder at the trapper's cabin

Fort McMurray's police blotter remained relatively quiet until the morning of October 28, 1914 when trapper Paul Miller came racing into the RCMP detachment, claiming that bushman Otto Bushner, who lived on the north side of the Clearwater River, had assaulted him with an axe. H.J. McColley and another guest were left behind in Miller's cabin. Suddenly, a shot was heard in the distance. By the time Constable Thorne made it to the scene, three of Miller's buildings were on fire. A doctor who happened to be passing through later identified the charred remains of two men, McColley and a second man believed to have been named Reis.

The search was on for Bushner. Businessman Jim Cornwall, former boxer Mickey Ryan and a number of others tracked the alleged killer and a few days later located Bushner in a clearing a few miles out of town. Rather than be brought to justice or trade gunfire with the posse, Bushner raised his weapon and took his own life.

The incident shocked the community and injected some realism in many residents who had come to believe that Fort McMurray was immune from crimes prevalent in the "city."

Sidney Ells gets down to business

In 1912, the federal government, under pressure from the British, slammed the brakes on private oil sands exploration. While during the early part of the century, oil exploration was permitted in an often wild and speculative manner; the British government was becoming increasingly sensitive to the strategic, economic and military value of fuel, and strongly encouraged Ottawa to develop a policy on oil exploration. In 1913, the federal government placed the Turner Valley, south of Calgary and the oil sands near Fort McMurray in a reserve.

Private exploration could continue, but until the federal government could assess the full value and potential of the oil sands, it would maintain the right to appropriate land and equipment if required. At the same time, Alberta MLA J.L. Cote asked that Canada's best geological talent be sent to the Fort McMurray area to establish the value and viability of Athabasca oil deposits. The oilsands remained under reserve status until the end of World War I.

Sidney Ells, a geologist with the Federal Department of Mines was dispatched on behalf of the federal government. In 1913, Ells began exploring oil deposits in the area. He surveyed about two hundred miles of river frontage and assembled more than two hundred core samples. He mapped areas where oil appeared to be most abundant, and focused his attention on developing ways to separate oil from the sand.

Ells immersed himself into the oilsands with the same passion and zeal that had propelled Cornwall and Von Hammerstein. Aside from his own survey work, Ells visited ten plants in the United States which had some experience with mineral separation techniques. Among those were two California plants operated by the Alcatraz Asphalt Company. The Carpinteria plant processed deposits that were similar in composition to those of the Athabasca oil sands. In the late 1890s, the company's general manager, had patented a process to turn natural material into asphalt.

Ells returned to the Athabasca region in 1913 brimming with new scientific ideas that he eagerly applied to the Fort McMurray oil sands deposits.

The extensive survey work conducted during the spring and summer months of 1913-14, exhausted his crew members who fought their way through tangled brush and rough beaches. Tied together with metal twine, they would drag heavy equipment and samples along narrow paths carved along the steep Athabasca River banks. Ells wrote that "scow-tracking," as the practice was called, was one of the most "brutal forms of labour."[11] There were also the elements to contend with: mosquitoes, black flies, swamps, long dry days and cold. Ells also wrote of the tremendous physical pain endured. "On one survey, I stood for three days in muskeg, my legs underwater the whole time. I had to be carried out and couldn't walk for a week."[12]

In addition to developing an oilsands separation technique, Ells became obsessed with "asphaltum" as a potential source of paving material. Ells gathered samples from the Horse River, transported them to Edmonton and in 1915 oversaw the paving of a downtown sidewalk. Additional paving was completed in Jasper, Alberta.

Scientists and "dreamers"

John Wilfred Barker was thirty-two years old in 1914 when he was hired by Ells as a handyman on a wildcat oil rig near the House River, about ten miles from Fort McMurray. On the eve of his hundredth birthday in 1982, Barker recalled how scientists like Ells, who were "cooking" the ground to extract oil, were regarded as pipe dreamers. "I handled it once just as they were prepared to ship it to Edmonton to pave roads. But no one ever imagined what could be done with it."[13]

At the Horse River site, Barker handled a team of oxen, removed logs from the river, operated an eighty-five foot rig and swung a sixteen-pound sledgehammer. "There was also all kinds of gas," he recalled. "You could see it bubbling in the river."[14]

In 1917, Ells published a two volume book titled "Notes on Certain Aspects of the Deposits of Bituminous Sands in the Province of Alberta." The document served as "bible" for future oil sands explorations, and a catalogue of possible techniques that could be used to separate oil from oil sand.

In the early 1920s, Ells would pioneer a radical process that involved hot water flotation. He would add water to vats of oil sand and cook the mixture to separate it into sand, water and oil.

Remarkably, when Great Canadian Oil Sands (Suncor) and Syncrude began operation in the mid 1960s and 1970s respectively, it was Ells' basic technique which was used on a massive scale.

While Ells worked quietly during the mid-1910s solving the great oilsands mystery, the world to the south was about to enter into a frenzy.

The world catches on

In 1913, explorers and entrepreneurs returned from the Athabasca oil sands with tales of the rich business opportunities that awaited the sharp investor. Oil companies, governments and investment groups quickly grasped the importance of the Athabasca Oil Sands and its potential to provide fuel to heat homes and businesses, to power locomotives and even to fuel the military. In a June 24, 1913 article in the Vancouver Sun, Guy R. Andrews, a local official of some reputation, states that aside from fuel oil and asphaltum "the country near Fort McKay is worthless." But Andrews observes that "everything is soaked in oil. The rocks actually exude oil and the streams glisten with it."[15]

Andrews then expounds on the military potential of the Athabasca oil find: "The value of the district to the British Empire is the fact that it is the only place in the British Empire where fuel oil has been found.... Battleships of the future are to be equipped for burning oil fuel and the ships of the navy are to be converted into oil burners, according to latest advices."[16]

The following is a sampling of newspaper quotes, which appeared during 1913 throughout western Canada and the United States.

"The asphaltum beds stretch for a great distance toward the north, and the material is so plentiful that a prospector is reported to have declared that he walked them for one hundred and fifty miles and if he had chosen could have stepped upon natural pavement every foot of the way." *California Oil World, January 1914*[17].

"So marvelous are the oilfields of Athabasca, so extensive the measures of asphaltum, that as soon as transportation is provided and, therefore greater incentive and capital for development work, that (this) will be the greatest country in the world in the amount of fuel oil and asphaltum produced." *Vancouver Sun, June 24, 1913*[18].

"Within the next six months, boring for oil will be commenced in the Fort McMurray district on a hitherto unprecedented scale, if the report of A. Fonberg Hamilton, oil expert of Victoria B.C., is approved by the syndicate of English financiers whom he represents." *Edmonton Capital, Aug. 28, 1913*[19].

"Edmonton is wild over the find, 300,000 acres have been filed on." *Northern News, Nov. 28, 1913*[20].

"The highest grade of asphaltum base oil on this continent has been found in three wells near Fort McKay about thirty miles north or down river from Fort McMurray. One of the wells operated by this company (Athabasca Oils Limited) produces more products from one hole in the ground than probably any mine which has ever been sunk. Well No. 1 which was drilled in 1911 to a depth of five hundred feet struck oil in Eighteen feet below the surface of the ground and this oil continued for one hundred and fifteen feet." *Edmonton Bulletin, Nov. 18, 1913*[21].

"Whatever may be the outcome of the work of the companies engaged in prospecting for oil along the Athabasca River in the neighborhood of Fort McMurray, the visible asphaltum deposits of that region are practically inexhaustible." *Victoria Colonist, Sept. 1913*[22].

Under the headline "Prospectors Rush to the Northwest," a Seattle, Washington newspaper announced on Aug. 24, 1913 that "scores of prospectors and experts"[23] from United States, Canada and Mexico were preparing to set up camp in the Fort McMurray area.

Even small investors were invited to get on board. A boxed newspaper ad which appeared on June 24, 1913 in the Vancouver Sun announced "You Can To-Day Profit by the development and prosperity which will come out of the development of the enormous Athabasca Oil Fields by joining the Athabasca Petroleum Company Ltd. Write for full information to NorthWest Underwriters, Vancouver, British Columbia." Another ad reminded investors that "tarsand is liquid gold."[24]

Oilsands samples were carted around the world to demonstrate how rich the oil deposits were. But the biggest challenge of all, remained unsolved: how to separate the oil from the sand.

The frozen trapper

While Fort McMurray proved to be a godsend for many new arrivals, it was not the land of milk and honey for many others.

Many southerners came north hoping to cash in on the fur trade or the oil business, however, without proper northern skills, some of their attempts ended in near disaster. In 1914, after three successive years of crop failure, farmer Harry Sykes, travelled to Fort McMurray from Lethbridge to try his hand at trapping. On November 10, Sykes, his uncle and a group of friends set up a base camp near the Firebag River and ventured out to set their individual traplines

The next morning, each man set off to check his traps. Sykes was deep in the bush when he heard a rustling in the woods. It was a moose, and Sykes began to prepare his weapon. However, the moose proved more skilled in bush navigation than Sykes, and after some time pursuing him through the forest, Sykes became disoriented.

A fresh snow was falling, making it difficult to retrace his steps. Sykes realized he was hopelessly lost. For five days, Sykes' friends scoured the woods without success. On the sixth day, the search party came back and found Sykes at the cabin doorstep, weak from lack of food, and suffering from severe frostbite.

For a week, Sykes' comrades tried to keep him warm, however, with frostbitten feet and hands, Sykes was in agony. Sykes was loaded on to a sleigh and transported by a local native to the NWMP detachment in Fort McMurray.

According to an account of the incident in J.G. MacGregor's *Paddlewheels to Bucketwheels*, the native handed Sykes to Thorne who spent the next week transporting him by dog sled to Lac La Biche and then to Athabasca. Throughout Thorne's heroic journey, Sykes moaned in constant pain. Gangrene had set in.

Sykes was successfully delivered to Athabasca. Doctors amputated a number of toes and treated his wounds. After a few weeks recovering, Sykes returned to Lethbridge, where he resumed a much safer profession: farming.

Board of Trade and the Women's Institute

Residents of Fort McMurray continued with their business, largely unaware of the frenzy that was building to the south.

As Fort McMurray began to gel as a community, the need was identified for an organization to promote economic development, and to serve as a forum for local government. In 1914, the Fort McMurray Board of Trade was formed. At the outset, it served as a gathering point for local merchants and entrepreneurs interested in developing the oil sands. However, due to a lack of other community groups, the all-male board began taking responsibility for minor and unofficial law-making. While the town was governed on an outreach basis from Edmonton, the Board of Trade initially served as an advisory group.

The idea of an all-male club controlling all aspects of the community was not greeted with unanimous enthusiasm. Soon after the formation of the Board of Trade, a group of women met and formed the Women's Institute. An official division of responsibility was established between the two groups. Monthly meetings of the Board of Trade would provide businessmen with an opportunity to network and discuss news of the day. The Women's Institute would organize charitable campaigns and social events.

As pharmacist Walter Hill recalls, "the Board of Trade and that Women's Institute were responsible for everything that was done in this town. Those women were wonderful. They had some opposition and a lot of people didn't like them because they were non-denominational, but everything worthwhile in this town was gotten through the auspices of the Women's Institute or the Board of Trade."[25]

Sam Kushner, a McMurray fixture

In 1913, a heavy man with bushy eyebrows and an eastern European background arrived in Fort McMurray. Sam Kushner was a Jew of Lithuanian descent who came to Canada in the early 1900s. He made his way across Canada and eventually settled in Edmonton. In the early 1910s Kushner became intrigued by some of the optimistic news trickling south from Fort McMurray, and decided to venture north.

In the "old country" Kushner's surname meant "furrier," and although his immediate descendents were not involved in the trade, Kushner quickly immersed himself in his namesake profession. Kushner's easy going style and his respect for native people quickly won him friends in the community. In 1914, his brother-in-law, Ephraim Allman, joined him.

From his freestanding store on Franklin Avenue, Kushner bought and sold furs, and provided a variety of services including axe sharpening. Every type of clothing, tool or foodstuff was either stacked on his shelves, or hung from his rafters. Kushner's Store would later become Hanson's Store, and then Haxton's Store, which continued serving Fort McMurray until the late 1970s.

Kushner was one of the founders of the original 1914 Board of Trade. His sons Laz and David were raised in Fort McMurray and were both fixtures at the Kushner store and within the community. Kushner remained in Fort McMurray until the mid-1940s and died in Edmonton in 1947.

"He was easy to get along with and always spoke of his love for the Indians,"[26] recalled daughter-in-law Martha Kushner.

First Chinese residents

During the mid-1910s, Fort McMurray began to show additional signs of cultural diversity. The community had a small but distinct French community, and Charlie Eymundson proudly boasted his Icelandic heritage

A History of the Chinese Community in Fort McMurray states that the first person of Chinese descent to settle in the community was David Mah, who arrived in Fort McMurray around 1915. Mah was eighteen when he settled in McMurray, and two years later, he built the Union Café and Rooms on Franklin Avenue. His next door neighbors to the west were Edmonton Rooms, and Scotty Morrison's barbershop and general store. The three businesses were located on the south side of Franklin Avenue between Main and Morrison Streets.

By the early 1920s, there were three Chinese residents living in Fort McMurray. Charlie Mah came to town to help his brother run the Union, and was joined by Charlie Young. After a dance or a late night social, folks would wander over to the Union Café for a sandwich and a coffee. Later, Charlie Mah would try his hand at trapping before moving back to China in 1947.

Other members of the Mah family would later establish the Athabasca Café and Mah's Hall in Fort Chipewyan. Both would remain in the family name until the mid-1980s.

McMurray connects

In 1915, Fort McMurray entered the age of communications technology as the Dominion Telegraph completed its connection from Athabasca to McMurray. Businesses, investors and residents were now able to connect by telegram to the outside world.

Later that year, the SS Fort McMurray, a sternwheeler steamer was launched on the Clearwater River. Service was initiated thereby enhancing the connection between Fort McMurray and the northern river system.

The Waterways railway controversy

Few events would shape the development of Fort McMurray more than the construction of the Alberta and Great Waterways Railway (A&GWR). Soon after the Rutherford Liberals were re-elected in 1909 under a slogan of "Rutherford, Reliability and Railroads," the Edmonton business community began clamouring for a northern rail route. Although the federal government subsidized two east-west railway lines, the seeds of western alienation were already taking root. Provincial politicians, fuelled by pressure by the Edmonton/Strathcona business community, wanted to expand commerce north. At the time, the Athabasca rapids posed a tremendous natural barrier to moving goods to and from the Arctic.

In addition, the country's interest in oil development was mounting quickly. In an attempt to prove how rich the area was in oil potential, and to demonstrate the difficulties of getting product to market under current circumstances, James Cornwall hired some crewmen to drag a large quantity of oil sand upstream to Athabasca Landing, which is now the town of Athabasca. From there it was carted to Edmonton, for display and promotional use.

Facing pressure to live up to its election commitments, the legislature moved into action. Although the possibilities for commercial development of the oil sands were still remote, the potential of accessing the Arctic through Edmonton captured the province's imagination. The federal government remained unconvinced. In a letter written in March 1912, a federal government official stated that supporting an "expensive railway at the public expense" made little sense "in order to help out a few needy promoters."[27]

Although the provincial Liberals agreed in principle to support an Edmonton to Fort McMurray railway in 1909, its own bungling and internal squabbles delayed the start of construction until 1914. Controversy revolved around a sweet plan, under which the Province agreed to guarantee loans to an American consortium of up to twenty thousand dollars per three hundred fifty miles of track, and four hundred thousand dollars to build the Edmonton terminal. In February 1910, Rutherford's own Minister of Public Works, W.H. Cushing, publicly expressed the opinion that the loan guarantees were too rich, and would enable American backers to reap rich profits from the railway's construction. In a letter which was tabled in the legislature on February 17, Rutherford was forced to read Cushing's letter of resignation. Rumours began to spread about government graft. Cushing offered to put up a personal bond for five million dollars to prove that the railway could be completed for twelve thousand dollars a mile.

Rutherford appointed a royal commission, which later cleared his government of wrongdoing. However, the controversy around the Waterways railroad had two important results. In 1913, the American interests pulled out of the project, and control of the project was handed to the J.D. McArthur Company, the same contractor who had been laying track from Edmonton to the Peace River area. From then on, the Alberta and Great Waterways Railway (A&GWR) became unofficially known as the "McArthur Railway."

On Sept. 23, 1913, the Edmonton Journal announced that "the A&GWR is taken over by J.D. McArthur. Construction will begin at once and completed within two years from December 31st next. Government receives interest earned on money in bank, but pays past interest on bonds to date. The company settles all claimed filed with the Government and properly payable."[28] Railway experts Harry Warner and Louis Scott were placed in charge of the project's engineering.

The controversy over the A&GWR ended Rutherford's political career. Rutherford was never considered to be a charismatic leader. His main strength lay in his ability to unite the fragmented Alberta Liberal party. With Rutherford's party splintered over his handling of the Waterway's railway affair, the Premier resigned and was succeeded by lawyer Arthur Sifton who won subsequent majority governments in 1913 and 1917.

Construction of McArthur's Railway began in 1914, using initial portions of the Peace River railway. The A&GWR line crossed the Redwater River, passed through Boyle and in July 16 ended its initial construction phase at Lac La Biche at Mile 113.1.

The task of building the next hundred and seventy miles would be the most difficult. About two thirds of the northern line had to be built along muskeg, which presented workers with immeasurable obstacles. Trees to support the line had to be cut and laid in terrain covered up to twenty-five feet deep in mud, oil sands and swamp. Carloads of fill were brought in to stabilize large muskeg holes. The mosquitoes were unbearable.

Retired railroad employees tell the story of a worker named Edwards who was with a pre-survey crew that preceded the construction gangs. As the story goes, five crew members jumped into an unnamed lake at Mile 180, but only four came out alive. Edward's gravestone stands to this day between the tracks and the lake that is named in his memory. Many residents of the area still refuse to fish in the lake partly due to superstition, and as well in tribute to those who carved out the Waterways railway. Until the Northern Alberta Railway run was eliminated in March 1987, passing trains would lower their speed as they passed the Edwards grave.

The railway was built to Lynton in 1915 and then extended to Draper, or Little Waterways, in 1917, to a point about six miles upstream from the town of Fort McMurray. It was felt that road and river navigation were stable enough to allow goods and passengers to be transported to town. Others felt the railway should continue all the way to Waterways. The controversy resulted in the resignation of its two main engineers, Harry Warner and Louis Scott. In 1919, the "end of steel" was established in Waterways just upstream from the McMurray townsite.

At the time, Waterways consisted of a general store and hotel, and a rooming house and cafe named "Bunkhouse villa – Two Bits a Flop." It had taken five years to build the basic rail line from Lac la Biche to Waterways, and it would require an additional year to stabilize the rails and their foundation.

Three days before Christmas, 1922, the Alberta & Great Waterways Railways was approved for operation by the Province of Alberta. However, in the early years, mudslides and track slippage caused frequent delays inspiring the residents of McMurray to unofficially rename the A&GWR the "Arrive God Willing."

The Ryan Brothers

As the A&GWR tracks began creeping towards Fort McMurray, two brothers, Mickey and Pat Ryan, emerged as local players. The Ryans were ex-boxers and bouncers from Muncey, Indiana, known to be in the Fort McMurray area around 1914. In 1917, their company, Ryan Brothers, Freighting and Transportation Agents, became a vital cog in Fort McMurray's economy, as they began transporting mail and freight by "speeder" north from Lac La Biche. Although the end of steel reached Lynton located near Waterways, in 1917, the new track and unstable ground were not yet ready to support passenger and freight service.

The Ryans equipped a Packard with flanged wheels and attached a flatbed trailer so that both goods and passengers could be transported in various classes of comfort. The mail, supplies and freight were first loaded in the back. Then, First Class passengers were escorted into the Packard. The remainder of the passengers jumped on board the flatbed trailer for open-air transportation to the north.

The Ryans also controlled transportation once passengers disembarked at Lynton. The Ryans shuttled passengers to McMurray along the final eleven miles by horse and sleigh.

The Ryan brothers were extremely opinionated regarding the political climate in Ireland, and it was not uncommon to hear the shouted voices of Mickey and Pat Ryan bellowing from beer halls in McMurray, and later Waterways.

The Ryans' shed was located on the north side of Franklin Avenue between Fr. Mercredi and MacLeod Streets and was moved during the early 1980s to Heritage Park.

World War I

World War I was partially responsible for a plunge in Fort McMurray's population during the mid-1910s. In 1916, a census showed that Fort McMurray's population had dropped in half since the last count held in 1911. Fort McMurray's population in 1916 stood at one hundred and fifty-eight.

Many men left the community to enlist from their towns or cities of origin. McMurray sent two native sons, Gilbert Decharme and Modest Powder. Both returned safely.

Walter Hill, a seventeen-year-old from Edmonton, snuck into the Canadian forces and fought on the European front. Hill would move to Fort McMurray soon after the war ended and would become one of its major boosters and raconteurs. "In 1917, I saw men beside me literally drown in mud," Hill said in 1979. "It was stupid, bloody, blundering butchery. In one day, in one battle, we lost fifty-seven thousand men."[29]

As for James Cornwall, he answered the call of World War I with his usual flair. He travelled to Edmonton where he formed the #218 Infantry Battalion. But Cornwall was very particular about the type of soldier who could join his battalion. Recruits had to be of Ukrainian origin or have married into a Ukrainian family. The unofficial name of Cornwall's battalion was Jim Cornwall's Irish Darts.

The town's first "chemist"

In 1918, a short man of Scottish descent ventured north to work for Jim Cornwall and the Northern Trading Company. The company transported goods from Athabasca north and when "Peace River Jim" needed someone intelligent and honest to manage his McMurray operation, he turned to Angus Sutherland, a graduate in pharmacy at the University of Winnipeg.

Sutherland arrived in Fort McMurray during the winter of 1918 to look after the company's affairs. It was not long before local residents learned that Sutherland had a "medical" background. Faced with a devastating flu epidemic that year, McMurrayites turned to Sutherland, the best "medical expert" they could find.

Sutherland began to order and stockpile medical supplies, and is credited with saving many lives during the epidemic. Sutherland is particularly recognized for having provided drugs free to those who could not pay.

Sutherland soon realized there was a need for a small pharmacy in Fort McMurray, and set up shop in the O'Coffey family's Franklin Hotel, located where the Oilsands Hotel stands today. Sutherland continued to act as a purser when Cornwall's river boats operated during the summer.

With Fort McMurray and Edmonton now connected by rail and the river boat business beginning to grow, business at Angus Sutherland's pharmacy boomed. In the early 1920s, a two-storey frame building was constructed next to the hotel. That site would eventually become Hill Drugs and would serve the community until October 1988.

In the late 1910s, a photo of the Fort McMurray Board of Trade was taken. It featured many of the important businessmen and "movers" of the day including, William Biggs, D.C. McTavish, Bill Gordon, Sam Kushner, Angus Sutherland and Jim Cornwall.

The "Great Flood" of 1918

Fort McMurray's new and confident community learned an important lesson in April 1918. As the community burst with new development, the town was dealt a harsh reminder that in the north, nature often has the last word.

During the 1918 spring river breakup, ice along the Clearwater River jammed, pushing water over its banks and into the townsite. While historically, ice jams and flooding along the Clearwater and Athabasca rivers was common, this was the first time that a major settlement was involved. Waters backed up to Franklin Avenue and beyond.

Although details of the flood are sketchy, the Roman Catholic Church reported that "the Great Flood damaged all of the northern mission supplies at the river dock."[30]

In search of salt

In 1919, the provincial government became interested in a resource whose importance had been previously overshadowed by the quest for oil.

Senator Jean L. Cote, an Alberta cabinet member and a former land surveyor, began to promote the possibility that salt could be mined in the Fort McMurray area and shipped back to Edmonton by rail. Increasingly, salt was becoming a valuable commodity. Before the days of commercial refrigeration, it was used to preserve animal and vegetable products. Salt also had great value in the manufacture of bleach, plastics, solvents and glycols.

Cote sent geology professor J.A. Allan to Fort McMurray to investigate. Allan quickly became aware of Von Hammerstein's work that had been completed nine years earlier. Historian Darlene Comfort, in her book Pass the McMurray Salt, quotes long time resident George Golosky's recollection of a conversation between Allan and one local resident:

When he (Allan) inquired of one individual if it was rock salt that was found, the terse reply was, "Hell, no! It was table salt. The drill dropped exactly one hundred feet through this table salt."[31]

Allan was convinced and recommended further tests. In October 1919, a salt well operated by the Alberta government began operation near the Snye waterfront, located about a half mile east of downtown Fort McMurray. William Pickles managed drilling operations. A channel of the Clearwater River, which flowed nearby, hampered initial drilling of the site. As well, Pickles had to negotiate how to transport salt he extracted to the railway that had not yet reached Waterways.

Like its sister oil industry, the new salt operation posed technological and transportation problems. Government officials would continue sporadic drilling into the next decade, and these efforts would eventually lead to a full-fledged commercial operation.

McMurray becomes home

As the 1910s closed, Fort McMurray was perched on a wave of excitement.

Opportunists, investors, speculators and entrepreneurs flocked to McMurray, looking for a quick investment return. But as these opportunists came and went, something unique and magical began to occur. Many newcomers opted to remain and participate in the founding of a permanent community. While many had been attracted to the town's riches, it was Fort McMurray's natural setting, coupled with the warmth of its residents, which enticed many to stay.

It was a trend which would be repeated through a dozen economic peaks and valleys through to the end of the century. As the 1910s closed, the oilsands industry appeared poised for a technological breakthrough. A railway had come to town. Churches and social clubs were beginning to take shape. Fort McMurray and the fledgling community of Waterways were buoyed by unbridled optimism that would carry them into the Roaring 20s. Already, the tiny settlement of McMurray had endured an unprecedented economic boom.

As the corner turned on 1920, Fort McMurray's population stood at just below four hundred. The coming of rail and river travel, resource investment, government interest and hundreds of new residents was almost too much for such a young community to bear.

Fort McMurray was about to split in two.

Chapter Three:
The rise of Waterways

As Fort McMurray turned the corner on the 1920s, a familiar trend began to emerge. Fort McMurray would live within two realities. While analysts, scientists, opportunists, newspapers, oil companies, and governments focused on Fort McMurray's economic potential, the community's permanent residents occupied themselves with daily living. Institutions such as churches, schools, social clubs and small businesses began to take shape.

With the big steel rail now running between Edmonton and Fort McMurray, the prospect of northern settlement, commerce and exploration became more realistic for residents of other Alberta regions, and those beyond. Once per week, the Ryan brothers would meet the train in Draper, and shuttle wide-eyed newcomers to Fort McMurray. This perpetual flow of new recruits brought fresh ideas and excitement to the community.

During this period, Fort McMurray's attention shifted from its traditional fur trading roots towards the influx of new residents, ideas and technologies which would arrive weekly aboard the train. While the "fort of the forks" had provided an ideal location to conduct commerce with Fort Chipewyan and points north, the Fort McMurray townsite remained three to ten miles short of the new economic wave which had been generated by the Alberta & Great Waterways Railway (A&GWR).

Within a few years, a sister settlement would rise, rivaling and temporarily surpassing Fort McMurray in activity and influence. The community, known as Waterways, would flourish around the economic opportunities created by the railway. Much to the chagrin of Fort McMurray business interests, ongoing economic and housing activity would be split between two townsites.

The rise of Waterways began with the arrival of the A&GWR, and further accelerated with renewed interest in river transportation, oil exploration, and the development of other prized resources such as asphalt, lumber, fish and salt. At this point, its future remained linked to the provincial and federal governments, and their "hot and cold" interest in the Athabasca oil sands.

Federal government turns away

A provincial government decision in 1920 produced a flurry of economic activity within the region. After years of tests and study, the Province decided to fund oil sands research conducted by Dr. Karl A. Clark. Clark had lured the Province into supporting his petroleum experiments by touting the economic potential of bitumen as a road paving material.

Although Clark recognized the oil sands' vast petroleum potential, he realized that until the secret of extracting oil from sand could be unlocked, research needed to be sustained. Booming demand to pave Edmonton roads provided fertile conditions for Fort McMurray to increase its profile within media, business and government circles

During the previous four decades, the federal government had taken a strong interest in the Athabasca oil sands. But following a trend that would repeat itself for decades to come, Ottawa's taste for oil sands development would fluctuate between unbridled enthusiasm and indifference. With the passing of World War I, the federal government downgraded its strategic interest in the region, and looked for ways to pass its flickering torch to the provincial government.

The resource divorce

In 1919, a series of meetings took place at the University of Alberta aimed at forming a research agency to study the Athabasca oil sands, and the abundant coal deposits which had been identified elsewhere in the province. A steering committee was formed made up of University President Henry Marshall Tory, Professor of Engineering N.C. Pitcher, Professor of Geology John A. Allan, Provincial Inspector of Mines John Sterling and Provincial Secretary J.L. Cote. The five, along with federal representatives, established the groundwork for a research council which would help develop new oil and coal deposits.

In the spring of 1920, the federal/provincial research romance began to fade. Ottawa's interest in the oil sands plummeted following release of a McGill University study which concluded that bitumen found in the Fort McMurray area belonged to the "naphthalene series" and was more suited to asphalt than petroleum. While the Province's resource committee bubbled with enthusiasm over Fort McMurray's potential, Ottawa continued to downgrade the area's importance. The federal government began to express concerns that oil sands development was too expensive, and that its "hands on" role could not be sustained from Ottawa. University of Alberta president Henry Marshall Tory publicly denounced the federal government's lack of commitment.

Tory penned an angry letter to Ottawa pointing out that the McGill study had examined bitumen which did not contain the same properties as those found in the Athabasca region. The stage was set for Alberta to take the lead role in oil sands development.

Birth of the research council

Tory fervently believed that the key to private investment in Alberta's resources rested with the development of new mining technologies. In the face of new and less expensive oil discoveries in Texas, Oklahoma and the Middle East, national and international interest in the mysterious and expensive oil sands continued to wane. However, the provincial government and the University of Alberta remained steadfast.

Since the early 1920s, Dr. Karl Clark had experimented with hot water extraction in the Fort McMurray area. He had collected a number of promising theories from projects in Europe and the United States, and appeared ready to put them to work.

In 1920, the federal Mines Branch officially backed out of Tory's research initiative. In response, on January 6, 1921, the Alberta government launched the Scientific and Industrial Research Council of Alberta (SIRCA) which combined the Province's strength in legal and financial matters, with the expertise of University of Alberta scientists. The Athabasca oil sands, whose vast potential had been dangling for decades, provided an excellent initial opportunity for SIRCA to prove its worth.

SIRCA would later become the Alberta Research Council, an organization which to this day plays a vital role in the development of oil sands technologies. The launch of SIRCA created renewed interest in the oil sands, and in turn sparked a fresh wave of business activity. Dozens of newcomers arrived weekly to assess Fort McMurray's economic potential.

The great rail disaster

The completion of the Alberta and Great Waterways Railway did not solve all of the Fort McMurray's transportation problems. It had taken more than a decade for the *Muskeg Special* to push through swamps, mosquitoes, political controversy, construction problems and financial challenges.

So perhaps it was the ultimate insult that after the investment of untold resources, the A&GWR stopped about six miles short of Fort McMurray. A terminus was established along the Clearwater River, in the valley below where the community's Vista Ridge ski facility operates today. The provincial government had previously washed its hands of the costly railroad project, and decided that it would be up to Fort McMurray's resourceful residents to navigate the remaining distance. At first, local residents weathered the challenge. After so many years of complete isolation, a six mile trek from train to main seemed like a small price to pay. But one disastrous event would soon change the government's attitude.

While work crews had successfully planted tracks downstream from the junction of the Clearwater and Christina rivers, the rail line literally rested on unstable ground. Engineers and workers observed that in places, tracks would tilt, or disappear into the muskeg. Concerns were voiced that the moist earth could not safely support the full weight of a freight or passenger train. In response, workers were hired to cart earth and timber to support unstable areas. However, in mid-1919, the worst concerns of engineers, work crews and local residents were realized. An empty train was climbing a steep grade when suddenly the soft hillside collapsed causing the locomotive and an outfit car to topple. Engineer Jim Donnelly and two construction workers were killed.

The Province's judgment was immediately called into question. Faced with public outcry, and ongoing concern about track stability, engineers began designing an alternate route, south of the original terminus location. The new construction phase began later in 1919 and was completed in 1921.

The "naming" of Waterways

When John Moberly named the Hudson's Bay Company fort at the junction of the Athabasca and Clearwater rivers, he chose to honour his mentor, William McMurray. As towns, villages and other settlements began to spring up throughout the west, names of kings, queens, saints, pioneers or explorers were often adopted to either honour the past or set a course for the future.

The naming of Waterways was considerably less thoughtful. By 1921, a settlement had emerged at "end of steel." After a long journey from Edmonton, many passengers and freight haulers required a landing station before continuing their journey to Fort McMurray. The new community consisted of a combined general store, hotel, bunkhouse and café known as *Bunkhouse Villa: Two Bits a Flop.*

The area was informally named after local entrepreneur Thomas Draper who had mining interests in the area. However, the A&GWR appeared reluctant to name a rail station after a private businessman. The name *Alberta and Great Waterways Railways* was too long to place on a railway station, so the simple word "Waterways" was etched on a sign above the front door.

In 1925, when the railway was extended from Draper to a location about two miles east of Fort McMurray, the wooden station house was hoisted and barged down the Clearwater River. As pharmacist Walter Hill recalled, no one ever got around to removing the station sign, and the name stuck. Local residents called the new location *Waterways.* The former A&GWR terminus became known as *Old Waterways.*

Thomas Draper's dream

In 1921, Thomas Draper secured a formal lease near Old Waterways, and the following year opened up a bitumen quarry under the name the McMurray Asphaltum & Oil Company. Although Draper became one of the oil sands' most fervent supporters, he had little interest in petroleum. Draper believed that Fort McMurray contained enough bitumen to meet Alberta's growing need to pave newly developed roads and highways.

While Draper's enthusiasm helped focus the provincial spotlight on Fort McMurray, his dream to develop a local paving industry never materialized. In 1924, Draper's plant was destroyed by fire. The Old Waterways area would later be known as Draper Station, and would continue to serve as a rail stop until the early 1990s.

While the fire of 1924 halted Draper's production plans, he steadfastly pursued his vision of Fort McMurray supplying paving material to markets across Canada. Draper spent the next five years promoting Athabasca asphalt throughout the province, most notably at the Edmonton Exhibition. Despite the fact that his plant had been destroyed, Draper continued to quarry material from his lease and ship it through the A&GWR which crossed his property. Later in the decade when Dr. Clark needed oil sand to provide material for further Edmonton paving projects, he and his University of Alberta associate Dr. S.M. Blair acquired material from Draper's old lease.

In the early 1930s, Fort McMurray asphalt was transported to Ottawa after Draper was awarded a contract to pave Parliament Hill and a small portion of Wellington Street. Draper also earned street and sidewalk paving contracts in Vegreville, Medicine Hat and Camrose.

Meanwhile, as Draper and others touted the advantages of bitumen as a paving material, scientists such as Clark and Blair reported that they were making progress in the area of petroleum extraction. In August 1921, Clark wrote to Tory "something definite had been accomplished and a very considerable glimmer of daylight has been let through the problem."[1]

Clark also reported to Edmonton authorities that "most of the purely inventive work has been done. There remains to be accomplished the practical application of the new method to the production of bitumen from the tar sands. This means....on a commercial scale."[2]

While Clark may have addressed the scientific issue, larger challenges loomed. Clark's work still needed to be adapted from the safe world of a university laboratory to the harsh realities of commercial development.

The "voyage" to Fort McMurray

While Fort McMurray residents appreciated their new southern rail link, the journey was by no means luxurious. It often took more than a half-day for the *Muskeg Special* to rattle along the sagging tracks between Draper and Lac La Biche. Derailments were commonplace. Rail historian Cecil Swanson observes:

Getting from Lac La Biche to Waterways or vice versa was more of a "voyage" than a trip. The one hundred sixty-eight miles took fourteen hours according to the schedule, if everything went normal – an average speed of twelve mph. To complete the distance without getting a few derailments was regarded as a very good run. The passengers and crew were always on friendly terms and ready to help out even if it meant one should be prepared to procure trees and brush along the right of way and drive these under the track to keep it from sinking out of sight in the muskeg[3].

Stops along the way were so frequent, that some of the crew members laid down animal traps, and harvested furs while tracks were repaired. During a number of scheduled and unexpected stops which often lasted up to two days, passengers would disembark and fill makeshift containers with nearby blueberries and raspberries. During extreme conditions, passengers and crew would raid the freight car for food, or send a hunting party into the bush.

Winnie Hutchinson was a passenger on one of those troubled trains. She was riding with her mother and young brother in 1922, when the *Muskeg Special* derailed in a remote area. While the crew waited for extra manpower and equipment to arrive, passengers made themselves at home. "Mother had to wash my baby brother's diapers, and she hung them on the willows," Hutchinson recalled in a 2001 interview. "We picked berries and found other things to eat."[4]

During the 1920s, the "mixed" train between Draper and Edmonton consisted of a sleeping car, the *Waterways*, a dining car named the *MacKay* and a number of freight cars. As challenging as the *Muskeg Special* was for passengers, it offered a considerable improvement over previous alternatives.

Movers and shakers

By 1921, Fort McMurray's population had grown to four hundred and eighty-three. Business was booming. During the summer of 1921, members of the Fort McMurray's Board of Trade posed for a photo which included some of the local business, community and political leaders. They included George Golosky, Ed Clausen, Jan Laboucane, Frank O'Coffey, Pat Ryan, D.C. McTavish, Member of Parliament Frank Falconer, Billy Loutit, Sam Kushner, Tom Conn, Cecil Potts, Charlie MacDonald, Bill Pickles, Tommy Woodman, Jack Sarcee, Gus Leister, Fred Murray and Cleve Cinnamon.

Also included in the photo was Walter Reamer who later drowned in the Athabasca River. Reamer's widow, Olive, subsequently wrote an account of her ordeals in the north which was later adapted into a screenplay. For three weeks during the fall of 1979, a Hollywood production crew and a team of actors led by Ellen Burstyn, descended on Fort McMurray, recreating 1920s life in the region. The movie, Silence of the North, was released in 1981.

First vehicle arrives

The arrival of the railway so close to Fort McMurray opened new possibilities. In late summer 1921, the town's first motor vehicle arrived. Pharmacist Angus Sutherland had arranged for a Ford Model T truck to be shipped by rail, and then barged it to Fort McMurray. In a 1985 interview, pharmacist Walter Hill recalled the importance and fanfare surrounding the vehicle's arrival.

It was September 11. I remember the date because I put it on a postcard...A bunch of the local citizens including the Alberta Premier (Herbert Greenfield), and the local Member of Parliament (Frank Falconer), and some big local cit-

izens including local barrister Cecil Potts and Jim Cornwall were all there. There was great excitement[5].

The truck was paraded down Franklin Avenue, and for months residents cozied up to Sutherland in hopes of earning a ride.

Young Hugh Stroud and his amazing work day

In many ways, the story of Hugh Stroud parallels the story of Fort McMurray. From the time of his arrival in 1921 at age six, to his death in 2000, Hugh Stroud was recognized as a hard-working resident who survived by the credo of "hard work never hurt anybody." He began on the trap line at age seven, helped his mother run a dairy at age twelve, went north to search for gold, launched a number of business ventures, and participated in an endless list of councils, boards and community organizations.

Stroud was thrust at an early age into a life of independence and self-sufficiency. Soon after his birth in Edmonton in 1914, Stroud's father, Arnold, enlisted in the 49th Edmonton Battalion and was sent to France to fight in World War I. Hugh and his mother, Christine, moved back to native Scotland to be closer to the front. But in 1916, Christine received the devastating news that Arnold had been killed in battle. Brokenhearted, Christine and Hugh returned to their small home in Edmonton.

In 1917, Christine met and later married Fred Furlough, a trapper from Wisconsin, and in March 1921, the family boarded the *Muskeg Special* with hopes of cashing in on Fort McMurray's growing prosperity. Fred Furlough had worked in Norman Wells in 1914 where he participated in the area's initial oil explorations. He craved to return to the slower pace offered by the north.

The family spent a few initial weeks in Fort McMurray where Hugh attended a one-room school, which served grades one to eight. During his travels through the community, Furlough met local trapper Charlie Eymundson. The two built a scow and sailed "down river," to Lake Athabasca to participate in the spring fur hunt.

During the 1920s, the weather and the northern rivers cooperated with local trappers. Each spring, the Athabasca and Peace river delta around Fort Chipewyan would jam with ice, backing waters into nearby ponds and sloughs. These marshes and perch basins provided ideal feeding and breeding grounds for a variety of fur bearing animals which were ripe for "harvesting" by enterprising trappers

During the *Roaring 20s*, large urban centres such as New York, Paris and London were bubbling with prosperity, and the market for furs was booming. A good fox pelt would fetch thirty-five dollars. A muskrat pelt would earn about a dollar, and on a good day, one hundred "rats" could be trapped. An experienced trapper like Furlough could snag three thousand muskrats per season. Some trappers could snare up to four thousand. The conditions were excellent, the profits were great, and soon the Furlough family settled near the south shore of Lake Athabasca.

At age seven, from a small cabin in the bush, Hugh Stroud began to learn the family business while receiving a basic education from his mother. "My mother gave me my A,B,Cs in the morning and I went out hunting in the afternoon," Stroud recalled in a 2000 interview. "My stepfather would give me a handful of ammunition and I looked for rabbits and ptarmigan."[6] Each spring, Hugh would come to Fort McMurray where he joined other children at school.

Life on the trapline was tough, especially for Christine. She was isolated within extremely basic surroundings and acted as cook, housekeeper, mother and teacher. After about three years along Lake Athabasca, the hardship and isolation became too much, and in 1925, she and Fred parted ways. While Fred remained in the north, Christine Furlough, Hugh and her new son Fred moved back to Fort McMurray. Thanks to almost five years of successful trapping, the Furloughs had acquired significant land holdings in Fort McMurray. They owned a number of river lots along the Clearwater, along with a half dozen lots along Franklin Avenue, and a sizable chunk of MacDonald Island. In those days, land was relatively cheap. Furlough would later sell his seventy-six acres on MacDonald Island to hotel owner Frank O'Coffey for three hundred dollars.

Christine Furlough maintained a large parcel of land along the Clearwater River area, and launched a dairy business. From their small cabin, the single mother and her two sons eked out a hard living.

Hugh Stroud would rise each day at five a.m., and would gather the cows. Because Christine Furlough could not afford an animal pen, cows often wandered up to a mile away. Hugh listened for cowbells, herded the animals and began milking. Stroud would bring the milk to his mother, load up his dog sled, and begin to deliver milk to homes and businesses in Fort McMurray. As the dairy became more established, Christine Furlough bought her son a pony to pull the cart. Once his McMurray deliveries were complete, Stroud would dash to school for a full day of classes. After school, he would return home, reload his wagon and make deliveries to Waterways, and then return home to complete his schoolwork.

During all of the years he assisted his mother, Hugh Stroud never took a sick day from work or from school. "I guess I was a pretty healthy kid. I don't ever remember being sick,"[7] he later recalled.

At age fourteen, Stroud was sent south by his mother to negotiate a major purchase. His mother loaded him on a southbound train to Lac La Biche where he bought a team of horses and walked them back one hundred and fifty-six miles along the train tracks to McMurray. Despite all of the hard work and responsibility, Stroud never resented his tough life. "I guess it didn't do me any harm," he said. "We had to live."[8]

In come the bankers

In early 1921, the amount of commerce passing directly through Fort McMurray became too much for Edmonton financiers to ignore. Goods and equipment were beginning to flow into the town aboard the new railway. The telegraph was in operation and steamships were beginning to push north from Fort McMurray along the three thousand miles of rivers leading to the arctic.

In early-1921, the decision was reached to open a Union Bank of Canada branch in Fort McMurray. The branch's designated manager, E.G. Parsons was sent to McMurray and spent five months examining the town's business potential. On September 25, the Union Bank opened on Franklin Avenue with a staff of two – Parsons and a teller/clerk. Mail and financial records were brought in weekly from the train by dog sled or horses.

From the start, Parsons recognized Fort McMurray's potential and on the day the branch opened penned the following words:

The day is September 25, 1921 and we are very excited to be opening the Fort McMurray branch of the Union Bank of Canada. Interest in the bank is so high I've had to accept deposits even before we've opened. Fort McMurray is a community dependent on, and rich with, vast natural resources....Our natural resources and the continuous strength of the fur trade industry give promise that Fort McMurray will find prosperous days ahead. After spending five months at Fort McMurray, I am more optimistic than ever regarding its future[9].

Parsons served as manager until November 1924 when he was replaced by Robert MacLeod who served the community until 1931. In September 1925, the Union Bank became the Royal Bank of Canada.

Bay moves uptown

During Fort McMurray's initial years, the Hudson's Bay Company served trappers and residents from its headquarters along the Athabasca River.

However, in 1921, the Hudson's Bay made an important business decision in response to the growing number of businesses locating on Franklin Avenue. The Bay vacated its Athabasca River base and set up shop on Franklin Avenue, west of current day Morrison Street.

From its new location, the Hudson's Bay store continued to buy furs, however, it began to shift its attention to the main street needs of Fort McMurray's growing population. Its larger store in "downtown" Fort McMurray was stocked with food, clothing, firearms, trapping supplies and building materials.

The arrival of Walter Hill

In March 1922, a young man stepped off the train in Draper and filled his lungs with the fresh spring air. Walter Hill quenched his thirst with water from a nearby barrel, and paused for a moment to survey the flurry of activity surrounding the train's arrival.

Crews were unloading trunks, suitcases, boxes and furniture. The Ryan brothers were loading their sled with people and freight. Nearby, the general store and café were doing a brisk business as passengers filled their bags with sandwiches and sweets before embarking on the final six mile journey to Fort McMurray.

As Hill would later reflect, the combination of fresh air, new opportunity and economic excitement somehow felt right. At age twenty-two, Walter Hill arrived in Fort McMurray to join pharmacist Angus Sutherland to run the town's pharmacy. Sutherland, whose chronic arthritis had begun to limit his ability to deliver services, had beckoned Hill north.

The decision to settle in Fort McMurray was not clear-cut. Prior to his arrival, Walter Hill appeared destined to set up a business in California. A friend had described the "abundant opportunities" which awaited entrepreneurs in a growing town named Hollywood. "We can't go wrong, he told me,"[10] Hill recalled. However, Hill's path to becoming "pharmacist to the Stars," was detoured by the call to assist Angus Sutherland.

Immediately following Hill's arrival, Sutherland left by train for the Mayo Clinic in Minnesota. Sutherland believed he had only a short time to live and told Hill to either "wind down the business or buy it."[11] Hill refused, but agreed to buy half of the pharmacy. The deal was sealed with a handshake and was not put to print until the early 1950s. The arrangement lasted until 1951 when Sutherland died at the end of May. In 1958 the pharmacy was renamed Hill Drugs.

Those initial Fort McMurray moments were forever etched in Walter Hill's memory. He recounted to the *McMurray Courier* in July 1970 what he observed when he arrived in 1922.

The original Hudson' Bay post built by Henry J. Moberly was still standing at the Athabasca River where the present bridge starts to cross. This was a one and half storey log building about twenty by twenty-four feet and was in 1922 being used as a residence by John Sutherland, chief engineer of the HBC transport. Alongside was the newer two storey house housing the Bay staff and the HBC warehouse where their steamers and boats used to unload. On Franklin Avenue there was a scattering of frame and log buildings occupied as dwellings, stores, post offices and telegraph office, bank and the two storey Franklin Hotel. Other stores, shops, a café, market garden and a log building used by the Board of Trade were scattered from west to east.

A Presbyterian Church, a one room log schoolhouse and small house for the minister, Rev. D.C. McTavish and his wife who taught the school were close together. At the Prairie there was a small collection of frame and log dwellings, a sawmill and a new boat yard where the HBC river steamer "The Athabasca" was being built[12].

In a community which seemed to turn over its entire population each decade, the presence of Walter Hill on Franklin Avenue until his death in October 1986 provided the one thing past and current residents could count on. The Hill Drugs guest book, now in the care of his son, Ken, provides a "who's who" of individuals who dotted the Fort McMurray landscape through almost seventy years of growth, challenge and change.

The man they called "Uchulah"

In 1922, a Jewish/Russian immigrant, Edward Hanson, moved to town and launched a second hand store. The new business, "Uncle Sam's," was located on Franklin Avenue west of Morrison Street, and served as a meeting and departure point for both new and departing residents looking to buy or sell furniture, tools, firearms or work clothing.

Soon after his arrival, Hanson immersed himself in northern culture. His daughter, Ann- Zoe, recalled he learned to speak six languages, including Cree and Chipewyan. His store was a constant hotbed of activity as trappers and local residents gathered around the store's wood stove to trade stories.

Hanson married wife Lillian in 1925, and with their children Julius and Ann-Zoe would become fixtures in Fort McMurray. In 1927, the Hansons moved to Fond du Lac where they continued trading. In 1944, they returned and purchased the Paul & Leggett General Store which the family continued to operate until selling their business to Alec and Alice Haxton in 1960. The comfort and trust native people felt towards Hanson earned the endearing Chipewyan nickname "Uchulah," meaning "Rags."

Escape from the Klu Klux Klan

There was no person more closely identified with the *Muskeg Special* than Len Williams. For almost fifty years, Williams was employed as the train's porter, serving as a host, caretaker and messenger to both passengers and residents along the rail line.

As the train regularly crept along the tracks from Waterways to Lac La Biche, Williams and crew would slow down as they approached trapper's cabins or small settlements and wait for a wave or a gun shot to signify that all was well. The crew would also deliver mail or gifts up and down the track, and would bring news of friends and relatives to those trapping in isolated areas.

When McMurray residents needed special medicine, fresh produce, dry cleaning or even a tuxedo rental, Williams would gladly ride into downtown Edmonton and perform the favour. He was known as a sweet and caring man. But few knew about the background of hatred and violence which brought him to Fort McMurray.

Williams was born in Mississippi in 1885, and like thousands of other blacks, left the United States to escape the lingering hatred and racial violence which followed the American Civil War. Many blacks who remained in the south bore the brunt of vigilante groups such as the Klu Klux Klan.

In 1910, Williams watched from the forest as members of the Klan lynched his best friend. The following day, he borrowed money from his sister and headed for Oklahoma to join the "underground railroad" to Canada. Williams made his way to Winnipeg and west to Alberta where he first homesteaded near Wildwood.

Although details of this journey remain sketchy, it is believed he came to Canada to survey the country on behalf of a community of southern blacks who would later immigrate and homestead in Amber Valley, near Athabasca.

By 1922, Williams had landed a job with the A&GWR, and over his many decades with the railway remained a loyal and trusted employee. Children would remain in his gentle custody during the twenty-eight hour train trip to Edmonton. For many years, any dignitary or important piece of cargo travelling between Edmonton and Fort McMurray would pass under his care.

He helped ship the original buffalo which would stock Wood Buffalo National Park. During the early days of oil exploration, Williams would also assist his friend "Sid" hauling oil sand by horse and wagon. Later, residents realized Williams was referring to oil sands explorer Dr. Sidney Ells.

Throughout, Williams remained tight-lipped about his Mississippi roots. His son, Gilbert, has spent a number of years piecing together his father's story, and notes that during his sixty-five years in Alberta, Williams refused to go back and visit his birthplace. "He didn't believe anything had changed," recalled Gil. "This was in the 1960s when there was a lot of racial reform and violence, and Dad saw this on television and refused to go back."[13] Williams died in 1977 at age 92.

"He didn't harp on his hardships or on the discrimination," his son recalled. "He just wanted to protect his family and to get away from the hatred."[14]

Morimoto and family

Katsuhei (Tom) Morimoto may not have been the tallest man, but that didn't stop him from thinking big.

Morimoto arrived in Canada from Japan in 1906, and soon made his way to Edmonton where he ran a rooming house. Frustrated by high rents in Edmonton, Morimoto came to Fort McMurray in 1920, and launched a similar business on Franklin Avenue.

Upon arrival, Morimoto contracted Sven Swanson who built a two-storey house on Franklin Avenue, just west of the current day Morrison Centre. In a community where shacks and small homes were the norm, the Morimoto house stood as a mansion.

Later in the 1920s, when the rooming house failed, Moromoto tried his hand at trapping, and then at farming. Morimoto cultivated ten acres in an area known as Hudson's Bay Flats, located where Franklin Avenue meets the Athabasca River. Each year, Morimoto would produce tons of potatoes, carrots, turnips, cabbage, and corn, and used the nearby Hudson's Bay steamboat to transport his fresh vegetables to the north.

In her diary, Ellen "Granny" McDermott, wife of Hudson's Bay Company manager Bob McDermott, noted that "today (Aug. 26, 1926) Mr. Morimoto filled thirty five bags of potatoes for the north steamer."[15] Morimoto was barely five feet tall, but was known as one of the strongest men in town. It was said that he could sling a hundred-pound bag of potatoes "like a rag doll, and could easily complete forty pushups on one hand."

One of the biggest events on Fort McMurray's social calendar was Morimoto's corn roast. Morimoto would call on some of the town's youth in late summer to help his family pick crops, and when it was over, Morimoto would say "thanks" by throwing a big bash for the community. Morimoto's wife Mitome would cook pot after pot of sweet Fort McMurray corn.

During the winter, the Morimotos served as Fort McMurray's ice providers. Moromoto and his sons would cut blocks of ice from the Clearwater River, and sell them at ten cents a block for use in ice houses. During the days before refrigeration, ice would be packed in small huts filled with sawdust, and this would keep perishable items like butter and cheese cool during the long blistering summer days.

Tom and Mitome also believed in big families. They produced seven sons. However, in July 1938, tragedy struck the Morimotos as Mitome neared the end of her eighth pregnancy. A workman completing repairs to the Morimoto home fell off the roof and hit the ground breaking his back. Mitome saw the man drop by her window and immediately went into shock and labour. Neither she nor the couple's eighth child, a girl, survived.

The Morimotos continued to be active members of the Fort McMurray community well into the 1950s.

O'Coffey takes over

Frank O'Coffey was known as a fiery Irishman who was never afraid to walk an extra mile. When O'Coffey's real estate career faltered in Edmonton in 1917, he turned his sights to the province's northern frontier and in spring boarded a train in Edmonton and rode to "end of steel" at Lac La Biche. With no further transportation available, O'Coffey packed his belongings, turned his feet northward, and over the next seven days, walked the one hundred and fifty-five miles to Fort McMurray.

Upon his arrival, O'Coffey began working for Northern Transportation, a company which shipped freight by barge to Fort Smith, NWT, and points north. Using money he had earned selling real estate in Edmonton, O'Coffey bought a rooming house, in 1922, and began operating the Franklin Hotel. In 1924, the hotel became the town's most prestigious address when the Province granted O'Coffey a liquor license. The hotel dining room was split into a restaurant and a beer hall, with a large wood stove built into the wall which separated the two sides.

Although at the time, Fort McMurray existed as a dusty frontier community, Frank O'Coffey did his best to ensure his hotel provided visitors with a "touch of class." O'Coffey owned a gramophone, and incoming guests would usually be greeted with classical music or the tenor tones of opera singer Enrico Caruso.

During the next thirty years, the Franklin Hotel would serve as Fort McMurray's primary meeting point. During the 1930s, severe arthritis and hearing loss hampered O'Coffey, however, he remained an active and influential member of the community until his death in 1945 at age seventy-three. The Franklin Hotel remained under the O'Coffey family's ownership until 1952.

The 1923 land revolt

In early 1923, Fort McMurray experienced its first citizens' protest. When the first settlement plan was drawn in 1910, the town was divided into huge river lots and placed under the control of about a dozen local residents and speculators. Some, like businessman William Manning, were eager to subdivide and sell small residential lots. But others preferred to hold their undeveloped land, waiting for the market to improve.

The lack of developed land did not sit well with the town's newer arrivals, many of whom were interested in establishing homes and businesses. In January 1923, members of the town's business community launched a strategy to free downtown land for development. One morning, eleven growly town residents gathered in front of the old public school board cabin and posed for a photo hand inscribed with the caption "Smashing the Land Monopoly, January 12, 1923."

The Board of Trade and the Public School Board took up the cause, and armed with the Land Monopoly photo travelled to Edmonton requesting that the Province apply pressure on passive landowners to either sell or develop. The Province adopted a crafty policy to address the problem. It noticed that one major land holding company had not paid its land taxes. The government eventually seized the land and allowed it to be subdivided.

Fort McMurray's first citizen revolt had succeeded. Organizers credited the January 12 photo with helping to press the government into action. The photo's impact was further enhanced by the restless look of the residents, and by the visual impact of one man with his fingers bandaged, supposedly due to frostbite.

The man with the bandages was D.S. MacKenzie who two days earlier had lost his fingers in a power saw accident.

Scotty Morrison, "unofficial" lawyer

A second prominent individual pictured in the 1923 photo was Scotty Morrison who made his living cutting hair, but like many others in the community operated a series of side businesses.

While Cecil Potts served as a criminal lawyer and later as a magistrate, Morrison unofficially took care of civil matters. When residents needed someone to prepare a bill of sale for property or a major piece of equipment, it was Morrison who prepared it, ensuring that it included the proper language and conditions.

Morrison also achieved popularity with local youth during the 1930s, when he provided a piece of downtown land to build a ball diamond. The sports field was located just northwest of the current day Morrison Centre, a professional services building which bears his name.

Research shifts to Edmonton

In 1923, Karl Clark and his associate Dr. S.M. Blair moved their research efforts to Edmonton. The team built a hot water separation plant in the basement of the University of Alberta power plant and over the next three years transferred about eighty-tons of material from Fort McMurray to Edmonton for study.

The following year, the Province provided Clark with a second Edmonton area laboratory, this time at Dunvegan to test the oil sands' paving potential. In 1924, about one hundred tons of bitumen was shipped south for treatment, most of it provided by Thomas Draper.

Pavement material from the Dunvegan plant was used to surface St. Albert Trail. Meanwhile, Clark and Blair continued working in the basement of the University of Alberta power plant perfecting their hot water process.

New York police arrive

In the late 1910s, the call of Fort McMurray reached New York City. A group of policemen working in a New York stationhouse read an account of the Athabasca oil sands, picked up stakes and boarded a west bound train. Sometime in 1917, the squad arrived in Fort McMurray with drilling equipment, and proceeded north to mine a lease it had acquired near Fort McKay. The lease was located on the east banks of the Athabasca River on a site known as "Old Fort", or Calumet which had been used as a trading site during the times of the North West Company.

While the New Yorkers confirmed the vast potential of their oil sands deposit, their ability to cash in was limited by a lack of technology. By 1923, the Americans had exhausted their resources. Their money had been spent and the area's harsh climate, and persistent mosquito population had thwarted their initial enthusiasm.

In 1922, a Prince Edward Island native arrived in Fort McMurray, lured to the area by stories of great oil deposits. Robert Fitzsimmons arrived in Fort McMurray after leaving his Vermilion real estate company and soon after acquired the Alcan Oil Company lease. In 1927, Fitzsimmons incorporated the property under the name International Bitumen Company. During his initial years of exploration, Fitzsimmons joined many of his predecessors by attempting to find the elusive source of liquid oil. However, by 1927 it had become apparent to Fitzsimmons that a yet to be developed technology held the key to his future success.

Fitzsimmons purchased fifty dollars of materials and began building his own hot water separation plant. He placed shares of International Bitumen Company on the stock market and despite the challenging investment conditions created by the depression was able to finance his ongoing excavations. In 1929, using a hot water injection process Fitzsimmons was able to skim eighty-four hundred gallons of bitumen. Fitzsimmons was able to produce immediate results for his nervous investors.

Soon after, Fitzsimmons signed a deal with Edmonton's Marshall-Wells store to distribute his product. Following the example of aboriginal people who had used the oil sands to waterproof canoes, Marshall Wells marketed the product as a material to waterproof roofs. Some of the bitumen was also shipped for paving operations in the Jasper area.

As historian J. Joseph Fitzgerald noted in his book *Black Gold with Grit*, the business deal marked the first commercially profitable oil sands recovery operation. The location of Fitzsimmons plant was called Bitumount, and included a nearby store and post office operated by American Al Wheeler who was associated with the original New York crew. Although the Bitumount site has been long abandoned and looted, many maps still carry its mention.

Almost sixty years later, in March 1984, a construction foreman named Gord Hnatiuk heard accounts of a decaying metal structure tucked in the woods near Bitumount. Hnatiuk scoured the area and eventually stumbled on Fitzsimmons' abandoned Cable 2 oil rig. Alberta Culture was dispatched to the site and matched the rig with some of Fitzsimmons' documents which it had acquired. The records show that the original rig cost seventeen hundred and sixty-five dollars, and a further two thousand dollars to transport it from Chicago.

Other documents provide a window into the high operation costs of the day. A bill from the early 1920s shows it cost Fitzsimmons thirty-three hundred and forty-three dollars to buy one load of horse feed and other incidentals. Camp supplies and labour totaled six thousand dollars. Incorporation of the original International Bitumount Company cost nine hundred dollars, with three hundred in additional fees.

Fitzsimmons also possessed an oak boat equipped with an OX5 airplane engine and propeller mounted at the rear. Some local residents recall the noise and the speed in which Fitzsimmons shuttled between McMurray and Bitumount. Fitzsimmons could navigate the fifty-five miles between the two sites in under ninety minutes.

"You could also smell him coming a mile away," recalled longtime resident Hugh Stroud. "He made his own gasoline and it smelled like skunk oil."[16]

Oilsands Champion

By 1942, with an aging and abandoned Bitumount plant on his hands, it was time for Robert Fitzimmons to take drastic action.

While Fitzsimmons lacked working capital, he did possess expertise and a plant shell which he believed could be of value to a perspective investor. That investor turned out to be Lloyd R. Champion, a Montreal financier, who was also a friend of Nathan Tanner, the Alberta government's Minister of Land and Minerals.

In 1942, Champion arrived in Alberta and offered Fitzsimmons financial assistance in return for control of the Bitumount operation. Champion proposed to form a new company, Oil Sands Limited, with a limited share transfer from Fitzsimmons' old company, International Bitumen. The offer was five shares of International Bitumen for one in Oil Sands Limited. In 1943, a deal was completed which enabled Champion to take full control.

But if Fort McMurray residents believed that Champion would dig into his pockets to upgrade the Bitumount plant, they were wrong. Bitumount's new owner initially refused to provide money for improvements. By the time Champion realized that a major investment was needed, the 1943 mining season had passed, much to the frustration of Robert Fitzsimmons, who in March 1944 resigned his advisory position with Oil Sands Limited.

Champion pursued Fitzsimmons to return for the summer of 1944 which provided the new owner an opportunity to train new managers. In late summer. Fitzsimmons was dismissed as chief architect and left the Bitumount plant and Fort McMurray.

While the Bitumount plant never resumed full production, Champion continued to lobby the Provincial government to become actively involved in the oil sands. Champion enticed Premier Ernest Manning to provide Oil Sands Limited with working capital and on December 6, 1944 a board of Trustees was appointed made up of W.A. Fallow and Nathan Tanner from the provincial cabinet, and Lloyd Champion from Oil Sands Limited.

The deal was almost identical to the one signed by the federal government with the Abasand project. Again, the provincial and federal governments were in direct competition. In the end, neither plant proceeded, due partly to the amount of duplication and error expended by both plants attempting to perfect an experimental technology.

Until 1948, the provincial government attempted to secure additional investors, but was not successful. Later that year, Bitumount was abandoned as a commercial project. For the next thirty years, its buildings and other assets remained idle, often the target of vandals and souvenir hunters.

Province returns to salt

In 1923, the provincial government decided that conditions were ideal to resume its hunt for salt in the region.

Between 1919-22, it had conducted tests near the Snye, just north of downtown Fort McMurray; however, due to the distance between its mine and the A&GWR, the project never progressed past the experimental stage. With the extension of the railway to Draper, the province's enthusiasm increased. It located a site between the Draper station and the Clearwater River where it felt the product could be easily transported to the railway.

Unfortunately, while the Province had completed its homework on transportation, it had failed to properly assess location. Tests were shut down in 1923 when after drilling seven hundred and eighty-nine feet, no salt deposits were found.

"McTavish University" burns

In spring 1923, students in Fort McMurray received an unexpected one-day holiday. One morning, the town's one classroom school caught fire, and within two hours was reduced to ashes.

As Real Martin, a nine-year-old student at the time recalls, the town's youth celebrated all day, but soon received sobering news. Classes would resume the next day, outdoors in the laneway behind the school site. A few days later, students moved indoors to a classroom set up in the nearby teachers' residence. Students would eventually be placed in a nearby warehouse until a new school could be built.

The town school was nicknamed McTavish University after its teacher, Cassia McTavish. Martin remembers McTavish as being a good teacher, although somewhat strict. In an interview a few months before his passing in 2000, Martin recalled his only encounter with "the strap," which occurred soon after the fire.

Guys were fooling around having lunch and somebody threw a piece of chalk at somebody, and someone threw one back and the next thing you know they were in to a big box of chalk, and the older guys started breaking off pieces and started throwing it at each other. After awhile, they had a civil war going on. There were only about three girls and the rest were guys. All the boys got a strapping. I didn't even throw a chunk of chalk. Make sure that your history book records that I was innocent[17].

Done.

Radio and telephone links

In 1924, Fort McMurray's world became just a bit smaller. That year, Edmonton radio station CJCA improved the power of its signal, and its programs could be received in Fort McMurray during the late evening and early morning. CJCA began targeting northern audiences with programs like *Calling the North* which aside from providing music and other programming, enabled family and friends to send important messages to northern communities.

That year, telephone service came to Fort McMurray. Trapper and entrepreneur Charlie Eymundson purchased an old crank phone system and subsequently strung a three mile telephone line from Waterways to McMurray. Each phone was connected to the main trunk and was operated by two dry cells. Each home was given a code which consisted of a series of short and long rings. Although no one was supposed to lift the receiver unless they heard their signal, it was common practice until the arrival of Alberta Government Telephones in 1958 for local residents to engage in the popular pastime of eavesdropping. "There were no secrets,"[18] recalled Hugh Stroud.

The railroad inches closer

While the Province remained firm that the A&GWR would end at Draper, the pressures of nature, and the clout of the Hudson's Bay Company would soon force a shift in direction. During the early 1920s, the Clearwater River experienced a decline in water flow.

The once mighty river was reduced to a series of sand bars and water paths which could only be navigated by experienced captains. On many occasions, shallow waters prevented boats from reaching the rail link at Draper. Frustrated by problems moving materials from Edmonton to Fort McMurray, the Hudson's Bay Company threatened to bypass the A&GWR in favour of a longer but more dependable route through Peace River. Combined pressure resulted in the Province extending "end of steel" from Mile 282 to Mile 285.5 where the community of Waterways would soon be established. The Province approved regular rail traffic from Edmonton to the Waterways station house on July 11, 1925.

Return of the Count

With rail service from Edmonton now reaching Fort McMurray's doorstep, entrepreneurs began to dust off projects and schemes which had been shelved due to previous transportation challenges.

In 1924, Count Alfred Von Hammerstein returned to Fort McMurray with plans for a massive industrial project. Von Hammerstein had been a minimal player in the community during the previous decade, due mainly to his dubious oil exploration practices. This time, Von Hammerstein was back as a minority shareholder in a new venture supported by the financial weight of Edmonton businessman John Gillespie, and other southern investors. Gillespie operated the Alberta Grain Company and also owned a brokerage firm in downtown Edmonton.

Gillespie announced that a full salt production plant would be built on Von Hammerstein's abandoned oil lease at the mouth of the Horse River. The plant was located below where the Fort McMurray subdivision of Abasand Heights is today. From there, salt would be mined, granulated and shipped to Edmonton. By September 1925, the Alberta Salt Company had secured lease rights from the federal government to a forty-four acre parcel area officially known as the La Salina mineral claim.

The Horse River operation was massive by 1920s standards. It included a large wooden processing plant, three thirty-thousand gallon tanks, a dining room, bunkhouse, and a number of houses.

Darlene Comfort, author of *Pass the McMurray Salt* please described the plant's production method.

The process was simple and was based on a system of shallow wooden evaporating vats heated by steam piping first introduced in Canada in 1874. Fresh water from the river was pumped down the old Northern Exploration Company well. This became saturated with salt and the brine was then pumped up. The subsequent brine was then placed in large shallow vats which were steam heated. The water was evaporated off and the settled salt was shoveled by manual labour[19].

The salt was separated into various grades and was shipped south by rail to Edmonton.

The plant provided a major economic jolt to Fort McMurray. An estimated twenty five to thirty men were hired to operate the plant and to shovel salt. A team of women was employed to sew fifty-pound gunnysacks. As well, crews were imported to carve road links from the Horse River, along the Athabasca River to Fort McMurray.

Rail dispute shuts plant

In the beginning, it was the opportunity created by the new railway which launched the Alberta Salt Plant. In the end, it was a dispute over the railway which closed it.

In July 1925, the Alberta Salt Plant began full operation, but transportation remained a major issue. Shipping tons of salt out of the Horse River valley presented a huge challenge which was further aggravated by rainy conditions during spring and summer, and brutal cold during winter. Gillespie and the Province locked horns over who would pay for a rail extension from Draper to the salt plant.

Since the plant was located in a valley, a rail link to Waterways "end of steel" would have involved climbing the steep slope through future Abasand Heights, and then descending back into the Clearwater River valley. Moving salt south directly to Draper was identified as a safer and more efficient route. Gillespie agreed to pay for the rail link, but he wanted sole ownership of the Draper to Abasand spur. The province would not agree.

In 1926-27, with the government and Gillespie at an impasse, the Alberta Salt Plant began to drastically reduce production. While the plant lost money during its initial two years, it proved that large quantities could be efficiently mined from the Fort McMurray deposit.

During 1925, eight hundred and thirty-three tons of salt were sold to outside companies. That figure climbed to over two thousand tons in 1926. However, without a reliable rail link out of the Horse River valley, costs dramatically exceeded revenues produced. The company continued to mine a limited amount of salt until 1928. Salt was transported out of the valley by horse and cart by entrepreneurs who included Syd Hawkins and the Ryan brothers.

The coal footnote

Although the Alberta Salt Plant enjoyed only a brief period of success, it facilitated a major shift in the way in which local residents heated their homes.

In 1925, most residents used wood burning stoves. However, the cost of wood had become a problem. The price of a cord of wood had recently risen from four dollars a cord to twelve dollars. The Board of Trade negotiated a deal with the Alberta Salt Company to purchase coal from the plant at a cost of ten dollars a ton. The salt company regularly imported coal by rail from Carbondale, and soon, the Ryan brothers transported a portion of each shipment for use in Fort McMurray.

To take advantage of the new heating opportunity, most Fort McMurray residents converted their stoves from wood to coal. Following the departure of the Alberta Salt Plant, coal continued to be transported north by rail.

Runaway logs from Athabasca

During the summer of 1925, Fort McMurray unwillingly became northeastern Alberta's lumber capital.

A sawmill operator in the Town of Athabasca named Omar Tutty had lined up about two million feet of logs along the nearby river. His crews were in place to turn the logs into timber, and ship the product to markets throughout North America.

But before his sawmill crew could begin, the boom which held the logs in place snapped, sending a huge wall of lumber down the Athabasca River. Tutty had no way of stopping the massive flow as it pressed north, but he soon developed a backup plan to save his investment. Tutty and his logging crew secured a team of horses, and raced north to Fort McMurray arriving just a few hours ahead of the log flow. The team positioned itself at the entrance to the Snye, a small waterway which flows off the Athabasca at Fort McMurray, and built an impromptu wing dam.

"The dam was completed just as the logs arrived in Fort McMurray," recounts George Waterhouse, a longtime local sawmill operator. "Tutty and his men steered the wood into the Snye, and held them there."[20] From the banks of the Snye, Tutty set up a sawmill, turned most of his load into lumber and quickly completed a deal to ship a huge quantity of wood to the arctic.

"He had quite a good head," said Waterhouse. "He wasn't about to lose two million feet of logs."[21] Waterhouse, who turned 88 in February 2001, heard the story from Charlie Fix, one of the Tutty's crew members.

Hudson's Bay boom

It did not take long before the "end of steel" at Waterways became a hotbed of economic activity. The Hudson's Bay Company rewarded the Province for its decision to extend the A&GWR by building a major warehouse. A second warehouse was added in 1926.

The Hudson's Bay Company then cancelled its Grande Rapids steamer service from Athabasca, and consolidated its shipping operations in Waterways. The HBC's marine branch operated from the banks of the nearby Clearwater River under the name Mackenzie River Transport. A Waterways store also opened making Fort McMurray the only northern community to support two Hudson's Bay Company stores within its boundaries.

Both Hudson's Bay Company stores remained extremely active. The Waterways store was supported by the rail and by the growing community of Waterways, while the McMurray outlet profited by supplying dry goods to local trappers and residents, and by serving as a freight and passenger hub for steamboat travel to the north.

During the mid-1920s, Bob and Ellen "Granny" McDermott ran the Fort McMurray Hudson's Bay Company store. McDermott joined the Hudson's Bay Company in 1885 and served the company for fifty-one years in a variety of locations along the Mackenzie and Athabasca rivers. Another person of note during that period was Doug Ferrier, an accountant, who initially worked with the Hudson's Bay Company and over the next twenty years was employed in the Fort McMurray area with a number of companies including the Ryan Brothers and Robert Fitzsimmons' International Bitumen Company.

Granny McDermott kept a diary between 1925-26, and two excerpts provide a glimpse into the mid-1920s. McDermott records a forest fire, a rail speeder collision and the sighting of one of the first airplanes to pass over Fort McMurray.

May 16, 1926: Fine, hot windy day. Another fire down the other shore. Looks wicked. I thought of Sodom and Gomorrah. The fire boat came rushing down the Athabasca and came back tonight.

August 22, 1926: Doug Ferrier camped here. He is telling me about the speeder that ran into another one by mistake running off on the wrong track. Nobody hurt. The Flying Machine passed over while we were at dinner. I was the first to see it.[22]

Town rushes to the Snye

One of the biggest events during the summer of 1927 was the landing of a double winged plane on the Snye. Although a Vickers Vedette, flown by a Royal Canadian Air Force pilot, landed in 1924, it was the 1927 event which caused a local frenzy. Seventy-four years later, Alvina (Laboucane) Strasbourg recalled the event:

I was six years old and we were living in a little shack just about where the highway runs now behind Zeller's. It was early in the morning and my mother was feeding us breakfast. All of a sudden we could hear something humming. My mother went outside and she said "come on, it's a flying machine." She grabbed the kids and we ran down to the Snye. Every person was there. It was early in the morning. Some had their nightgowns on and they were all lined up along the shore. It was a double winged plane, and they taxied up and down the Snye to show us. That was the first of the bush pilots — the first time they landed there. That was the greatest thing that ever happened to us[23].

In the months to come, the appearance of bush planes became more frequent. Soon after, a hangar was built along the Snye.

It wasn't long before Alvina and her enterprising brother Ambrose developed a small business to support the bush pilots. Over time, most pilots would rent or build small cabins in the Fort McMurray area, and the Laboucane kids would earn fifty cents a trip keeping the cabin fires burning while pilots were away.

Chicago develops a taste

Fort McMurray's economy continued to diversify as rail service into Waterways became more dependable. The next company to fuel the local boom was the McInnes Fish Products Company.

In 1926, McInnis brought six boats from its Lesser Slave Lake operation to fish the teeming waters of Lake Athabasca. The company set up an elaborate and sophisticated operation using a series of boats and barges. Its staff was stationed on floating barges at the southern tip of Lake Athabasca and as fishing boats arrived, fish were gutted, graded, packed and iced in wooden boxes and shipped by iced barge to Waterways.

The fish were unloaded in Waterways, placed on a conveyor system and packed for shipping by rail to Edmonton. *The Muskeg Special* was met in Edmonton by a crack team of freight handlers who transferred the rail cars to a high-speed train which in Calgary linked up with the national railway network.

Ten days after being plucked from Lake Athabasca, northern pike, lake trout, pickerel and white fish were on the table at homes and restaurants in New York, Chicago and other major urban centres. Based on the superior taste of the Lake Athabasca product, and McInnes' reputation for dependable delivery, a contract was signed with Bird's Eye Foods, and this sustained the Waterways operation until its closure in 1969. Over time, McInnis learned to develop some "niche" products for sale to "upper crust" clients. In 1965, Lake Athabasca pickerel cheeks sold in New York fish markets for $16.95 per pound.

McInnis also developed a series of smaller industries to support its fishing operations. The company launched a sawmill in Draper and organized logging operations at three camps along the Clearwater River. A plant to produce fish boxes opened in Waterways which employed twenty residents.

McInnis also built a Waterways shipyard which produced three tugboats: the Noralta, Norlac and Norbasca. The company bought a number of Hudson's Bay barges and soon began shipping lumber and freight from Waterways to Fort Fitzgerald. Steve Brooks, Jr. who served for six summers on the Norbasca, recalls unloading freight at Fort Fitzgerald, hauling cargo over the sixteen mile portage to Fort Smith, and reloading it on to barges for transport north along the

Mackenzie River. Many of McInnis' fishermen, Brooks recalls, were of Scandinavian origin who travelled from Manitoba each spring to fish the lakes.

By 1929, McInnis' yearly haul from Lake Athabasca had reached one hundred sixty-five tons. While most of the area's stores and services were located in Fort McMurray, expansion by McInnis and the Hudson's Bay Company propelled Waterways as the area's employment hub. Houses began to spring up around the warehouses and factories, and Waterways began to take shape as a distinct and vital community.

The Fort McMurray Board of Trade later coined a marketing phrase to describe the Waterways link between the barges and the railroad. It advertised Fort McMurray as the place "Where Steel Meets Keel."

Nursing station, church and school

Economic activity in Waterways placed increased pressure on Fort McMurray's existing community structure. New workers and their families arrived each week, and soon Fort McMurray's churches took steps to expand services.

The Presbyterian Church established a two bed nursing station in 1925, staffed by nurse Olive (Dolly) Ross. The following year, a new Roman Catholic Church was built on Franklin Avenue at the present site of the Fort McMurray Public Library.

In 1928, Fort McMurray's public school finally reopened. During the years which followed the 1923 school fire, students studied in a room furnished in the teachers' residence. In the fall of 1928, Gerald Card, Chair of Fort McMurray School District #2833 proudly opened a new two-room school which would later become Peter Pond School. The new school began with about forty students and by 1935 had expanded to ninety-four. Grades ranged from one to nine. Students wanting to attend higher grades were sent to Athabasca or Edmonton.

It didn't take long for students at the new school to run into trouble with teacher John Hammond, who came to Fort McMurray to teach grades six to nine. Hammond quickly gained a reputation as a strict disciplinarian.

One day at the close of recess, some of the boys decided to carry their game of schoolyard football into the classroom. "They started kicking the ball inside and then Mr. Hammond came in," recalled Alvina Strasbourg, a six-year-old student at the time. "He lined up the boys and starting strapping the big guys first. I still remember the little ones starting to cry as they waited for their turn."[24] Students spent the rest of the day washing the school ceiling.

Although Hammond was known to be tough, there was no mistaking his teaching commitment. Every Friday afternoon, students would sit back as Hammond would read excerpts from Shakespeare, or a great novel like Ben Hur. It was Hammond's way of connecting children of Fort McMurray with the outside world. In 1939, when a number of his former students prepared to enter World War II, Hammond went to the Greisbach Barracks in Edmonton to help send them off. "He was a good teacher and he wanted to get the information in your head," recalled student Roy Hawkins. "I credit him with giving kids a good education." [25]

Hawkins himself felt the strong hand of Hammond's law. Hawkins was smacked more than once for knotting the braids of Peggy Skelton, who sat in front of him. There were other ways teachers would administer justice. On cold winter days, students who misbehaved were sent to the back of the classroom, far away from the stove which heated the school.

How cold was it? Hawkins remembers some days when the ink would freeze in the ink wells.

The legendary "Punch" Dickins

For ten years, Fort McMurray had relied mainly on rail and barge service to connect with the "outside" world. During the latter part of the 1920s, Waterways became the meshing point between rail service from Edmonton and a growing fleet of barges and steamers moving north to the arctic. Planes landed frequently along the Snye, but were still viewed as a novelty.

In early 1929, a new form of commerce began to make its mark. On January 3, 1929, Clennell "Punch" Dickins raised air service to a new level. He loaded his single-engine Fohker monoplane with a sack of mail and took off from the Snye for an historic journey along the Mackenzie River. The flight marked the beginning of airmail service between Fort McMurray and the north, and further propelled the town into a dominant position as a gateway to the arctic.

On his maiden flight, Dickins immediately encountered problems. While landing in Fort Resolution, NWT on his return flight, Dickins broke a ski. The mechanic in Fort Resolution, Lou Parmenter, constructed a new ski from a dog sled and then trimmed eight inches off of the propeller to balance the plane. Later that day, Punch Dickins safely landed his "trimmed" airplane on the Snye.

Despite his difficulties, Dickins' maiden voyage was deemed a success and Canadian Airways Limited was born.

Wop May and the Red Baron

Punch Dickins was not alone for long in the northern skies. Shortly after Canadian Airways Limited launched regular flights to and from the north, Dickins' long time friend, Wop May, began a competitive service, Commercial Airways, which in December 1929 was awarded commercial air mail service rights to the north.

Winifred "Wop May" became a fixture in Fort McMurray. He lived in a home at the corner of Morrison Street and Franklin Avenue and when he wasn't flying, he would join in a game of pond hockey or fastball, or dazzle local children with stories of his flying exploits. In 1918 he had been fighting the Germans over the skies of Europe when his guns jammed. May was ordered away from his unit when suddenly

German flyer Baron Manfred Von Richtofen appeared on his tail. Von Richtofen, known as the Red Baron, was the Germans' most feared World War I pilot and to that point had successfully downed two hundred allied flyers. May led the Baron to his own unit where squad leader Roy Brown fired and ended Richhofen's spree.

Wop May also achieved a degree of notoriety at home. He was once reprimanded by the Edmonton police for flying under the High Level Bridge. However, the story, which most impressed McMurray young people, involved his stint in 1932 as a sky sheriff when he guided the RCMP in the chase of Albert Johnson the "Mad Trapper" of the arctic.

Wop May was made an officer of the British Empire and was named to the Canadian Aviation Hall of Fame. He died in June 1952 at the age of 60.

"You had to be nuts"

When flyer Lewis Leigh visited Fort McMurray during the early 1980s, he admitted that during the early years of aviation "you had to be totally nuts"[26] to fly. Leigh was one of Alberta's legendary open cockpit flyers challenging the minus forty degree temperatures during the days of Canada's northern expansion. During the early 1930s, flyers like Leigh, Dickins and May flew open cockpit to transport food, furs, merchandise or medicine to their final destinations.

"We had no weather reports or radios," he once recalled. "There were no comfortable seats, seat belts or heat. It was the Depression and we had to make money to eat. You had to do these things to get business."[27] Leigh later became the first pilot with Trans Canada Airways (TCA) which later was renamed Air Canada.

As a sign of respect for those who braved the early years flying in and out of Fort McMurray, the streets of a new subdivision, Dickinsfield, were named in the 1980s after those employed during the early years of flying. Streets were named after Punch Dickins and mechanic Lou Parmenter. Oaks Crescent was named after Harry "Doc" Oaks, an employee with Northern Aerial Mineral Exploration, who in 1926 piloted the first monoplane into Fort McMurray.

Streets were also named for Andy Cruickshank and Duc Torrie who both died after crashing into the side of a hill during a snowstorm while on a mercy flight. Grant McConachie was honoured for his dedication in delivering mail, medical supplies and clergy. McConachie flew extensively throughout the north in his plane known as the Tin Goose.

Other noted flyers included Marlowe Kennedy, Cy Becker, Con Farrell, Leigh Brintnell, Matt Berry and Archie McMullen.

Northern Waterways Company

Cy Becker flew as a pilot during the late 1920s, assisting Wop May in the launch of Commercial Airways Ltd. However, in spring 1931, when May's company sold out to Canadian Airways, Becker planted his feet and turned his sights to the area's northern rivers.

In 1931, Becker bought a small boat and accepted a contract to move gasoline in forty-five gallon drums down the Mackenzie River. The gasoline arrived by rail at Waterways, and it was there that Becker built a narrow forty feet long scow powered by a forty horsepower engine. In mid-1931, a single Northern Waterways Company boat set course from the Clearwater River. On board was crew mate W.S. Kelly Hall who later became a purser, mate and skipper. Soon after the Northern Transportation Company Ltd (NTCL) was established in 1934, Hall became Superintendent of Operations.

From Fort McMurray, barges would eventually move north along the Athabasca and Slave rivers towards the arctic. For the next fifty years, the NTCL would transport fuel, equipment, supplies and passengers from Waterways, and later the Prairie to points north.

The NTCL provided opportunities for local residents to gain summertime employment packing and loading barges. Some seasonal workers made special arrangements to have their pay cheques cut into twelve equal payments so that while the NTCL was shut down during winter, their income would continue to flow.

In July 1937, 22-year-old Real Martin was hired as a deck hand on an NTCL barge. For the next three summers, Martin unloaded cargo along the rivers from Waterways to Fort Fitzgerald. He recalls that while the barges were licensed only to carry freight, the captain would often turn a blind eye to passengers who hitched a ride. "The NTCL was pretty lax about passengers," Martin recalled. "There was no other cheap way to get up north."[28]

While Waterways continued to grow as a commercial centre, its prosperity was largely limited to the summer months when barge activity was most active. Martin recalled:

The only problem with that kind of work is that there was plenty to do during the summer, but during the winter you would barely survive doing a few days of work for this guy or that guy. During the winter you earned just enough money to keep the wolves away[29].

New wave of research launched

By the mid-1920s, Karl Clark had gained valuable insight regarding the commercial viability of the Athabasca oil sands. While conducting research at the University of Alberta, Clark concluded that although a scientific formula could be developed to produce oil from the Athabasca oil sands, concrete challenges such as heat costs, labour and transportation needed to be overcome.

During Clark's travels throughout eastern Canada and the United States, fellow scientists confirmed that oil extracted from the Athabasca deposit had commercial potential. In particular, a respected researcher at Sarnia's Canadian Oils Limited concluded in 1926 that oil extracted from the Athabasca deposits could be used as an "excellent" lubricant. However, much to his disappointment, Clark learned that refineries in Chicago, Toronto and Sarnia were cautious about working with experimental oil providers. At the time, abundant supplies of conventional oil were being developed throughout North America.

In 1927, Clark wrote directors of his research council that he had successfully developed an effective and "economical" oil extraction process. Clark began pressing for a new and aggressive scientific initiative in the Fort McMurray area.

Soon after, conditions and personalities began to line up in his favour. In 1928, one of Clark's strongest supporters, Henry Marshall Tory, was appointed to a high-ranking research position in Ottawa as president of the National Research Council. Tory was replaced on the Alberta Research Council by Robert C. Wallace, a research expert who had gained a respected reputation in northern Manitoba as a promoter of northern resource development. At the same time, the Premier of Alberta, John E. Brownlee, expressed his support for renewed oil sands development. This was not surprising, since earlier in the 1920s, Brownlee had served as chair of Alberta's research council. Clark now had a network of strong supporters placed in positions of influence at both federal and provincial levels. It wasn't long before these sympathetic individuals would converge behind Clark's research efforts.

In May 1929, the Bituminous Sands Advisory Committee was formed, led by Wallace, Deputy Mines Minister Charles Camsell, and Henry Marshall Tory. The committee's initial two-year mandate was to experiment with hot water extraction techniques, and to further explore the use of oil sand as a viable road paving material.

The committee appointed a scientific "dream team" to lead the initiative. Clark was paired with fellow oil sands pioneer Sidney Ells, who for almost twenty years had served as the federal government's lead oil sands scientist in the Athabasca region. While Ells and Clark had devoted considerable personal effort towards developing the oil sands, their efforts had never been formally linked.

Sidney Ells' stellar reputation

While Karl Clark spent a significant part of the 1920s in Edmonton developing an oil sands separation process, Sidney Ells had occupied himself in the Fort McMurray area mapping the full breadth of the Athabasca deposit. Ells originally came to Fort McMurray in the early 1910s and initiated work at a number of experimental drilling sites. In 1917, he tabled an extensive report describing the content of the Athabasca oil sands which he estimated at 250 billion barrels.

Pharmacist and historian Walter Hill knew Ells well and recalled how thorough Ells was in mapping the area.

He travelled to Poplar Point where Billy Loutit had a stopping place for the dog team. He went north and mapped trading posts which Dan Patterson and Bill Gordon ran. Sid Ells was making a memo of all these things and named all of these places. He stopped all along the way making a survey and a plan of the oil sands. He was going down the river all the time making observations and drawing maps of it and where it was. He'd try and test the sand and evaluate the richness of it. He did that all the time, that man. He never stopped working[30].

Ells established a camp near Fort McKay at a site which would later become Bitumount and would routinely sign up students from the University of Alberta to three-month agreements to assist him mapping and analyzing the oil sands deposits. Ells quickly gained a reputation for frugality. On one occasion, while in the Fort McKay area, Hill saw Ells walking along the Athabasca River with an empty sled in tow. Ells told Hill that he had run out of "grub" and that his men had eaten only rice for the previous five days.

Ells feared that his recruits would get lost if he sent them to Fort McMurray to buy food, so he took it upon himself to walk the fifty-five miles to town and then drag the new supplies back to camp. When Ells returned, he was approached by the camp cook who said he was tired of the job, and requested a dog sled to trans-port him back to McMurray. Ells refused. Hill referred to the story as an example of how strongly Ells took his responsibility of managing federal funds.

Ells told him "that's the way it is. You signed up, you're supposed to stand through thick and thin." Ells would never spend five cents, whether it was his money or the government's money. He was more careful with the government money than with his own because he wanted to get every cent's worth of value out of what he spent. Another time I saw him on a hill hand drilling to see how much overburden there was before he hit the oil sand. He went one hundred feet down by hand. He wasn't popular for the simple reason that he watched every penny[31].

Hill recalled another incident where after over-turning his canoe on the Clearwater River about eighty miles east of Fort McMurray, Ells paddled up river on his own to retrieve his equipment, rather than send one of his crew.

The Bituminous Sands Advisory Committee combined Ells' field knowledge with Clark's scientific expertise. The federal/provincial initiative appeared poised for success.

Waterways test plant

One of the committee's first tasks was to dismantle the Edmonton/Dunvegan paving plant, and ship its components to Waterways. The plant was reassembled along the banks of the Clearwater River and in October 1929 was deemed ready for production.

In late fall, 1929, a limited amount of bitumen was produced at the Waterways plant, however, the product contained higher than acceptable water content. Led by Clark's associate, D.S. Pasternack, scientists began developing a series of addi-tives to reduce moisture in the bitumen produced.

In May 1930, the Waterways plant resumed operation. However, despite occasional periods when Clark and Ells produced rich crude oil, reoccurring problems with the feeder, dehydrator and other components shut down the plant for extended periods. In his 1930 report to the Alberta Research Council, Clark admitted that the plant faced significant technical problems, but noted the fact that a high quality of oil was being produced which provided reason for optimism. "This has had psychological as well as technical value," he reported.

Despite some initial successes, Clark and Ells' initiative soon ran out of steam. The research council was disbanded in 1933 due to funding pressures brought about by the Great Depression, and was not re-established until the early 1940s. As the federal and provincial governments occupied themselves with larger economic challenges, a group of private investors began moving to the forefront, and announced their willingness to pick up the ball.

The arrival of Max W. Ball

In his 1940 book, This Fascinating Oil Business, entrepreneur Max W. Ball stated that the Athabasca oil sands possessed the potential to fuel three distinct oil booms. He made note of the immediate economic opportunity that existed in the Fort McMurray area, as well as the possibility of extracting additional material by shafting into lower deposits. Ball also predicted that one day, when oil prices reached higher levels, oil that lay at the deepest levels of the Athabasca oil sands would attract oil companies and other investors. Ball referred to Fort McMurray noting:

Canada has three distinctions; it has the world's most northerly oil field, the world's largest known oil deposit, and world's only city that has based three oil booms on one field[52].

Ball, a Denver oil executive, first became interested in the oil sands in 1929 following a visit and presentation by Sidney Ells. Ball, a graduate of the Colorado School of Mines, originally worked for the United States government and had acquired strong credentials as both a lawyer and businessman. This combination of public and private sector experience had prepared him with excellent negotiating skills and a calm global perspective on investment and government relations. Ball was immediately convinced of Fort McMurray's potential and began exploring investment possibilities. Ells and Ball discussed potential lease sites, and although it was known that higher quality oil sand existed in the Fort McKay area, due to projected transportation challenges, a decision was reached to explore sites closer to the "end of steel."

Using Ells as an intermediary, Ball approached the federal and provincial governments with a request to develop Alfred Von Hammerstein's former oil and salt lease. The reserve contained confirmed oil sand deposits which were linked by roads cleared by the Alberta Salt Plant to Fort McMurray and the Northern Alberta Railway.

In September 1930, the Canadian Northern Oil Sands Products Limited was formed and Ball was officially granted rights to the Horse River lease. The federal government, which soon would hand jurisdiction over natural resources to the

Province, added one option. It gave Ball the right to pick ten square miles any-where within the Athabasca oil sands to develop an additional oil lease. Ells advised Ball to claim land in the Mildred Lake area, located about twenty-five miles north of Fort McMurray. Although the lease was never developed, it would serve as the launch point thirty-five years later for the world's largest oil sands opera-tion, Syncrude Canada Ltd.

While world economy struggled during the Great Depression, Max Ball con-tinued to boldly invest in the Fort McMurray area. In 1931, he changed the name of Canadian Northern Oil Sands Products Limited to Abasand Oils Limited, and during the next four years pressed research centres in Denver and Toronto to develop a reliable oil sands extraction process.

In December 1935, plans were completed for construction of a two hundred and fifty-ton separation and refining unit on the Horse River and the following year the pilot plant was completed. Subsequent operations revealed the need for modifications and in 1937 construction began on a second separation unit with a capacity of four hundred tons per day. In his memoirs, Ells observed how sig-nificant Ball's accomplishments were in the face of world economic conditions. "The above operation had been courageously carried out in the face of prejudice and skepticism and during a period of depression when financing had presented exceptional difficulties," Ells noted.

Ball spent the remainder of the 1930s perfecting his extraction process and navigating challenges such as transportation and overburden removal. The plant was eventually opened in 1940.

The Hungry '30s

While Fort McMurray was largely isolated from the Great Depression, residents were not completely untouched. While large centres such as New York, Montreal and Toronto bore the weight of a collapsing economy, Fort McMurray's fortunes were still tied to the rail and to the river system which continued to carry goods to and from the north.

In 1929, an eighteen-year-old, Gabrielle "Gibby" Comeau, walked off the Waterways train with two brothers, and her parents, Arzelie and Joseph Fontaine. The family had ventured north from Lac La Biche to work at Nick Moore's sawmill, but soon after, due to the economic slowdown, Moore's sawmill ceased operation. The Fontaines found shelter with Arzelie's brother, Louis Phaneuf.

Work was available, but it wasn't glamorous. Arzelie was hired by Frank O'Coffey to work at the Franklin Hotel at forty dollars per month. She was employed from four a.m. to ten p.m. daily, cooking meals and cleaning rooms. Joseph found work as a handyman with the Hudson's Bay Company. He earned fifty dollars per month. Comeau recalled those difficult times.

You look back at the Hungry 30s, and it was hard. There was no welfare and there was no assistance of any kind. You had to make it on your own. When you had a job in those days even if you hardly got nothing, you're going to hang on to it because you could hardly get anything anywheres[33].

When the NTCL or Hudson's Bay Company needed cheap labour, there were scores of men available, eager to work for low wages. Comeau continued:

The Hudson's Bay and the NTCL had big warehouses in Waterways right on the river bank and they used to take all the freight that used to come on the train, unload it in those big warehouses. When the boats would come up with the barges, then they would hire at twenty-five cents per hour to truck the groceries and everything from the train to the warehouse and from the warehouses to the barges. That was my brother's work at twenty-five cents an hour. And if you had to work the barges you'd have to work all night, until the barge was ready to go[34].

While jobs were not plentiful and wages were low, many McMurray and Waterways residents filled their pantries by turning to the land. Each home had a garden. For many, this was not an option but a necessity. As winter approached, women and children would furiously pick potatoes, tomatoes, cucumbers and berries, and begin canning. Many families used to can their vegetables in the same boilers they used to wash clothes. In the fall, some men would take to the "bush" and bring home a moose to feed the family for the winter. Families who had more than what they could use shared with others.

In the early 1930s, sharing became more difficult following a string of cold summers. Comeau remembered one year when only potatoes could be harvested since early frosts had destroyed most of the green vegetables. Through a combination of gardening, hunting, and wages earned from local employers, no McMurray or Waterways resident starved during the Great Depression.

"You could count on other people, but you had to work hard yourself to survive," Comeau said. "I didn't get these tough hands playing the piano."[35]

The Constable and the Prime Minister's brother

Kentucky had the Hatfields and McCoys. Fort McMurray had George Bennett and Jack MacDonald.

Throughout the 1930s, two of Fort McMurray's most prominent citizens became embroiled in a feud, much to the amusement of local residents.

George Horace Bennett was known as a "remittance man." He was the "ill-behaved" brother of Prime Minister R.B. Bennett who was lifted out of the national spotlight and dispatched to Fort McMurray, which was viewed as a safe and isolated location. Each month, a hefty cheque arrived from Ottawa, and this more than paid for Bennett's living expenses and his bar habit.

Bennett moved into a home on Manning Avenue between Main and Morrison streets next door to the Provincial Police barracks, where officer Jack MacDonald lived. It was MacDonald who was frequently called upon to collect Bennett, drunk on the street, or passed out at the Franklin Hotel. Bennett would flash his federal credentials at MacDonald who in return would assert his Police authority. Over time, a feud developed.

Bennett had a pistol and was fond of firing it into MacDonald's back yard. One time the two were arguing over the fence when Bennett lit up a cigarette. MacDonald slapped it out of Bennett's mouth and told him "don't blow smoke in front of me."[36] Bennett lit another cigarette and MacDonald slapped it again. Bennett retaliated by hooking MacDonald around the neck with the handle of his cane.

Residents recall both Bennett and MacDonald once arguing on the Snye pier when suddenly Bennett grabbed the constable's hat and threw it in the water. MacDonald calmly hired a local youth to retrieve it.

Bennett frequently accused MacDonald of condoning the manufacture of local liquor and publicly referred to him as "Moonshine Mac." When one would enter the front door of the Franklin Hotel, the other would exit through the rear.

With time, amused local citizens began to agitate the situation. It was customary for local residents to pay each other visits on New Year's Eve. As visitors exited Bennett's home, they picked up a piece of firewood from his front porch, carried it next door and presented it to MacDonald. At the end of the day, Bennett bemoaned his lack of firewood, and fingered MacDonald as the culprit.

MacDonald was transferred to another detachment in 1935. Bennett died in 1938 and is buried in the Fort McMurray cemetery.

Cow Carnage

In mid-1931, Fort McMurray experienced its first fatal car accident. The collision involved pilot "Monkey" Sherlock and a pair of Mrs. Furlough's cows.

Sherlock was a former World War I ace who was fond of performing aerial stunts. "He used to scare the hell out of us," recalled Alvina Strasbourg. "He used to take his plane up and he would go tail spinning and come down on the road."[37] It was rumoured that the swashbuckling Sherlock was responsible for two airplane ski tracks which appeared one winter day on the roof of the McMurray Hudson's Bay Company store.

One night, an intoxicated Sherlock along with a fellow pilot and a few "local girls" packed into a car and raced down Franklin Avenue. As they approached the mid-point of Franklin Avenue, a number of cows happened to be crossing the road. The ensuing collision caused a mess of animal parts which spread across Franklin Avenue. The occupants of the car were unhurt, but two of Mrs. Furlough's cows had to be shot.

Believe it or not!

During the early 1930s, one McMurray resident received worldwide attention. In her family biography written in 1988, Gwen Iris Spearman, daughter of

Charlie Eymundson, refers to three brothers from Iceland, Sig, Barney and Fussi Arnfinson, who "worked on steam boats, trapped, hunted, prospected for gold or did anything to turn a dollar during the Depression years."[38]

One day, the oldest Arnfinson, Sig, was alone in the brothers' cabin cleaning his rifle when he accidentally shot the gun's ramrod through his chest. Without anyone to assist, Arnfinson apparently "cut it out, or cut off both ends, then pulled it out with the pliers and stuffed the hole with towels."[39] The following day Arnfinson was on the river cutting a hole in the ice to gather water to boil to nurse his wounds, and to make coffee.

News of the incident raced through McMurray and eventually to London, England where Arnfinson's amazing heroics received global attention in a worldwide newspaper column of oddities known as Ripley's Believe it or Not.

Birth on Cooking Lake

One of the community's best-known families weathered a major crisis in August 1932. Pregnant with her second child, Gladys Hill unexpectedly went into labour, and her husband, fearing that she would encounter complications decided to transfer her to Edmonton for the birth.

Pilot Lewis Leigh, who flew for Explorer Air Transport, loaded Mrs. Hill and husband Walter into his aircraft and took off for Cooking Lake, just southeast of Edmonton. As the plane approached South Cooking Lake, the weather turned sour, and Leigh desperately searched for a hole in the fog to land. "Every few minutes Walter Hill would knock on the window and ask me to hurry up," Leigh later recalled. "Mrs. Hill was in pain."[40]

Finally, Leigh located a "window" through the clouds, and landed on South Cooking Lake. Gladys Hill was rushed to Leigh's nearby home and within ten minutes, Ken Hill was born. Before an ambulance and nurse arrived, the baby was wrapped in a makeshift nightie torn from a pillowcase.

The bear attack

Sometimes it takes a near death experience to help a person assess life's priorities. Sven Peterson learned that lesson in 1932.

Peterson was a quiet middle-aged Swede who came to Fort McMurray during the Depression to work as a trapper. After a few months, Peterson began living with a local woman, known as Mrs. St. Arnaud, in a cabin outside Fort McMurray. Mrs. St. Arnaud was a stocky woman who smoked a corn-cob pipe.

Early one morning, Peterson left the cabin and shuffled through the snow to check his trapline. As Peterson entered the bush, he heard squealing noises and eyed two bear cubs rolling in the snow. Peterson suddenly felt a piercing pain from behind, as a long sharp claw raked the back of his neck.

Peterson had inadvertently positioned himself between a mother bear and her cubs, and within seconds found himself being tossed like a rag doll by the incensed black bear. Peterson was attacked until he was chewed, bleeding and defenseless. Hearing the commotion, Mrs. St. Arnaud ran from the couple's cabin and clubbed the bear with a rifle. She dragged Peterson into the bush and then shot the bear between the eyes. St. Arnaud then threw Peterson over her shoulder, carried him back to the cabin and began nursing him back to health.

It didn't take long after his recovery for Peterson to realize what a dedicated partner he had in Mrs. St. Arnaud. Immediately after Peterson recovered, the two were married.

On Valentine's Day for years to come, the Peterson and St. Arnaud story was told in homes, schools and bars as an example of "true Fort McMurray love."[41]

Arrival of the Signal Corps

By 1932, Fort McMurray had established itself as an important launching point for northern air travel. Canadian Airways and Mackenzie Air Services had developed permanent bases and homes along the Snye for pilots, mechanics and their families.

Mail and express was received by train in Waterways, trucked to Fort McMurray, reloaded on airplanes and sped to northern outposts. With the volume of air traffic increasing each month, the need was identified to establish a reliable signal system to advise pilots about weather conditions. In addition, the Canadian government had become sensitive to the security threat posed by foreign countries, and looked for a way to link isolated northern settlements with the rest of Canada. In the late 1920s, the Royal Canadian Corps of Signals' Northwest Territories and Yukon System was established.

In December 1932, Sgt. Jim Lilly and Sgt. "Red" Scharfe arrived in Fort McMurray, and installed radio equipment in the former "Indian Agency" building on Franklin Avenue. By January 1933, a local station was on the air. Fort McMurray was now linked with a chain of signal posts which extended from Edmonton to the Beaufort Sea. During the mid-30s a permanent Signal Corps building was erected on Main Street, which was also known as the Snye Road.

Aside from providing weather reports, the radio system enabled isolated communities to summon assistance in the case of medical crisis or other emergency. Pilots could receive up-to-date weather information before they left, and could communicate by Morse code with stations during their flight path.

Tourism to the arctic

In 1932, Hudson's Bay Company, under its shipping wing Mackenzie River Transport, advertised river tours from Waterways through Fort Smith to Aklavik, NWT. A promotional brochure claimed that "this interesting and enchanting trip through Canada's North Western Waterways can be made—Edmonton to the Arctic and back—in a calendar month. Total cost for the month's journey including meals and accommodation was three hundred and twenty-five dollars."[42]

Freight rates from Waterways were set at twenty-five cents per hundred pounds to Fort McKay, seventy-five cents to Fort Chipewyan and eight dollars to Aklavik.

Mackenzie River Transport's fleet included the SS Athabasca River and SS Northland Echo which were based in Waterways. The MS Pelly Lake and the MB Canadusa served Lake Athabasca. Other boats included the SS Distributor, the SS Mackenzie River, the MS Slave River, the MT Liard River, The MS Buffalo Lake and MB Weenusk.

Fire destroys Franklin Avenue

On July 16, 1934, the resourcefulness and gumption of Fort McMurray residents was tested to the limit. It began with a mournful cry at four a.m., and produced monumental effects on Fort McMurray for months to come.

Roy Hawkins, who was thirteen-years-old at the time, vividly remembered the first sounds of the devastating fire which gutted the south side of Franklin Avenue. The Hawkins family lived across the street from the RCMP barracks, on Manning Avenue between present-day Main and Morrison streets. It was a hot summer night just before sunrise. Suddenly, Hawkins was awakened by the sound of Lowry O'Coffey, son of Franklin Hotel owner Frank O'Coffey, moaning "fire, fire, fire."[43]

"It was a mournful wail," said Hawkins. "I still remember that. He was alerting the RCMP but since there was no fire department, there was nothing anyone could do."[44] The fire began in the Franklin Hotel pool hall and soon spread west to Sutherland Drugs. Gladys Hill was asleep in the apartment above the store, and barely had enough time to rescue her children. She instructed her son, Dave, to tuck the store's books under his arm, and run.

With the fire now licking at the store's eastern wall, Hill was asked by onlookers which items should be saved. She replied, "anything worthwhile."[45] A number of rescuers knocked down the front door, and gathered the items of most value including cigarettes and some counter displays, before smoke and flames seared through the store walls. Hill sent a telegram to her husband Walter, in Edmonton, and within a few days, new stock arrived by rail.

To the west, John Parry's general store faced an additional complication. Some of the town's folk began looting items. Parry's stock, including a number of firearms was passed out the front door, but the pilfering came to an abrupt conclusion. "There was gunpowder in the store and I remember it went up with a boom," Hawkins recalled. "The looting ended after that."[46]

Occupants of the hotel made it out safely, but there was one close call. Hotel employee Celeste "Fille" Auger, heard the noise, and ran outdoors to safety, however, a second hotel worker, remembered only as Dee, remained asleep. Volunteer firefighters hacked through the smoke and flames, and pulled her out of bed. Moments later the hotel collapsed.

The fire completely destroyed the hotel and surrounding buildings, but there was one glimmer in the aftermath. When the icehouse adjacent to the hotel caught fire, the sawdust ignited and subsequently cooked hundreds of pounds of meat which had been earmarked for the hotel dining room. While fleeing the burning hotel, "Fille" Auger had grabbed a drawer of cutlery. As Marie O'Coffey would later tell her daughter-in-law Mary O'Coffey: "The meat was perfectly cooked and ready to slice and eat."[47] Amidst the ruins of Franklin Avenue, residents sat down to a meal of fresh meat, eaten with shiny hotel cutlery.

While Rome burned

Another casualty in the 1934 fire was McVittie's Dance Hall. McVittie's was a place where town residents could kick back and dance to songs played on a large wind up gramophone. The cover charge was fifty-five cents for men, and women were admitted free.

While Franklin Avenue burned, twenty-year-old Ronnie Morrison son of town barber George "Scotty" Morrison, dashed into McVittie's and rescued what he thought was the most important item – the town gramophone. On his way out, Morrison scooped a number of records including a violin concerto and set up the gramophone across the street from the blaze. As the RCMP and town residents wrestled with the fire, they suddenly heard the squealing sound of a violin coming from across Franklin Avenue. One of the RCMP yelled at Morrison to shut off the music.

"Just pretend I'm Nero," replied Morrison. "Rome is burning."[48]

McMurray rebuilds

A total of fourteen businesses were destroyed in the fire of 1934 including the hotel, Sutherland Drugs, John Parry's store, McVittie's, Skelton's Meat Market, the Government Telegraph office and the Gem Confectionary Store. Although the fire had disastrous consequences, the rebuilding of Franklin Avenue provided the community with an economic spark. While most businesses were restored, John Parry used the insurance money to build three small dwellings on Morrison Street, known as Parry's Houses.

The closure of John Parry's store was a particularly bitter pill for the town's youth who had come to know Parry as a kind old man who could be counted on for a free candy or a cookie. As Myrtle (Paquette) Graham recalled: "He was a nice old fellow. Sometimes I'd come there after school and drop in to warm my hands. He'd give me an apple or candy. He loved all of us kids."[49]

Frank O'Coffey brought in his brother in law, Frank Dusseault, to rebuild his hotel. The New Franklin Hotel opened in 1936.

Carpenter J.W. Mann who three years earlier had completed the St. John the Baptist Anglican Church, returned to town and was immediately hired to rebuild Sutherland Drugs. "He was digging out the basement while the ashes were still hot,"[21] recalled his daughter Enid McDonald.

Mann remained in the community, and later became a town councillor. Mann found steady work as a carpenter, and soon landed a contract hauling freight to and from Bitumount. Soon after, Mann and son-in-law Alex McDonald launched an important sideline business. It began with Mann building coffins for the town's churches. Eventually, Mann and McDonald began offering a full funeral service. Mann and McDonald would prepare the coffins and the burial site, and Enid McDonald would attend to the deceased and cover the caskets. It was a sacred business which the McDonalds would continue until the late 1960s.

The McDonalds had an additional claim to fame. When Mann built his family's home near the corner of current day Morrison Street and Highway 63, he included a cistern which would capture rainwater during spring and summer, and serve as a holding tank during the winter.

This provided the community with its only indoor toilet which proved very popular with local kids especially during Fort McMurray's long and numbing winter months. The McDonald's indoor throne was a popular resting-place, and highlighted the spirit of sharing which existed among neighbours.

Enid McDonald recalled awakening one morning at three a.m. to find next-door neighbour Jack Cockerill rocking in the family's living room. "Jack's propane was broken and he decided to come in and sit in our living room until he could find someone to fix it. That's the way things were in those days. No one was better than anyone else. The door was always open and we shared what we had."[50]

The "power" of cooperation

In 1936, Joe Durocher brought a Fairbanks Morse Stationary Diesel Engine to Fort McMurray and launched the town's first commercial power plant. Durocher offered nightly service between seven p.m. and ten p.m., with an extra hour added on "movie night" at the McMurray theatre. Power was sold at a rate of twenty-five cents per kilowatt-hour.

The following winter, Durocher played a key role in building the town's first "lit" skating rink. For years, local residents used the Snye as a community rink, but with so many airplanes now taking off and landing, an alternative site had to be located.

Land was identified on Fraser Avenue just east of Morrison Street. One of the local sawmills donated the lumber, Hugh Stroud provided the horse team to help level the land, and Joe Durocher hooked up a lighting system which enabled games to be played at night. The lighting system was popular with most hockey players and fans, but proved a nightmare for goalies.

Goalie Real Martin recalled: "Every ten feet they hung a hundred watt bulb and when you're playing goal and they shot that puck from the blue line you'd lose it. If they shot it close I could see it, but from far it would come in and out of sight."[52]

Fans would line the snow bank surrounding the ice and between periods help scrape the surface. When conditions allowed, the ice was flooded with a heated water barrel drilled with small holes. Some fans also served as medics.

One night, Martin was delayed in Bitumount, and Roy Hawkins was called upon to suit up in his place. During the second period, an opposing Waterways player streaked for the net, and Hawkins sprawled out to stop the shot. Hawkins was caught under the chin by the player's skate and began to bleed profusely.

"I didn't have stitches put in," recalled Hawkins. "The girls just grabbed a whole bunch of tape and taped it up and I carried on playing. I couldn't quit because we didn't have a another goal keeper."[53]

The flood of 1936

As far as Fort McMurray floods go, the disaster of 1936 will forever be known as the "big one." In late April, the Athabasca River broke sending a huge carpet of ice and water through the Snye and up the Clearwater River.

Within minutes, the Clearwater began to back up, sending tons of huge ice chunks into the lower townsite, in some areas past Franklin Avenue. The lower portion of Waterways and the Prairie were submerged. More than seventy homes were destroyed. Houses were flattened like soft drink cans. An eight-foot high building along the Snye was completely under water.

There had been some warning. That year, the winter was mild, and snowfall had been heavy. The Board of Trade feared these were ideal conditions for flooding and warned local residents through "word of mouth" and over CJCA radio from Edmonton. Few residents paid attention.

Alvina Strasbourg and her friends were watching the river close to the junction of the Snye and the Athabasca, "when all of a sudden we heard a terrible roar. The chunks of ice were unbelievable — the size of a house. So we took off and started running. The water and ice were coming right through the buildings."[54]

As they raced to dry ground, Strasbourg and her friends realized they were not alone. Halfway to Franklin Avenue they were overtaken by few dozen mice fleeing the advancing waters.

Longtime resident Garnet Ross recalled in a 1981 interview how quickly the flood forced him and wife Margaret out of their Morrison Street and Manning Avenue home.

"The water was in our house in a flash and the ice chunks in our yard were taller than me. We grabbed a lantern and some papers and just headed up the road ahead of that ice."[55]

A tent town was set up on high ground above present day Hospital Street. Frank and Marie O'Coffey came by daily to provide soup to those who were displaced. Air and rail traffic were halted, cutting Fort McMurray and Waterways off from vital supply routes. Residents in other areas of McMurray and Waterways began making plans to evacuate. Suddenly, the ice jam broke, and floodwaters began to subside.

A few days after the jam broke, Florence Bird, sister of riverboat captain Billy Bird, suffered a ruptured appendix and she was ordered to Edmonton for emergency surgery. However, all of the town's planes had been lifted on to the Snye banks, and a massive tangle of ice blocked the path to the water. Every able-bodied man was summoned to the Snye.

"Everybody brought an axe, and a path had to be cut for the plane's wings to pass through," recalled Real Martin. "There were also three or four canoes on the Snye pushing the ice aside so that the plane didn't hit anything on takeoff."[56]

As a crowd of townsfolk held their breath, the small plane carrying Florence Bird took off and made it to Edmonton in time.

Rival schools

In 1936, attending school in Fort McMurray became more competitive with the opening of the newly built St. John's Roman Catholic School. The school, located south of Franklin Avenue near current day Haineault Street, opened with forty-five students.

Sister Agnes Sutherland in her book *Northerners Say: Thanks Sisters*, notes that raising funds to build St. John's was not difficult. However, staffing the school was another matter. It soon became evident that the parents and the newly formed Catholic school board had a building and lots of school aged children, but no teachers. Low salaries, lack of staff housing and Fort McMurray's isolation deterred many teachers from venturing north.

In desperation, Father Joseph Turcotte appealed to the Grey Nuns in Edmonton for assistance. Sister Marie Boulet was dispatched to Fort McMurray and became St. John's first teacher and principal. She was joined by teacher Mary Redmond. The new school allowed older students who had been studying in Athabasca or Edmonton to come home. St. John's eventually offered grades one to ten, and later grades eleven and twelve.

Redmond was coaxed to Fort McMurray by Frank O'Coffey and flown north by Wop May. In a 1986 interview, Redmond recalled the challenging conditions when she arrived.

The school wasn't ready when I got there. It wasn't finished. The first three weeks I taught in the main body of the church and the children sat on the kneelers and wrote on the benches. I was the junior teacher. The senior teacher and class were up in the choir loft. I was supposed to get eighty-four dollars a month but there were months when I got nothing. The Catholic Board did not have the money. They had no firm tax base at the time, and in some ways, I suppose they should never have built a school, but the Bishop said if they built a school, he would build the hospital. So the school was built and he built St. Gabriel Hospital[57].

Within months of its opening, a strong rivalry developed between the Public School and St. John's School. Scholastic and athletic competition between the Catholic and Public School became more fierce as St. John's became more established. This was especially true during the May 24 Victoria Day weekend as the community shut down for Sports Day. Young athletes from St. John's and the Public School competed head to head in a variety of events.

During the late-1940s, Merle (Golosky) Rudiak experienced the heated rivalry first hand when her parents transferred her from St. John's to the Public School.

"There were names we had for students at the other school," she said. "St. John's students were called "Catlickers," and those at the Public were "Potlickers." All of a sudden my parents switched me and I was on the other side. It was devastating at first but I eventually got over it. I was really upset at having to move to the rival school, but I never said anything. In those days you never talked back to your parents."[58]

The Salt Plant

By the mid-1930s, the Great Depression had subsided, and investors looked for new areas to invest. With the Northern Alberta Railway now running smoothly between Waterways and Edmonton, transportation challenges, which had previously hampered earlier economic development, dissolved.

Both the Bitumount and Abasand Oils plants were under construction and in 1936, the prospect of renewed salt mining activity was advanced by the Dominion Tar and Chemical Company Ltd. (Domtar). The company had gained a national profile for developing resources in northern communities, and expressed its eagerness to invest in the Fort McMurray area.

An elaborate salt plant was built at the western edge of Waterways. The plant was a highly efficient but somewhat unsightly operation, described in 1939 by the *Calgary Herald* as "a Turkish mosque designed by a Canadian lumberjack."[59] The salt plant was built where current day Ptarmigan Drive turns north into Waterways. The once mighty Domtar salt plant is now a children's park, but from the mid-1930s until its closure in 1951, the salt plant was a major employer and producer of table salt for Canadian and American markets. "Fille" (Auger) Jenkins worked at the plant for thirty five cents an hour, first filling bags with salt and later operating a high pressure machine which created red salt blocks for cattle. She noted that during the 1930s, thirty-five cents an hour went a long way, and that the wages earned at the salt plant contributed to the economic boom which swept the region.

By the close of 1936, the Fort McMurray/Waterways area boasted a rich and diversified economy which included two oil sands plants, a salt factory, sawmills, a box factory, air and river transportation, a fish plant, rail service and a growing array of small businesses.

Gold, water and wood

In the early 1930s, Hugh Stroud and a number of other local residents ventured to the northeast corner of Lake Athabasca where gold had been discovered near Uranium City in an area known as Goldfields. While the opportunity for instant wealth was great, by 1936 the Goldfields area had been flooded by prospectors and opportunists, and Stroud and friends soon returned to Fort McMurray.

One year later, the Ryan Brothers hired veteran prospector Tom Payne to investigate a rumoured deposit in the area. Payne spurned the use of aircraft which had become popular with "modern" prospectors. Instead he followed the old practice of tapping on rocks with his hammer. In August 1937, Payne's "old ways" paid off when he confirmed a rich gold deposit near Goldfields. One month later, Consolidated Mining and Smelting Company agreed to pay five hundred thousand dollars for sixty per cent controlling interest. The profits were distributed among the Ryans, Payne and accountant W.R. Wilson who maintained forty per cent interest. After years of backbreaking work hauling freight and mail throughout the north, the Ryan Brothers had finally hit their payload.

Meanwhile, the less successful Stroud returned home, and at barely twenty-one years of age, decided to start his own business. He bought some used equipment and soon launched the town's second wood and water service, running into direct competition with the experienced Ryan brothers. Stroud's strong work ethic quickly earned him a number of customers, and in 1942 before heading off to World War II, he sold his business to Jack Cockerill for seven hundred and fifty dollars. His equipment included two horses, three sleighs, a water wagon, a woodcutter, some barrels and a pump.

"My business began with a tank, a pump, a heater and an endless supply of water from the Clearwater or Athabasca rivers," he recalled. "It took thirteen five-gallon pails to fill a barrel. I remember the number of pails very well since I had to carry their full weight across many slippery kitchen floors."[60]

Price for a barrel of water in 1936 was fifty cents. Inflation would later cause Stroud and the Ryans to raise their price to seventy-five cents.

The fighting Irish

Fort McMurray was not completely isolated from the philosophical battles which raged elsewhere in the world. Each night, Tom Conn and Frank O'Coffey brought the debate over Ireland home to Fort McMurray.

Conn was a railroad man turned trapper who hailed from Northern Ireland. He was a Protestant. O'Coffey was a proud Catholic. After work each day, the two would lock horns over "the Irish question." At the time, the issue of whether England should continue to govern Ireland was a passionate topic.

"They would argue for hours,"[61] recalled Walter Hill in a 1980 interview. Conn and O'Coffey would bombard each other with facts and opinions until sometime in the early morning hours the two would part company before resuming their discussion the following day.

"Conn was so stubborn, he once needed a fact to win his argument so he walked twenty-three miles there and twenty three miles back to find the man with the answers," recalled Hill, a frequent observer. "He won that argument."[62]

Conn and O'Coffey would continue their verbal brawling daily, pausing only on St. Patrick's Day. On March 17, the two would toast Ireland with the rest of Fort McMurray's Irish community. It was a special time and the only night of the Lent period when the Catholic Church would allow its members to tip back a few beers. "It was all very unofficial," recalled Hill. "But it went on anyway without being frowned on."[63]

Conn died in Fort McMurray in 1945, and is buried at the Biggs Avenue cemetery. O'Coffey passed away that same year in Edmonton.

St. Gabriel Hospital opens

Since 1925, medical services in Fort McMurray had been limited to a two-bed infirmary run by the Presbyterian Church. Between 1917 and 1933, Dr. George Ings served the community and the north. The community remained without a physician until Dr. "Mac" McCallum arrived in 1938.

As early as 1930, the Board of Trade began lobbying for a hospital or other medical care facility. In 1930, residents petitioned Bishop Grouard for a local "Sisters' Hospital", similar to the one run by the Grey Nuns in Edmonton. Five years later, a full hospital was approved for Fort McMurray with funds provided by both the Church and the Province. Construction began in 1936.

The facility was built by the Oblate Brothers and was named in honour of Bishop Gabriel Breynat. St. Gabriel Hospital officially opened in 1937, at the corner of Franklin Avenue and the present Hardin Street, with sixteen beds and four bassinettes. Its original staff included sisters Marie Nadeau, Rose-Anna Henri and Aldera Roberge. The plaque on the hospital's brick façade carried the French words "Hopital St. Gabriel." In 1984, Sister Agnes Sutherland interviewed Sisters Nadeau and Roberge about St. Gabriel Hospital's early days. As ninety-six year old Sister Nadeau recalled:

Fort McMurray's was very different from all the other hospitals in the north. It served a different kind of people. There were Crees, Montagnais, Metis and more non-aboriginal people than other northern missions. We had a more balanced diet and we were never in want. There were no long-term tuberculosis patients in our hospital. We had a good supply of medicine and hospital equipment. We had a good supply of water though it was quite a rusty kind of water from a well[64].

The sisters originally lived on the second floor but when there was a need for extra patient rooms they would often give up their rooms and share accommodation. The church eventually built a sisters' residence next door.

Sister Nadeau recalled that weeks ahead of the hospital's opening, three foundresses arrived to prepare St. Gabriel's for operation. "We worked almost all day and night to unpack, open and place all the donations we received from the Catholic Women's League, the Ryan Brothers, the Salt Plant, Doctor Blais, Northern Transportation, the Hudson's Bay Company and the Cooper Corporation of Edmonton."[65]

Sister Aldrea Roberge, who managed the housekeeping, recalled that although short staffed, the sisters worked tirelessly to supply the hospital staff and patients with clean linen and immaculate rooms. She noted that the laundry was located off the hospital grounds. "We had to do the work of at least two persons so we worked hard and long hours,"[66] she recalled.

Food was transported upstairs by a "dumb waiter." A hole was drilled from the top floor to the basement, and meals were lifted by a rope between floors.

While the community rejoiced over the opening of St. Gabriel, it was quickly sobered by news of the hospital's first case. Rachel Bourque, mother of Sister Delia Bourque entered the hospital with severe labour pains. Brother Laurent Bruyere, head of the construction crew, rushed to assist. He tore a new mattress from its packing box and quickly assembled it. Because Dr. McCallum was occupied with another emergency; the sisters delivered the baby. Shortly after birth, the mother lost consciousness and died. The baby survived and was baptized as Gabriel. Although the sisters had lost their first patient, it was widely recognized that the child would not have survived without the care and assistance of the new hospital staff.

"That was a terribly sad moment for me and for the family," recalled Sister Nadeau. "We were heartbroken and we all wept and tried to console the family. We had very few deaths in the hospital from then on. With God's help and our best efforts we did miracles without antibiotics and modern day medicines."[67]

St. Gabriel Hospital served the community until the late 1960s. The property sold in 1972 to a team of developers for two hundred and sixty thousand dollars and was demolished in 1979. The original hospital cornerstone laid in 1936 was incorporated into the construction of Fort McMurray Regional hospital which opened in 1979. The cornerstone remains embedded in the wall just outside the hospital cafeteria.

Bitumount's rise and fall

Throughout his forty-year involvement with the Athabasca oil sands, Robert Fitzsimmons never shed his reputation as an industry outsider. With limited resources and no major oil company investor, Fitzsimmons was never able to cross the threshold of acceptance within the Canadian business establishment. Fitzsimmons was regarded by many as an amateur who merely adapted the technology of others to produce bitumen for short-term profit.

While rich oilmen like Max Ball continued to pump resources into research, and great scientific minds such as Dr. Karl Clark and Sidney Ells mulled over scientific formulas, Fitzsimmons enthusiastically went about his business, armed with a keen sense of observation and a knack for surrounding himself with committed and energetic staff.

During the early 1930s, Fitzsimmons had successfully duplicated the successful components of Dr. Clark's Clearwater River test plant, and built his own experimental plant in Bitumount. While Max Ball's Abasand plant required dynamite and drilling to reach oil sands deposits, Fitzsimmons' product was located a few feet from the surface.

Clark wrote:

It is the same type of plant we had on the Clearwater River. The sand is heated and mixed with water in a pug mill and discharged into a second pug mill filled with hot water. The bitumen is skimmed from the surface of the water into a reservoir. This bitumen is next put into a third pug mill and stirred around in cold water. This operation removes clay and some water from the crude bitumen The bitumen is then passed on to a dehydrator where the water is boiled out of it by heating with steam coils. It is then run to a final storage and settling tank[68].

Fitzsimmons knew his deposits were superior in richness, but he lacked the resources to promote his lease on the national and international scale. That was soon rectified during the mid-1930s when Fitzsimmons travelled through United States, Canada and Great Britain and attracted the interest and financial backing of a number of investors.

In 1936, Fitzsimmons hired American oil engineer, Harry Everand to develop an advanced oil production system at the Bitumount site and in spring 1937, crews began a plant overhaul. During tests conducted in June, Everand reported that good quality crude was being produced. However, questions remained whether the plant's outdated equipment could support production demands. Despite their concerns, Fitzsimmons and Everand remained optimistic, and Bitumount's sales representative began taking orders for oil and paving material in Edmonton and beyond.

In August 1937, Governor General Sir John Buchan and his entourage visited the Bitumount site as they returned from an arctic excursion. While at the plant, a forest fire broke out nearby and Sir Buchan and his party where rushed to McMurray by Bitumount employee Doug Ferrier, where they spent the night aboard the SS Echo and were later shuttled by plane to Edmonton.

During the late summer of 1937, conditions began to turn sour. Plant breakdowns were frequent and replacement equipment was delayed or did not appear. Before plant operations were temporarily suspended in September, the plant had produced only a third of its projected capacity. Bitumount was also plagued by lack of operating funds. Crewmembers, Everand in particular, received their wages late, or in some cases not at all.

Everand and Fitzsimmons began squabbling over the lack of working capital and plant design flaws. Everand was dismissed and in October, Fitzsimmons hired

Elmer Adkins, a recent engineering graduate from the University of Alberta who had worked in previous years at both the Abasand and Bitumount plants. For a time, the future looked less cloudy for Fitzsimmons' plant. The company's sales representative secured a contract with Consolidated Mining and Smelting to supply seventy thousand gallons of fuel to be shipped to northern Saskatchewan. A roof asphalt contract was also signed with a company in Gary, Indiana.

By summer 1938, Bitumount was producing bitumen, and employed between fourteen and forty workmen. Employees tolerated late pay cheques and missing equipment, and remained on the job. During 1938, International Bitumen earned revenues of over twenty thousand dollars.

However, by late 1938 Adkins' good will had reached its limit. Because Fitzsimmons was not able to pay him for months at a time, Adkins began to encounter personal financial difficulties and eventually accepted a position with another company. Adkins remained in touch with oil sands developers, and from 1948-49 returned to run an experimental plant at Bitumount on behalf of the Province.

In late 1938, remaining staff at Bitumount walked off the site. Fitzsimmons' charisma, hard work and ingenuity had overcome significant technological problems; however lack of capital to sustain his plant and to pay his employees soon forced International Bitumen into insolvency. Fitzsimmons was advised to leave Fort McMurray and departed for Chicago in late 1938. Two years later, he returned to the region in an unsuccessful bid to relaunch the plant. International Bitumen was sold in 1942 to Montreal financier Lloyd Champion.

In assessing Fitzsimmons' contribution to the development of the oil sands, it is noteworthy that the one time real estate agent was able to survive for twenty years during the Great Depression, and within the highly competitive oil business. He succeeded in capturing the imagination and loyalty of his staff and of financial backers. Fitzsimmons' major error was rushing his plant into operation without long-term financing and production issues.

Oil company conspiracy?

Following the demise of his Bitumount dream, Fitzsimmons declared in a twenty-six page pamphlet issued in 1953 that oil companies and governments had conspired against him. The pamphlet, titled *"The Truth About Alberta Tar Sands: Why they were kept out of production,"*[69] accused the federal and provincial governments of treating the oil sands like a novelty, rather than as a bona fide source of oil.

He noted that while politicians from Edmonton and Ottawa, and dignitaries such as the Governor General visited his plant and expressed verbal support for his efforts, their words did not translate into action. Fitzsimmons accused the government of supporting large oil companies who conspired to thwart the efforts of smaller producers. Fitzsimmons' pamphlet states:

As soon as the feasibility of production became established, we were obstruct-

ed in every move we made towards financing the installation of a refinery....the blocking tactics seemed to follow a well-defined pattern on the part of both the Dominion and Alberta provincial governments regardless of which party was in power which means that both were subject to the same pressure groups. One of their favourite methods when issuing official reports on developmental work of the tar sands was to completely ignore us and what we had accomplished[0].

Fitzsimmons claimed that prospective customers had told him "big interests" threatened that further supplies would be cut off if they dealt with International Bitumen. He also claimed that in 1936 he had successfully secured two hundred and fifty thousand dollars from British investors to erect a refinery.

"The deal was called off as soon as they had contacted Canada," Fitzsimmons accused. "Several other substantial deals were built up, but all were cancelled after contacting the Alberta Government and receiving adverse reports, evasive replies, or not receiving any replies to their enquiries."[1]

In 1968, Fitzsimmons made a brief and noisy return to Fort McMurray when he announced he was considering a lawsuit against Great Canadian Oil Sands for allegedly copying his extraction process. Fitzsimmons eventually dropped his legal plans. He died on Sept 11, 1971 in Victoria, one week after his ninetieth birthday.

In 1983, Elmer Adkins returned to Fort McMurray and visited the abandoned Bitumount site. Despite disappointments and lack of financial reward, Adkins remained fiercely proud of what had been accomplished at Bitumount.

"We shipped the first commercial tar sand out of there in 1938," he boasted. "If you look at what we had then and look at even what Syncrude has, they're pretty analogous. Old Fitzsimmons pretty well had it solved."[2]

Waterways churches and schools open

By the end of the 1930s, there were signs that Waterways had achieved parity with Fort McMurray. In 1938, the Waterways School District was formed and opened a school on property where the Royal Canadian Legion stands today. There were two teachers on staff and thirty-nine pupils who attended grades one to seven. Opening of the Waterways school brought total enrolment in the Fort McMurray area to one hundred and sixty-one students.

That same year, St. Aidan's Anglican Church opened. An Anglican congregation had been active in Waterways since 1936 and held services during summer in a small building with a tent roof. The new church also housed a day school from 1939-1942. It offered classes to twenty-two students. In 1939, Roman Catholic services came to Waterways with construction of St. Peter's Catholic Church and rectory.

During the late 1930s, two important businesses opened in Waterways. The Waterways Hotel was built opposite the railway station and offered lodging, meals, a lounge and a pool hall. In 1938, Sutherland's Drugs began business next door.

With construction of schools and churches in Waterways, residents no longer had to travel to Fort McMurray to receive most services. Indeed, Waterways had come of age, and in the eyes of its residents deserved equal status with Fort McMurray. Efforts also began to subdivide Waterways into its own autonomous townsite.

Abasand nears completion

After spending the majority of the 1930s in research and development, by 1936 plans were being finalized to complete Max Ball's Abasand plant. By 1937, construction and improvement costs had reached over three hundred and seventy thousand dollars. Ball found that deposits were mixed with rock and that his quarrying equipment was not totally adaptable to minus forty-degree temperatures. A refinery still had to be built, and the issue of developing a final process to extract oil from the deposits still had to be addressed.

As the 1930s closed, Ball still struggled with financial and technical complications. In 1939, he requested that the federal government waive its lease royalty fees for a thirty-six month period. In return, he agreed to commit a further two hundred thousand dollars to upgrade the Abasand plant, bringing his total investment by the close of the 1930s to seven hundred thousand dollars.

A fourth community rises

In early 1939, a large group of new residents began to cluster around the Abasand oil sands plant. By some accounts, close to two hundred residents lived in homes and dwellings which surrounded the plant. Particularly during winter months, it was difficult for Abasand students to travel out of the Horse River valley to attend St. John's or the Public schools.

Residents of Abasand lobbied the province for their own school and in mid-1939, the Province agreed and established the Abasand School District #4865. Abasand Oil furnished a house for daytime classes, and a teacher was hired. Over the next few years, Abasands would develop some limited commercial activity and would spawn a number of hockey and ball teams which competed against those from Fort McMurray, Waterways and the Prairie.

The Prairie consisted of lands located between Waterways and McMurray just south of the Clearwater River. The area provided fertile ground for lush gardens and small farming operations, and was settled by a number of families including the Goloskys, Castors, Augers, Fontaines and Bacons.

Whereas at the start of the 1920s, McMurray residents were concentrated within one townsite, and paid taxes to one school district, by the close of the 1930s, ratepayers were spread between public and Catholic school boards in Fort McMurray, along with one in Waterways and an additional board in Abasand. Although the Abasand division did much to enhance local pride, it further spread thin educational resources throughout the community.

Fort McMurray/Waterways rivalry

By the close of the 1930s, a fierce municipal rivalry had developed between Fort McMurray and Waterways. While Fort McMurray was seen as the community where those of higher position and standing lived and worked, Waterways residents viewed themselves as hard working and resourceful residents who carried the economic momentum for the entire region.

While residents were friendly enough during regular work hours, during the evening and weekends, the two lifestyles clashed on the ball diamonds and on the hockey rinks. By the late 1930s there were five hockey teams in the area. McMurray and Waterways each fielded a team, along with Abasand, the Signal Corps, and the Cubs.

The Cubs were made up of young players like Stroud, Martin and Hawkins who could not land a position on established adult teams. The Cubs formed their own squad and began challenging teams throughout the community. The Cubs' wives and girlfriends knitted sweaters similar to those worn by the Chicago Black Hawks. Goalie pads were fashioned from local materials.

A few years later, when Hawkins set off to join World War II, he loaded his Cubs sweater with him. "To me it was an important piece of my heritage and being a young guy I didn't want to give it up,"[73] he said.

Games were usually played Sundays, Tuesdays and Thursdays and residents from all townsites lined the snow banks which surrounded the ice surface. The action was spirited, and the rivalries were intense.

"There was rivalry, never kid yourself," recalled Hawkins. "It got pretty serious. I remember getting into a fight with Cal Vince who was a tall gangly guy who played for the Signal Corps. I weighed one hundred and thirty pounds soaking wet. We were up against the boards fighting and his wife was standing in a snowbank on the side and she had a purse with a big long strap on it. She swung that purse and whacked me on the back of the head. That was rivalry, I'll tell you."[74]

Men of the cloth

Aside from his popularity as priest Father Patrick Mercredi quickly became known as one of the town's most talented sports figures.

Mercredi was a hard-hitting defenseman with the Cubs and would also spend endless hours at the outdoor rink refereeing and practicing with local youth. Mercredi would often take to the ice and dare local kids to wrestle the puck from him. Oldtimers recall Mercredi stickhandled up to thirty youth for twenty minutes without any of them successfully touching the puck. It was widely held that if Mercredi had not become a priest, he could have played professionally.

Often when an opposing player muscled Mercredi, the Cubs would step in and pick up the fight for him. Mercredi was a tough player, but he realized that he had a reputation to maintain in front of the town's youth. Roy Hawkins recalled:

During May we would be playing ball and then church bells would ring and the Catholics would all have to go to Benediction. You couldn't play ball because everyone else was gone, so all of us, regardless of religion, used to go to Benediction whether you were Protestant or whatever. After Benediction, he used to throw parties for us with candies and such. Differences between people didn't matter much then[75].

There was only one dent in Father Mercredi's public armour. When Rev. Richard Ruch of the Anglican Church was on the ice, Ruch and Mercredi would settle their philosophical differences in a rather unholy manner. As Real Martin recalled: " When they got each other in the corner those two didn't spare each other, I'll tell you. Bodies and sticks."

A strike for womanhood

During the 1930s, two local women made a dent in the previously male-dominated world of sport. One of the Cubs' most consistent ball players was Anne Morrison, daughter of Scotty Morrison, who patrolled right field. Waterways also had a woman player, Viola "Sissy" Burton, who was also popular in the community as a basketball player.

Father Patrick Mercredi, Real Martin and the Arnfinson brothers were all feared pitchers. On the other end of the spectrum was Harry Morimoto, a small boy who played left field. Opposing pitchers would have difficulty finding the strike zone when Morimoto was at the plate. In those days, outfielders were not permitted to wear gloves; however, because Moromoto's hands were so small, special provision was made for him.

Headlines from 1939

Fort McMurray and Waterways residents began reading hometown news first hand in March 1939 with the launch of the *Northwest Review*. The four-page broadsheet newspaper cost five cents a copy and was edited by H.A. Dalmer. St. John's School principal J.E. Duchak moonlighted as the *Review's* advertising manager.

Merchants of the day supported the venture with advertising. Frank O'Coffey bought an ad promoting "The Comforts of Home at the New Franklin Hotel." Kushner's Store featured "four dozen ladies hats, latest style, at *outside* prices."[76] Other advertisers included McInnes products, J.W. Mann Builders and Painters, Sutherland's Drugs, Frank's Waterways Café, Boivert's General Merchants, the Waterways Hotel, Josie's Barber Shop, the Paul & Leggett Store, Demers' Taxi and Transfer, and Gordon Lumber. The Fort McMurray Board of Trade purchased an ad which proclaimed, "if it will help the north, we're for it."[77]

The following are headlines and excepts from the May 15 and 22, 1939 editions of the Northwest Review.

New equipment for Waterways Hall

Modernization of radio equipment with the purchase of more expensive loudspeakers equipped with amplifiers is promised by A.R. McNeill, manager of the Waterways Theatre and Dance Hall when the building is more nearly completed. The introduction of expensive dance records more suitable for reproduction than those already in use is contemplated in order that the dancing enjoyment of patrons may be increased[78].

First summer mail planes

The first 1939 summer mail went north from McMurray Friday, May 5 when Bob Randall took off for Fitzgerald and Stan McMillan in CF-BBB left for Yellowknife...Canadian Airways made their first trip Wednesday May 10 when Jack Crosby came north with three passengers[79].

Fairbairns back home

Mr. and Mrs. Jack Fairbairn who recently returned to Waterways after an extended winter vacation in Central and South America were relating their experiences to friends last week[80].

Hubaco burns

Fire broke out aboard the Hudson's Bay Company Hubaco 12:30 p.m. Sunday, May 14 ending in her complete destruction. Deckhand Jackson who boarded the vessel just as the fire started escaped with a scorched face. The only man aboard the boat at the time of the outbreak was Engineer Hartley who was asleep in his bunk but awakened in time to get ashore uninjured. A crowd of approximately one hundred people, many of them armed with cameras lined the river bank and watched the tongues of flame lick away the life of the little yarding boat[81].

Salt plant to re-open

Contrary to the vague rumours that were playing around town recently that the Industrial Minerals Salt Plant had shut its doors for good, it was reported last week that the plant will swing into operation again soon. Lay off of employees and ceasing of operation was due to the large reserve of available salt on hand[82].

Air field meeting subject

A special meeting of the Fort McMurray Board of Trade Tuesday May 16 attracted most members and the turnout to discuss a landing field for wheel equipped aircraft was very good... An area of 4,000 by 800 feet to be fenced in would be required in the first place, according to Mr. Lawson, but arrangements would be necessary to ensure possibility of lengthening the field to 5,000 feet at any future time[83].

Waterways fights for incorporation

Negotiations between Waterways Citizens and Mr. R. Huggard, agent for the Northern Alberta Exploration Company in an effort to reach satisfactory agreement regarding the sale of lots in the townsite to local residents were not progressing as favourably as desired here last week[84].

Notice

The tennis courts of the Fort McMurray Tennis Club are now ready for use. Members are requested to pay their fees at the earliest possible moment. Fees: ladies $3. Men $5[85].

Flying dentist on the way north

The north's flying dentist, Dr. Lee R. Dodds arrived here last Thursday on the first leg of his journey to down river points. Dr. Dodds is expected to spend about five days in Waterways and several in McMurray before flying to Fitzgerald and Smith on Wednesday of this week[86].

McMurray tar sands lauded

Enough heavy oil to supply the British Empire for one hundred years is contained in the tarsands of the Fort McMurray district if the oil could be rid of sand and mixed with the fine oil from Turner Valley, according to A. Von Hammerstein, veteran operator at McMurray, in a recent statement made in Winnipeg[87].

Pigs versus the King

The May 15, 1939 edition of the *Northwest Review* made mention of a unique opportunity for Fort McMurray and Waterways residents. The Northern Alberta Railways announced that it would add a special June 1 train to enable local residents to witness the June 2 visit of King George VI and Queen Elizabeth to Edmonton. A special adult return fare of six dollars and seventy-five cents was announced. Children could ride for three dollars and forty cents.

Five schoolteachers were chosen from McMurray and Waterways schools to escort the seventy children who signed up for the trip. Miss K. Olsen and Miss K. Weldon were assigned to accompany the McMurray public school students. Mrs. L. Brodie chaperoned the twenty-seven Waterways students, and Miss Mary Redmond joined the nine students from St. John's School.

For most students, it was their first time outside Fort McMurray. And while most only caught a brief glimpse of the Royal Couple while sitting on grandstands on Kingsway Avenue, it was an event en route which caused the most excitement. Weeks earlier, St. John's students participated in "Enterprise Day," a day to set up facsimiles of small businesses throughout the school. The most popular enterprise was "the farm." Although there were some cows and horses around McMurray and Waterways, few students had ever seen a live pig or chicken.

In 1986, when former teacher Mary Redmond returned to Fort McMurray to celebrate the fiftieth anniversary of the Fort McMurray Catholic School District, she recalled the day when "the farm" came alive.

We had built this farm on the floor of our classroom out of old boxes and paper and had little toy animals in it. On the train when we got near farming country, they looked out and screamed "The farm, the farm." And I thought, "Well I haven't done a very good job teaching them. They think there's only one farm." And the pigs! The Royal Couple were people and the children had seen people before, but pigs? They ran from window to window on the train looking at the pigs[88].

Former St. John's student Doris (Somers) Mirkovich was on the train and recalled, "the Royal Couple had nothing on those pigs."[89]

The rude awakening

As the 1930s came to a close, a feeling of stability washed over the communities of McMurray and Waterways. Companies like McInnes, Dominion Tar and Chemicals, Hudson's Bay Company, the NTCL and a variety of support services provided permanent and seasonal employment. With the oil sands finally showing commercial results, Fort McMurray burst with optimism. The area, which hosted twenty-six people at the beginning of the century, now boasted eight hundred and twenty-five residents.

Meanwhile, some thousands of miles away, across the Atlantic Ocean, events in Europe were beginning to take shape which would draw Fort McMurray out of its naïve isolation. The guns, which were beginning to fire in Europe, would eventually be felt in Fort McMurray.

In the immediate years to follow, thousands of American troops would bring World War II to the main streets of Fort McMurray and Waterways. In return, Fort McMurray would send some of its youngest and finest aboard southbound trains to fight on Canada's behalf. Most had never travelled further from home than Edmonton. They were armed with visions of patriotism and a burning desire to see the world. Many would leave. Not all would make it home alive.

Chapter Four:
The War Years

They wanted to get out of Fort McMurray and see the world. Who knew what was going to happen? Who knew about the world? Who knew about the war?[1]
- Alvina Strasbourg.

While Fort McMurray's economy continued to expand, this growth did not translate into increased opportunity for young residents. Work was often seasonal and sporadic. Tommy Paull, who served as Fort McMurray's RCMP commander from 1938-1942, recalled how hundreds of hungry transients would arrive each summer in search of work. "This was the end of the Dirty Thirties – the Depression," he recalled. "In the summer there were jungles of people camped in Waterways looking for work on the docks. They rode the freights and lived in makeshift shanties."[2] Competition for available work was fierce, and often Fort McMurray's young men were passed over in favour of the more aggressive and desperate men living in the bush.

In late 1938, Walter Hill, a veteran of World War I, received a letter marked "confidential and private" from his former commanding officer, Colonel Louis Scott. The hand-delivered letter asked Hill if he would be prepared, at a later date, to raise a company of young northern Alberta men to participate in a future military campaign against Germany.

One year later with Adolf Hitler's armies advancing across Europe, Hill boarded a plane to Edmonton with World War I ace Wop May to discuss with Scott how northern Alberta could contribute to the war effort. Hill was asked to be involved in recruitment, and to help coordinate the sale of war bonds. Fort McMurray did not have to look far for recruits. By 1939, Fort McMurray's population had reached about eight hundred and twenty-five, and dozens of the town's young men answered the call. Some were motivated by patriotism and others by the opportunity to see the world.

Bolstered by stories of patriotism and heroics from World War I veterans such as Hill, May and local businessman Syd Hawkins, Fort McMurray's young men prepared to travel overseas. Others followed in the early 1940s. They included: Edward Auger, Willie Malcolm, Ernie Clark, Archie Goodwin, Eddie Plamondon, Walter Malcolm, Roy Hawkins, Real Martin, Buster Martin, David Hill, Johnny Webb, Howard Mein, George Waniandy, John Waniandy, Gabe Castor, Pat O'Coffey, Romeo Eymundson, Oliver Eymundson, Joe Desjarlais, Bill Woodward, Roy

McKinnon, Fred Lissoway, Glen McKinnon, Don Gallagher, Al Dusseault, Henry Dusseault, Hugh Stroud, Ambrose Laboucane and Tommy Morimoto. Others joined from the nearby communities of Anzac and Fort McKay.

Riding the rails to Edmonton

The first five to leave for war were Pat O'Coffey, Real Martin, Johnny Webb, Roy Hawkins and Alphonse Dusseault. Their adventure began on September 18, 1939 as they assembled in Waterways to board the *Muskeg Special*. However, not all could afford the train fare to Edmonton, so in solidarity, the five waited down the tracks and as the train crawled by, jumped into an open freight car. About thirty relatives, friends and townsfolk lined the tracks as the train picked up steam. "No one was actually at the train station," recalled Roy Hawkins. "They were all standing one hundred yards down the tracks waving at the water tower."[3]

For the first miles, the men sat tucked in the freight car, riding the rails, enjoying the fall colours, and the sandwiches that had been packed for the journey. But as the train pulled into Lac La Biche, a local RCMP officer filed by and noticed them hiding in the freight car. He ordered them off.

Rather than pay full train fare to Edmonton, the five hatched a scheme to get back on board. Real Martin, who was over twenty-one years of age, entered the local saloon and bought a case of beer to barter with the train's brakeman, remembered only as Slack. Slack agreed to stop the train one-mile outside of Lac La Biche in exchange for the beer. Once the transaction was complete, the five jumped back on board and continued their journey to Edmonton. As the train approached Dunvegan, porter Len Williams invited the recruits into the passenger car. The five entered Edmonton in First Class, and later pooled their money for a hotel room.

On December 15, 1939, they set sail for Europe aboard the Batory, a small Polish vessel. During the upcoming months, the first five would be joined by dozens of others. Most who served were employed in ground combat while others were engaged in the air force, navy and in counter-intelligence.

Life at home

While Fort McMurray's young men battled overseas, the communities of Waterways, McMurray and Abasand carried on their daily business amidst an air edged with uncertainty. Barges continued to run between Waterways and the arctic. The Northern Alberta Railways ran goods to and from Edmonton, and salt continued to be mined from the Waterways plant. Both the Abasand and Bitumount projects struggled to overcome financial and technical difficulties, however technological advances provided cause for optimism.

A twinge of tension wafted through the community each morning as telegraph operator Charlie Somers and his children set off to deliver the day's telegrams.

Local residents held their breath, hoping that none would stop at the homes of those men fighting across the ocean. From 1939 to early 1943, none did.

Managing with coupon books

Like everywhere else in Canada, rationing was in effect in Fort McMurray. Items such as meat, sugar and butter were distributed in limited quantities through a system of coupon books. Supplies of other commodities such as gasoline, tires and liquor were also controlled. Some materials, such as fuel and rubber, were diverted to Europe to assist the Canadian army, and their availability to Canadians strictly limited.

Foods such as meat and butter were plentiful in rural areas, but had to be managed so that cities could be supplied during a time when production of many agricultural items was limited. As for liquor, each person over twenty one years of age was allowed a maximum monthly ration of one gallon of wine, a bottle of hard liquor and two cases of beer.

During the war years, gasoline ration coupons were often valued higher than the vehicles they fuelled, and once a person's gasoline rations were depleted, they would hand the keys to a friend or family member. "Once you used up your gasoline coupons for the year, you weren't going anywhere," recalled Bill Hyska, who moved to Fort McMurray during the war. "You gave your car to a friend and he got a new book of gas coupons."[4]

There were also strict rules against selling unused rations, particularly those for alcoholic beverages, and gasoline. Although family members or boarders were permitted to share rations, the sale of coupons on the street was strictly forbidden, and was known as "black-marketing."

Led by Walter Hill, Frank O'Coffey and others, the effort to sell war bonds continued. Even schoolchildren participated, bringing spare change to school each Monday to buy war stamps. Between 1939 and 1945, some Fort McMurray children accumulated up to fifty dollars in war stamps which were converted to cash when the war ended.

News of the day

While Fort McMurray's young men battled overseas, life remained relatively normal at home. Here are some examples of what made the headlines in the April 4, 1939 edition of the local *Valhalla Star*.

Redecorating

The Waterways Hotel is redecorating and remodeling the rooms, dining room, and lobby because spring is here and they are expecting the spring rush.

The Coffee Pot is varnishing and intends to redecorate the interior. The outside will be painted when the slush is over[5].

Renting milk business

Mrs. Giguere is renting her milk business and selling five cows to Mr. Dunbar from Saskatchewan. He will take over some time in May[6].

Local boy makes good

On March 31, Mr. and Mrs. Hawkins received word that their son Roy had been promoted to the rank of Sergeant. He was formerly a Lance Corporal[7].

Playing at the Waterways Theatre

Swanee River starring Don Ameche, Andrea Leads and Al Jolson[8].

Mr. Mercier returns from Outpost Island

Mr. Mercer returned from Outpost Island by the Mackenzie Air Service. When asked why he returned, he said, "I came home for a visit and if the wife and I get along, I may stay awhile. I like the north fine especially Outpost Island as there is nothing but bachelors there and we get along fine[9].

Paul Schmidt, the heartbroken German

Within the community, every resident was expected to contribute in some way to the war effort, and this created a dilemma for Paul Schmidt, one of Fort McMurray's most upstanding citizens, and a fiercely loyal German.

Schmidt came to Fort McMurray in the early 1910s to work for oil sands pioneer Sidney Ells and was later employed by Dr. Karl Clark. When World War I broke out in 1914, Schmidt was frequently taunted by some of Fort McMurray's more patriotic residents, but he continued to be respected in the community by virtue of his hard work ethic. During the mid-1930s, Schmidt publicly declared himself to be a loyal follower of Adolf Hitler and was often involved in heated discussions at the New Franklin Hotel. Schmidt publicly applauded Hitler's ability, to as he termed it, "to pick Germany up by its bootstraps and put it back on its economic feet."[10]

However, when news of Germany's invasion of peaceful countries such as Belgium and Holland reached Fort McMurray, Schmidt's attitude changed and his personal conflict began. Although known for his strong and vocal political views, he withdrew from the hotel and other public places. It soon became public knowledge that Schmidt had not contributed to the war bonds effort, and many privately questioned whether Schmidt was more loyal to Germany than to Canada.

One day in 1941, Schmidt walked into Sutherland Drugs and collapsed in tears on Walter Hill's desk. As Hill would later relate, "the man was heartbroken. He cried that Hitler had ruined his country and that Germany had become a "stink in the nostrils of civilized man."[11]

As a proud German, Schmidt could not buy war bonds to fund attacks against fellow Germans, but he also believed that the Nazis needed to be stopped and ultimately defeated. Schmidt and Hill worked out a solution. Schmidt pulled out his wallet and wrote a cheque for five hundred dollars, his total life savings, and donated it to the Royal Canadian Red Cross to aid war victims and injured soldiers. Other Germans living in Fort McMurray followed suit. With this compromise, Schmidt was able to hold his head high for the remainder of World War II. Schmidt became known in subsequent years as an experienced and dependable oil field worker, an upstanding citizen, and was eventually elected mayor of Fort McMurray, a position he held from 1951-55.

Johnny Shemko's pickle jar

One of the most colourful characters who lived in Waterways during the war years was barber Johnny Shemko who arrived in Fort McMurray in 1938. Shemko and his brother rented a shack from businessman Louis Demers for eight dollars per month, and Johnny soon launched a haircutting business from the lobby of the Waterways Hotel.

One of the great stories about Johnny Shemko involves the pickle jar which sat next to his cash register in Waterways. During the early 1940s, few Fort McMurray charities were linked with national organizations, so it was up to local businesses and volunteers to raise funds from local donors. Often, Shemko's customers would pay for their thirty-five cent haircut with two quarters, and an empty pickle jar was placed on the front counter for clients to deposit their change. A sign was posted on the jar which read "FOR THE BLIND."

For weeks, community-minded customers deposited their nickels and dimes in the jar until one day the jar overflowed with coins. Shemko carefully gathered the funds donated for the blind, hung his "out for lunch" sign, and then disappeared for two hours.

Later that afternoon, Johnny Shemko's customers noticed something different. Rather than having the midday sun glare through the front window of the Waterways Hotel, the sunlight was now blocked. Shemko was now able to cut hair without having to squint.

Town's people suddenly realized that the cash donated to Shemko's pickle jar was not earmarked for the visually impaired, but to buy a Venetian blind for Shemko's front window. "I told everyone it was for the blind,"[12] Shemko insisted.

Matchmaker, matchmaker

In early 1941, Mary O'Coffey was a twenty three-year-old nurse working at the Edmonton General Hospital, when she was asked by the Order of Grey Nuns to consider moving to Fort McMurray. From the moment she accepted the offer, a number of events lined up all leading to one destination, her future husband, Lowry O'Coffey.

Before moving north, Mary travelled to her home town of Warspite to visit her parents and on the train back to Edmonton sat next to a woman, remembered only as Mrs. Dupre. When Mrs. Dupre learned that Mary was moving to Fort McMurray, she insisted, "you must visit my friend Mrs. O'Coffey. She has some lovely boys which you should meet."[13] It was not the first time that Mary had heard of the O'Coffey boys. During World War II, Radio Station CJCA featured a nightly segment which enabled army recruits training in Camrose to greet their family and friends. As Mary listened one night in January 1941 with her family, a recruit, Lowry O'Coffey came on air and sent his regards to his family in Fort McMurray. At the time, Mary turned to her brother Russell and predicted, "he's going to be my boyfriend when I get there."[14]

On February 4, 1941, Mary arrived in Fort McMurray and was shown to her new quarters at St. Gabriel Hospital. Soon after, she met Mrs. O'Coffey at the New Franklin Hotel as Mrs. Dupre had suggested, and the two discussed Fort McMurray, the war, St. Gabriel Hospital — eligible men. On February 14, Mary attended the Valentine's Day dance and attracted the attention of the man behind the voice she had heard weeks earlier on the radio, Lowry O'Coffey.

Nuns at St. Gabriel Hospital stood in for Mary as she bicycled on dates around Fort McMurray during the summer of 1941 on a two-wheeler provided by Father Chouinard. Exactly one year after their first meeting, the couple was married. Mary joined one of Fort McMurray's premier families, and remained in the community until the early 1950s.

"I guess it was fate and the help of a lot of people who just wanted us to come together,"[15] Mary O'Coffey recalled.

The Abasand setback

While at home and overseas, Fort McMurray battled World War II, the Abasand oil sands plant shone as a bright light from the Horse River Valley. However disaster struck in November 1941 when a fire destroyed the entire plant. An investigation concluded that damage caused by the fire could have been avoided with better fire fighting equipment.

Rather than shut down, Ball opted to rebuild, and a new Abasand plant was ready for operation in August 1942. During the next three months, the plant produced eleven thousand tons of oil sands.

Federal government takes an interest

In early 1942, the federal government began to revisit its largely passive position on the oil sands. During the previous two decades, Ottawa had dedicated itself to developing conventional oil supplies, and had left management of the oil sands to private business and to the Province. However, the allies' worsening position against Adolf Hitler in Germany, coupled with the entry of the Americans into World War II forced a change in Ottawa's thinking. The United States government had two military fronts to consider. While by mid-1942 it was involved and committed to the European campaign, it kept a watchful eye on the increasingly aggressive position of the Japanese government. With the United States and Canada dependent on the Middle East and other foreign countries for oil supply, Ottawa began to focus on Max Ball's promising oil experiments north of Fort McMurray.

In order to protect Alaska, Canada and the continental United States from northern attack, the American army descended on northwestern British Columbia and began building the Alaska Highway. The Canadian and American governments also began investigating ways to secure an oil supply which did not involve extensive transportation by sea or over land. A decision was reached to develop extensive oil deposits in the Norman Wells area, and to further study developments north of Fort McMurray.

The Northern Wells development was good news for Fort McMurray and its position as the shipping gateway to the north. Millions of tons of materials would soon be shipped from Edmonton to Fort McMurray for transport by barge to Norman Wells. A one hundred and thirty-four million dollar venture known as the Canol Project was launched, which, during 1943-45, carried three thousand barrels of oil a day to a Whitehorse refinery.

While the American government showed some initial interest in investing in the oil sands, Prime Minister Mackenzie King expressed some concern about giving up control of a major resource to a foreign country. In early 1943, the federal government began examining ways to support the development of the Athabasca oil sands.

In early 1942, the federal government's oil Controller, George Cotrelle, concluded that oil sands development could assist the allies in their war efforts. As he noted to C.D Howe, the federal Minister of Trade and Commerce, "if anyone is likely to solve the problems attendant on this deposit and which at one time seemed insurmountable, Mr. Max Ball and his associates will do it."[16] Cotrelle also noted that the Abasand plant had yet to show sustained success, and concluded that even if its technological problems could be overcome, it would be necessary to invest ten million dollars to produce a ten thousand barrel per day plant near Mildred Lake.

A report tabled in April 1942 to the federal Mines Department-National Research Council committee concluded that oil sands could be mined, separated and refined for a dollar thirty-one per barrel, about thirty five per cent less than the estimates developed by the Geological Survey's George Hume. Based on its untested technology, varying cost estimates and delivery challenges the committee noted that oil sands production was feasible, but that further study was needed.

At roughly the same time, one of Abasand Oil's partners and clients, Consolidated Smelting and Mining (CS&M), began experimenting in the Steepbank/Mildred Lake area, which would in future become the site of Suncor and Syncrude Canada Ltd. CS&M had gained a strong reputation in the region for developing resources in northern Alberta and the Northwest Territories. Preliminary drilling showed rich deposits in the Mildred Lake area; however, a technology had to be developed which could provide large quantities of oil sands within a safe and reliable process.

Based on the need to develop new and costly technologies to support oil sands development, the federal government reversed its previous position and announced it would take an active role in the development of the Athabasca oil sands.

Federal government steps in:

The federal endorsement of the oil sands was by no mean unanimous. Strong concerns were expressed that operations at the Abasand plant were "haywire." Managers often became embroiled in operational disputes, and the plant continued to be plagued by outdated equipment and the absence of its majority shareholder, Max Ball. As well, due to the drain of manpower by the Alaska Highway and Norman Wells projects, employees working at the Abasand were among the least skilled in the province. Employees were often unproductive and disgruntled. Sabotage of equipment was common.

Thus, in April 1943, the federal government took action forming the Wartime Oils Ltd., a Crown Corporation dedicated to developing additional conventional oil sources. More importantly, the federal government incorporated Abasand Oils Ltd., under which Max Balls' plant became a Canadian government holding. Ottawa appointed a board made up of government and business officials, and committed five hundred thousand dollars to upgrade the plant. Abasand Oil also retained the right to repurchase the plant and to participate in management and operational decisions.

The American invasion

They came with little warning, but for days there had been whispers on the street.

A number of strangers with American accents had been surveying the community, identifying large tracts of undeveloped land. No one knew why, but these were war times, and this was Fort McMurray, and people had come to anticipate the unexpected.

It began with a large advance party. One spring morning, an unscheduled freight train pulled into Waterways carrying a group of American engineers equipped with a full compliment of trucks, jeeps, bulldozers, tents and building materials. Also on board was a team of intelligence officers.

The group comprised of an advance party assigned to gather information about Fort McMurray including its climate, physical layout and transportation links. The scouting party eventually identified a flat area near the east end of Franklin Avenue, known as the Prairie, near where Keyano College stands today. Within days, two more advance battalions arrived.

Throughout that spring and summer, Fort McMurray experienced an invasion which would change the community forever. At first, a few thousand men arrived. They were engineers and technicians who were transported to the Prairie where they erected tents, and a number of small buildings include a stockade, a mess hall, administrative offices, a community hall and various storage facilities. That was the beginning.

Then, one day in July, a massive rumble shook Waterways. Residents rushed to the railway tracks in time to observe two huge Pullman coaches rolling into Waterways packed with black soldiers. As Northern Alberta Railways worker Harry Miseck would later observe, "it was unbelievable that there were no derailments since these were big Pullman coaches and all we had was sixty pound steel. Trains had to inch in at twenty-five miles per hour."[17]

Veteran rail workers also recall some of the initial American troops dashed off the train and assumed defensive military positions. Some troops had been told they were being transported to the Japanese front lines.

By the time the trains had finished arriving during the following few weeks an estimated five thousand troops were in the area. Their duties were many. The troops were pressed into duty to support the development of the Norman Wells Canol project. Troops were also involved in shipping materials, providing engineering expertise, and assuming a military presence to protect construction.

Soon after their arrival, the Americans identified two major transportation flaws in the community and two major projects were initiated. In 1942, the Americans extended the Northern Alberta Railway line from Waterways to the Prairie, at a point where current day Hospital Street extends to the Clearwater River. For years, the area had been used as a loading ground by Northern Transportation for barges heading north to the arctic. While Waterways continued to be a passenger terminus and loading station for general freight, the Americans needed an easier way to transport incoming materials from end of steel by barge to the arctic.

In addition, Fort McMurray's air landing facilities were seen to be lacking. The Snye served as a landing point for small aircraft equipped with skiis, but there was limited opportunity for larger craft to land. Although a dirt runway had been discussed in Fort McMurray since the late 1930s, it took the initiative of the American army to make those plans a reality. Bethtel-Price-Callahan of San Francisco was brought in to build a series of ground strips in Fort McMurray and in communities such as Grande Prairie, Fort St. John, Fort Nelson, Watson Lake and Whitehorse. In mid-1942, legendary pilot Matt Berry was brought in to begin clearing an airstrip in Fort McMurray, which was eventually used to land Canadian Pacific's DC3 aircraft. This project marked the beginning of the Fort McMurray airport.

The arrival of the troops also signaled a further economic growth for the community. General labourers, housekeepers, groundkeepers and other non-military jobs were filled by Fort McMurray residents. The soldiers also proved popular with the town's young people. Troops and engineers always had pockets filled with candies. "The soldiers always had goodies," recalled Merle Rudiak. "Kids were always following them."[18]

Some the children and local residents, especially those living in the Prairie would frequently attend dances and movies put on at the soldiers' mess hall. And some of the mischievous teenagers would also steal into the camp at night, jump into military jeeps and joy ride throughout the community.

But the arrival of thousands of American troops did not come without complications. From the start, eligible women in the community were subject to the aggressive advances of both troops and their officers. Native women, most of whom had never mingled with those living outside Fort McMurray, were particularly vulnerable.

Hugh Ross, former manager of the Waterways' Hudson Bay Company store recalled in his book *The Manager's Tale*, that at one point a local woman set up a side business just south of Waterways. She apparently enlisted a number of women from a local settlement and set up a professional establishment at the edge of town. Much to Ross' dismay, following a few days of non-stop activity in the tent area, the American army erected a tent across the street on Railway Avenue just opposite the Hudson's Bay Company store. A sign hung outside which read "Prophylaxis Tent." Realizing this was not the type of economic development which the community of Waterways wanted, Ross insisted that the army's condom dispensary be moved to a less prominent site.

During evenings and on weekends, the Americans troops packed into beer halls at the Waterways Hotel and New Franklin Hotel. Because beer was rationed to the hotels based on previous year's population, it didn't take long each month before beer and liquor ran out. Attracted by American dollar bills which troops waved, waiters gravitated to the Americans before they served Waterways and Fort McMurray regulars. This caused tension within the community.

Although some soldiers became involved in church and community activities for the most part the presence of the Americans produced widespread social stress. Fort McMurray had within a few months grown in size from barely nine hundred to almost six thousand.

Corporal Thompson, head of the local RCMP detachment, surveyed the situation and called in for four reinforcements. The RCMP sent four additional constables, two to be stationed in each Waterways and Fort McMurray.

Strong hand of the law

Hugh Ross also tells the story of how one Waterways RCMP officer established physical dominance over the hordes of American troops milling after hours on the streets of Fort McMurray,

One Friday night, Smitty, one of Waterways' two constables, ran into a group of drunken American soldiers who were harassing patrons outside the local dance hall. The group had already been ejected for disorderly behaviour. Smitty approached the men and asked them to "move on," however, the troops responded with taunts, and began to encircle him menacingly. Before the soldiers could cause Smitty any harm, a Military Police van arrived on the scene, and carted the offenders away.

The next day, Smitty and his partner Joe, went to visit the American commanding officer to ensure that the offenders would be properly dealt with. The Colonel assured Smitty and Joe that military authorities would handle matters, but this did not satisfy the local RCMP. Joe, a heavyset muscular man, identified six men who had been particularly offensive, and demanded that they be brought to the local detachment office to be charged under Alberta law.

The Colonel refused to submit the men for local prosecution, however, he and Joe agreed on a compromise. Joe asked that each of the six be presented to him privately in front of a full gathering of American troops and engineers. Joe then removed his RCMP tunic and Stetson, and handed it to his partner.

One by one, as Ross recounts, the men appeared, and as Ross writes "Joe beat the living daylights out of each soldier in front of his buddies. He meticulously adjusted his Stetson, saluted the Colonel and bade him a formal good day. There was no trouble for the Mounties after that."[19]

White versus black

Not only did American troops bring social problems to Fort McMurray, they also brought deep racial tension. These were still the days of racial division in the southern United States, and many of the white troops stationed in Fort McMurray hailed from segregated states.

Meanwhile, the black troops sent to Fort McMurray hailed from the American northern states that placed blacks on a more equal footing.

One day in the summer of 1942, of group of white soldiers came in to Bill Mitchell's Waterways Cafe. The cafe was crowded and the troops rudely ordered a black soldier to give up his seat. The black slowly turned and chopped the white soldier's tie off with a razor. As Hugh Ross recalls, "for a long time that tie was pinned up on the wall behind Bill's counter as a sign that there was to be no racism in his café."[20]

Soon after the incident at Bill's cafe, a brawl ensued between blacks and whites. There were numerous broken bones, injuries and damage. American Military Police and town leaders met to assess the problem and a solution to keep the peace was agreed on.

White and black troops would be segregated. On alternate weeks, black and white battalions would alternate their recreational activities between Waterways and McMurray. Blacks and whites would never socialize again. Segregation had come to Fort McMurray. Although many residents were uncomfortable with the racial division, in the interest of peace, they agreed to support and enforce the division.

There were other incidents that occurred. Later in the war, a soldier who had been reported missing from his battalion, sexually attacked a schoolteacher crossing with her children from Abasand into Fort McMurray. This raised some suspicion and concern within the community of the American "outsiders."

Evelyn White, a Fort McMurray resident who married one of the American troops, recalled walking on the street one day with some white soldiers as they approached a number of blacks walking towards them. The blacks were told to get off the sidewalk and walk on the street. White also recalled one day when, while on a date with a white soldier, a member of the black battalion opened the door for her. "I smiled and said "thanks" and then my date got quite annoyed at me. And I told him "look, this is my country and I'll do my thing here. It brought the whole racial thing to our door and we weren't used to it."[21]

White would eventually marry a soldier form North Carolina who tragically drowned a year after their wedding. White would remarry, and later in her life would experience the grief of losing a loved one in a foreign war. Twenty-five years later, her son Gordon left Fort McMurray to enlist in the American Marines. Gordon White was killed in Vietnam in 1968.

Charlotte Mitchell and destiny

When Charlotte Mitchell left Colinton, Alberta in early 1943, to visit family in Waterways, she had no idea that soon the hand of fate would dramatically alter her life, and the life of those around her.

In early 1943, Charlotte Mitchell left the farm she and her husband owned near Athabasca to visit relatives in Waterways. Born in Boston, Charlotte moved with her parents to Alberta in 1911. Her brother-in-law, Bill Mitchell ran Waterways Cafe, and family members thought it would be a good idea for the couples' children to spend some time together. In February, Charlotte and her daughters Shirley and Elva boarded a train in Boyle with thoughts of spending a week in Waterways. It didn't work out that way.

Five days after her arrival in Waterways, Charlotte's muscles began to stiffen, and within days she was paralyzed and bedridden. She had to be hand fed. Charlotte Mitchell lay helpless in Waterways, stricken by rheumatic fever. She was unable to move, and physicians feared the worse. Family members, in particular her husband Abe, felt it was time to rally the family's resources around her.

"There came a sense that if I was going to be that sick and helpless that we should all move to Waterways for the family to be together,"[22] Mitchell recalled.

In April 1943, Charlotte began to regain feeling in her fingers, and limbs and eventually to the rest of her body. Her mysterious illness subsided during the summer of 1943, but by then her family had become accustomed to Waterways. They decided to remain and sold the farm.

Over time, the Mitchells became one of the most respected and well-liked families in Waterways. Abe worked for the American Army, the Salt Plant and Imperial Oil, and performed other jobs within the community. Charlotte Mitchell worked at the McInnes fish plant during the late 1950s, then became a sales clerk at Haxton's General Store from the early 1960s to the time the store burned down in December 1979.

Her optimistic attitude and her ongoing interest in politics and community affairs made her one of the most well liked and influential citizens of Fort McMurray. In a 2001 interview, at age ninety-three, she credited her optimism with that fateful illness in 1943.

"How or why did it happen. I'll never really know," she recalled. "It doesn't make much sense and sometimes I think I dreamed it. But it is the truth.

"When I was crying and alone in 1943 I told myself that if I ever got better, I would never complain about anything to anyone. I just made up my mind that I was lucky to be alive and healthy. I have always lived by that."[23]

The birth of Guiding

Males were not the only ones to don uniforms during World War II. Since the 1930s the Boy Scouts had been active in Fort McMurray, and in early 1943 a similar organization was launched for girls.

That year, the Anglican Women's Auxiliary sponsored a Girl Guide company that was officially registered on March 24, 1943. Led by Verna Morrison, wife of Anglican Minister William Morrison, local young women were taught a variety of outdoor and safety skills.

The Guides represented an important step in opening opportunities for local girls aside from cooking and sewing skills traditionally taught in the home. Morrison enlisted the support of a number of high profile women of the day including Ethel Bird, Gladys Hill, Margaret Ross and Edith Heslop.

Within four years membership in the Fort McMurray movement had reached about fifty with meetings held in both McMurray and Waterways. It didn't take long for local guides to focus attention on the war effort.

A 1945 edition of the Guiding newsletter, Woodsmoke, reports that Fort McMurray Guides supported the sale of War Savings Stamps within schools and throughout the community. In particular, the efforts of Girl Guide Janet Head were featured. "Janet Head had the largest number of customers and will soon have her War Service Badge for having put in one hundred hours of service towards the war effort. She also conducted the sale of stamps one day each week at the school."[24]

Other activities included hikes along the Clearwater and Hangingstone rivers, box socials and badge stitching.

When the Morrisons moved out of McMurray to eastern Canada in 1946, Anne Rankin took over as Captain of the McMurray Guides. Gladys Hill's sister, Marjorie Percy who arrived from England in late 1945, later assumed the position of Captain of the Waterway Guides. Kathleen Millar served as Lieutenant.

A Life Saved

The community reaped the benefits of Girl Guides training one day in 1950. On an ongoing basis, Gladys Hill taught a lifesaving course along with swimming instruction to Girl Guides.

That training may have helped save a life seven years later. During World War II, the American army had dug into the bed of the Hangingstone River near the east end of Franklin Avenue creating a swimming hole where troops and local residents could cool off during hot summer days.

One day in 1950, three-year-old Margo Shanks was swimming in the Hangingstone River when she disappeared under the surface. Using her lifesaving skills, nine-year-old Brownie Joyce Switzer dove in and pulled Margo out of the water. Joyce Switzer was later awarded Guiding's second highest award – the Gilt Cross.

The Switzer family had a second claim to fame. Around 1945, Wilmut Switzer purchased an old school bus and launched service between the New Franklin Hotel and the Waterways Hotel. Cost was twenty-five cents to the Prairie, and an additional twenty-five cents to either Waterways or McMurray.

The service was especially handy for those employees working on barges in the Prairie area.

McMurray's boxing contender

Growing up in Fort McMurray as a small boy of Japanese descent, Tommy Morimoto was mercilessly teased by children at school and on the street. Morimoto was short for his age, and as an adult grew to five foot two inches.

"I was called a Jap and that kind of thing,"[25] he recalled. Unable to defend himself against constant schoolyard taunts, Morimoto one day in the early 1930s tucked a dollar bill into an envelope and mailed it away to an American address. Soon after a book arrived titled "Learn How to Box." Guided by instructions and diagrams, Morimoto practiced tirelessly in his home, until "one day it all started to click."[26]

In the late 1930s, Morimoto moved to Yellowknife where he attempted to join the Royal Canadian Air Force but he was rejected due to his height. "You had to be five feet four inches and one-hundred and thirty-five pounds, and I fell short."[27] Morimoto recalled. Morimoto enlisted in the regular army in June 1940 and served with the Canadian armed forces for the remainder of the European campaign.

It didn't take long for Tommy Morimoto to turn his hand fighting skills to good work. When the Canadian forces announced a competition to crown the best Canadian boxers stationed in Europe Morimoto stepped into the ring. One night in 1942, the short but tough soldier from Fort McMurray stepped into the ring and knocked aside virtually all of his opponents.

Tommy Morimoto made it to the finals of the Canadian Armed Forces Bantamweight championship where he was defeated in the final bout. Morimoto brought his silver medal back home after the war, and his toughness was never again questioned.

Fort McMurray women support the fight

Throughout the war, Marie O'Coffey co-owner of the New Franklin Hotel served as a rock of support for families of troops serving overseas. O'Coffey, with assistance from hotel staff, local families and children, raised money to support Fort McMurray's fighting men and would organize major campaigns to pack and send parcels overseas.

The parcels were stuffed with cigarettes, chocolate, tea, coffee, items of clothing and souvenirs from home. Her fund raising efforts were tireless and culminated with a major project in the summer of 1944. This funded her activities for the remainder of the war.

Aided by a number of local residents, O'Coffey brought a carnival to town. The carnival was intended as entertainment for the entire community, and featured rides and games of chance. While local residents and their children enjoyed carnival atmosphere, American troops lined up to throw darts at balloons, throw softballs into milk containers and pitch coins on to flat plates.

A total of fifteen hundred dollars was raised. Funds that were not used to ship parcels overseas were used to launch the Fort McMurray Royal Canadian Legion when the troops came home.

The heartbreak hits home

Of those who went to war from Fort McMurray, many were of native descent. These men were tied closely to the land and to their families, and that made what they experienced overseas additionally difficult to endure.

The experiences of the Waniandy brothers speak directly to the experiences of native men within the European battles. Caroline Waniandy sent three sons to war. John and Jim returned safely. George Waniandy did not. He is remembered by the family only by a picture of his grave in Italy which was sent by the war department to his mother shortly after the war.

In a shoebox still treasured by the family, George's letters remain. Copies of his letters hang at the Royal Canadian Legion. The letters express the personal side of combat. The Fort McMurray Express published some of these letters in 1979.

June 1942

I'm hoping the war ends soon so I can come back home. I got a letter from John yesterday saying he's coming overseas. It's warmer now. We are back in short pants.

January 1943

Just a few lines to let you now I've been wounded again but this time it's not bad at all. You'll be getting telegram soon but I hope this letter reaches you first. It sure is cold out here – lots of snow and rain, I hope you had a good time at Christmas.

January 1943

I'm so glad Johnnie got home on leave. I wish I could have been there. We may all be home together by New Year's, I hope. From what I hear Jimmy's become a real lady-killer. I wish he wasn't so hasty about getting in the army. He's much too young yet. I got a ribbon today – it's blue, green and red with a maple leaf on it. It's supposed to represent eighteen months of combat.

February 22, 1944

We're still in Italy and I don't think much of it. I go out and get a feed of spaghetti once in awhile. We get a few eggs and all kinds of wine, but I don't like it. I sure wish you would send me a pipe. I've been smoking so many tailor made cigs I'm getting a cigarette cough.

March 31, 1944

The guns are always going at night. I'm getting quite used to the banging and the mud. It's like hunting muskrats at home in the spring, and the mud and water is always up to our knees, but it isn't bad. We now have lots to eat. I must move out. I hope to hear from you soon. It doesn't look like I'll get home for awhile yet[28].

George Waniandy was killed in combat August 31, 1944.

Men of valour

One night in 1941, while on leave, Roy Hawkins and some friends decided to spend an evening at the movies. As they left, Hawkins was drawn to an auburn-haired English woman. The two began talking outside the movie house and eventually Hawkins mustered the energy to ask her on a date. The two would eventually marry, and Rowena and Roy settled in Fort McMurray when the war ended.

Rowena Hendry's house, located in Epsom, Surrey became a gathering point for Fort McMurray servicemen while on leave in England. Rowena's mother, Mary, was happy to provide Fort McMurray servicemen with a warm bed, and a home cooked meal. The war was progressing and for a time the Fort McMurray soldiers remained safe.

In 1944, two McMurray servicemen, David Hill and Howard Meins paid separate visits to the Hendry home. Shortly after, each perished in battle. Mary Hendry looked at their deaths as an omen, and asked Hawkins to refrain from bringing Fort McMurray soldiers to their home.

Pat O'Coffey was the first to be claimed. He died a hero in early 1943. In the heat of battle in Sicily, O'Coffey, an infantryman, was attempting to take out a German position with a machine gun when he was cut down by enemy fire. O'Coffey was one of Fort McMurray's hometown heroes, born and raised in the community, popular in school and a fixture on the ball diamonds, hockey rinks and at his father's New Franklin Hotel. His passing was a devastating reminder to Fort McMurray residents that war had a harsh and brutal side.

David Hill was a pilot for the Royal Canadian Air Force and a highly visible and beloved member of Fort McMurray's closely knit community. He was shot down in February 1945 while flying a mission over Germany.

During the war years, Charlie Somers, the telegraph operator, had the most heart-wrenching job in Fort McMurray. From 1943-44 he personally delivered five tragic telegrams to families of those serving overseas. In a 1979 article in the Fort McMurray Express, David's father, Walter Hill, recounted how he heard the news of his son's death.

I was in the drug store. I used to open on Sundays from ten to noon. The telegraph operator came in and didn't say anything but "I'm so sorry Walter." I left the store and went for a walk in the bush. I walked and walked trying to think of a way I could go home with the news. After two hours I realized that my wife Gladys was going to be worried that I hadn't come home for lunch. When I came into the house she looked at me and knew right away. "It's David," she said. I handed her the telegram. She read it and let it drop. Then she put her arms around me and we both wept[29].

Howard Meins was a navigator with the Royal Canadian Air Force and was wounded while on an airborne mission. He survived for a period with his wounds, but eventually succumbed in a British hospital. Meins was a middle-aged man, known as a good local citizen, who served as an agent for Mackenzie Air Services.

The Fort McMurray's Royal Canadian Legion officially recognizes Fred Lissoway as a local resident who died while serving in World War II. Lissoway was a watchmaker who lived in Waterways during the late 1930s. He eventually moved to Goldfields, Saskatchewan and enlisted in the army in 1944. Lissoway was killed in combat on March 30, 1945.

Fort McMurray would learn more about Fred Lissoway during the 1970s and 80s, thanks to the efforts of his niece Maureen Paquet who managed the Fort

Theatre. Each year on Remembrance Day Paquet would make a display in the theatre window of her uncle's photos, memorabilia and the letter received from the Canadian government advising the family of his death "I never met him but I wanted people to know that he once lived and that he served his country and that he gave his life for it,"[30] she recalled.

The D-Day Assault:

On June 6, 1944, Allied forces staged an assault on the beaches of Normandy, France which served as the turning point in World War II. That morning, allied forces struggled across the stormy English Channel and during the ensuing days pushed back the German troops who lay in wait. It was a brutal period of blood, death and sacrifice remembered and replayed perpetually by those who were there.

George Cochrane, who moved to Fort McMurray after World War II stormed the Normandy beaches and was the only one of his detachment who survived. He was a private, later a corporal, whose job it was to aim ten-pound mortar shells towards the enemy. Cochrane fought on the Normandy coast for two months. He recalled in a 1984 interview his memories of that military assault, and the moment his body was shattered by a German shell.

You're not looking back, behind or sideways. You were looking ahead. And your were always in the line of fire – from the time I got in until the time I got out at two p.m. on August 16. We were out in an open field. We were shot by a German with an '88. He got us on the third shot. He killed the rest of the detachment. My sergeant was killed right alongside of me. So was the rest of the detachment. I was blown twenty to thirty feet by the gunfire[31].

Cochrane lay in a field for an hour before he was discovered. Medics picked him up and transported him to a British hospital where he recovered from fractured bones and serious wounds to his shoulder, hand and chest. He returned home to Berwyn, Alberta after the war and soon after moved to Fort McMurray.

From the beaches of Normandy, Allied forces moved inland, and painstakingly inched through Europe, liberating countries previously occupied by Germany. The assault marked the beginning of a long and arduous march to victory, and the eventual end of World War II.

American troops bury it

In mid 1945, with victory assured both on the European and Japanese fronts, the American army began to plan its departure from Fort McMurray. However, completion of the Americans' stay in Fort McMurray did not come without controversy. Fort McMurray residents had been conditioned by years of hard winters and isolation to value and share food, utensils, tools, materials and other supplies. As shocked Fort McMurray residents stood by, American troops bulldozed the

FMHS Collection

Over 50 people in front of Paul Fontaine's Teepee at West End of Franklin Avenue ca 1913

Smashing the Land Monopoly in Fort McMurray, January 12, 1923

Personal Collection /Jerry Bussieres

FMHS/Bern Brown Collection

1911 RC Mission relocated to Peter Pond Shopping Centre by Fr. Brown in 1959

St. Aiden's Anglican Church at Waterways - ca 1945

FMHS/Thelma Houston Collection

FMHS Collection

West End of Franklin Avenue - HBC buildings on shoreline of the Athabasca - ca 1930

Looking West from present day Reidel Street area along Franklin Avenue - Late 1940s

Personal Collection/John Ross

FMHS/J.A. Mills Collection

SS Athabasca stern wheeler pushing barge - ca 1942

FMHS Collection

Old & the New - Wooden Stern Wheeler & Steel Tugboat - ca early 1940s

SS Northland Echo docked by barge at Waterways Shipyards - ca 1939

FMHS/Dorothy Pollock(Hutchison)/Robert R. Leggett Collection

FMHS/Eugene Burton Collection

South side of Franklin Avenue before July 16, 1934 fire

FMHS Collection

North side of Franklin Avenue before Dec 25, 1945 fire - Parade - ca 1938

First changes to south side of Franklin Avenue - Aug 1964

Personal Collection/Hill Family

FMHS/Walter Hill Collection

Flat Sleighs at West End of Franklin Avenue leaving for the North - winter 1924-25

First Horse drawn Flat Sleighs heading North from Snye - John MacDonald's house in background - ca 1922

FMHS/Mrs. Harry Halliday Collection

FMHS Collection

York Boat with a crew of 9 men shooting the Grand Rapids - ca 1912

FMHS Collection

Shooting Little Cascade Rapids - ca 1910s

MV Beaver Lake & SS Northland Echo at Tar Island Shipyards - ca 1940s

FMHS Collection

Building Wooden Barges - Oakum & tar used to seal bottom and sides

FMHS/J.A. Mills Collection

FMHS Collection

Waterways Waterfront looking West downstream from Upper Wing Dam - McInnes, MRT, Imp Oil & NT - ca 1950s

NTCL Prairie Shipyards looking west - now commercial area north on Hospital Street - early spring late 1950s

Personal Collection/Hill Family

Personal Collection/Jerry Bussieres

Abasand Oil Limited - operated late 1930s until June 18,1945 when fire destroyed Separation Plant

1926 construction in Waterways following the railroad extension from Old Waterways (Draper) in 1925

FMHS/Norma Gray Collection

Abasand Oils Limited
Waterways Alberta Canada

FMHS/Ken Hill Collection

North side of Franklin Avenue after Dec 25, 1945 fire - late 1950s

Old Peter Pond Shopping Centre with Sunoco - late 1960s

FMHS/Lynda Rodger/Lester H. Stahike Collection

FMHS/Annette Culp Collection

West End of Franklin Avenue - note bill in background - 1917

Looking East on Franklin Avenue from HBC building - 1921

FMHS/Mrs. Harry Halliday Collection

Ladies' Ball Team at Prairie - ca 1936-37

Outdoor Rink between Main & Morrison on north side of Fraser Ave - ca 1938

FMHS/John Ruch Collection

Salt Plant Men's Hockey Team - Wtys - winter 1940-41

FMHS/Roy Hawkins Collection

Boy Scout Troop organized by Fr. Chouinard - ca 1937

FMHS/Mary O'Coffey Collection

CPA - DC3 at Airport ca 1957

Personal Collection/Jerry Bussieres

Illegally parked Helicopter on Franklin - ca early 1960s

Personal Collection/Hill Family

FMHS/Alex Mair Collection

PWA Airport Terminal (south side of runway) - ca 1960

First New North Side Airport Terminal - early 1960s

Personal Collection/Hill Family

Personal Collection/Hill Family

First Vehicle in Fort McMurray - owner Angus Sutherland - 1921

Grant MacEwan bridge under construction looking west - winter 1964-65

Personal Collection/Hill Family

Personal Collection/Hill Family

A &GW Steam Engine on Old North rail bed to Clearwater -ca 1920

D.P.W. Dredges #250 & #252 in Clearwater River at the Prairie - ca 1960

Personal Collection/Hill Family

D.P.W. DREDGES 250 & 252, FORT McMURRAY, ALBERTA

HILL PHOTO

Raphael Cree & Family up Clearwater ca early 1920s

FMHS/Ben Powder/Alberta Riedel Collection

Treaty Time in front of RNWMP Barracks - ca 1916

FMHS Collection

Pack Horse Team for Telegraph Line - ca 1915

FMHS Collection

West End of Franklin Avenue - Post Card - Oct, 1914

FMHS/Rose/George Reidford Collection

FMHS Collection

Dog Team in front of Ryan Bros cook house and bunkhouse

Joe Durocher's Power Plant by Hangingstone River - 1942

FMHS/R.E. Duncan Collection

FMHS Collection

West End of Franklin from Hill - Note Paul Fontaine's Tent and RC Mission

George Golosky's Sawmill on Clearwater River bank at Prairie - ca 1920

FMHS/George Golosky Collection

FMHS/H. Stroud Collection

Hugh Stroud in front of his home - note roof shape - ca 1928

Dog Team at West End of Franklin Avenue - winter 1921-22

FMHS Collection

Personal Collection/Hill Family

Governor General Lord Tweedsmuir Visit - lawn party - Jul 25-1937

Swimming down at the Snye from Airplane docks - ca 1940s

FMHS/Mrs. Harry Halliday Collection

FMHS/Chamber of Commerce Collection

First General Hospital on Hospital Street which opened Aug, 1966

FMHS/Mary O'Coffey Collection

Laundry & St. Gabriel Hospital (closed 1969) - 1941

First Airmail flight leaving Snye for Aklavik - Dec 10-1929

FMHS/Ethel Bird Collection

Early Airplanes during the 'Hay Days' of the Snye - 1929 to 1932

FMHS/Collection

FMHS/Mrs. Harry Halliday Collection

Students in front of Fort McMurray Public School

FMHS/Mrs. Harry Halliday Collection

Students at desk and tables outdoors after first schoolhouse burned - 1923

St. John's Catholic School after 1st expansion

Personal Collection/Hill Family

Waterways Public School sports day - ca 1950s

FMHS Collection

Waterways Baptist Church (now Waterways Community Hall) - late 1960s

Personal Collection/Jerry Bussieres

FMHS/A. Kucy Collection

Abasand Oil Townsite with plant in backgroud - 1945

St.John's Anglican Rectory; Church & Hall (old Presbyterian church) - ca 1947

FMHS/Collection

Their first church built in 1950 - Morrison Street at base of Hill

McMurray Gospel Assembly File

1963 Clearwater & Snye Breakup

Fort McMurray File

1963 Clearwater Breakup at Waterways

Fort McMurray File

Fort McMurray File

1963 Breakup of rivers - Snye view

1963 Prairie view looking south on King Street

Fort McMurray File

Personal Collection/Hill Family

View from Hill at the end of Morrison Street - ca 1963

Personal Collection/Hill Family

Town Office, Library & Garage (NW corner Jubilee Centre) - ca 1963

View from Hill of Waterways from Cliff Avenue - ca 1963

Morimoto, Simone & Maynes buildings west of Morrison St on Franklin Ave

Personal Collection/Hill Family

Personal Collection/John Ross

Forestry & RCCS along Main Street (Snye Road) - Late 1940s

Start of new construction along Franklin Avenue - May 1965

FMHS/R.E. Duncan Collection

FMHS/Carl & Helen Nelson Collection

Alberta Salt Plant - Horse Creek - capacity 75 to 100 tons per day - ca 1925

Dominion Tar & Chemical Salt Plant at Waterways - ca 1941 (operational 1937 to July, 1950

FMHS Collection

FMHS Collection

US Army troops along side train passager cars at Waterways - ca 1942

FMHS Collection

US Army Camp at Prairie (present Keyano College site) - ca 1943

US Army Equipment at Waterways - ca 1942

FMHS/J.A. Mills Collection

entire Prairie camp. The troops, according to standard military procedure 'buried food, pots and pans, building materials and supplies.'[32]

"We had been taught to consider waste of food to be a sin,"[33] recalled Merle Rudiak. Aside from items left underground in the Prairie, the troops also earthed barrels of unknown materials in a landfill area near the current location of Alberta Drive and Peden Crescent.

Prior to their departure the army sponsored a major party for Fort McMurray residents. Hand shakes and "thank yous" were exchanged. In late 1945, a caravan of trains arrived in Waterways and carried the troops back home to the United States. By the time the dust settled from the departing trains, Fort McMurray's population had returned to its pre-war population of less than one thousand.

In later years as housing subdivisions, mobile home parks and Keyano College were built, construction crews dug up barbed wire, building materials, wood, utensils, barrels and other long-buried items.

Abasand burns

By 1942, a third community had developed within the boundaries of Fort McMurray. Along the Horse Creek, not far from the Abasand plant, a settlement of about one hundred and fifty took root.

Those who lived in the area were either involved with, or working at the Abasand plant, or within the company office. Frieda Milne came to Fort McMurray that year with her husband Jarvis, and remembers that the community was close knit. Evenings would be spent socializing, singing and playing cards. Despite very spartan conditions, women wore high heels and flowing dresses both to work and to local functions.

The community consisted of about ten log homes and shacks, a bunkhouse for the single men, a general store and some storage shacks. Houses dotted both sides of the river, and a swinging bridge ran across the river.

Although in 1945 the plant was not making money and was producing only a small quantity of oil, there was optimism that both the plant and the community could be sustained. That was until June 1945. Frieda Milne was nearby when it happened and observed the event which spelled the end for the Abasand oil sands project.

I was standing at the grocery store and I was talking to somebody and looked across and suddenly this big flare went up inside the building. Evidently there were people working with welding torches and the sparks went flying and everything was covered with that oil. Then all of a sudden there was a big bang and I stood there with my mouth open yelling, "fire, fire, fire" and nobody looked at me. Somebody eventually got wise to what I was hollering about[34].

As the residents of the Abasand community watched in horror, their homes and their dreams vanished. Residents of Fort McMurray saw the smoke coming up from the valley and immediately realized what had happened.

When the fire eventually subsided, all that was left was charred equipment and some fireplaces which jut from the Horse River banks behind Abasand Heights to this day. Jarvis Milne and Joe Pint were hired for a short period to watch over the abandoned site, but within a few months both were gone.

The fire proved the last straw for the controversial Abasand project. The plant was never rebuilt.

Childhood memories of Abasand

Jean (Milne) O'Connor was barely four years old when her family moved to Abasand. As a child growing up in a quiet isolated community within Fort McMurray, she retained a number of childhood memories. Many of those tranquil images helped shape her career as an accomplished artist[35].

***

There was oil from the plant on the ground, and I saw rainbows in the puddles. Oil was magic. There was no radio, so you had to have imagination. To me all puddles have rainbows[36].

***

Everybody would wear rubber boots and it was a fashion statement to roll the tops of your boots down like pirates[37]

***

When we first moved in we had an open cellar and we went down in the cellar and there were mice. So we got a big old cat and the next day they were gone. We were three little girls. If we caught one by the leg or the tail we would throw them outside, otherwise we'd throw the ones in a trap in the stove and toast our bread over it[38].

***

We had a net tucked under our hats and into our necks to protect ourselves from the mosquitoes. Sometimes they were so bad we couldn't go out. And we used to pick raspberries. Big beautiful raspberries[39].

The Americans army had sprayed the area with something and for a long while there were no birds[40]

***

We had wild Indian horses that would come along and roll in the yard. Native people would often let their horses and sled dogs go free during the summer and they used to come up to the cookhouse[41].

***

The James family had three or four kids and they found a little bear and they brought it home and the bear would play with the kids. The cub grew up with their kids[42].

***

You'd get just about anything looking in your window. One day I looked up and there was a moose and an owl both looking in[43].

***

There was heat from the stove and so we were never cold in our pajamas, but you learned not to move in your bed. I don't remember cold but I remember not turning over. I still don't turn over in my sleep[44].

***

My dad Jarvis played in a band. He played saxophone along with Roy Gamble. There were lots of bands. The Royal Bank manager Mr. C.J. Palmer would play the drums. Somebody who worked for the Hudson's Bay Company in Waterways played the piano. They made a noise anyway and people came to their dances. I think they earned five dollars per night[45].

The healing begins

By-mid 1945, Fort McMurray's young heroes began to arrive home. In many ways they were scarred. They had seen bodies and souls destroyed, and brought those tainted visions home. Shortly after their return, Marie O'Coffey took the fifteen hundred dollars she had raised through the town carnival and launched the Fort McMurray Royal Canadian Legion which initially met at the Franklin Hotel.

As each serviceman returned home, the O'Coffeys sponsored a welcoming party. Each service man was presented with an inscribed gold ring thanking them for their service to their community and to their country.

During the immediate post war period, the Legion served as a vehicle to help young people readjust to home life. Each day at the Franklin Hotel, Fort McMurray's young veterans traded memories, stories and horrors. Some say this helped dull the pain and help counter the lingering nightmares of combat. A Veteran's taxi service was organized to help provide the returnees work until permanent positions could be found. While Fort McMurray's young men had left the isolation of a small community to see the world, most had seen more than they had anticipated.

In a 1979 Fort McMurray Express article, Roy Hawkins summed it up:

War is a dirty, messy, lousy business. There is no glory. All of us joined up because the rest did. We played hockey together and we went to war together. From the time we were little guys we were taught to honour King and country – you lost track of reality. When we got into combat we realized what was happening. You didn't run because the guy next to you wasn't running. He didn't run because you weren't running. If you had both thought about it at the same time you would have ran together. We always thought it would be the other guy — but not your friends. It was stupid butchery. Deep down we didn't understand. If we would have known everything that was happening around us we probably would have said to hell with it and come home[46].

As Fort McMurray's young men, and the families who had been torn healed, the community embraced them. At small social gatherings or at kitchen tables the pain was shared. The communities of Waterways and Fort McMurray dusted off from the war years, and prepared to enter a period of quiet and stability. "We knew there would be other times of frantic growth in the future," recalled Marie O'Coffey. "Some of us just needed a time of peace in order to heal."[47]

Many of those who returned became prominent members of the community. They served as town councillors, fire chiefs, presidents of community organizations; were fathers, husbands and friends. But there is not a day that goes by that those who returned to Fort McMurray do not think about those who perished.

"I once thought during the 1970s when Fort McMurray was growing so quickly that we could have used some of those guys who didn't make it," recalled Roy Hawkins. "We could have used some more people who cared to help us keep the values of Waterways and McMurray. It is such a tragedy not just for them and their families, but for the entire town. Who knows what they could have been."[48]

Chapter Five:
Calm before the storm

By early 1946, Fort McMurray's young soldiers had returned home. As each arrived, a celebration was held at the New Franklin Hotel, but once the fanfare had died down, reality set in. During the European conflict, many of the local young men had witnessed misery and destruction beyond anything they could have imagined. They had changed, and so had Fort McMurray.

The community had become more stable and reflective than at the start of World War II. The word "boom" had been unofficially scrapped from the town's collective vocabulary. Both the Abasand and Bitumount projects were commercially dormant, and in 1946 prospects for additional oil activity appeared bleak. In 1946, an official census placed the population of the Fort McMurray area at one thousand one hundred seventy-three, and that figure would not significantly change until the early 1960s.

During the next fifteen years, Fort McMurray would remain a relatively stable Alberta community. People went about their business, worked their jobs, socialized, and established schools, churches and other institutions. The post war years provided a sobering period of calm and stability which although void of major economic development, helped prepare Fort McMurray for the feverish times which lay ahead. In the years to come, Fort McMurray residents would look back at the two decades prior to the 1964 launch of Great Canadian Oil Sands as both peaceful and satisfying.

It was a period when locking one's door was unheard of, when people could wander in and out of each other's homes at will, when a record player, a fiddle and a deck of cards were all you needed to have fun, and when a colourful collection of local characters dotted local streets, bars and coffee shops.

These were the years when memories and lifelong relationships were made.

Approach of the Sun

Sometime in 1946, a small group of engineers arrived from Edmonton on a private airplane, travelled north to Bitumount, and dug their bare hands into the Athabasca oil sands. The visit was short and the results unspectacular, but its effects would be felt for decades to come.

Since 1944, Oil Sands Limited president Lloyd Champion had been enticing international oil companies, including Sun Oil, to invest in the Athabasca oil sands.

Champion understood that involving companies like Sun, either in his Bitumount operation, or in their own venture, would improve overall interest in the region, and in turn enhance his own prospects for government loans, private investment and other support.

In 1946, Sun Oil sent a team of engineers to Fort McMurray to assess first hand the economic potential of the area. Sun Oil was a Philadelphia company which maintained a Canadian operation based in Toronto. Sun was a conservative company, traditionally reluctant to invest in risky and unproven ventures. Its main strength lay in conventional oil exploration, refining and shipbuilding.

The arrival of Sun Oil's engineering team in 1946 was regarded as unusual because to that point, few oil companies had sent representatives to view the oil sands first hand. After careful inspection, the Sun Oil team came to a predictable conclusion; commercial development of the oil sands would require an additional twenty years of study and technological development.

Statements made at the time by Sun Oil engineers may have been mistaken as a declaration of non-interest, however, Sun kept a close watch on the Athabasca oil sands, and in 1954 acquired a seventy-five percent interest in a lease along the Athabasca River near Mildred and Ruth Lakes. True to prediction, almost twenty years later, Sun Oil launched the Great Canadian Oil Sands plant, located just north of Fort McMurray.

Fort McMurray and Waterways amalgamate

One of the first orders of business after World War II was to bring stability and efficiency to Waterways and McMurray. During the 1930s, the rivalry between the communities produced parallel sets of schools, churches, and other institutions, often creating frantic competition for grants, tax revenues and community support. After World War II, a more sober and realistic attitude prevailed.

In early 1947, meetings were held between McMurray and Waterways community leaders, and soon after the Province was approached to amalgamate both under one municipality. To that point, the Province had governed Fort McMurray as an Improvement District, with advice from the local Board of Trade.

However, even these local discussions created controversy. The question rang through both communities; what would the new municipality be called? Waterways residents refused to lose their identity, and balked at being absorbed under the name Fort McMurray. A compromise was reached. The combined communities of Fort McMurray and Waterways would be known as McMurray, until 1962 when the word Fort was reinstated. The Village of McMurray was incorporated on May 6, 1947.

Soon after, the Fort McMurray Board of Trade announced it would be focusing its entire efforts on encouraging and sustaining economic growth in the region. It was officially renamed the Chamber of Commerce.

Fort McMurray's first election

On May 30, 1947 residents of the Village of McMurray went to the polls to elect a village council. Although no record remains of the vote, minutes record that Alfred Penhorwood, the operator of the Waterways Post Office, led the polls, followed by businessmen Albert Riedel and Bill Mann.

On June 2, 1947 the Village of McMurray held its first council meeting at the home of hotel owner Lowry O'Coffey and confirmed Penhorwood for a three-year term as McMurray's first mayor. Riedel was named deputy mayor for a two-year period, followed by Mann who would serve for one year.

The new council appointed local resident John Buck as the village's first secretary-treasurer at a salary of ninety dollars per month. Buck accepted the job on the condition that he be permitted to pursue additional work within the community. Aside from acting as the village's secretary-treasurer, Buck also sold insurance, acted as agent for the federal department of native affairs, and provided general accounting services.

Buck immediately began developing the village's first budget, which for the remaining seven months of 1947 totalled twelve thousand dollars. That included salaries, the upkeep of public works equipment and the doling out of social assistance within the community.

Fort McMurray's first mayor

Fort McMurray's first mayor, Alfred Penhorwood was known as a distinguished English gentleman with a stubborn streak. Penhorwood arrived in Waterways in 1930 as an employee of the Mackenzie River Transportation, a division of the Hudson's Bay Company, but soon after left the company to take over operation of the Waterways Post Office.

Among working class residents of Waterways, the tall and distinguished Penhorwood stood out in both stature and education. Penhorwood was a pillar within the Waterways Anglican Church, and an avid curler.

As John Buck recalled, Penhorwood was also a man who disliked change. Up to the late 1940s, Fort McMurray received mail service once per week. On Mondays, mail sacks would arrive from Edmonton on a plane which would continue to the arctic. On Tuesdays, the plane would return and fill up with outbound mail.

In the late 1940s, the federal government announced that mail service would begin on a daily basis. Buck recalled Penhorwood fuming over the introduction of daily mail service. "I remember him insisting that McMurray did not need daily mail,"[1] Buck recalled.

In 1952 Penhorwood retired from the post office and he and his wife took a trip to England.

First town offices

An odd financial arrangement enabled the Village of McMurray to establish its initial municipal office.

On Christmas day, 1945, a fire ravaged the north side of Franklin Avenue, destroying the Royal Bank, Albert Riedel's pool hall and the Richardson family residence. The Royal Bank immediately initiated plans to rebuild, but according to bank policy, the financial institution was not permitted to own its own building. Royal Bank manager C.A. Palmer approached the owner of the New Franklin Hotel, Lowry O'Coffey with an irresistible offer.

The bank agreed to lend O'Coffey the entire sum to build the Royal Bank of Canada and an adjacent building, both to be located on Franklin Avenue across the street from Sutherland (Hill) Drugs. The bank offered him the lowest possible interest rate, agreed to serve as the building's primary tenant, and paid enough rent to cover loan payments.

O'Coffey's sweet deal translated into good news for the Village. There was enough room in O'Coffey's new building to accommodate additional tenants, and at the Village of McMurray's third meeting, it was agreed to pay O'Coffey fifteen dollars per month to rent municipal office space.

Leigh Brown: Doctor of everything

If you were a doctor in Fort McMurray in 1946, you were responsible to heal anyone or anything, including humans, animals and broken dolls.

In 1946, Dr. Leigh Brown and wife Nan came to Fort McMurray as newlyweds and spent their first few months living and treating patients at the New Franklin Hotel, before moving into their own home on Main Street just north of Franklin.

Brown, who went on to become Director of the Gynaecology Department at Edmonton's Cross Institute for Cancer Research, brought an air of professionalism to Fort McMurray.

He was responsible for a number of firsts. He brought antibiotics to Fort McMurray in 1946, and in 1947, using a new drug called streptomycin, is credited with saving the life of a child who had been dying of tubercular meningitis. Brown also preformed the first emergency caesarian section in Fort McMurray with use of an anesthetic.

Brown admits that not all of his activities related to strict medical practice. "You had to pull teeth, or tend to a wounded dog or even patch up a doll if a little girl brought it to you,"[2] he recalled.

In 1947, Brown was appointed Health Officer by the Village of Fort McMurray and began accepting patients in the municipal office. Brown's duties as Health Officer included ensuring that local restaurants and cafes followed proper sanitary regulations. This was a challenge considering Fort McMurray had no running water.

Winston the wonder dog

Although Dr. Leigh Brown was credited with saving dozens of lives during his stay in Fort McMurray it was his dog, Winston, who in mid-1948 had the town talking. Winston was a British bulldog who was occasionally mocked as a lazy animal in a community that was used to dogs who were put to work pulling sleds.

That was until one summer day as Brown and a number of Fort McMurray residents lay sunning on a beach along the Clearwater River. While Brown, dentist George Clarke and others dozed in the afternoon heat, no one noticed Clarke's eighteen-month old son wandering into the Clearwater River, headed for deep water.

Winston noticed the child and raced to the riverbank to intercept. Winston's running and barking alerted adults, and within seconds, just inches from catastrophe, the baby was plucked from the river. Winston became a local celebrity after the incident.

The job no one wanted

One of the first challenges Fort McMurray's new council faced was assembling a local police force. Until that time, the RCMP had provided law enforcement. At the Village's third council meeting, Constable Jack MacGregor advised the municipality that the RCMP would only address law enforcement until the fall of 1947, at which time policing would become the Village's responsibility.

However finding a Chief Constable for the Village proved a difficult task. A number of local residents were offered the position, but each declined. After all, Fort McMurray had two major town sites with a population spread over a substantial area. The job of Chief Constable, in spite of is official sounding name, often involved being a dog catcher, or gathering drunks from the street.

In addition, Waterways required considerable attention with a constant influx of transient workers coming to town to take advantage of work opportunities. In April 1948, the job of Chief Constable was offered to former RCMP officer Sid Hawkins at a salary of two hundred dollars per month. Six days later, Hawkins advised the Village that after consulting with his wife he would be unable to accept the position.

On April 26, 1948, a motion was passed to hire William Charles Anderson on a one-month trial basis. Two months later, Anderson resigned due to ill health. On June 22, Don Violette was hired as Chief Constable, but on August 16 he resigned. Violette agreed to be rehired only after council agreed to grant him a special allowance of fifty dollars every three months, over and above his normal two hundred dollar monthly rate of pay.

At one point during the summer of 1948, Violette raised eyebrows over the way he handled a Waterways drunk. On one evening, a local businessman was standing outside the Waterways dance hall reveling after too many beers. Violette attempted to arrest the businessman at which point the man darted into the woods. Violette pulled his revolver and fired a shot into the air, much to the horror of the businessman, and those partying at the dance hall.

On June 29, 1949, Violette resigned and the job was offered to Forestry Officer Jack Roy who in turn declined. The position was finally re-offered to Sid Hawkins.

Hawkins accepted the job to start August 1, 1949 on the condition that he be paid two hundred and twenty-five dollars per month, plus a uniform consisting of a regular coat, two pairs of pants, great coat and a raincoat. Council agreed, but added that in the event Hawkins resigned his post before a year ended, he would be charged a percentage of the cost for his uniform. Sid Hawkins served as Chief Constable until he resigned eleven months later. Town records don't say whether he paid for the clothing.

Highlights from 1947/8 council meetings

Other highlights from meetings held during 1947-48 include:

- Phoebe Penhorwood, Art Hardman and Hugh Stroud appeared before council representing school boards in Waterways and McMurray, asking that land in the downtown area be put aside to build a high school. (September 6, 1947)

- Len Williams' application to renew his license to operate a cafe in Waterways was approved. (September 6, 1947)

- Jack Wood of the Skating Rink Committee of Waterways requested a grant to cover the cost of lighting the outdoor rink. (November 10, 1947)

- Council passed a bylaw to provide a two-dollar meeting honorarium for councillors. (February 10, 1948)

- Frank Harris, who had purchased Albert Riedel's Franklin Avenue pool hall and barber shop, was granted permission to add a coffee and lunch bar (February 10, 1948)

- John Funk was hired as the Village's first General Utility Man. (March 15, 1948)

Fire fighting concerns

One of the reoccurring hardships which plagued Fort McMurray was property damage due to fire. Since its inception, fires caused by wood or coal heaters had been responsible for gutting schools, homes, hotels and other businesses. On November 24, 1947, the Chamber of Commerce, led by President Hugh Ross, appeared before the Village council and requested that measures be taken to improve fire protection.

Council told the delegation that it was not feasible to purchase fire equipment, however Councillor Mann advised the delegation that he owned a portable hand-pumping machine that was capable of throwing a stream the height of any building in the village. He offered to make it available for use at any time. It was also suggested that the village drill a well in a central location in order to be assured a steady supply of water.

On December 15, 1947 the Village ordered one hundred feet of hose with coupling and nozzle, and council discussed contracting Hector Demers, James Dowd and John Wood to act as fire marshals.

Hair stylist to the north

The community of McMurray provided a fresh start in 1945 for a single mother and her daughter. Alexandra (Nowicki) Taylor arrived in town just after the end of World War II, and immediately launched a beauty salon in downtown McMurray.

However, after a month, it became apparent that Waterways was the place to be to operate a business. "The boats and train would come in, and there were wives and also plenty of native people who wanted their hair cut,"[3] she recalled.

Taylor moved to Waterways in 1946, and from there her business literally soared. Her friend, Ethel Bird suggested that Taylor try cutting hair in Fort Chipewyan. Taylor flew north and was so enthusiastically supported in Fort Chipewyan that she continued on to Fort Smith and to Fort Fitzgerald. During the spring of 1946, Taylor became hair stylist to the north.

In particular, she loved cutting the hair of native people who she recalled appreciated the service and did not request "fancy perms." Taylor also recalled how soft the water was in Waterways.

On Monday mornings, it was common for women to line up at the Waterways salt plant and fill pails with the soft water which had been produced by the plant's turbines during the salt production process. "It was beautiful soft water from the salt plant which we stored in barrels and heated on wood stoves in big kettles,"[4] Taylor recalled.

Clark's last stand

Towards the end of the 1940s, the provincial government began to become impatient over lack of activity at the Bitumount oil sands site. In 1945, it had provided Lloyd Champion's Oil Sands Limited with thousands of dollars in loan guarantees.

Early in the decade, Oil Sands Limited owner Lloyd Champion had secured loan guarantees from the provincial government, but by 1947, Ernest Manning's government became impatient over a lack of activity in the area.

On behalf of Premier Ernest Manning, oil sands pioneer Dr. Karl Clark was brought in to assess the situation, and in 1947 concluded that an additional seven hundred and fifty thousand dollars was needed to bring the plant up to working order. That was a commitment which Champion was not prepared to make.

Relations between Oil Sands Limited and the government became strained and in 1948, under pressure from the provincial government Champion's company was dissolved. Shortly after, the Bitumount project became entirely government-owned, and Clark was brought in to oversee research and production.

At the outset, hours of operation at the Bitumount plant were extremely limited, and the separation process that Premier Manning had been so enthusiastic about proved much slower than anyone anticipated. Costs were higher as well, but ultimately confidence remained high that the plant could work effectively once operational problems would be identified and solved.

In 1949, a comprehensive series of tests were conducted to assess the viability of oil sands' development. The tests told investors and government officials that the oil sands were an area with potential, but conclusions about the Bitumount plant itself were not as promising.

One of Bitumount's biggest problems was a clash among personnel. Pay cheques were often up to a month late, and this fostered disloyalty and anger among the men working at the plant. A test of the competence and teamwork of staff came on July 29, 1949, when there was a serious explosion at the plant. One man suffered serious burns due to the overuse of gasoline while cleaning the machinery, and the incident highlighted the disastrous inexperience of some of the men working on the project.

Clark's diary recorded the event:

July 29. 1949

"This was a bad day. Everything was going smoothly up till about 3.30 pm. Then the report of an explosion was heard. It sounded just like a dynamite blast in a quarry. Sharp sound rather than a dull thud. In fact everybody thought at first that it was just that and wondered who would be blasting and for what purpose. Then men started running. It became known that the explosion was in the separation plant and that Sam was hurt – the welder. The stretcher was taken down. The truck went too and Sam was got up to the laboratory which seems to be the First Aid station. He was badly burned on the face and was burned on his body too. It was learned later that the face burn was the bad one but that his eyes were ok. The body burns were bad enough but were "flash burns" whatever that means exactly. Sam complained of pain in his stomach but there were no internal injuries. Trouble with his stomach was shock. I heard that his face was bloody but that does not seem to have been particularly significant. Word was got to McMurray as soon as the radio time (4 pm) came and a plane arranged for. The CPA contacted a plane at the Embarass and it was in about half an hour later. Sam was put aboard and Bill Arnold went with him. Bill sent word back later that the doctor had been at work on Sam and that there was nothing wrong with him that would not heal in time.

The [cause of the explosion] seemed clear. Sam and his helper cleaned the place where welding was to be done with gasoline. They probably used plenty."[5]

Despite this setback, the summer of 1949 was a relatively successful one for Bitumount, and forty members of the Alberta legislature who visited the plant in August were impressed.

Although construction and operation of the plant were approximately half as costly as those for the Abasand project and strategies were developed to increase its success, the Bitumount venture was shut down in 1955. After nearly eight years of operation under government scrutiny, the plant failed to produce financial or technological results.

Manager W.E. Adkins proposed that the oil separation process be halted and that Bitumount be turned into a government research site, but the idea came too late. Northern Alberta was becoming less of a focus for the provincial government, because oil reserves were being found in more southern areas such as Leduc. As a result, the government became more focused on conventional oil production and less on research and experimentation. Circumstances and the packaging of proposals regarding its work obscured the Bitumount operation's progressiveness and relative success.

The plant site remained dormant until the early part of the next century when True North purchased the lease and announced plans for commercial development.

Broken beer bottle

In the fall of 1948, the Village of McMurray faced its first lawsuit.

William Koski, an employee of Oil Sands Limited, told council that he had suffered a cut on his foot from a broken beer bottle in front of Arnold Skelton's office. Skelton owned a meat market just east of Morrison Street and Franklin Avenue. On the top floor of his market, Skelton had an office from where he served as town magistrate.

Koski told council that he had required medical attention, which cost him two dollars, and had also ruined a pair of shoes and socks. Koski demanded restitution. Minutes record that Mayor Penhorwood questioned Koski as to how old the shoes were. Koski replied that he had purchased them two weeks earlier and was prepared to produce the sales slip.

Councillors sided with Koski and agreed to pay six dollars and ninety cents on the understanding that no further claims would be made against the village.

One for Waterways, one for McMurray

Until the fall of 1948, the streets of Fort McMurray remained dark after sunset. But a motion passed on September 27 changed that. Council gave consideration to installing a streetlight in front of both the New Franklin and Waterways hotels.

The discussion highlights how even though Waterways and McMurray had amalgamated, residents of each community kept a close watch to ensure that neither gained the upper hand.

"If one community had a street light then the other needed to get a street light," recalled Ken Hill. "If McMurray got sand on their streets then Waterways would have to get sand on their streets. There were people watching this very closely. Everything had to be even."[6]

On September 29, 1947, a special council meeting was held and Joe Durocher and George Milne were approached to cost out installation of streetlights in Waterways and McMurray. The lights were installed later that year.

Fort McMurray becomes a town

It didn't take long for the Village of McMurray to grow out of its britches. After careful study by the secretary-treasurer, it was concluded that McMurray would benefit from increased grants and provincial support if it were to become a town.

On November 8, 1948, the Village applied to the Province and on December 30, 1948 was officially incorporated as the Town of McMurray. Alfred Penhorwood was appointed mayor.

In elections held in February 1949 six councillors were elected to serve with the new mayor, Albert Riedel. They included: Lowry O'Coffey, Hugh Stroud, Hector Demers, Bill Mann, Ernie Couture and Bill Mitchell.

Council Highlights 1949-50

The hottest issue at town council during 1949 was an application by Steve Workun to open a cafe in Waterways. The application was energetically opposed by Garth Moore, owner of Moore's Cafe who claimed that Waterways could not support a fifth cafe.

The debate raged over four meetings with council each time attempting to delay or pass the buck to provincial authorities. Councillor Ernie Couture backed the Workun application noting that Waterways would appreciate a new cafe since sanitary conditions at the Empire Cafe were less than ideal. Health Officer Dr. Leigh Brown subsequently inspected the Empire Cafe and told council on July 25 that the eating and cooking utensils at the Empire were kept in a clean condition. Brown did however tell the owners to paint their ceilings and walls, and install a screen door to keep the dust and bugs out.

Based on its conclusion that there was already sufficient cafe competition in Waterways, Council ultimately refused the Workun application.

First woman elected

McMurray voters crossed gender lines in February 1950, and elected Gladys Hill as the town's first female municipal councillor. During the same election, Hugh Stroud and Lowry O'Coffey were re-elected to council. Hill was active in a number of community organizations and proved the popular choice of Fort McMurray and Waterways residents. Hill was soon assigned special duties which in council's view required a "woman's touch."

At the time, there was no provincial welfare department, so the municipal council managed local social services. Council became concerned about the amount of money being spent to support the community's unwed mothers, and Hill was assigned to track down the men who were responsible.

"It was one of my jobs to visit all unwed mothers," Hill recalled in 1980. "Then I'd try to find the man and make him pay child support. A woman was better equipped to handle some of these cases. And because everyone knew me, they could open up knowing nothing about their problems would be blurted out all over town."[7]

Hill would also accompany the health inspector who on a regular basis would travel north from Edmonton. In those days, recalled Hill, attention to health standards was considerably more lax and on one occasion she watched the inspector scrape an inch of grease from the stove at the Franklin Hotel.

Mrs. Hill recalled that in the early 1930s, the process of civic government was significantly less structured and local residents were expected to play their part. If someone wanted to build a garage or fence, there was no permit required from the town office. One weekend, a group of residents appeared on Franklin Avenue with tools and timber, and built a wooden sidewalk from Morrison Street to the Franklin Hotel. The project was organized without any municipal or provincial funding. "It was needed so people went ahead and built it,"[8] said Hill.

Each councillor was paid forty-eight dollars per year and cheques were issued between Christmas and New Year. "It came in awfully handy," she said. "That money bought a lot of things."[9]

Other highlights of 1950 include:
- Earlier in 1950, the province had agreed to reduce motor vehicle licenses from five dollars to two dollars. Councillor Gladys Hill initiated a motion that motorists be approached to donate two thirds of the amount to help maintain "the road," namely Franklin Avenue. At the time, there were thirteen vehicle owners in the town. Four complied.
- The position of Chief Constable for Fort McMurray attracted thirteen applications. Council agreed to offer the job to Steve Craddock "as he is a local man." Craddock was hired at one hundred and eighty-five dollars per month, and would be provided living quarters at the police house in Waterways. The town agreed to pay him two dollars and fifty cents towards his power bill to offset the lights used when police cells were full. Council also agreed to furnish Cradock with one uniform per year.
- Wettlaufer was granted permission to hold a dance beginning at 12:05 a.m. January 1, 1951.

How curling used to be

During the late 1940s, a third sport began to take its place in popularity alongside hockey and fastball, and again the old McMurray/Waterways rivalry came into play.

In Fort McMurray, residents banded together and on one weekend in 1949 built a one-sheet outdoor curling rink. Not to be outdone, the same year Waterways residents responded with a one sheet rink which in 1950 was knocked down and replaced with an indoor two-sheet rink at the corner of Tomlinson Street and Bulyea Avenue. The Waterways rink allowed spectators to stand behind a sheet of glass and watch the game in progress. Long before the availability of artificial ice, the surfaces at both rinks were kept solid by the natural cold, and residents attempted to play into the spring when the temperatures didn't always support good curling.

"In the springtime, you'd be curling in water," recalled Jack Leirdal. "You'd throw rocks and the water flew." [10]

Longtime Waterways resident Charlotte Mitchell recalled how seriously local residents took their curling. "We never missed a game in those days because of the rivalry between Waterways and McMurray. Those of us behind the glass had as much fun as the curlers. We made big fifty cent bets on some of the important shots." [11]

In order to flood the Waterways ice, curlers took a water truck to the station and were able to heat the water through the steam engines. The heated water was then taken to the curling rink and the surface was flooded.

Two challenge cups: the David Hill Memorial Cup and the Canadian Propane Mixed Challenge Cup spurred a rivalry between Waterways and McMurray. As longtime resident Jerry Bussieres recalled, "it was a lot of fun. Back in those days, there was no road out and in winter curling was the thing to do." [12]

One of Fort McMurray's best-known landmarks burned down during the winter of 1949-50. The Club Cafe joined the seemingly never-ending list of landmarks, which were destroyed by the wave of fires, which plagued Waterways and McMurray. Another cafe, the Union Cafe, had burned down in 1943. The fire which destroyed the Club Cafe was a spectacular sight due to the kitchen grease which fed the flames, and the event was even captured on film by Health Officer Dr. Leigh Brown.

The Club Cafe was run by Charlie Mah who was known throughout town for his exceptional hospitality. It was usual for McMurray residents to go to Mah's cafe for coffee after a movie or social gathering. Meals were reasonably priced. A dinner of roast beef and mashed potatoes cost about thirty-five cents.

Mah was also known for the New Year's party which he threw every year for the entire town. Those who attended recall that Mah would "drown all his guests with scotch, whiskey and mounds of Chinese food." [13] Long time residents also recall that in 1948, when Fort McMurray experienced a wave of forest fires in the vicinity, Mah prepared piles of sandwiches and delivered them to firefighters on the front lines.

Following the fire, Charlie Mah opened a cafe next to the New Franklin Hotel but soon after left the community and returned to China.

Gus Strandberg: Photographer and mechanic

Some of the greatest memories of the 1940s and 1950s were recorded by Gus Strandberg, a mechanic and businessman who during the 1950s owned and operated the Esso station at the corner of Main Street and Franklin Avenue.

Strandberg originally came to Fort McMurray during the 1930s to work on the Abasand project and later at the McMurray salt plant, and soon after gained a reputation as a master technician. People from Fort McMurray and Waterways would bring Strandberg their radios and other appliances to repair.

But aside from fixing cars, trucks and radios, Strandberg gave the community something more. He gave them memories. Strandberg was the town's unofficial photographer and whenever families would gather, or a major community event occurred, Strandberg would load up his camera gear and record the event. Strandberg developed and printed these photographs in a home darkroom.

During the late 1990s, Judy (Strandberg) Mitten, Gus' daughter returned to Fort McMurray with dozens of photos which had been stored for decades in old steamer trunks. She knocked on doors throughout Fort McMurray and in some cases delivered portraits which had been taken fifty years earlier. The remainder were donated to Heritage Park.

Growing up "inside" Fort McMurray

Judy Mitten was born and raised in Fort McMurray, and like so many local residents who have since departed, carries hometown memories which she relives virtually everyday.

She still remembers the experience of going "outside", the term used by local residents when they travelled to Edmonton or other communities. The following are some of Judy Mitten's memories growing up and living in Waterways and McMurray. Her memories are similar to many who were brought up in Fort McMurray and left, but still referred to the community as home.

- The train travel was very important to me. It was a very exciting aspect of my life – especially the comings and goings. It was a big part of our life. The sound of the train was so exciting. We were so few and there was so little happening.

- As soon as we heard the train coming we would run to the tracks because practically everyone was expecting either someone or something to arrive that would affect their lives in one way or another. It would be fresh milk at the very least, or a friend who had been away who would come back with great stories. It was very exciting.

- The smell of the coal on the train was wonderful. Being on that sleeping car I remember the sheets being crisp and everything being clean and white.

- We always referred to going out of the community as going "outside."

Business people, my dad for example, would refer to being away from our isolated community as being "outside." They would say, "oh he's 'outside' for a few days." That gave greater definition to the isolation because you were either "inside" or "outside" McMurray.

- The moms would pack picnic lunches and take us little kids down to the river and we would picnic and the men would come after work and fish. And I would kill now for some fresh pickerel. To this day, I can imagine the smell and still crave fresh pickerel.

- The sense of community was quite wonderful. Mom belonged to the Women's Institute which was a very active ladies group. There were wonderful afternoon tea parties which were held at the Waterways community hall. The sandwiches were teensy and great. And there were bean suppers and other events which you find in any isolated community. These are all nice memories.

- I'd work at the Hudson's Bay store and save my money to get a hairdo or some clothing in the city. All the girls would go to Edmonton to the Paul Pierre hair salon. Elizabeth McCormack, Eileen Somers and my other friends would come back with lovely new clothes and there was competition for me to get there too and I would save my money to go and shop.

- Everyone looked out for each other. I'm sure that my Mom told this big nasty cop to send me home at a certain time. After a movie and we'd all be at the Oilsands Cafe, he would embarrass me with his flashlight and tell me to go home.

- If I would transfer or transport myself anywhere, I would transport myself to a small community where everyone had simple values and cared for one another.

- Life in McMurray in the 1950s was quite wonderful. It was quite simple. I loved it. It was a splendid isolation for me and prepared me for life[14].

Salt plant closes

For more than a decade, Waterways appeared to be invincible as the area's major economic hub. Industries like fishing, transportation, and lumber provided employment and economic strength for the entire community.

However, that economic armour sustained a major dent in early 1950, when it was announced that the Waterways salt plant would be closed and demolished. About fifty local residents would be laid off or transferred to the company's other operation. In a community of barely one thousand, the news was catastrophic.

The plant, which had operated since the late 1930s, was a victim of economics. The cost of both importing coal to heat the plant, and shipping the salt out by train proved prohibitive.

Bill Hyska worked at the plant and was a shift supervisor at the time of its closing. He recalled that at its peak, the Waterways plant produced one hundred and ten tons of salt per day. The technique used was simple. The salt plant relied on two wells, one roughly situated where the Waterways skating rink stands today, and the other located to the northwest. Steam was pumped in one well about one thousand feet deep, and travelled along a natural canal until it mixed with salt deposits and exited the other well in the form of brine. The liquid was treated, filtered and dried until table salt and salt blocks were produced. The salt blocks were mixed with iodine and colorants for use as animal salt licks. Elsie Hyska who worked packaging the salt recalled that the plant produced a variety of boxes and packages of two to one hundred pounds.

"When you think that in those days a two pound box sold for six or seven cents, you had to sell a lot of it to cover your costs," Bill Hyska recalled. "Sometimes the cost of shipping the coal in was worth more than the coal itself. Even though the salt was some of the purest anywhere in the world, the freight costs were too much."[15]

Employees of the salt plant had been expecting the news. Salt had recently been discovered in Unity, Saskatchewan and it could be mined and brought to market for less. On June 9, 1950, salt production ceased at the McMurray plant, and on February 9, 1952, demolition began.

Closure of the plant produced an eerie silence in Waterways. The community had become used to three shift whistles – at seven a.m., four p.m. and nine p.m. The nine p.m. shift whistle was also the curfew signal for young people to return home.

Caribou by the thousand

One of the oddest wildlife occurrences happened during the spring of 1951, when one day local residents woke up to find the town completely overrun by caribou.

Caribou were common in the area north of Fort Chipewyan, but it was almost unheard of for any to venture as far south as McMurray. That all changed with an invasion of tens of thousands of caribou along the Athabasca and Clearwater rivers and the Snye. Some ventured into the town's back yards and as far south as Franklin Avenue.

The herd of caribou was so thick that airplanes could not land on the Snye. For many residents who relied on wild meat to sustain them through the summer and winter months, arrival of the caribou was like manna from heaven. Local resident Arthur Harpe recalled the scene:

"The area was black with barren-lands caribou. They were everywhere. These caribou aren't that bright and I remember one guy walked right into the herd, and hit a few over the head with an axe. He cut their throat and skinned them right there."[16]

Harpe recalled that so many caribou were in the community people began killing animals just for specific body parts, like tongues. A lot of meat was left rotting on the rivers.

Dr. Leigh Brown and wife Nan became caught up in the excitement. They walked across the Snye to the Clearwater River and with her first shot ever Mrs. Brown felled a caribou. The Browns shipped their caribou stew as far away as Montreal.

Waterways Hotel burns

On October 31, 1951, an event took place in Waterways which would have a monumental impact on McMurray.

Earlier that day, as was the tradition, the Waterways Hotel had organized a Halloween penny scramble for the town's children, but later that night, Halloween ghosts would linger and cast a darker spell.

Just after midnight fire broke out in the adjoining pool hall owned and operated by Garth Moore. Within minutes the fire had spread to the hotel and east to Sutherland's Drugs. McMurray's inferior fire fighting equipment was no match for the heat and speed of the blaze. The airport fire truck driver, who apparently had been drinking that night, turned his hose on a power pole rather than on the hotel itself. Half the block was destroyed and would not be redeveloped until the mid-1970s.

As with every tragedy, there was a silver lining. While the fire spread through the hotel, a number of Waterways residents raced into the hotel bar which remained untouched during the fire's early stages. Dozens of cases of beer were removed from the hotel, and when the insurance company tallied the final damage, the beer was included as a write-off. For months to come, there was free beer at parties, weddings and other functions throughout the community.

However, after the beer dried up, the fire's impact began to be felt. The Waterways Hotel had served as a social hub for the entire community and without it Waterways seemed to lack focus.

The closure of the McMurray salt plant and the loss of the Waterways hotel were two major economic blows from which Waterways never recovered.

"It was a bad thing for Waterways," recalled Bill Hyska. "Waterways was the prosperous community, and McMurray was the dead one. You'd go into the hotel in Waterways and it would be packed, whereas the New Franklin Hotel would have three or four people. Things started to turn downward after the salt plant closed and the hotel burned down."[17]

New Franklin Hotel sold

In 1952, one of McMurray's most prestigious addresses changed hands. That year, the O'Coffey family sold the New Franklin Hotel to businessman Jack Wagner who along with a partner took over operations, and changed the name to the Oilsands Hotel.

Following the death of Wagner in 1952, Mike Kolawaski assumed controlling interest of the hotel. It the early 1960s it was brought to Kolawaski's attention that although his hotel was known as the Oilsands he had never bothered to register the name. Kolawaski scrambled to register the name prior to another entrepreneur adopting it.

The O'Coffey family remained in the community another two years concentrating its efforts on land holdings and its sawmill. At the time, Fort McMurray's economy was sagging, and as history would later show this downturn would provide Fort McMurray with two important land acquisitions.

Faced with a heavy tax burden, the O'Coffey family left town. Their property on MacDonald Island, which they had purchased from Fred Furlough, reverted to the province. Eventually it was annexed by the town.

Some town council highlights which occurred during 1951-52:

- Paul Schmidt is elected mayor. George Ciunyk and Wilmot Switzer are elected to town council. (February 26, 1951)

- Dr. Leigh Brown and wife will be leaving the community soon and an invitation was extended by council to attend a community gathering in their honour on May 30, 1951.

- Dempson Cross is acclaimed as town councillor, replacing Wilmot Switzer who was leaving the community. Dr. J.M. Wesolowski was appointed the new Medical officer of Health. (June 11, 1951)

- Constable Craddock is given permission to purchase a sawdust burner and to install it, at his own expense in the kitchen stove at the police house. (June 11, 1951)

- Council decided to place flagpoles in McMurray and Waterways. The McMurray flagpole was placed in the middle of Franklin Avenue at the corner of Morrison Street. This was done to prevent planes from using Franklin Avenue as a runway.

Hawker and the Queen

It must have been a curious site when Gus Hawker, his spouse and planeload of children arrived in London in 1953 to witness the coronation of Queen Elizabeth II. After all, the Hawkers had spent most of their life in the bush in Waterways and Uranium City areas, and were not exactly cultured in the ways of royalty.

During the 1940s, Hawker operated a store at the corner of Bulyea Avenue and Bishop Street which sold everything from cans of peas, to snowshoes, ammunition and candy. Residents would order items from the front counter, and Hawker would disappear into the bowels of the store and return with the product. Cans of Spam would be stored behind the underwear or trapper's snare wire underneath the cans of sardines.

"If you remember how packed full of items Haxton's Store was in later years," recalled long-time resident Elva Bussieres, "Haxton's was like Saks of Fifth Avenue compared to Hawker's."[18]

In later years, Hawker would be remembered for two "claims to fame." He and spouse, Marie Townsend, would produce a large family and each would be named after a month of that child's birth. Names of the Hawker children included April, May, June, August and October.

During the early 1950s, Hawker and family left Fort McMurray and moved to the Uranium City area where, as the story goes, Hawker amassed considerable wealth by "grub staking" new prospectors. In return for furnishing initial prospecting supplies, Hawker would accept shares in each company. Although only a handful of these companies ever achieved success, Hawker waited until his shares rose on the market and sold them at their peak.

Hawker's profits mounted and in June 1953 he decided to indulge in a royal fantasy. Following the death of King George VI, Hawker chartered a plane, loaded up his family, and flew to London where the Hawker clan participated in the festivities surrounding the Coronation of Queen Elizabeth II.

When Fort McMurray residents heard about Hawkers' royal adventures, disbelief raced through the community.

"Here was a family who lived all their lives in a cabin and in the bush, chartering an airplane to participate in the royal coronation," recalled David Brooks. "Like most things about Hawkers, it was very odd and very unpredictable."[19]

Gun toting bankers

Jim Stephen, manager of the Royal Bank of Canada seemed an unlikely gun slinger as he and a teller travelled three times a week to provide services in Waterways. During the 1940s and the first part of the 1950s, banking services were provided Mondays, Wednesdays and Fridays in Waterways, and Tuesdays, Thursdays and Saturday mornings in McMurray.

The Waterways branch consisted of a small room just off of Maciver's store. In order to ensure that the bank remained secure, Stephen packed a revolver and with teller Doris (Somers) Mirkovich took a taxi three times a week to and from the Waterways branch.

"You wouldn't normally think of a bank manager carrying a gun, but I guess because there were a lot of transient people in Waterways he had to be careful,"[20] Mirkovich recalled. Providing banking services in Waterways also proved to be a dirty business. Stephen and Mirkovich would enter the branch wearing clean white clothing, but especially during winter, Maciver's stove would cough soot into the air and both would leave each day covered in black.

In 1955, the Royal Bank's new manager Bill Cormack took Stephen's place and soon after petitioned his head office to close the branch. Cormack recalled that with the salt plant closed and the Waterways Hotel gone, keeping a branch no longer made sense.

"The Royal Bank gave me permission to break the lease," Cormack recalled. "The landlord didn't seem to mind since there was a liquor store ready to move in."[21] As for the famous Royal Bank gun, Cormack saw it as a necessity.

"The gun sat on the counter where everybody could see it. It wasn't hidden. When you went to the post office you took it with you. The bank had canvas bags and anytime you went to the post office nobody knew whether you were going with mail or money. This was a smart move when you think of it."[22]

Cormack, who served in McMurray from 1954-57 recalls that it was important for the Royal Bank to establish a highly visible presence in the community.

"We were providing a service and not making money," Cormack recalled. I had a limit of about five thousand dollars but I'm sure I never had to get anything approved because everything up there was so small. Everyone had money on deposit and there were few loans. The Royal Bank knew that McMurray was in a holding position. They knew that some day the oil sands would be developed and they wanted to be there."[23]

Council highlights, 1953-54

- Paul Schmidt is re-elected mayor. (February 23, 1953)

- Council authorizes a phone to be installed in the police office and in the town office. (December 28, 1953)

- Constable W.P. Elliott replaces J. R. Riddle as the town's chief constable. (May 31, 1954)

- Council is informed that Dr. Gordon Maynes recently passed away (August 9, 1954)

- Minutes record the death of former meat market owner and magistrate Arnold Skelton (September 27, 1954)

- Council is informed that Chief Constable Elliott has polio in his left arm and is under quarantine. Councillor James Hutchinson agrees to look after the police duties in the interim (November 8, 1954)

The Humes of Waterways:

In 1955, Waterways welcomed two important new businesses. Frank Hume, recalled as Waterways' first permanent resident of Chinese descent, moved to town and soon after opened both Hume's Meat and Groceries and the Liberty Cafe. Both businesses were located on Bulyea Avenue just east of current day Marketown. Their sons, Benny and Hughie, came to join the family soon after.

Benny Hume recalled that the idea of bringing fresh meat and groceries to Waterways was enthusiastically welcomed by local residents. He noted that the family's goal was to sell fifty dollars worth of meat each day; instead most days the cash register rang in between one hundred to three hundred dollars a day.

Church in a box

Fort McMurray's Baptist church took shape in 1954 with the arrival of Art Hoehne, a student from a Vancouver Bible College, who quickly became known for his ability to work a variety of jobs, while providing pastoral services.

He came to work as a summer labourer on the expansion of Fort McMurray's airport. That year, the federal government had agreed to expand the airstrip which had originally been built by American forces during World War II, in order to accommodate the C46 and DC6 aircraft which were now being used by Pacific Western Airlines and a number of private flyers. Hoehne often worked from noon to seven in the morning, extending the runway and greasing the heavy equipment. "It was so bright during the summer months we could work overnight without using extra lighting,"[24] he recalled.

When his fellow students left in the fall Hoehne remained behind to begin a Baptist work in Waterways. He was instrumental in building Waterways' Baptist Church, a tin building, which was shipped to Fort McMurray in seven boxes and assembled on one weekend. The church was located on land formerly occupied by Hawker's store and would later become the Waterways Community Centre.

During their stay in Fort McMurray, Art Hoehne and his wife Ella, watched the Fellowship Baptist Church grow to be one of the community's largest. In the early years his salary was fifty a month. To help supplement the family income, both parents drove school bus; Hoehne managed Swanson's Lumber and later they operated a chicken farm.

"In order to make the church work in a new community, you had to juggle the whole time," Hoehne recalled. "But we made it."[25]

Winter road to Fort McMurray

Since it was founded as a community McMurray always had been completely cut off by road from the outside world. Transportation in and out of the community was limited to rail, river and air. However, that changed slightly in 1955, when British American Oil began to express an interest in oil deposits which were buried between Wandering River and McMurray.

Since these deposits were not accessible by road, British American began planning a meandering winter road which would wind its way along the Athabasca River and eventually reach McMurray.

The company contracted a heavy machinery operator who had a reputation of successfully completing difficult assignments. The operator would become one of the most colourful and dedicated Fort McMurray residents, and would one day serve as its mayor.

During the winter of 1955, Claire Peden arrived in Wandering River with three "cats" and a small crew and began clearing trees, shrubs and snow. Later that winter, the winter road was completed to the top of Beacon Hill, known as Willow Lake Road.

Peden's company had succeeded in punching through a road which theoretically connected McMurray with the outside world. It would be an additional two years before anyone would actually try navigating the road.

As Peden's son, Torchy, recalled, "you could do it, but it was a big gamble you were taking. If you ever got a snowfall you'd never come out. It was a pretty risky situation."[26]

In 1956-57, Peden returned to McMurray, this time under contract from Shell. Peden shipped heavy equipment by train to McMurray and then barged it north to Lease C13, which had been purchased by Shell during the mid-1950s. Although the provincial government would build a bridge during the 1980s across the Athabasca River to the Shell site, it was Peden's road building and land clearing which would form the basis for Shell's explorations.

Keystone fire men

McMurray's proudest acquisition in 1956 was a three-ton fire truck equipped with a thirteen hundred-gallon tank and a small pump loaded on the back. But if McMurray firemen were looking for credibility with their new acquisition, their first episode with the fire truck appeared more like a comedy routine.

First of all, the town's new fire truck was so heavy that only one person in town, Oil Sands Hotel owner, Mike Kolawaski, could drive it. These were the days before power steering, so it took a person of considerable physical strength to turn the steering wheel.

"It was a three-ton truck with about six and a half tons of water loaded on the back," recalled former fire chief Roy Hawkins. "There were no baffles on the tank, so as the water sloshed back and forth, it would jerk the truck forward and backward."[27]

On the truck's first assignment, Kolawaski and deputy fire chief Archie Goodwin dashed into the front seat, turned on the siren and rumbled towards the downtown area. But as they approached Franklin Avenue and Riedel Street, they noticed something odd. The back wheels of the fire truck had fallen off the axle, and were rolling down Franklin Avenue ahead of the fire truck.

Within seconds Fort McMurray's new fire truck ground to a halt, its rear axle embedded into Franklin Avenue. The truck had to be towed back to the station. Eventually the tank was trimmed to one thousand gallons and bolted to the back of the truck. The homemade fire engine served the community until the early 1960s when a used vehicle was acquired from the town of Vermilion.

Transit service, and tragedy

Bus service returned to McMurray in 1956. Taxi owner Johnny Sandulac purchased an Edmonton school bus, shipped it north by rail and converted it for adult passenger use between McMurray and Waterways.

Cost from the Oilsands Hotel to Waterways was fifty cents. For twenty-five cents, the bus would drop you off in the Prairie.

The town's taxi operators, who complained to town council that there was not enough business for everyone, met Sandulac's bus service with less than unbridled enthusiasm. In an April, 1980 interview, longtime resident Bob Duncan recalled the furor the new bus service created. "I remember the hassle we had with the cab drivers about the bus. Cabs would shadow the bus and pick up customers ahead of the bus."

The wreck of the Clearwater

For decades, river traffic had proceeded along the Athabasca and Clearwater Rivers with very little loss of human life. But in August 1956, Fort McMurray was shaken by the wreck of the NTCL riverboat, the Clearwater.

During a fierce storm on Lake Athabasca, a cable tangled around the Clearwater's boathouse, twisting the vessel and causing it to capsize. Lake Athabasca was known for its violent storms, but nothing of this kind had occurred before. Captain Ken "Tiny" Holden and seven crewmembers perished.

The tragedy served as an everlasting reminder of how river and lake travel, which local residents took for granted, could produce fatal consequences.

"It was the only major accident on Lake Athabasca," recalled Captain Billy Bird in a 1986 interview. Fellow captain Gilbert Auger remembered how his son, Roy, had become friends with Tiny, the boat's captain. Roy would lie awake at night mourning his lost friend.

Tin Can Charlie and Lovely Mike

Like any small community, Waterways and McMurray had their share of bona-fide characters. Because the cost of living within the community was relatively low, and fresh vegetables and fish were easily obtainable, a number of unemployed or semi-employed residents wandered through town, sharing stories over a cup of coffee or glass of cold beer.

"These were guys who didn't do things like everyone else," recalled longtime resident David Brooks. "They never really had a full time job so they did odd jobs around town, and would often be seen on the street, at the liquor store or at the bar."[28]

The most famous of these characters was "Tin Can" Charlie Anderson who lived in Waterways during the 1950s. Anderson was a tall bearded man who lived in a shack covered with metal siding made from flattened oilcans. Anderson was an educated gentleman who could have played an important part in the community; instead he became a public nuisance. He rarely bathed and was always covered in dust and grime. On occasion, he would be shipped to St. Gabriel Hospital for a full scrubbing.

Anderson also kept dozens of cats, and this created a health concern. One night, when Tin Can Charlie was out of his house, the town sent a piece of heavy machinery to his residence, lifted it off the ground and carted it to the end of Bulyea Avenue past the current location of the Royal Canadian Legion.

In the early 1960s, Tin Can Charlie's luck changed. His poverty came to the attention of the Grey Nuns in Edmonton who paid for him to travel to Edmonton and move into a room at a seniors' centre.

One day in the early 1970s, longtime resident Alwyn Tolen recalled the train pulling into Waterways, and a distinguished English gentleman, wearing a three-piece black suit, disembarking. He stepped into the streets of Waterways and walked around the community and spent a night in McMurray.

"It was Tin Can Charlie," recalled Mrs. Tolen. "It was obvious that the Grey Nuns had taken good care of him. He looked good and was well dressed."[29] The next morning, the dapper Charlie Anderson got back on the Northern Alberta Railways train and returned to Edmonton. Months later, Fort McMurray residents received the news that Charlie Anderson had passed away in Edmonton.

"He just wanted to come up here before he died," Tolen recalled. "He left here for the last time very much a gentleman."[30]

Lovely Mike

Another colourful Waterways character was "Lovely Mike" Hrychuk who was best known for his drinking antics. Lovely Mike received his nickname because of his habit of ending every sentence with the phrase "for lovely Mike."

It was not unusual for Lovely Mike to convene a meeting of drinkers on the day when pension cheques were delivered. On one occasion a crowd gathered outside an outhouse located at the centre of Waterways.

"We looked and there was this biffy just rocking," recalled Tolen. "There were eleven people in there drunk and fighting, including Lovely Mike."[31] Before any harm could be done, the outhouse was cleared and the drinking party disbursed into Waterways.

During part of the 1950s, Lovely Mike lived in the bowels of an abandoned boat parked in Waterways on the shores of the Clearwater River.

Town council highlights, 1955-57
- Council agrees to install nine street lights in both McMurray and Waterways (October 11, 1955)
- Albert Riedel is elected mayor for a two-year term. John Fairburn and Lawrence Tolen are elected to council.
- A letter is received from the Dominion Bureau of Statistics advising that Fort McMurray's population in 1956 is 1,103. (September 26, 1956)
- A letter is received from the Alberta Liquor Control board asking permission

to open a liquor store in the old Maciver store in Waterways. Council agrees. (November 27, 1956)

Base 800 radar installation

In early 1958, four young men stood on a corner in a village near Belfast, Northern Ireland. Their lives were going nowhere. Prospects for jobs and a bright future appeared bleak.

One of the four made the suggestion that they leave Northern Ireland for another commonwealth country. A coin was flipped between Australia and Canada. The luck of that Irish coin toss produced a series of events which brought Larry McArdle to McMurray. In March 1958, McArdle, one of the four, caught a plane to eastern Canada and then to Edmonton. He then turned his sights north and boarded an eighteen-dollar flight to McMurray.

Within days he landed a job at Base 800, located south of Fort McMurray on Stoney Mountain Road. Fanned by the cold war, Base 800 was part of a national effort establishing a mid-Canada early warning radar system. The self-contained base, located not far from Anzac employed about one hundred and thirty staff members, most of them residents from the Fort McMurray area. Facilities included an infirmary, dormitory, fire hall, officers' lounge and canteen.

Hours after arriving in Fort McMurray, McArdle reported to a spot in the centre of the town. A helicopter appeared, plucked McArdle and shuttled him to Stony Mountain Road where McArdle worked as a labourer, cook and bartender.

He recalls that by the time the radar equipment was installed in 1961, it was deemed obsolete and was shut down soon after. Many of the buildings were sold and ended up being used for storage in McMurray. Some were moved to Anzac and later formed the basis of the Regional Campsite, used by schools and churches.

Aside from the experience he gained, McArdle will always remember Base 800 for the helicopter crash he survived:

We were going in and the pilot started turning around. I thought he must have forgotten something. The next thing I know we were going down, losing altitude. Helicopters are usually safe but this time we came down in the middle of the camp among wires. As soon as we hit the ground someone was looking after us. We were lucky because there must have been two feet of snow. The blades broke off and the helicopter fell forward and pushed into me. It was a write off and nobody was hurt but a lot went through my mind when were going to hit the ground. I thought, "I am never going to see Ireland again and I probably said a little prayer. The next day they made us go up again. Forever after I had butterflies in my stomach when we went up, especially if it was windy[32]."

McArdle has remained in the community and became an active businessman and member of a number of non-profit organizations.

Wayne Chow's near death experience

Wayne Chow is a lucky man to be alive.

In 1959, he and cousin Danny Chow arrived in Fort McMurray from Lac La Biche and began to search for a restaurant to either buy or launch. Within days, the Chow cousins acquired the Oilsands Cafe for thirty-five hundred dollars. The purchase price included stove, fridge and inventory. The restaurant had no running water; it was piped from a well across the street to his basement. The quality of the water was known across McMurray as the clearest and freshest tasting.

In June 1959, Wayne Chow was involved in an accident which is still talked about among old-timers. In those days, businesspersons, in particular restaurateurs, relied on the Northern Alberta Railway to bring in their supplies from Edmonton. Each Tuesday and Friday evening as the train pulled in, residents would rush to the Waterways station to view who was coming and going, and what interesting boxes and other freight would be loaded off the cars.

One bright evening in June, Wayne Chow was driving towards the train and became distracted about the following day's menu and drove through a stop sign at the Waterways train crossing.

"There were a couple of big trees, it was bright and I wasn't paying any attention," he recalled. "I kept on going not bothering to look — which was a little bit of a mistake."[33]

It could have been a life-ending mistake. Chow looked to his right just in time to see the huge engine of the Muskeg Special bearing down on his vehicle. The train hit his pickup flush against the right-hand side driving the vehicle down the tracks at a ninety-degree angle.

Had Chow brought along a passenger, that passenger would have surely been killed. Had the train hit Chow's vehicle other than at a ninety-degree angle, the truck would have likely been sent into a fatal tailspin.

"I had no time to be scared and I had no time to think,"[34] Chow recalled. Dr William MacDonald treated Chow for a forehead cut. There was some damage to Chow's knee and some glass to remove from his hair. The next day he was back in the Oilsands kitchen.

Because many of the town's residents routinely went to the train station to greet the train, within minutes everyone in town knew about Chow's close call.

A few weeks later, an envelope arrived from Edmonton. It was a bill for thirty-seven dollars and fifty cents to cover damages to the train.

Over the next four decades, Wayne Chow and his wife Anne, went on to own a series of businesses including the town's first dry cleaning business. During the 1970s, his store, Chow's Varieties served as a meeting ground for local business people, along with members of the Fort McMurray Chinese community.

Residents for years to come would continue to make fun of Chow and his close call.

Council highlights, 1958-59

- a motion is passed to appoint Ron Henriet as Fire Chief who is mandated to establish a fire brigade. Members are to be paid $2 for each fire attended. The secretary is instructed to order one pole, two fire axes, six flare pots and two road signs. (April 28, 1958)
- Roy Hawkins is appointed town fire chief (March 9, 1959)
- Shell Oil applies to operate a bulk plant in Waterways. (July 27, 1959)

The emergence of GCOS

Patience, as history would reveal, proved to be a major component in the success of Sun Oil, which during the mid-1950s began developing the Athabasca petroleum deposits in partnership with Great Canadian Oil Sands (GCOS). Sun engineers had concluded in 1946 that it would require about twenty years of research and development before the oil sands would be financially attractive to investors.

During the next decade, Sun Oil continued to assess the potential of oil sands development and in 1954 Sun acquired seventy-five per cent interest in Lease 4, just west of the Athabasca River near the Mildred and Ruth Lake area. Sidney Ells had originally identified the land during the 1930s as being rich in oil content.

Meanwhile, events were occurring in eastern Canada, which two years later would produce an historic business relationship which would eventually change the face of oil production in Canada. In 1953, a group of Toronto businessmen formed GCOS with hopes of one day developing an oil sands project. GCOS investors began immediately assessing some of the technological challenges and concluded, as others before, that it would require considerable financial resources to overcome the obstacles which lay head. In 1954, GCOS hired Dr. Karl Clark, who had recently retired from the Alberta Research Council, to act as a consultant.

GCOS began immediately lining up its investors and its technology. In 1954, Montreal businessman Lloyd Champion offered GCOS Robert Fitzsimmons' Bitumount patent, plus Lease 14 in return for three hundred seventy-five thousand GCOS shares. In 1957, GCOS raised working capital when Rio Tinto Mining bought eighty thousand units of GCOS stock at three dollars per share.

While GCOS and Sun began assessing their options north of Fort McMurray, events in the Middle East came into play. In 1956, during a Middle East war, the government of Egypt blocked the Suez Canal, a major oil-shipping thoroughfare. Governments and private investors within North America began to explore ways to reduce their dependence on Middle Eastern oil.

At last, both the political and economic climate appeared right for oil sands development. 1958, a contract was signed between Sun and GCOS which provided GCOS with rights to mine and process half of Lease 4. GCOS would receive a rich royalty deal, while Sun Oil agreed to buy seventy five percent of the oil produced. The remaining twenty-five per cent went to Canadian Oil Companies Limited, which eventually became owned by Shell Oil Canada.

During the early 1960s Sun would acquire controlling interests in GCOS, setting the stage for Canada's first mega project, the GCOS plant, which would open in 1967 north of Fort McMurray.

Perhaps a New York Yankee

They could have been contenders.

During the late 1950s, Fort McMurray produced two ball players who many believe could have made it to the major leagues. By the time Cliff Waniandy and Roland Harpe graduated from St. John's School in 1957, both were highly sought after players on local ball teams.

Cliff Waniandy was shortstop whose hitting and fielding earned him a local following and an attractive living during the summer months. During the late 1950s and early 1960s, teams in Yellowknife, Hay River and other locations would recruit Waniandy. He would be placed on local company's payroll and required to do nothing else but play baseball. As well, Waniandy was recruited by teams participating in the tournaments held throughout Alberta and the Northwest Territories. These events attracted All Star teams with the lure of huge prize purses.

A second player, Roland Harpe, pursued his career outside Fort McMurray. Harpe left Fort McMurray, and in the late 1950s pitched for the Edmonton Eskimos in the Pacific Coast League (PCL). In 1959, Harpe landed a starting position with the Spokane Indians, earning the respect of PCL batters with his blazing fastball. The following year, Harpe joined the New York Yankees system and played Triple A ball with its affiliate in Columbus, Ohio. He attended spring training with the Yankees in Clearwater, Florida and it appeared he was destined to join the New York dynasty. Then homesickness struck.

"It was my first time breaking away from my small community," he recalled. "You'd travel all over by bus and stay in these lousy hotels. I just wanted to be home."[35]

Harpe longed for his family and friends, and in 1961 left the Yankees organization and returned to Fort McMurray. There are days when he regrets the decision. Teammates such as Ron Fairly enjoyed successful careers with the Los Angeles Dodgers, Montreal Expos and Toronto Blue Jays.

"I know I could have made it no trouble," Harpe recalled. "But I missed the small, safe and friendly place I grew up in."[36]

The dawn of Syncrude

Although the Bitumount oil sands plant has been dormant since the early 1950s, its role within the region was by no means complete.

In 1955, a New York-based company, the Can-Amera Oil Sands Development

Company, took over the Bitumount site in order to further test a centrifugal process developed by Gordon R. Coulson which it was believed could successfully separate oil from the oil sands. Both Can Amera and the Royalite Oil Company Limited financed the hundred and eighty thousand dollar acquisition. As part of the deal, Can Amera was granted the rights to acquire ten per cent of all production, while Royalite received the rights to Gordon Coulson's separation process.

That year, Royalite also secured the rights to Lease 17 northwest of GCOS, however little development occurred until June 1958 when Cities Service Company bought ninety per cent of the Royalite. In turn, Cities Service sank major financial and technological resources into the oil sands. This commitment which eventually would bring about the development of a large consortium which would one-day launch Syncrude Canada Limited. Cities Service had developed a warm water separation process at its plant in Louisiana, and felt that the idea had potential north of Fort McMurray. In 1959, Cities Service built an eight and a half million dollar plant near Mildred Lake, and accepted Richfield Oil Corporation and Imperial Oil as partners.

Cities Service's Mildred Lake investment produced a boom within Fort McMurray. Oil money to purchase supplies and services began flowing into the community. The town, which had existed in stable condition since World War II began to feel the effects of increased economic activity.

Sun Oil, Richfield Oil, Imperial Oil, GCOS and others were now major investors in the oil sands, by extension in the future development and stability of Fort McMurray. After nearly fifteen years of sleepy existence, the pieces were now in place for Fort McMurray to become an oil capital.

As the 1950s drew to a close, a number of new residents began to arrive. They were fresh and open to the new business and community possibilities which existed. They brought with them new expectations of what a community should offer. Fort McMurray's existing residents watched the new developments with both excitement and concern. Many of the newcomers, some from larger cities such as Vancouver, Edmonton, Calgary and Toronto were perceived as being aloof, and critical of the Fort McMurray's small town flavour, and divisions between two classes of residents began to emerge. However, after almost fifteen years of slow economic activity, residents appeared ready to seize jobs and new economic opportunities.

During the late 1950s, a number of these newcomers began to dot the community landscape. Many of these individuals, young, eager and hungry, would grow with the community and would eventually take up positions of responsibility. Some of these included Jack Shields, Norm Weiss and Claire Peden.

One of most notable arrivals during the winter of 1959, was a camp manager who one night slipped into Fort McMurray, downed a meal at the Oil Sands Cafe and took up residence in a freezing trailer. His name was Chuck Knight, a former skid-row drunk, who would later become the mayor of Fort McMurray.

Chapter Six:
The GCOS decade

During the fifteen years prior to 1960, Fort McMurray existed within a relative calm. Although oil companies attempted to excite the town with plans and pronouncements, many residents remained skeptical. After all, this was the community that had seen the Abasand and Bitumount oil sands projects rise and fall, again and again.

But something seemed different at the start of the 1960s. Multi-million dollar test plants were being approved. Residents observed heavy equipment arriving by train and being barged north. Newcomers employed by oil companies began arriving, along with waves of businessmen and others eager to take advantage of ground level opportunities.

However, the increase in activity did not occur without some collective soul searching. Although the 1950s had been referred to as the "poorer times," when prosperity finally arrived, a degree of apprehension gripped many longtime residents. The shell of isolation that had nurtured a sense of self-reliance in the community also protected it from outside influences.

Fort McMurray has often been compared to Brigadoon, the Scottish fictional community made famous on Broadway and film. Brigadoon remains isolated from the larger more complex world and comes alive only one day per century, when strangers are able to stumble upon it. For decades, the much-fabled community of Fort McMurray had remained isolated from the outside world. But strangers were on their way.

Since the 1940s, Fort McMurray's cast of characters remained stable. Families, friends, relationships, celebrations and even disasters could be experienced with a degree of predictability. However, during the first half of the 1960s, Fort McMurray appeared to be swallowed up by newcomers. Although these new residents brought optimism and fresh ideas from the "outside," they also challenged the status quo, and demanded that additional services and comforts be provided, similar to what they were accustomed to in cities like Edmonton, Calgary, Vancouver and Toronto.

As well, Fort McMurray began to develop social classes. In late 1966, Canadian Bechtel, the company contracted to build Great Canadian Oil Sands, held a Christmas party at the Peter Pond Hotel. Much to the amazement and insult of longtime residents, the guest list was limited to Bechtel employees. It was inconceivable to many, that a function be held in McMurray which was not open to all.

In addition, upper crust neighborhoods began to emerge. The small cluster of houses built at the top of Crescent Heights, and occupied largely by Bechtel families, became known as Snob Hill. From there, "rubber boot glamour" was born. During a decade when heavy rains and road construction often turned the lower townsite into a quagmire, rubber boots were compulsory footwear. Dinner parties, brunches and card games were held on Snob Hill which attracted women dressed in the finest clothing who had to make their way through heavy layers of mud. Some local residents were invited to these parties, and recalled some of the bizarre clothing combinations. "I was invited to Mrs. Phyllis Humphreys' for tea, and everyone arrived with fancy dresses with lacey gloves and hats, complete with massive mud boots," recalled Audrey Petruk. "It was actually quite comical as people tried to be sophisticated in their gumboots."[1]

Often, local residents felt overshadowed by the new arrivals. Many felt minimized and forgotten. As the heavy machinery rolled into Fort McMurray towards Great Canadian Oil Sands, some residents chose this period to move south, or to relocate in Anzac or other quieter communities.

Peter Hanson summed it up, "It seemed like it was us and them, with all these new guys coming in and it was a long time before it started integrating. It always seemed there were two groups: the outsiders, ones who worked for Bechtel and GCOS, and us guys who had been here all our lives and worked for NTCL or McInnes. I thought they would come in and do this stuff, and leave again and leave us as a little town again." However, in time, the two social classes would become one. In spite of their initial reservations, jobs and economic opportunity did emerge for Fort McMurray residents.

As dignitaries cut the ribbon in September 1967 to officially open Great Canadian Oil Sands, Fort McMurray unofficially broke with the past. The quaint and tiny community of eleven hundred was about to embark on a frantic and memorable journey, which would lead it out of its days as a local transportation centre, towards its destiny as an oil capital of international importance.

GCOS makes its move

It is usual within the oil industry for great plans to be developed based on optimism and speculation. Such was the case in 1960 as GCOS prepared to launch a commercial oil sands operation north of Fort McMurray.

GCOS believed it had acquired a rich oil lease supported by reliable technology. However, what GCOS did not have was money. Faced with pressures by shareholders and the Province to begin construction, GCOS needed to locate the financial resources to both build its multi-million dollar plant, and to financially float its operation while anticipated glitches and production problems were addressed.

In spite of its questionable funding situation, GCOS decided in 1960 to embark on its historic journey. Early that year, it applied to the Alberta Oil and Gas

Conservation Board for funds to build a one hundred and ten million dollar oil sands complex on Tar Island which would produce up to thirty-one thousand five hundred barrels of oil per day. Hearings were held in Edmonton during the fall of 1960, and in September 1962 the Conservation Board offered its conditional endorsement. Two months later, the Alberta government formally approved construction of GCOS, Canada's first oil sands project. It set royalties at eight per cent for the first nine hundred thousand barrels produced each month, and twenty per cent for oil produced above that total. The Province also stipulated that GCOS complete its financial arrangements within one year.

Stock options had been purchased by Canadian Pacific Oil and Gas, Sun Oil, and Canadian Oil Companies Limited, but these options did not necessarily translate into cash. The short time frame identified to shore its finances produced challenges. Faced with construction cost estimates that had risen to one hundred twenty-two million dollars by late 1962, the prospect of raising short-term capital seem nearly impossible.

The scope and cost to build GCOS exceeded anything that had been undertaken in Canada to date. To further complicate matters, in mid-1963, Canadian Pacific Oil and Gas, and Shell Oil, which had taken over Canadian Oil Companies Limited, dropped their GCOS stock options. It soon became clear that if the GCOS plant was to proceed, it would require a giant leap of faith and a massive cash injection by the remaining potential investor, Sun Oil Limited, a company not traditionally known for its eagerness to risk money on untried or unfamiliar ventures.

The future of GCOS would be decided by J. Howard Pew, Sun Oil's Board Chair, who at age eighty-one, would be asked to risk the security of his precious family company, and a rumoured one-third of his personal fortune on an untried project far from his Pennsylvania base of operations. There were those who predicted the demise of GCOS. But those people did not know J. Howard Pew.

The Pew visit

Within a company as cautious and conservative as Sun Oil, J. Howard Pew stood as a contradiction. Pew was known for his sense of adventure and his ability to cut through formalities. He possessed the ability to speak plainly to front line employees and experts, and quickly gain an understanding of a situation or opportunity.

Pew was also prone to make decisions based on instinct. There is a story told about Pew during one of his later visits to Fort McMurray which demonstrates his willingness to invest financial resources supported by emotion rather than cold facts.

During the mid-1960s, while GCOS was under construction, Pew and a colleague rented a car in Edmonton, and began driving the muddy road north to Fort McMurray. Miles south of Fort McMurray, the vehicle's windshield washer fluid hit empty, and at various intervals, Pew's driver had to exit the car and throw water from the side of the road on the windshield. When Pew's vehicle finally arrived in

Fort McMurray, the driver paused at the downtown Esso station to fill up with gasoline. The driver asked the attendant to clean his caked windshield. The attendant demanded five dollars payment for the service.

Pew apparently turned to his associate and said "when we get going at GCOS we are going to build our own service station here to keep everyone else on their toes. And there will be no charge for window washing."[2] Shortly after, the Franklin Avenue Sunoco station was approved.

When news of GCOS' funding problems reached Sun Oil offices, Pew demanded to be flown to Fort McMurray to personally assess the oil sands. Sun Oil and town officials immediately began preparing for Pew's visit.

Pew's arrival in Fort McMurray on July 3, 1963 was treated by the Province, GCOS and town with the attention and preparation of a royal visit. Pew was known to have a deep love for Canada, in particular Alberta. Both he and Premier Ernest Manning were devout Christians and would spend time together in Jasper each summer discussing politics, oil and religious matters. However, Pew's first hand knowledge of Fort McMurray was limited.

In his book *Black Gold with Grit*, former GCOS field manager J. Joseph Fitzgerald recalled how residents and GCOS employees scrambled to make Pew's visit a first class experience – Fort McMurray style. Five chrome imitation-leather chairs were expropriated from the Oil Sands Hotel and placed on the deck of Mayor Claire Peden's twenty-foot skiff. As Fitzgerald recalled:

I even located caterers for the executive luncheon. George and Mavis Caouette prepared a lunch to be served in a special tent. Special meant clean and large. The entire taxi fleet of McMurray, three cars, was to be ready at the airstrip for the motorcade to the Snye where Peden's yacht rested at anchor. The event was to be photographed by Bill Hill, son of Walter, the town druggist... This assignment I hoped would make its own history. The Sun Oil Gulfstream landed precisely on cue on July 3[3].

The entourage, which consisted of Pew, Senior Vice President Clarence Thayer, Sun's Calgary manager G.E. Dunlap, and Lloyd Miller, Dunlap's assistant, made its way to the Snye.

On the trip by boat north to the GCOS site, Pew apparently brushed aside his company associates and spent much of the trip locked in conversation with Mayor Peden who was known for his honest and straighforward talk. Peden would later recall that Pew did not want a sugar coated public relations tour; he wanted hard facts and a real assessment of potential problems that the plant would face.

During the visit, in private conversations with his senior vice presidents, Pew expressed concern whether a qualified project manager could be located to oversee project construction. Former Sun CEO Clarence Thayer, who was approaching retirement, agreed to take on the job provided he could retrieve his yacht from Singapore.

"Go get your boat," Pew is quoted as saying. "And get back up here and get this job done."[4]

Soon after, Pew appeared before the Sun Oil board in Philadelphia, and in one of the shortest company meetings on record uttered the historic words, "lets go out there and build this thing."[5] Sun Oil subsequently agreed to invest up to sixty-seven and a half million dollars and arrange for financing for an additional one hundred and sixty-six and a half million dollars. In turn, the province agreed to raise the maximum number of barrels per day to forty-five thousand. Sun Oil subsequently became GCOS' major shareholder and would assume six of eleven positions on the GCOS Board. Sun Oil was clearly in a position to launch the Great Canadian Oil Sands project.

In subsequent years, many Sun Oil shareholders and board members would question the decision reached in late 1963. It would take many years before GCOS would overcome initial production problems, labour challenges and a number of fires. As late as 1990, the financial viability and future of the plant was called into question.

However, it is likely that without the vision and faith of J. Howard Pew the history of the Athabasca oil sands and the community of Fort McMurray would have stalled in 1963. Pew and Sun Oil were willing to venture into the unknown, trail blazing new technology for companies like Syncrude Canada to follow.

The Minister who sang and danced

Fort McMurray would be forever touched by a remarkable man, Peter Gamble Harris, who spent three years in Fort McMurray during the early 1960s.

During the late 1940s, Harris earned his living in England as a song and dance man in pubs and show halls. There, he met his wife Thirza, a dancer, and the two appeared destined to spend the rest of their lives as entertainers.

However, fate altered those plans when a serious motorcycle accident left Harris with a crippled leg. Harris was forced to leave his career, and attempted to earn a living selling fruit and vegetables on the streets of London. Due to his crippled leg, Harris became the target of a number of thieves who knew that it would be difficult for him to pursue them.

Harris realized he needed a new start and in the early 1950s immigrated to Canada under an agricultural visa. He eventually made his way to Beaverlodge, near Grande Prairie, where he proved to be a dismal failure as a farmer. Harris was a dedicated Anglican and an inspiring orator, so when he began making plans to leave Beaverlodge, local businessmen gathered to find a way to keep him in the community. An opportunity for Harris soon emerged. The town had recently been approached by the government to test a new type of grass seed, creeping red fescue, and Harris was invited to lead the experimental planting.

Creeping red fescues soon became one of the popular grass seeds in North America. Harris became rich and before he reached sixty was in a position to retire. But Harris was not content to remain still, and when the Anglican Diocese suggested he become an ordained minister, Harris seized the challenge.

Harris was dispatched to Fort McMurray in 1961 to lead the Anglican Church and quickly gained a local following. Harris was also known for his fondness for song and drink. He would often arrive at the home of a parishioner, or at the Legion where he served as pastor, and lead lusty choruses of British show tunes until the early morning hours.

Some of this natural ability to entertain came in handy during the early 1960s when Harris became the president of the Fort McMurray Chamber of Commerce. In 1962, it was Peter Harris who delivered the initial presentation at the provincial hearings convened to consider the Great Canadian Oil Sands application. Harris impressed the provincial panel with his sense of humour, and his ability to deliver a point with passion. It is recalled by those in attendance that Harris outshone the lawyers present with his ability to speak eloquently and convincingly.

Sun Oil president J. Howard Pew was so appreciative of Harris' supportive comments, that months later, through his personal foundation, Pew arranged for a sixty thousand US dollar cheque to be delivered to Harris' church. The funds enabled the congregation to tear down the church built in 1931 by Bill Mann, and replace it with the All Saints Anglican Church that stands today.

Edmonton historian Alex Mair recalled how in the early 1960s, Harris led a delegation to the Legislature to lobby the Province to establish a paved road from Wandering River to Fort McMurray. Mair, a journalist with CBC at the time, took Harris, Mayor Claire Peden and Alberta Power manager Bob Duncan to the Edmonton Petroleum Club to celebrate the town's successful presentation. As Mair recalled:

The waitress came around and asked each of us what alcoholic drink we wanted. When she got to Harris she noticed the collar he was wearing and discretely asked what he would like to drink. Harris yelled his order so loudly that you could hear him across the club, "anything with gin in it."[6]

Peter Harris left Fort McMurray in 1964, and settled on Vancouver Island.

The case for a road

The case for an all weather road from Wandering River to Fort McMurray began to take shape during the late 1950s. A brief prepared by Walter Hill on behalf of the Fort McMurray Chamber of Commerce provides a window into the flurry of activity that surrounded the community at the dawn of the 1960s. A motion passed by the Chamber and later presented to an Edmonton conference on northern development lists the following reasons for a winter road.

- year round communication has now become vitally necessary for the continued exploration and development of our great natural resources, such as timber, pulpwood, oil, gas and bituminous sands

- The Royalite Company of Calgary has already commenced preparation at their site near Fort McMurray for construction of a large commercial separation plant and subsequent pipeline to refineries in the Edmonton area.

- A Pipeline is more readily built, serviced and maintained when constructed in conjunction with a road.

- A road connecting the present Highways #2 and #46 with McMurray will transverse large areas of forest land, thus facilitating the better development of the lumber and pulpwood industries.

- This road would also then connect with a winter road built in February and March of this year by the Provincial Department of Highways from the McMurray district northward to Lake Athabasca in order to provide winter transportation to the Uranium City mining district[7].

Extensive lobbying by the Fort McMurray Chamber of Commerce and the town led to the approval of a highway which would at last provide a land connection between Fort McMurray and the outside world.

Yoo hoo surveying

Receiving approval from the Province to build Highway 63 involved a series of high level meetings, but when it came down to actual construction, the effort involved proved considerably more basic.

During the late 1950s, Germain Routhier was employed to cut a forestry road that would eventually serve as the starting point for Highway 63. Routhier and Anzac trapper Lawrence Whitford would clear the road by a process that would later be called "yoo hoo surveying." Whitford cut into the bush on snowshoes and a dog sled beginning at the House River. Whitford would then yell or send a signal to Routhier who would mark the path and then clear it with a D6 or D7 cat. Often, Whitford discarded the map and used his instinct to mark new paths for clearing.

In this manner, mile by mile, the forestry road that later became Highway 63 was initially cleared. As Routhier recalled:

Whitford had some kind of glass that he used to hold over the map and he could tell the height of the land and the muskeg spots. We tried to keep the trail on the highest land possible. We lived in a bunkhouse and moved it two or three miles every few days."[8]

Curlers get last laugh

In 1960, Fort McMurray's economy was so slow, first prize for the community's most prestigious curling bonspiel consisted of two gag prizes. However, as time marched forward, one of those prizes would eventually yield a remarkable return.

As organizers prepared for the 1961 Tar Sands Bonspiel, attempts were made to provide the eventual winners with an entertaining prize which could be acquired at a minimum cost. Community leader Bob Duncan decided to approach Mayor Jack Wagner with a unique idea.

Four lots, which sat in a flood area near Gordon Avenue and Main Street, would be awarded to winners. Wagner endorsed the idea realizing that the bonspiel winners would be forced to pay taxes on the vacant land.

After two days of fierce competition, the rink of Jackie Kreutzer, David Brooks, Stan Pawelek and Art Giroux emerged victorious. "We actually were given two prizes, " recalled Brooks. "We were each given a lot and a pee pot. For years we four had to pay one dollar each in taxes."[9]

However, as Fort McMurray's economy began to heat up, so did the value of land in the Gordon Avenue and Main Street area. In 1975, the four lots were sold to an apartment developer. The price each lot was sold for was twenty-two thousand dollars.

Legendary Curlers

It was an experience to watch Lawrence Tolen of Waterways and Hugh Stroud of McMurray curl against each other. It was not a matter of their curling ability but the length of time it took them to play the game.

Lawrence would lean on his broom while tapping the toe of his shoe on the ice and consider his options over and over again. Finally, he would tighten up his lips, nod his head, and go to the other end to throw his rock.

Hugh would look over the house, debate which shot to make, then gradually back up to the hog line, then slowly walk back to the house to check how the rocks were lined up. This would go on for awhile and then he would slowly walk to the other end to throw his rock.

The problems came for other curlers. Tolen and Stroud curled the seven o'clock game. The nine o'clock curlers knew they'd have a late night.

Haxton traditions

When Alex and Alice Haxton bought Hanson's Store in 1960, they inherited a Fort McMurray tradition, and launched a few of their own.

Alex Haxton arrived in Fort McMurray in 1957 as manager of the downtown Hudson's Bay Store. From its location at Morrison Street and Franklin Avenue, the Hudson's Bay sold food, trappers' supplies, fresh meat, hardware and clothing. The Bay also continued a two hundred-year tradition, buying furs from local trappers and shipping them to markets in western Canada. As Hudson's Bay Store manager, Haxton learned valuable skills about buying furs which came in handy in 1960 when he and wife Alice bought Hanson's Store which had originally been built in the early 1920s by Sam Kushner.

"When we bought the Hanson's Store, there was still merchandise left from 1922,"[10] recalled Alice Haxton. Half of the store consisted of groceries, meat, and a walk-in cooler, while the other side was devoted to hardware and clothing. While the Haxtons continued selling dry goods, clothing and trappers supplies, they also introduced an important change for shoppers. Previously, general stores in Fort McMurray required that customers line up at a counter and wait for items plucked by clerks from store shelves. Haxtons changed that. Customers could now go through the store and gather their own items.

Alex Haxton quickly put his buying skills to good use and was soon able to out-bid the Hudson's Bay for local trappers' furs. Haxton made his store a one stop shop for local natives offering basic items such as snare wire, traps and bush foods such as flour, lard, tea, jam and sugar. Around Christmas, Fort McMurray and Fort McKay trappers would park their dog sleds on Franklin Avenue, sell their furs, and purchase their holiday presents.

"Everyone came in at Christmas," recalled Haxton. "They would sell furs and buy things, and then kept coming back as they thought of other things. They did-n't make shopping lists like people do today. Books were kept on what they owed, and we never thought about not trusting them. People eventually paid."[11]

The policy of trust which the Kuschners and Hansons began was maintained by the Haxtons. For example when forest fires broke out north of Fort McMurray, firefighters arrived with paycheques to cash, requesting an advance on their money. The store was trusted to keep the rest of the cheque until the firefighter's return, and would keep detailed books in the back office. Alex Haxton died in 1973, and within a few months, Alice, who had been originally trained as a book-keeper and an agricultural seed analyst, quickly became a fur expert.

During the 1960s, despite the fact that shopping centres and chain stores sprung up around them, Haxton's Store remained a Fort McMurray institution. However, on Christmas Eve, 1979, a lit cigarette ignited a macramé hanging, and within a few minutes, Haxton's store was destroyed. Longtime employees Charlotte Mitchell and Gerry Furber escaped out the front door, but for many nervous minutes, Alice Haxton could not be located.

Haxton had run into the back office and retrieved the box of accounts owing, and had slipped out the back door to safety.

The Paris Connection

Long before the days when Fort McMurray exported petroleum outside of Alberta, it was sending an important oil product to international markets.

While native men would usually set traps and catch fur-bearing animals, women would often skin, clean, cook, tan and otherwise prepare animals for sale. Often the pay received from their husbands consisted of beaver castors that Haxton's, Hudson's Bay and other stores would cash for women to spend as "pin money." At the back of Haxton's Store were jars of castors which were later sold to the Hudson's Bay, and then shipped to Vancouver.

From the west coast, the castors were sent to factories around the world and used in the highest quality perfumes. In those days, ingredients were not listed on expensive fragrances. Had they been, many women would have noticed that their perfume had been manufactured from musk squeezed from castors, otherwise known as beaver testicles.

Haxton's phone book

Romeo Eymundson's phone monopoly in McMurray came to an end in 1958 when Alberta Government Telephones (AGT) moved in with a full dial and long distance service. There were initially only a handful of phones in the community, but by the early 1960s, there were hundreds. One day, Alice Haxton had an idea.

It was a local Christmas tradition that businesses hand out calendars, thermometers, blotters, pens and other trinkets to their customers. During the days when Fort McMurray's white page phone listings were mixed with those from Lac La Biche, St. Paul, Athabasca and other locations, the Haxtons received special permission from AGT to publish a dedicated Fort McMurray phone book. At first, the directory consisted of a one sided card. Soon, there were two sides, and eventually dozens of pages.

In the beginning, since there was only one phone prefix, 743, only four numbers were listed next to each name. Usually the four final numbers began with a two or three and until the early 1970s, residents could make a local call by dialing these four numbers. The Haxton's phone book remained a Fort McMurray tradition until the late 1970s when the town's population swelled to about twenty-six thousand. Each year, the Haxtons printed one thousand copies and in 1978, its last year of publication, the book was snapped up for nostalgic reasons, and remains a valued collector's item within the community.

Alice Haxton remains proud of one achievement. The phone book was produced as a pure community service, and despite requests from local businesses, no paid ad ever appeared.

Dim Silin stories

When longtime Fort McMurray residents recall "characters" of the 1960s, the name Dimitri Silin immediately comes to mind. Silin was a man of Russian aristocratic descent who came to Canada in the early 1920s after escaping the Russian Revolution. It was said that he and his brother fled Russia steps ahead of sword-wielding Bolshevik soldiers. Although Russian was Silin's first language, he fluently spoke four other languages,, including "the King's" English.

To say Silin was an "original" is an understatement. In the early 1950s, he and his family came to Fort McMurray and purchased a three hundred and forty acre parcel of land which extended from the west bank of the Athabasca River near the current water treatment plant, up into Thickwood Heights.

Soon after his arrival , Silin began life as a trapper and earned additional revenue selling wood. His family remained at home in McMurray while Silin lived with his dogs and horses on the west bank of the Athabasca River. Residents became used to seeing him wearing his black "foreign legion" style hat with flaps running down his cheeks. Although the hat was worn to protect his sun-sensitive skin, it gave him the appearance of a mysterious foreigner, a role Silin played to the hilt. With his dark clothing and accent, he appeared in the community as a fairy tale woodsman as he delivered cords of wood to his customers.

"My dad could be difficult and demanding," recalled daughter Ruth Schiltroth. "He wanted people to live up to his expectations."[12] His daughter recalled that one of the reasons he trapped on the west side of the Athabasca River is that he would go stir crazy if he remained in town too long.

Here are some of the stories which longtime residents tell as they fondly remember Dim Silin.

* * *

Silin did not have a great love for developers or oil companies.

One day, Silin noticed a truck pull up on his property. A well-dressed man exited the vehicle and began walking across his land. Silin's dogs, seeing the stranger, ran up to him barking. The man kicked one of the dogs away, and identified himself as a representative of an American oil company. Silin explained to him that oil companies were required to pay easement rights before proceeding across his land and reminded the man that he had not received recent payment from his paricular company. Silin also warned the man to never touch one of his dogs. Silin was famous for the way in which he loved and trained his dogs. With subtle commands his dogs performed a variety of duties, such as closing his cabin door.

The oil employee shrugged his shoulders and continued walking across Silin's land, explaining that he needed access, and that he had come a long distance to study oil deposits.

Silin went into his cabin and returned with a shotgun. The oilman turned around in time to see Silin take aim at his truck. First the headlights were shattered then the windshield and finally, the man's four tires were flattened. The oilman dashed off Silin's property and later sent a tow truck to retrieve his vehicle.

Later that week, Silin received a special delivery envelope from the oil company containing a few hundred dollars in overdue easement fees.

* * *

There are two Silin drinking stories which are told by locals. Although Silin rarely drank, when he did, the results were memorable. On one occasion, Silin rode into town on the back of Spider, his big gray horse, and began shooting his gun in the air John Wayne style. Silin rode off down Franklin Avenue before the RCMP arrived, or any damage was done.

On another occasion, Silin walked into the Oilsands Hotel, consumed a large quantity of beer and then flopped in the cart behind his horse team. Without a rider, his horses, Spider, Dick and Molly, pulled the cart containing Silin across the Athabasca River stopping in front of his cabin.

Silin woke up a few feet from his home.

* * *

Town Board minutes show that on July 15, 1965, Dim Silin was hired as Fort McMurray's dogcatcher. He was promised one hundred dollars per month, plus five dollars per dog destroyed, and one half of the revenue from the dog licenses he could sell.

Following his appointment, Silin attended a subsequent Town Board meeting. Board member John Polonuk noticed Silin's arms had been severely chewed by a dog, and ask him what had happened. Silin replied that he had grabbed a wild dog that had resisted capture. Polonuk asked why Silin didn't let the dog go. "I didn't want to lose the five dollars,"[13] replied Silin.

* * *

Silin was a very well read man who was a frequent patron of the Fort McMurray library. It is said that during the summer months, he would borrow hard cover books, and during the winter he would checkout soft cover novels. He explained that was due to the soot in the cabin during winters, he didn't want to dirty any of the library's better books.

Silin's cabin was a popular meeting place for some of Fort McMurray's teenagers who would gather to hear Silin's stories about trapping and the old country. One day in 1968 as Mark Jean and Steven Anderson sat at his table drinking tea,, Silin folded over and died of a sudden heart attack.

Silin was best remembered by his daughter Ruth as a Santa like figure who would always come across the Athabasca River on Christmas Eve with his dogs and holiday presents.

"He was like this mystical figure who we didn't always see a lot of, but who would appear on Christmas to be with us," she recalled. "It was like he was from another world."[14]

Kennedy and Getty come to town

If you wanted to know if anyone interesting had landed in Fort McMurray during the mid 1960s, you just had to ask Fred or Olive Woodward.

From 1964-1979, the Woodwards operated the Avis franchise at the Fort McMurray Airport. By keeping track of who was renting vehicles, the Woodwards could provide a reliable indicator of which segments of the economy were most active. The couple also felt a responsibility to be Fort McMurray ambassadors to those arriving.

"We felt it was important for us to make a good impression for people arriving," recalled Olive Woodward. "How they were treated we realized would say a lot about the community."[15]

That sentiment would never be felt more strongly than on September 30, 1967, the day that GCOS officially opened. The Woodwards ordered two trailers of additional rental cars, and as the private planes began arriving at six a.m., cars were driven out to the tarmac, and dignitaries loaded in. That day, their customers came from across Canada, the United States and Europe.

"We had men in uniforms standing by the planes to hand the keys to the incoming visitors," Olive Woodward recalled. "It was pouring rain, but luckily Fred had the foresight to order five hundred disposable rain coats so we handed four to the driver of every car."[16]

Later in the 1960s, the Woodwards rented vehicles to a number of high profile personalities. One of Avis' more important clients was an American promotions company which shuttled VIPs to a northern Saskatchewan fishing resort which was accessible only by airplane. One day, a plane landed at Fort McMurray which attracted considerable attention. A representative of the promotions company came into the airport and signed for a vehicle to drive to the Snye floatplane base. As Woodward would later find out, one of the passengers in the vehicle was United States Attorney General, Robert F. Kennedy. Other promotion trips would include a number of American astronauts.

However, Woodward's most prestigious customers appeared in Fort McMurray just after the opening of GCOS. As Woodward recalled:

I asked the man whether he had a letter of introduction to GCOS because it was known that no one got into GCOS without a letter. He said to me "young lady, I don't need a letter of introduction." When he returned he noticed me looking at his plane and asked me whether I wanted to look inside. The inside was the most beautiful I had ever seen covered in leather like you would see on the inside of a gun case[17].

Woodward never realized who the man was until two weeks later when she read a copy of the Edmonton Journal which had a picture of J. Paul Getty, titled "the richest man in the world."

"He was just a short little man," Woodward recalled. "I had no idea who he was."[18]

George and the bear

In spite of the fact that black bears inhabit the forest which surrounds Fort McMurray, recorded cases of bear attacks are quite rare. Black bears have been know to maul humans only when there is perceived danger to a cub, or when the animal is in pain.

However in 1963, Fort McMurray experienced a bear attack that involved George Sanderson, one of the community's most knowledgeable hunters and trappers. Late one afternoon, Sanderson remembered that he had left his rifle in his trapper's cabin located at the junction of the Horse and Athabasca rivers. Years earlier, Sanderson lost his leg when Hugh Stroud accidentally shot him during a hunting trip. Sanderson was determined that the same would not happen to a child wandering near his cabin.

Sanderson walked on crutches from his home between Saunderson Avenue and Highway 63 to an area beyond Abasand and retrieved his rifle. As he climbed the hill to Abasand he came face to face with an angry black bear. The bear immediately knocked Sanderson down and began gnawing on his leg. Sanderson grabbed the bear's tongue and held it while hitting it over the head with his rifle. Eventually, the bear fell back unconscious.

Because the black bear was lying on top of his crutches, Sanderson cut a stick from a willow, hobbled up the hill and then down to Highway 63. Sanderson was in pain and covered in blood, but made it home. George's wife Katie called cab driver Frank Leitner who rushed Sanderson to hospital.

News of the attack spread quickly. Father Bern Brown, the Catholic priest, located the bear near the Horse River hill and shot it. Brown said the bear was regaining consciousness when he reached it about an hour after the attack. When the bear was skinned Brown found buckshot in his back leg from a previous wound. That explained the bear's uncharacteristically nasty disposition.

Sanderson remained in hospital for about a week, and when he was discharged was given some of the bear's teeth as a souvenir.

Farewell to the outhouse

The battle over water and sewer service divided Fort McMurray in 1962. Three years earlier, an engineering firm had examined the feasibility of installing a municipal water and sewer system in McMurray and Waterways. Due to opposition of some taxpayers, town council shelved the 1959 report.

Residents appeared to be content with the existing system of wells and watermen. Once or twice a week, residents would pay a water delivery man to fill up their barrels.

In 1962, a petition was circulated demanding that a water and sewer system be installed. There were divisions in the community. The supporting side believed that with GCOS approaching and thousands of new residents expected, it was time to tear down the town's outhouses, and develop a more sophisticated water and sewer system.

However, a number of business leaders, particularly those who owned property on Franklin Avenue, remained concerned that frontage and usage taxes would cause an unfair financial burden. At times, the debate took on a carnival atmosphere as Bob Duncan and Claire Peden attached an outhouse and a toilet on a flatbed truck, and rumbled down Franklin Avenue asking residents to compare the comforts of current and future options.

In 1963, council approved a two hundred and fifty-eight thousand dollar loan for a water and sewer system to serve both McMurray and Waterways. Construction began in the spring and on November 1, 1963 a ceremony was held in front of Peter Pond School on Franklin Avenue.

With local and provincial dignitaries in attendance, a fire hydrant was turned on, and the streets and sidewalks were sprayed with fresh running water. The honor of turning on the hydrant was given to the deputy minister of health, Dr. Malcolm "Mac" McCallum who had served as Fort McMurray's doctor from 1934-39.

The New Town of Fort McMurray

By 1962, it became apparent that McMurray was on the road to unparalleled economic growth. However, town council and the Chamber of Commerce quickly realized that a population of barely twelve hundred could not finance Fort McMurray's anticipated expansion. New subdivisions and municipal services would have to be built to weather the incoming boom.

On June 11, 1962, the Chamber of Commerce sent a letter to the town council recommending that the word "Fort" be added to the town's official name. The council decided to seek New Town status from the Province of Alberta. Under New Town status, the Province would effectively assume control of the community, approving loans, schools, roads and other important services without having to lean too heavily on local home and business owners.

The name Fort McMurray was re-established, thus linking the community with John Moberly who almost one hundred years earlier had chosen that name for his original Hudson's Bay Company outpost.

New Town status would also shift ultimate management of the community to the Alberta cabinet, whose members had both the ability and power to cut lengthy bureaucratic delays, and enable McMurray to keep pace with the massive growth it was about to experience.

While the Province mulled over the request, a major event in 1963 helped tip the scales. In April, hours after the breakup of the Athabasca River, an ice jam formed at the junction of the Snye, backing waters into Waterways, the Prairie and parts of the lower townsite. Town council remained convinced that provincial intervention was necessary to help protect the community from future flooding. As well, the Canadian Mortgage and Housing Corporation (CMHC) announced that it would not approve mortgages in the lower townsite unless a dyke or other preventative structure was built.

In 1964, the Province approved New Town status, bringing to an end sixteen years of local government. The province also decreed that no housing development could take place in the lower townsite north of Franklin Avenue, with the exception of the general area surrounding Manning and Fraser Avenues, and Hill Drive. According to the terms of the New Town Act, town council was replaced by a three person board of administrators led by former mayor Claire Peden, Municipal Affairs official Bill Isbister and Provincial Planning Board secretary John Polonuk. The Alberta government also announced an expansion of Fort McMurray's municipal boundaries. MacDonald Island and most of what would later be known as Beacon Hill and Abasand Heights were annexed.

The Manning government also mandated that a dyke be built where the Snye met the Athabasca River. The dyke would also provide road access to MacDonald Island, while minimizing damage created by future flooding. Planners believed that if the Snye were cut off from the Athabasca River, any future ice jam would occur at a location three feet lower, downstream at the junction of Athabasca and Clearwater rivers. This in turn would cause a drop in flood levels, and would provide some protection to Waterways, the Prairie and the lower townsite.

The dyke decision infuriated Mayor Claire Peden. He predicted that the Snye, a key recreation area and landing strip for sea and ski planes, would dry up and become a pasture. In response, engineers agreed to install a larger culvert through the dyke which would allow for additional water flow. Peden predicted that this culvert would quickly become plugged, and continued his opposition to the plan. Peden quickly learned that under New Town status, while the Province would entertain opinions from local residents, its decisions were final. The Snye dyke was approved and over time, Peden's predictions proved correct. To this day, while small aircraft continue to land at the Snye, parts of the former wetland have dried up and have become a natural habitat to birds, small animals and other dry land wildlife.

Claire Peden complained that the dyke was launched as a make work project for engineers and consultants, and until his death in 1995 continued to refer to the engineering company which designed it, Stanley, Grimble and Roblin, as "Stab 'em, Grab 'em, and Rob 'em."[19]

Until July 1, 1980, Fort McMurray remained a New Town, administered by a Board of Administrators under the watchful eye of the Province of Alberta.

The rise of GCOS

In December 1962, Canadian Bechtel began developing a test plant that would serve as a prototype for future GCOS operations. Bechtel would be required to integrate mining, extraction, refining, movement of materials and employee housing and each component would require precision and a variety of logistical challenges. Bechtel operated the test plant from late 1963 to 1965, and this enabled GCOS to examine how Karl Clark and Sidney Ells' small-scale concepts would work within a more massive context.

Based on the lessons learned operating the Canadian Bechtel test plant, GCOS and its major backer, Sun Oil, appeared ready to proceed. On July 2, 1964, exactly one year after J. Howard Pew's historic visit, Premier Ernest Manning, along with a stream of officials from the Province, Canadian Bechtel, Sun Oil, GCOS, Mannix and others descended on Tar Island and planted a post, Datum Point, establishing Datum Point which would be considered "ground zero" for future GCOS construction.

Dr. Karl Clark, the great oilsands pioneer was hired as a consultant and until his death in 1966 provided both technical and moral encouragement. As Vern Hyatt, one of Bechtel's top managers recalled, "it was Clark who had done all of the work on a smaller scale. We increased the numbers, but in the end Clark, Ells and Fitzsimmons were right."[20]

In the fall of 1964 construction began on both the GCOS camp and plant site. Considerable site draining was required to provide a stable foundation for all building and plant components. As well, a dyke had to be constructed to support a tailings pond, which would contain waste products left behind by the oil production process.

In the fall of 1965, construction of a two hundred and sixty-six-mile pipeline began and was completed about one year later. The pipeline was designed to carry GCOS' licensed load of forty-five thousand barrels a day to refineries in Edmonton, where it linked up with the national pipeline which brought the Fort McMurray product to Sarnia refineries.

During the summer of 1966, two signature pieces of equipment arrived from Germany. Hundreds of employees were involved in assembling two bucketwheels each priced at over four million dollars. When assembled, the bucketwheels stood more than one hundred feet high. Transferring them across Canada required a forty-car train.

Library launched

Soon after her arrival in Fort McMurray in 1958, Fern (Ulmer) Brooks expressed concern about a lack of books in the community. As a teacher, she noticed that school shelves were nearly bare.

However, that situation changed in 1964 as news arrived that a large of number of books were available from the defunct Gunner Mines in northwestern Saskatchewan. In October 1964, the town made its play. Council agreed to purchase two thousand books from Gunner Mines at a cost of about two thousand dollars. The collection consisted of paperbacks, classics and contemporary books which arrived in Fort McMurray in late 1964.

The town asked the Waterways Women's Community Club to launch a library and provide volunteers to staff it. Fern Brooks was first in line.

Brooks may have had her books, but she did not have a location. She approached Town Council who informed her that the only place available was a corner of the municipal garage, roughly located where the Fort McMurray city hall stands today. A partition was set up between the heavy equipment and the library book. Brooks was hired as the town's first librarian, at a rate of one dollar per hour. The library would be open for three hours on Saturday mornings and for two hours on Thursday evenings. At the time, it seemed like a good arrangement, however, as Brooks recalled, a number of challenges emerged. "There was no heat in the building so at minus forty we had to wear gloves to stay warm. Also the partition did not completely enclose the library so fumes from the municipal vehicles would travel over."[21]

Despite the fact that Brooks was only paid for five hours a week, she worked countless hours cataloguing and shelving the books.

The new library was also boosted by the fund raising efforts of the Bechtel women, a group composed of wives of workers brought in to build GCOS. During Christmas 1967, a fair was held at the Peter Pond School which involved the sale of crafts and baked goods. Proceeds went to buy new library books.

During the next ten years, the Fort McMurray library moved to the Peter Pond Shopping Centre, back to the town office, to the Jean Building and then to the Caledonia Building just east of Haxton's Store. Brooks remained town librarian until the late 1970s when a new and permanent facility was built on Franklin Avenue as part of Fort McMurray's new city hall.

"It was a labour of insanity," she recalled. "I just loved books and it had always been a challenge for me to get them for myself and for anyone else. I saw starting a new library as a great opportunity to do just that."[22]

Bank with a back door

Think of a time long before automatic tellers, when you could knock on your banker's door at midnight and cash a twenty-dollar cheque. Now you have an idea of how in 1964, Art Avery and the Bank of Nova Scotia launched service in Fort McMurray.

Avery and wife Sylvia arrived in June to manage Fort McMurray's second bank. The Bank of Nova Scotia was the official financial institution of Toronto-based GCOS, and bank executives believed a local presence should be established. The branch launched operations in March 1964 with a senior clerk, John Jablonkay;, who conducted business from World War I pilot Wop May's old residence located near the corner of Morrison Street and Franklin Avenue.

Soon after, the bank purchased a doublewide trailer that was located on Franklin Avenue near the southeast corner of Morrison Street. When Avery arrived in June to manage the bank, he was advised that his furniture was delayed in transit, so his first night in Fort McMurray was spent in blankets curled up on the floor. Eventually, when their possessions arrived, Art and Sylvia Avery lived in half of the trailer, while conducting business on the other side.

In a community which since the 1920s had been used to dealing solely with the

Royal Bank of Canada, Avery had to travel the extra mile to attract customers. For many clients, that meant providing service which went far beyond today's limited hours of operation. In particular, when the Saturday evening Pacific Western Airlines plane arrived late, it was common for workers to appear at the Avery residence at midnight requesting banking services. As Avery recalled:

It was not uncommon for someone to knock at the back door at midnight and ask us to cash twenty dollars of a cheque and deposit the rest to their account. Even when I was not there, Sylvia would give them the money. We could do this because after awhile we began to know all of the people whether they were workers from out of town with a GCOS cheque or people coming in from Fort Chipewyan. When you think of it, that was real service, but it was also the way that business was conducted in those days[23].

Within months, through strong customer service, Avery and his new branch had attracted hundreds of clients and a respectable market share within Fort McMurray.

CIBC arrives

The Canadian Imperial Bank of Commerce was the next financial institution to come. Manager Fred Schindel was transferred from Fort Nelson, British Columbia, and soon learned that this assignment would be like no other in his career.

Three days before the branch was scheduled to open, Schindel and his teller/accountant Jorden Sviestrup were called to the CIBC's Calgary office and handed a bundle of twenties, tens, fives and ones along with a few rolls of quarters, dimes, nickels and pennies. The cash was packed in a briefcase and the two employees were sent north. Revolvers were issued to each.

Upon his arrival, Schindel learned that although a small singlewide trailer had been shipped north aboard Northern Alberta Railways to house the branch, a place for it had yet to be located. Schindel immediately met with druggist Walter Hill who agreed to rent the lot next to Hill Drugs for fifty dollars per month.

On May 16, local cab driver and entrepreneur Ken Cochrane moved the trailer to Franklin Avenue and within two days the bank was open for business. Schindel recalled the bank's first day.

We were able to hold three customers at one time and that was not a very confidential banking situation. We had one cash drawer and about two shelves underneath the counter to store all of the stationery. As a result the stationery would be up in the bedroom under one of the bunk beds in boxes and it came to good use with the bad back that I had as it supported my mattress. The first day of operation was on the 17th or 18th of May. Mayor Claire Peden was the only one that came in and welcomed us to town…..The first bank account was opened by Jorgen Sviestrup, my teller/accountant. He had account #1 and I took account #2[24].

The first few months of CIBC operations were so slow that it was common for customers to walk in and observe Schindel and Sviestrup locked in a game of chess. Sometimes, the bank safe was not opened for a week at a time, because, as Schindel recalled, "no one came in to do any business."[25]

The turnaround for the CIBC came in 1965 when three hundred Mannix Construction workers arrived to build the Athabasca River bridge. The bank trailer was temporarily moved next to the new Peter Pond Hotel and this proved to be a boon, as Mannix workers raced in to cash their paychecks en route to the bar.

In 1966, a new branch was opened in the Peter Pond Shopping Centre and within a few weeks the bank had attracted almost four hundred accounts.

Bridge across the Athabasca

The GCOS plant may have been approved and its financing in place, but some basic logistic problems remained. How would workers be transported from Fort McMurray to the GCOS plant site?

While engineers began designing a bridge across the Athabasca River, local entrepreneurs took advantage of business opportunities. George Caouette operated a barge and tugboat service that carried equipment and passengers between the Fort McMurray townsite and the west side of the Athabasca River. One of the tugs that carried passengers across the river was operated by Pat Shott, a descendent of Shott Fosseneuve, who piloted the first river craft down the Athabasca Rapids en route to Fort McMurray.

In the spring of 1964 work began on a bridge to permit Highway 63 to extend across the Athabasca River north towards Tar Island. It was a massive project that involved more than three hundred workers. Work included widening the highway on the west side of the Athabasca River from Fort McMurray to GCOS.

The contract to build the bridge was awarded to Mannix Construction which began the project by building cofferdams on the west bank of the Athabasca River. The dams rerouted the Athabasca allowing crews to construct the bridge foundation. Once the piers were completed on the west side, work shifted to the east bank of the Athabasca River. Due to high waters, the section in the middle of the river required some time to build, but eventually, in the spring of 1965, all bridge components were connected.

On July 1, 1965 the Honourable Gordon Taylor, Minister of Highways, arrived in McMurray and officially cut the ribbon to the bridge. In 1972 the bridge was named in honour of Lieutenant Governor Grant MacEwan, who for a number of years walked the twenty miles from GCOS to town in the Cosmopolitan Club's charity walkathon. At a ceremony in front of the town offices, Reg Humphries, vice-president of GCOS, unveiled a plaque that confirmed the bridge's official name.

The "real" bridge opening

Official records show that the bridge over the Athabasca opened on July 1, 1965, but in local legend, the actual christening took place a few hours earlier.

At about three a.m. that day, a number of young men gathered on the Fort McMurray side of the bridge, and decided to race Terry Street's 1958 Chevrolet station wagon. The car was extremely hot, built by master mechanic Tom Weber, and powered by a 348 engine. As Street revved his engine, he was primed for a lightening fast sprint across the new bridge.

Street carefully unhooked a metal line which blocked the bridge from traffic, popped the car in gear and floored the gas pedal. Street's friends hooted as the station wagon tore across the virgin pavement, until one unfortunate event abruptly ended his streak .

Unknown to Street and his friends, a similar metal line had also been placed at the structure's western end. At lightning speed, Street's vehicle slammed into the wire which seared through the vehicle's hood just above the headlights. Street slammed into the dashboard, but survived with no injuries.

Unfortunately his car and the bridge guardrail were not as lucky. At about four a.m., Street came knocking at Weber's door. Tom was an expert mechanic, the son of Don Weber, who owned a garage on Biggs Avenue where the Twin Pines Motel stands today. Weber quickly repaired the car, so no one could place the Chevrolet at the scene of the accident. The next day, as dignitaries arrived to open the bridge, few noticed that the guardrail on the bridge's western edge had been twisted and pulled up.

Alberta Transportation crews arrived soon after and repaired the damage. Officials always wondered what had happened to the guardrail and the truth remained a closely guarded secret among Fort McMurray's dragsters.

Until now.

Once the bridge officially opened, it became the town's late night racetrack. A quarter mile length was marked off, and on many Friday and Saturday nights, while most Fort McMurray citizens slept and the local police were occupied elsewhere, the town's hottest cars raced along the bridge.

"It was the only paved spot in town so it made for a good drag strip,"[26] recalled Weber, who went on to become Fort McMurray's fire chief.

Diversified convoy

There is no sight more familiar to McMurrayites than that ribbon of red Diversified Transportation buses rolling each afternoon in perfect precision along Highway 63.

In 1965, when GCOS began operation, Edmonton based Diversified Rentals was called upon to provide buses to shuttle workers to the plant. At the time, the

Athabasca River bridge was under construction, so buses would pick up and drop off workers at the west bank of the Athabasca River and from there, most workers would take Caouette's ferry across the river to the lower townsite. Some with more nerve would walk across the beams of the half complete bridge, high above the river's rapid current.

In 1965, ten buses were pressed into service. They were yellow school buses produced between 1948 and 1954, and were no match for the gravel roads, and the brutal cold. Diversified buses used during the mid-1960s were nicknamed "ice boxes." Small heaters located at the rear of each blew in futility as temperatures often plunged below minus forty degrees.

Orest the weatherman

In 1968, Allan Askeland was brought north by Diversified from Wetaskiwin where he had gained a reputation as an excellent welder and ace stock car mechanic. Askeland, who eventually became Diversified's local manager, recalled how Fort McMurray's bone chilling temperatures affected bus operations.

Orest Bodnarchuk, who ran the Esso bulk station near the Clearwater River, was known as the local weatherman. He had four thermometers scattered across the station. One night in January 1968, the mercury plunged below minus sixty, and did not come out of the bulb for four days.

Diversified left its buses running all night, but in the morning one vehicle could not be moved. The wheel grease had frozen solid. A second bus was called into service and "skidded" the first bus down Fraser Avenue for three blocks before the wheels unlocked.

How cold was it (really)?

For years, Bodnarchuk's Esso Bulk Station, located on King Street near the Clearwater River, was recognized as the coldest spot in Fort McMurray. Many mornings, Bodnarchuk would receive phone calls - not from businesses requesting fuel, but from residents asking how cold it was. Consistently, Bodnarchuk's thermometers registered colder than anywhere else in town. It was thought at the time that this was due to the fact that the Esso Bulk Station was located on low land near the river.

Bodnarchuk's status as the coldest spot in town was never challenged until one day, tired of the constant phone calls, he had his thermometers tested. Bodnarchuk learned that on average his thermometers registered ten degrees colder than the actual temperature. This was due to a defective batch of thermometers purchased by the business' previous owner. Bodnarchuk replaced the defective thermometers, and soon after, temperature readings at the end of King Street returned to normal. Bodnarchuk ceased being the town's weatherman, and focused his complete attention on selling fuel.

Claire's Peden's famous barbecue

One of Fort McMurray's great traditions during the GCOS construction boom was Claire Peden's annual barbecue. Each year Fort McMurray's top elected official would transport residents across the Clearwater River aboard NTCL barges and would entertain them on land he owned at the junction of the Athabasca River. The event was often held in cooperation with the Fort McMurray Chamber of Commerce.

Peden and Archie Brooks would roast a hip of beef in a gunny sack and let it cook for hours. Hundreds of local residents would travel across the river to enjoy the food, the beer and the camaraderie. Popularity of the barbecue peaked in 1966 when Premier Ernest Manning, along with a number of other political figures, attended the event. However, Peden scaled down the barbecue during the late 1960s after a number of drunken revelers while returning home fell off the barges.

Peden resigns

On October 19, 1965, Claire Peden resigned as chairman of the Town Board of Administrators. Although no reason was ever provided, it is believed that Peden had become increasingly frustrated over the lack of local autonomy during a period when the Province made most major decisions.

Although it was the Province's responsibility to name a successor, provision was made to allow local residents to suggest Peden's successor. A public meeting was held and three local businessmen were nominated including H.A. (Mac) McCormick, Al Campbell and Robert Chase. A majority supported McCormick who on November 30, 1965 was officially named Town Board Chairman.

At that same time, the Province decided that a three person Town Board of Administrators with two Edmonton-based members was not responsive enough to local needs. It expanded the Board to five members and included Gordon Munro, a manager from GCOS and Lewis Babcock, local provincial superintendent of lands and forests.

"Mac" McCormick

Henry "Mac" McCormick was a man of stature. Almost a half-century later, the man who succeeded Claire Peden as Town Board Chairman would be compared to Eric Newell, Syncrude's future president.

McCormack, who served as Fort McMurray's Town Board Chair until 1968, gained local respect for his community involvement and for his low key approach to leading the Town Board of Administrators. He was also active in the Chamber of Commerce, and both the Waterways and McMurray Anglican churches.

During the 1950s, often regarded as Fort McMurray's "poor" years, the McCormicks were seen as one of the town's more prosperous and well-respected families. They lived on "Prestige Hill" in a cluster of homes owned by prominent residents on Cliff Avenue in Waterways, overlooking the Clearwater River. McCormack originally came to Waterways in 1934 where he helped build the salt plant. In 1953, McCormack acquired the Imperial Oil bulk plant

In 1965, McCormick took the helm of the Town Board of Administrators providing it with a more low key, less confrontational approach than Claire Peden often offered.

"He saw getting into politics as his civic duty,"[27] recalled his daughter Elizabeth McCormick.

Watching the fights

Fort McMurray had never seen anything like it. At the height of the GCOS construction, twenty-five hundred workers were housed in on-site trailers while hundreds more remained in town.

This crush of transient workers created considerable strain on Fort McMurray law enforcement, which had been previously staffed to handle the needs of a population of about fifteen hundred. Construction workers adopted a "work hard, play hard attitude," and often this philosophy spilled into the downtown streets. During the mid-1960s, Fort McMurray was predominantly a male community with hundreds of workers converging on the town's major watering holes, the Oilsands Hotel, the Peter Pond Hotel and the Riviera Motel.

Some women recall being harassed during the day in parking lots or at bars, but for the most part, law and order was preserved. However, at night, Fort McMurray bars and the adjoining parking lots and sidewalks became the central area for brawls and other fisticuffs..

On weekend nights, RCMP were often scooping drunk and disorderly transients workers from the streets, throwing them into jail cells. Fort McMurray's longtime residents, who had been used to quiet and orderly streets watched with amazement.

During the days before radio and television, many Fort McMurray residents used this flux of street activity as a form of entertainment. The hundreds of construction workers who descended upon the community nightly during the mid-1960s provided fodder for a new Fort McMurray recreational pastime.

"We'd pack some sandwiches and park in front of the Esso Station and watch the fights across the street,"[28] recalled Fern Brooks.

"Fighting every night outside the bar was new to us, and since there wasn't much else to do for entertainment at the time we sometimes just parked there, ate sandwiches and laughed. It was definitely more fun that driving to the dump to watch the bears."[29]

In fact, fight watching became such a McMurray institution during the late 1960s that specific locations for each vehicle were unofficially assigned at Ed O'Neill's Esso station.

"It was kind of like reserved seats at the hockey game," Brooks recalled. "And there would be trouble if you moved into someone else's stall."[30]

Bank holdup rumours

In 1966, the Royal Bank of Canada and the Canadian Imperial Bank of Commerce formed an important business partnership which involved four hundred thousand dollars, a bottle of rye, a case of beer and a number of guns which no one knew how to use.

With GCOS under construction, managers at both branches agreed to share a vehicle to cash cheques at the construction site. Every Thursday evening, the two managers ventured north accompanied by a number of tellers. Each manager would pack a briefcase full of cash. The CIBC manager would carry a hundred and fifty thousand dollars, while the Royal Bank of Canada would load two hundred and fifty.

"We would have four armed guards in the vehicles with us which were bank personnel that didn't know how to handle revolvers, but we still had the revolvers with us," recalled Commerce bank manager Fred Schindel. "We always had a bottle of rye and a case of beer in the back because it was a twenty-five mile trip home and very cold at times."[31]

In late 1966, the two bank managers were called into the RCMP office and informed of rumours which been circulating about an impending bank robbery somewhere in northern Alberta. It was felt that because of the huge amounts of money being carried and the long distances travelled without armed guards, the GCOS cheque cashing expedition was a prime target.

For a period of one month, an elaborate convoy was set up. A police car would lead a three-vehicle procession made up of a private vehicle containing the bank employees and the four hundred thousand dollars, followed by a pickup truck with a movie camera mounted at the rear.

A robbery did take place, but it was in Onoway, located just north of Edmonton. Following the robbery, security was relaxed. In his memoirs, Schindel recalled the frantic scene at GCOS as employees lined up to complete their banking.

"People complain about bank line ups now, they should have been here then because there were at least three hundred men lined up at each of the teller wickets waiting to cash their cheques. This went on for five hours straight. We would go through as many as four hundred money orders in an evening as well as probably fifty to one hundred international money orders in different currencies because there was a variety of foreign workers at the plant."[32]

GCOS's practice of paying employees on Thursdays also produced a special tradition. Fort McMurray businesses remained open late on Thursdays to accommodate cash rich residents. This was a tradition that was maintained until the late 1970s when GCOS altered its payment schedule, and Syncrude came on the scene wuth a different payroll scheme.

Self taught judge

On paper, Fort McMurray was a community of fifteen hundred but in reality it generated the crime of a town three times its size. During the GCOS startup, the RCMP was consumed with nighttime brawls, disputes and other alcohol related offenses. It soon became apparent that a travelling judge could not handle the load, so the Province looked south for help.

In Lethbridge they found a candidate in Harry Aime, who was willing to move north and preside over the Fort McMurray court. The problem was that Aime was not a judge. He was an RCMP sergeant who was regarded as being both dependable and fair. In the summer of 1965, Aime arrived in Fort McMurray to serve as the community's first fulltime magistrate. He immediately immersed himself in law books, and following years of study was subsequently appointed a provincial judge.

At the outset, Aime handled petty offenses, but as the community grew in size he began judging more complex cases including robberies, assaults, murders, and during the late 1970s, a complex environmental trial involving Suncor.

"In those days, magistrates didn't have to have a law degree," he recalled. "You had to rely on your street knowledge which as an RCMP officer I had a lot of. Before the boom there were a lot of limitations but socially everyone knew everybody. The boom changed all of that."[33]

Aime served on the bench until 1988 and retired in Fort McMurray where he remained active in the Anglican Church, the Chamber of Commerce and Rotary Club.

Fort McMurray General Hospital

A period of soul searching swept Fort McMurray after the approval by the Province of the GCOS project. Many organizations assessed whether they could meet the influx of new residents. Included in that group was St. Gabriel Hospital which had served the community since the late 1930s.

On January 22, 1964, Mayor Claire Peden received a letter from St. Gabriel Hospital administrator Father Jean Lesage, announcing that the Grey Nuns would not be expanding their hospital to meet the demands of future population growth. The letter stated:

The impending oil development in our area may bring to this town a large population: thence the need of better and larger hospital facilities. The St. Gabriel Hospital's authorities do not plan nor intend to provide such facilities[34].

The letter confirmed that the Grey Nuns, whose mission had always been to provide health service in frontier communities, felt it was time for Fort McMurray to be served by a full provincial hospital. Town council agreed and soon after approached the Alberta government. Construction of a new hospital began in 1965, and in the fall of 1966 Fort McMurray General Hospital opened with thirty-four beds. A pediatric wing was added in 1970 bringing the total number of beds to fifty-four.

The new hospital changed the face of medicine in Fort McMurray. Slowly, the Grey Nuns were replaced by a team of nurses brought in from outside the community. Betty Golosky came to Fort McMurray in 1961 as a nurse, worked through the transition, and served for a period as Director of Nursing.

The old hospital had community spirit. No one ever said, "that isn't my job." There wasn't a lot of equipment, but we made do. When the new hospital came there still was a sense of community and patients got good care, but when Sister Cardinal, the last nun, left I felt a sense of loss. Things became less personal, more businesslike[35].

As new residents began arriving in Fort McMurray, the practice of medicine changed. With the opening of Highway 63 in 1967, the hospital began receiving injuries and fatalities from high-speed motor vehicle collisions. "The nature of accidents and illness changed," Golosky recalled. "We had to remember things learned in training. We had to learn new skills from some of the new nurses and doctors."[36]

Golosky recalled fondly times spent at Chateau Gai, a log house owned by the church, just above of the intersection of Highway 63 and Morrison Street. Father Brown built the cabin as a retreat for the sisters when he served in McMurray in the late '50s. "It was a good retreat where we had great parties,"[37] she recalled.

During the late 1960s, St. Gabriel served as a convalescent home. It later was used by the town for office space, and eventually became the first home of the Fort McMurray YMCA. St. Gabriel Hospital was demolished during the winter of 1979.

Why Hospital Hill?

The site where Fort McMurray Regional Hospital is currently located was not the original choice of the Province of Alberta. The debate where to locate the hospital was directly linked to a dispute between the Chamber of Commerce, Mayor Claire Peden and the Province over tits plans to build the Snye dyke.

The Fort McMurray Chamber of Commerce and the Mayor opposed cutting off the Snye from the Athabasca River. They initiated a series of letters to the Province objecting to the project based on cost and its "questionable" purpose. A hospital site had been previously identified west of Hospital Street, just south of Franklin Avenue. However the area was deemed vulnerable to flooding. The Province was faced with conflicting pressures. While it understood the urgency of launching construction of a new hospital, it could not build in its designated low lying location until the Snye dyke was approved.

A second site was ultimately chosen on higher ground, just north of Fitzgerald Avenue. The land originally designated for the new hospital eventually became the Willow Square housing project.

McMurray's new hotel

Approval of GCOS provided a green light to developers. At the forefront was

Edmonton millionaire Dr. Charles Allard who in 1964 began construction of the Peter Pond Hotel.

The Oilsands Hotel was for years Fort McMurray's prime entertainment, eating and lodging address. The Riviera Motel followed offering a cabaret, live entertainment and a dance floor.

In 1964 the Peter Pond Hotel opened with rooms and restaurants, and rented space for a pharmacy to future Town Board Chairman Sam Hardin, and to Tip Hlushak who opened McMurray Hardware. The hotel also leased space to Ken Cochrane who operated the Greyhound bus station.

Blueberry Festival

In the days when fastball was Fort McMurray's most passionate summer activity, respecting the environment was not always a top priority . This was never truer than during the late 1960s when organizers of the Blueberry Festival took extraordinary steps to ensure that ball games proceeded on schedule.

The Blueberry Festival was launched in 1965 by the Kiwanis, and was handed off the following year to the newly formed Kinsmen Club. The festival was seen as a way to both raise charitable funds, and to provide a party for the community during the Labour Day weekend. The initial festival consisted of a midway, a parade and what would become into one of western Canada's richest and most competitive ball tournaments.

Teams would arrive in Fort McMurray from as far away as the Northwest Territories, Saskatchewan and Manitoba to compete for a first place purse of more than five thousand dollars. The Playboys and the Edmonton Police team were regular participants, along with local teams which included GCOS, the Riviera and McMurray Lynks.

"It was something for all members of the family," recalled charter Kinsman member Tip Hlushak. "The Edmonton Marching Band would lead the parade. We'd all dress up as clowns and join in. It was a way for the community to have a good party while raising money."[38]

However, while Fort McMurray's spirit of cooperation shone, often the weather did not. Frequently the skies opened during Blueberry Festival weekend. The Kinsmen employed some dubious techniques to ensure that the ball field, located near the current Keyano Theatre site, was dry and ready for play. As former Kinsman and ball fanatic Ernie Yurkiw recalled, "it always seemed to pour when the Blueberry Festival came around." Said Yurkiw. "I was lucky enough to have access to a front end loader and we would get sawdust and a few thousand gallons of fuel from Jim Mutton who ran the Shell bulk station, and then spread it over the water."[39]

The oil mixture would burn for a half-hour and this would dry the playing area. In most years, while the stench of oil hung over the field, the tournament would proceed. "You did all this with great community spirit," recalled Yurkiw. "You took it in stride just hoping to get a ball game in. This was a social activity."[40]

The Blueberry Festival tournament created some longstanding traditions. Librarian Fern Brooks would serve as scorekeeper and umpiring duties fell on Nick Humeniuk, whose skill was respected, and whose eyesight was rarely questioned. "This was superb ball which was made even better by the great umpiring of Nick Humeniuk," said Hlushak. "He was the closest thing to a professional umpire we ever had. His calls were always fair so players respected him."[41]

The Blueberry Festival remains one of Fort McMurray's premiere community events, and is currently run by an exhibition society.

GCOS officially opens

September 30, 1967 will be remembered as one of Fort McMurray's most historic days. That day, more than five hundred dignitaries from around the world arrived in Fort McMurray to officially open the GCOS plant.

The previous day, the skies had been clear, but just before six a.m., rain began to pour, and this turned the site into a quagmire. This did not dampen the spirits of those assembled including the Premier, a number of cabinet members, plus officials from United States, Germany and many other countries who had played a part in GCOS's planning and construction.

While the rains poured, officials proudly spoke about the achievement of building such a massive industrial project. They acknowledged the apparent victory of expanding the basic hot water system developed by Clark, Ells and Fitzsimmons, into a forty-five thousand barrel per day operation.

There were three important pioneers at the ceremony. On hand was Sydney Ells who fifty five years earlier had arrived in Fort McMurray and had mapped and experimented with the Athabasca oil sands deposit. Also in attendance was Dora Clark, the widow of Dr. Karl Clark, who passed away the previous year.

The final speaker was J. Howard Pew who stood proudly surrounded by the massive structures which he had envisioned four years earlier. At eighty-five, Pew had been willing to risk his personal fortune and the future of Sun Oil on an untried technology. It could be argued that projects such as Syncrude Canada Ltd. and others would not have been possible without Pew's daring business decision.

While GCOS struggled with production problems, fires and other difficulties during the 1960s and early 1970s, Syncrude was able to build on these lessons, and moved into production during the late 1970s with a minimum of technological problems.

At the end of that historic day in 1967, dignitaries returned to the Fort McMurray airport, boarded their private jets and returned home. They left behind hundreds of GCOS employees who would be forced to overcome brutally harsh weather and technology that made sense on paper which had not been tested over a sustained period of time. There would be times when those dedicated GCOS workers and management would be brought to their knees.

Eventually, the faith of J. Howard Pew and the work and imagination of GCOS staff and management would be redeemed. Not only did GCOS pioneer the future of oil sands production for its own shareholders it also set the world stage for future development of non-conventional oil resources.

While the effects of the GCOS construction had far reaching impacts, its effects on the New Town of Fort McMurray were more immediate. The town flooded with new residents, new businesses and transient workers.

Fort McMurray would never be the same.

The Monday following GCOS's grand opening, the *Edmonton Journal* bubbled with quotes and comment. The following is a sampling of quotes from the October 2, 1964 edition:

There is no reason why the stretch along the Athabasca River cannot become an industrial valley in time. Synthetic crude is a natural for petrochemicals: *Robert McClements Jr. GCOS vice president of operations and plant manager.*

Oil from the Athabasca oil sands is naphthalenic and can yield generous amounts of aromatics, usable and welcome as feed to the chemical industry.....The original oil also contains trace metals such as vanadium and nickel which tend to concentrate during processing. In other words an extremely diversified industry could become based on oil sands operations: *R. E. Gishler, research director for Chemcell Edmonton Ltd.*

The best minds in the oil industry estimate that by 1985, the world's requirements of petroleum will be two and a half times what they are today....It is the considered opinion of our group if the North American continent is to produce the oil to meet its requirements in years ahead, oil from the Athabasca area must of necessity play an important role: *J. Howard Pew, Chairman, Sun Oil*[12].

The deep freeze

It took less than two months for GCOS to plunge from the high of its grand opening, to the lowest of lows. Amidst all of the optimism and hoopla at the September 30 grand opening, GCOS president Clarence Thayer sounded a cautious note when he told an *Edmonton Journal* reporter that "we need the experience before we know whether we want more capacity."

Experience slapped GCOS is the face in November 1967 when the plant powerhouse stopped working. The plant was crucial to provide heat to the thousands of miles of insulated components that kept production flowing. Within a short period, the entire three hundred and twenty-two million dollar plant was reduced to a block of ice that was further exacerbated by one of the coldest winters in Fort McMurray history. Some icicles extended two feet wide.

The plant freeze sent waves of panic through Fort McMurray. Rumours swept the community that the powerhouse had been built to run on coal, and that the use of coke had burnt the plant boilers. "Rumours were that we would lose our jobs and that this would be end of the whole thing," recalled Germain Routhier who worked twenty years with GCOS. "They asked operators if they wanted to help to clear off ice. Some did and some didn't." Routhier described scenes where inch by inch GCOS employees thawed pipes and other components until in March 1968 steam was restored to some areas.

"They gave us a copper tube with a point, connected the other end to steam," he recalled. "We dragged the pipe into the insulation and put the steam in. We then drained the water and continued." It would take until the following summer for the GCOS plant to resume full operation.

The freeze up produced a number of consequences which would deeply impact the community. Private developers who had been interested in building housing subdivisions for GCOS families suddenly pulled out. With private developers sheepish about providing housing for GCOS families, the role of Athabasca Realty Company (ARC), GCOS's housing wing took on increased importance. Although ARC had maintained an office in the Peter Pond Shopping Centre, its role was limited to providing housing for managers, along with a fixed number of employees. When it became apparent that private developers would not move in to establish new subdivisions, ARC's mandate was expanded. New subdivisions were planned for the downtown area and eventually Thickwood Heights, and Grayling Terrace located at the base of Abasand Heights.

The freeze up also brought together GCOS employees under one collective project, and demonstrated to the company and to Sun Oil the dedication of staff.

GCOS would face additional problems such as breakage of equipment due to cold weather and oil sand friction. During extreme temperatures, GCOS quickly learned that it was difficult to remove the overburden that covered the oil sands. GCOS's difficulties lead to a staggering sixty-eight million dollar loss during the 1968 fiscal year. Over the next decade, GCOS would work tirelessly to refine its equipment and its production process and in the mid 1970s began to register a profit.

"In the beginning it was a great experiment," recalled former ARC manager Al Burry. "This was new so there was no one they could call on. They couldn't borrow from other technologies so it all had to be learned. No one knew what this material would do to the equipment. No one knew what it would take to be profitable."

In many ways, future oil sands development and the provincial government were banking on the commitment and deep pockets of Sun Oil and J. Howard Pew.

The new business wave

As news of Fort McMurray's impending boom began to reach Edmonton and points beyond, a series of new businesses began to arrive.

During the mid-1960s, Alex and Alice Haxton had sold the grocery part of their business to Harold and Jeannette Tobin, who operated under the Red and White banner. Wolff's Men's Wear opened next to Hill Drugs, as did Karl's Jewellery Store.

Peter Pond Hotel owner, Dr. Allard, developed a strip mall, the Peter Pond Shopping Centre which housed the Fort McMurray Post Office, a new Hudson's Bay Store, Fort Drugs, McMurray Hardware, Athabasca Realty, Offereins Ladies Wear, Step Rite Shoes and Pond Flowers.

Further east on Franklin Avenue, Star Agencies Ltd. constructed a small strip mall that would serve as the forerunner of the future Park Plaza shopping complex. The initial Park Plaza strip mall housed the Solo grocery store, the Robinson's store, and Plaza Furniture and Hardware. Stu and Shirley Young operated the BA Service Station. Soon, Velma's Bakery opened, selling fresh bread and baked goods.

Ernie Wittke and Walter Diener opened the Macleod Store in 1968 next to the Bank of Nova Scotia on Franklin, and soon after the Jean family opened their gift and stationery store. Business was brisk in 1968; the new Macleod store set records for all of Canada and opening day saw seventy percent of its stock sold. By the close of the 1960s, lawyer Norm Simons had built the two-storey Professional Building that housed a dentist, lawyers and the health unit.

The face of McMurray changed dramatically in the late '60s. Most of the merchants who opened new businesses with high hopes of prosperity found with hard work, and long hours they made a living for their families but none grew rich; some moved from town and some lost their businesses during the economic lull which gripped the community during the 1980s.

A story of one business

As new GCOS employees arrived, Fort McMurray's expanded business community scrambled to meet the demand, often creating frantic and stressful times for both consumers and entrepreneurs. Many of Fort McMurray's new residents had left urban centres, and were aggressive in their demands for supplies and commodities to fill their new homes.

In the past, smaller businesses had served Fort McMurray's tiny population through crowded store shelves and easygoing service. But in Fort McMurray's accelerated economy, new rules applied. Both businesses and consumers were caught in a frenzy of activity and demands brought about by the GCOS boom. One of those businesses was McMurray Hardware which was owned by Tip and Betty-Anne Hlushak, first in the Peter Pond Hotel, and later in the Peter Pond Shopping Centre.

While residents initially embraced these new businesses, there soon developed an undercurrent that prices were higher than those in Edmonton, or that some entrepreneurs were taking advantage of Fort McMurray's isolation. Supply also became a problem. Prior to the 1967 opening of Highway 63, items had to be shipped by rail. Hlushak recalled how challenging it was to stock his shelves:

Our main problem was trying to get stock in. In those days, they didn't deliver the product to the store. You had to go to the railway station and ask what boxcar it was in. Then you had to dig it out. Half the town was there to watch the train come in. They were starved for stuff[33].

Stores like McMurray Hardware had to carry everything from hammer and nails, to radios and guns. Often, when a new service was added to the community, such as radio or television, the consumers stampeded stores like McMurray Hardware or Northwestern Electronics for product. Businesses were often willing to provide credit for such items as televisions and stereos.

While the business community clamoured to keep up with the demand, some tension developed with GCOS and Bechtel. Prior to Christmas, Diversified buses would load up, often in the Peter Pond Shopping Centre parking lot, and shuttle employees and their wives to Edmonton where hundreds of thousands of dollars were spent. A feeling developed that the plants were not doing enough to support local businesses. Some GCOS managers countered saying that Fort McMurray prices were too high. The practice of running buses to Edmonton prior to Christmas has continued down through the years.

Hlushak recalled spending long hours at his store keeping up with demand. The same can be said of most of other business operators during that period "The people from the larger centres really complained," he recalled, "Looking back, I know I didn't think much of them because we were working so hard, but we must have seemed like the end of the earth to them."[44]

Like many new residents who arrived during the mid 1960s, Hlushak remembers the mud.

In the Peter Pond, we used to have boots by the door so we could help our customers push their cars out. Once a lady drove up, probably somebody from Toronto, stepped out of her car and was just up to her knees in it. She let out a scream and dropped her purse. These people were not impressed with the community[45].

As Fort McMurray businesses rode the wave of boom and bust from the 1960s on, few left the community set for life. While periods of rapid population growth produced substantial profits during the mid 1960s and 1970s, lulls during the early 1970s and 1980s often wiped out those surpluses.

Memories of the Solo store

As a thirteen-year-old moving from Calgary to Fort McMurray, Glen Young had visions of what life in his new community would be like. He thought about being surrounded by native people, and learning how to hunt and fish.

Instead, when the Youngs arrived in 1965, Glen found a dusty community bursting at the seams with GCOS under construction. His father Stu Young took over the British American (BA) gas station near the Plaza Shopping Centre, and would eventually launch the Hertz Car Rental franchise, and Young Motors.

It still was an exciting time, full of opportunity for a young teenager. Within two weeks, Young was hired as a bagboy at the Solo store, a small supermarket that was run by Phil Poulin in the Plaza Shopping Centre. At the Solo, Young would learn some valuable lessons. On some Thursday nights, the Solo would take in ten thousand dollars in sales from two aisles feeding through one till. Those nights, the Solo store had more customers than the more established Hudson's Bay store. Why was the Solo store so successful?

"Before the customer had even paid their bill, I had their groceries out to their car," Young recalled. "Phil realized that you need good service and good meat."[46] The Solo store was a fixture in Fort McMurray until the early 1970s, paving the way for Harry Loo to open Harry's Food Market, a store which also focused on offering the best quality meat and service.

"At six dollars and forty cents per day pay, this was big stuff for a thirteen year old kid," said Young. "There were a lot of skills which we learned in those early days which would help us in later years."[47] Young would grow up in Fort McMurray and eventually would take over the Hertz Car Rental franchise and a variety of other businesses.

Digging up Franklin

Franklin Avenue was not the place to be from 1965-68. In 1965 the street was dug up to install water and sewer mains. No sooner was traffic flowing again than the street became off limits to motorists as crews battled against the rain and the terrain to provide the community's main thoroughfare with a paved surface.

Stanley and Associates oversaw the project that was completed by HB Contracting. While crews weathered two summers of steady downpours, Franklin Avenue was often reduced to a canal. Following one particular series of harsh thunderstorms in 1966, some residents were able to canoe down Franklin Avenue.

Ralph Fedorak was Stanley and Associates' project manager, and recalled how far crews had to dig in order to hit stable ground.

"The ground was very wet, and there was lots of silt, corduroy and trees," he said. "The trees and other materials were placed there when Franklin Avenue was first cleared because that was the practice back then."[48]

While the project fell victim to long rain delays, Fort McMurray residents became used to the site of manhole covers standing like small towers over the dug out Franklin Avenue ditch. Finally, after two long years of inconvenience the project was finally completed in late 1968.

Soon after, other paving projects were launched. Although Fedorak was not directly involved in the Alberta Drive project, he remembers one day being on site with the project manager when crews hit metal just below the surface. Heavy equipment eventually dug out the bodies of old army vehicles and other matter buried in 1943 by the American army.

Schools swell

The rush of new residents arriving daily soon began to choke the school system. Both Peter Pond and St. John's schools, which had been built to serve a small and predictable population, could not handle the crush of incoming students.

The Province, whose policy it had been to build a school only when a need could be shown, scrambled to approve construction of Dr. Clark and Father Turcotte schools located towards the east end of Franklin Avenue.

Although the Dr. Clark School officially opened in early 1968, during the previous year it existed as an unofficial entity. During 1967, the school was allocated six classrooms in the Peter Pond School, and six rooms above Haxton's Store. An initial six classrooms moved in to Dr. Clark School in January, with the remainder transferring around Easter. Father Turcotte School absorbed some of the pressure from St. John's School and opened two years later.

As Dr. Clark School Principal Dave McNeilly recalled, it was not unusual Monday mornings for a dozen families to be sitting in the school office waiting to register new students.

"There was a fantastic turnover," McNeilly recalled. "Transfers in and out were sometimes twenty to forty weekly. We began the year with two hundred students and at the end of the year we had five hundred. Classes were up to forty students."[49] It became impossible for teachers and administrative staff to keep up with the load, so parents and other volunteers were brought in to help supervise children, and in some cases to teach and grade exams.

It wasn't long before Dr. Clark School was filled beyond capacity. Trailers, known as portables, were added to the rear of Dr. Clark School. Prior to the opening of Clearwater School in 1974, one thousand and two students were registered at Dr. Clark School.

Sister Agnes Sutherland, who served as St. John's School principal during the GCOS boom recalled that in spite of classroom and school yard crowding, students were well behaved. "We were so crowded that we taught one group in the morning and one group in the afternoon," she recalled. "It worked out great because discipline problems were not as great. There were no problems in the schoolyards. Older kids would often look after the young ones. They just talked and played with none of the problems you would see today."[50]

The Father J.A. Turcotte Elementary School was soon built beside the Dr. Clark School to ease the crowding in St. John's, which remained as a high school. Frank Peters was named principal of Turcotte School and a friendly rivalry soon developed between the two elementary schools, which had adjoining playgrounds.

The Northlands School District, which since 1961 oversaw public school operations in Fort McMurray and northern Alberta, scoured the province and the rest of Canada for available teachers. After a Canada wide search proved unsuccessful, superintendent Bill Adams turned his attention overseas, developing a newspaper advertisement designed to pique the interest of adventurous recruits.

"No weaklings need apply"

Faced with teacher shortages and a student population which was growing daily, the Northlands School Division purchased space in newspapers throughout the United Kingdom. Elizabeth Kuhlen was a teacher in Scotland when she saw the ad in a local newspaper. She was intrigued by one line.

"It said they were wanting teachers in the Northland School Division in the Fort McMurray area and one little punch line got me," recalled Kuhlen. "It said, "no weaklings need apply."[51] Kuhlen and dozens of other teachers throughout the British Isles were intrigued by the "no weaklings" line, and within months many were on their way to Fort McMurray.

Kuhlen arrived at the new Fort McMurray Airport in August 1965. "I stepped off a stuffy plane into a brand spanking new airport and then outside into the mud."[52] At the time, crews were developing Highway 63 from the base of King Street to the top of Beacon Hill. One of Kuhlen's earliest memories involves loading up with groceries downtown, and having the vehicle she was riding in dragged up Beacon Hill by a "Cat".

Kuhlen was assigned to Northlands' school in Anzac and later to Fort McMurray where she eventually headed Keyano College's English program.

Another teacher who came to Fort McMurray during the British invasion was Danny Rampersad who arrived from Trinidad and was assigned to Fort McKay. Rampersad recalled that traditionally attendance at the Fort McKay school was poor. This was partially due to the fact that young people were expected to assist their parents in hunting, fishing and trapping. However, Rampersad recalls his first day in Fort McKay, when the school was packed.

"I was twenty-nine at the time and being from Trinidad I had darker skin," he recalled. "Everyone came out to see who this native teacher was."[53] Shortly after, residents realized he was not of native descent, but by that time Rampersad had established himself as a top-notch teacher and a valued member of the community.

About twenty teachers were hired during the British recruitment campaign. Most were pleasantly surprised that Fort McMurray was less primitive than expected. Teachers were thrilled to be provided with their own houses and for two years with tax-free status . The new teachers impacted the community in other ways. Along with a number of British expatriates working at GCOS, teachers formed a Fort McMurray soccer league, which in turn launched a parallel youth program.

Soon after, Fort McMurray became one of the Canada's smallest communities to operate a cricket league. Rampersad and Peter Kokaram launched a cricket program attracting local players from countries around the world.

Reality sets in

During the mid-1960s, Fort McMurray gained a distasteful name among new-comers. It was often referred to as *Fort MuckMurray*. While construction of new subdivisions, new houses and roads carried on, Fort McMurray experienced a string of rainy spring and summer seasons which often transformed streets to quagmire. During the spring, as the snow melted, new roads such as Biggs Avenue and Alberta Drive were reduced to muddy impassable trails, and often a variety of heavy machinery was kept nearby to help transport residents to and from their homes.

Neighbourhoods banded together to overcome boredom, loneliness and the over-whelming challenges Fort McMurray weather presented. In particular, mothers looked out for each other's children.

"If you heard a kid crying you knew they were stuck in the mud so no matter whose child it was, you pulled him out," recalled Phoebe Spice. "My son's boot sunk in one time, and we found it years later when we had our driveway paved."[54]

Fort McMurray's housing pioneers during the mid-1960s lived in an area known as Block X. This encompassed a subdivision which extended from the top of Crescent Heights to Biggs Avenue, Alberta Drive, Peden Crescent and Clark Crescent. Former city clerk Jerry Bussieres recalled the name Crescent Heights was actually suggested by Town Board member John Polonuk who was worried that Canadian Mortgage and Housing Corporation would not finance new mort-gages in a town so exposed to the northern elements.

"John figured that if we named the street where the first eight houses were located with the name Heights, CMHC would get the ball rolling," Bussieres said. CMHC did eventually agree on the condition that twenty-five per cent of the mortgage would be guaranteed by GCOS. The first eight houses built at the top of Crescent Heights were turned over to senior GCOS and Bechtel executives. The area was duly nicknamed "Snob Hill."[55]

In his memoirs, former CIBC manager Fred Schindel recalls a mud ritual that occurred each day at his bank:

One of the things that was a regular occurrence at the branch was in the morning shoveling out the mud from the office. This occurred on rainy and wet days when we had a lot of customers who would come in with their boots on and because of the gumbo which was on the streets they would leave large deposits of mud. At the end of the day we would have to literally shovel this out of the door and clear the premises of the dirt before we could proceed with enjoying our evening at the bank[56].

During dry summer days, the downtown core was covered in a layer of fine dust. Those who performed cleaning duties at offices and banks in the downtown core remember each evening cleaning dust from desks, floors and chairs.

"No one really remembers the mud being that bad before the GCOS development," recalled Bussieres. "But with the rain and construction during the 1960s it became a factor."[57]

New downtown residents who had been lured by the GCOS boom remained patient up to a point, but in 1967, the dirt hit the fan. On April 27, 1967, at the height of the spring meltdown, a delegation of women from the Poplar Subdivision appeared before Town Board, dressed in rubber boots. The enraged moms complained that roads were impassable, that building materials were being left behind by contractors and that muddy roads prohibited entry by the RCMP and emergency vehicles.

Town council told the delegation that it was Athabasca Realty, GCOS's housing wing which was responsible, and a meeting was eventually organized between GCOS, the town and the women to address their concerns. The meeting was significant in that it confirmed that there was a limit to what new residents were prepared to endure.

Although many new arrivals were prepared to weather some initial hardships, after a time, expectations began to rise that a certain level of comfort should be provided in return for the hard hours worked at the plant site. As well, by 1969, some of the glitter had worn off the initial Fort McMurray experience. While many had been excited to be moving to a place where employment and a home were assured by GCOS, many began to experience social problems which accompanied long, hard work hours, and isolation.

Men who worked at GCOS were often locked into shifts, which required twenty-eight straight days of work. Women were called upon to maintain the home, raise their children, and most importantly deal with the boredom. During the days before radio and television, many GCOS wives sunk into depression. Alcoholism, family disputes and dissolved marriages were commonplace.

"You had to rely on each other," recalled Caroline MacKay whose husband Bert was hired in 1966 by GCOS. "Those of us who had husbands on the same shifts would get together with our children and plan shopping or just enjoy each other's company. For others, especially when it was minus forty degrees, some didn't even bother getting dressed. It was the kind of thing which challenged you as a person, and also challenged your marriage. Our family stayed busy, but you would see many other families pack up because they couldn't take it."[58]

MacKay eventually conquered the boredom by returning to work. Others were not so lucky. Many believed that high wages and a new company house would alleviate family or marital problems which existed prior to their arrival. However, the isolation and long hours of work just irritated existing pressure points. For many, large paycheques were no match for the isolation, and these families did not last long in the community.

There were other families who found it easier to embrace the challenge. Bunny Philpott remembered with fondness how families banded together, founded sports and social clubs, and supported each other.[59]

"Remember, most families did not have their extended families with them" she recalled. "You rarely saw a senior citizen."[60] Philpott recalled how a few days after her arrival in Fort McMurray, her husband Fred's boss announced he was coming to their home for a social visit.

"We had nothing to serve so I ran out and knocked on doors and people were happy to give us things. I think that day we served Ritz crackers, cheese, kobasa and sardines."[61] The Philpotts also borrowed four hundred dollars to buy a stereo and one record, the Pearly Shells of Hawaii.

The spirit of adventure and survival attracted a special breed to Fort McMurray. People like the Philpotts would become instrumental in forming and sustaining organizations such as the Noralta Figure Skating Club and the Fort McMurray Band Association. It appeared that those families who survived the GCOS boom had the right stuff to help Fort McMurray develop into a permanent and sustainable community.

The courage of Marion Laird

Fort McMurray was rocked in October 1968 by the death of one of its popular residents, Colin Laird. Laird arrived in Fort McMurray during the late 1950s to work as an electrician with Cities Service, the forerunner of Syncrude Canada Ltd. In 1964, Laird and wife Marion began to wind down their work in the oil sands and launched Laird Electrix, providing electrical services and supplies to Fort McMurray builders.

"The town itself was opening up, and we saw the opportunity in the building of houses and businesses,"[62] recalled Marion Laird. While Laird Electric prospered on Franklin Avenue just east of Sutherland Street, Marion launched a laundromat nearby.

However, Marion Laird's world took a tragic twist in October 1968. Colin, a licensed pilot, was lifting off from Athabasca on the way home from a hunting trip when he suffered a heart attack and died during take off.

Marion was left alone to raise six children. With remarkable courage, Marion Laird took over Laird Electric, teaching herself bookkeeping and administration. She partnered with electrician Art Turnbull who had worked closely with Colin and continued the company's operation.

Within a few years, Laird had expanded her bookkeeping expertise and began to complete the payroll for Cities Service. From housewife to businesswoman, Marion Laird quickly earned a respected reputation within the community. In 1978 she sold her Laird Electric shares and eventually moved to Calgary.

The stakes were tasty

It was a muggy Sunday evening in 1968 when the Bay Beavers and the Riviera Wildcats took to the field. In those days, long before MacDonald Island, baseball players performed on a field located roughly where Keyano Theatre stands today.

There was little radio and no television for entertainment. At a time when Fort McMurray's population was barely three thousand five hundred, between four-hundred and six-hundred people would pack the stands to watch some of the best players in town. John Lambert, Al Fraser and Gary "Chicken Man" Palme were household names.

In those days, any player who could launch a home run over the left field fence would receive a package of steaks from the Red and White Store. The same prize awaited a player who pitched a no hitter. These stakes would add an air of excite-ment to each game.

And so it was that evening in 1968 as the Bay and Riviera met in front of hundreds of fans. On the mound for the Beavers was Jerry Bussieres, known for his fast ball and his paralyzing change up. He had one of the lowest earned run averages in the league.

Through six-and-one-half innings the teams played in scoreless futility. The Bay Beavers had a few runners on base, but none had crossed the plate. As the bottom of the seventh inning began, the Riviera Wildcats' scorecard was covered with raven's eggs. Bussieres had yet to yield a hit.

The first two Riviera batters were retired without incident. Bussieres appeared unstoppable.

Up to the plate came Ron Morgan. The two rivals locked sights and dug in for bat-tle. For three or four pitches, Bussieres and Morgan dueled. Change ups and foul balls.

But then the F-word sounded in Morgan's head. Morgan thought "fast ball." Bussieres delivered a blazing pitch and Morgan met it with an even cut across the letters.

The ball launched off Morgan's bat and soared. It did not stop until it landed past the left field fence. Bussieres' no hitter was gone. Morgan circled the bases and cruised home with a 1-0 victory for the Wildcats.

The duel would later be known as the "battle of the steak holders." The next day Morgan received his prize from the Red and White Store63.

The two players would remain archrivals on the diamond for years to come. Bussieres was already town clerk and would go on to serve the community as a municipal secretary until his retirement in 1994. Morgan celebrated his thirtieth year as a municipal councilor in 2001 and announced his retirement the same year. The two remain the best of friends

Vietnam claims local boy

On the wall at the Royal Canadian Legion in Waterways names are displayed of those Fort McMurray soldiers who perished in military service. Most of the names consist of young men who battled on behalf of Canada during both world wars.

However, the final name on that list refers to a local man who enlisted to fight in a war which some would argue had little relevance to Canadians. But Gordon White didn't see it that way.

In 1968, White announced to his family, friends and GCOS work mates that he would quit his job, leave his hometown, and join the United States Marines. Co-worker Bert MacKay remembers the passion White expressed for the Vietnam War.

"He was a very assertive and idealistic guy who wanted to go to Vietnam," recalled MacKay. "He was a gung ho kind of guy who wanted to go there for adventure and to kick those Commies."[64]

In March 1969, Fort McMurray received the tragic news that Gordon White, hometown boy, had been killed by a landmine in Vietnam. It was a crushing blow to White's family and friends, many of whom felt that White had no business being in that conflict in the first place.

For White's mother, Evelyn White, it was the second time she had been forced to deal with a military death. During the early 1940s, her first husband drowned in the Clearwater River while serving with American forces.

A boxing trophy awarded each year to the Clearwater Boxing Club's top boxer perpetuated Gordon White's memory. The boxing club initiated the Gordon White Memorial Tournament with a trophy donated by Gordon's father, Henry White.

The Place Burns

For nearly thirty years, the McMurray Community Hall served as a place for residents to dance, listen to music and hold public gatherings. In a matter of minutes in mid-April 1969 the hall was destroyed by fire. The adjacent Full Gospel Church was also gutted.

The hall was known as The Place, a hangout for young people to down a pizza and a pop after watching a movie at the adjacent Fort Theatre. The Place had been leased to Sigi Lucas and had gained notoriety as a late night pizza joint which attracted some of Fort McMurray's nighthawks. The Place also operated as a teenage dance hall.

For nearly three decades, the location served as a landmark. It was built in 1938 by a group of local residents who recognized the need for a downtown community hall. It opened on January 25, 1939 as the McMurray Community Hall.

During the early 1950s, businessman Dempson Cross purchased the hall, converted it to a movie theatre and allowed its use for public gatherings. L.W. Nelson purchased the Community Hall in 1959 and soon after built the Fort Theatre.

"The Place was a non-alcoholic place for us to go and dance and have a pizza," recalled Glen Young. "And when it burnt it seemed like there was something missing."[65]

Ski hill

During the late 1960s, businessman Sigi Lucas had a dream. As he stood at the top of scenic Abasand Hill overlooking the Athabasca and Horse rivers, he envisioned a European style spa, resort and housing development, which would eventually offer tourists and residents skiing, hiking and other recreational opportunities.

In 1968, Lucas and partner Norm Simons acquired rights to develop the property, but due to a variety of zoning issues, and resistance from the Town Board, no resort was ever built. Instead, Simons and Lucas offered use of the land to the town to develop a ski hill. The Mistie Sepee Ski Club was formed and a rope tow was installed. For a number of winters, skiers took advantage of the beautiful panoramic setting.

In the mid-1970s, the ski club moved to a hill off Highway 63 about five miles north of the Grant MacEwan Bridge, and eventually settled in the Saprae Creek area east of the Fort McMurray airport.

Why GCOS and not Syncrude?

At the start of the 1960s, it appeared that both GCOS and Cities Service Athabasca Ltd. were on equal footing to launch Canada's first oil sands plant. So why in the eyes of the province did it made more sense to support the GCOS proposal?

In all likelihood, it was pressure from conventional oil producers which drove the decision. In October 1962, following approval of the initial GCOS plant, the Province passed a policy that limited oil sands production to five cent of the province's total annual yield. As J. Joseph Fitzgerald hypothesizes in his book *Black Gold with Grit*, "in this way, Alberta assured its conventional producers that the marketing systems they had worked to establish would not be impinged upon by the oil sands producers[66]."

Within the conventional oil industry there was considerable hostility and concern over the emergence of the oil sands as a viable petroleum source. Fitzgerald, a former GCOS manager, recalled being accosted in 1962 at the Calgary Petroleum Club as "one of those guys from the tar sands." A member of the Petroleum Club demanded to know who had brought Fitzgerald to the club, and vowed to meet with the executive to ensure that "none of your kind"[67] would ever enjoy the club's privileges.

There was reason for hostility from the conventional oil industry. Oil sands plants held the potential to produce huge amounts of oil per day in comparison to conventional sources. Ultimately, the Alberta government chose the GCOS proposal which was initially one third of the per day total proposed by Cities Services. The reduced yield would allow oil sands production to remain within the five per cent ceiling.

The test plant

By 1959, Cities Service had built an eight and half million dollar test plant which ran until 1964. At one point, the plant employed more than one hundred and twenty five. Based on initial production successes, an initial application was filed with the Alberta Oil and Gas Conservation Board to begin work on a one hundred thousand barrel per day plant that would begin operation in 1969. The request was deferred until 1968.

On December 18, 1964, Syncrude Canada Limited was officially formed, and within two weeks a four company consortium had been assembled made up of Cities Service, Imperial Oil, Atlantic Richfield, each with thirty per cent. Royalite held ten per cent.

While the Province reconsidered its position on oil sands development, Syncrude continued monitoring GCOS' progress. Syncrude became increasingly encouraged that it would eventually build a plant which would not only produce oil, but also a variety of minerals and by-products.

By the late 1960s, it became apparent to the Alberta government and to conventional oil producers that sufficient markets existed to sell all oil produced within the province. In February 1968 the Oil Sands Development Policy was passed by the Alberta government which allowed oil sands producers to develop additional oil to serve identified new markets. This was a way to keep existing oil producers happy, while potentially improving Alberta's market share within the rest of Canada and the United States.

In May 1968, Syncrude Canada resubmitted its application to the Alberta Oil and Gas Conservation Board. Although various American import restrictions would have to be overcome, Syncrude proceeded with its application and on September 12, 1969, the company received permission to build an eighty thousand barrel per day plant which would begin production in 1976. Eventually that figure would increase to one hundred and twenty-five barrels per day.

Syncrude began to plan an oil sands plant to be developed near Mildred Lake. Fort McMurray braced for its second oil sands boom.

An incredible decade

Within the space of ten years, Fort McMurray had weathered an economic boom that had been unparalleled within Alberta. At the start of the 1960s, the community's population stood at about twelve hundred but by the close of the decade that figure exceeded six thousand.

Longtime residents had observed their calm and predictable towns overrun by outsiders who brought with them both new ideas, and a variety of social problems. Fort McMurray had annexed additional land, paved its main street, witnessed the development of two strip malls, and watched in amazement as thousands of transient workers stretched its police and legal resources to the limit.

But there were benefits which offset these discomforts. Jobs and economic opportunities were plentiful. GCOS employees were covered by generous benefits and housing plans. Residents and thousands of newcomers would have to endure the irritation of mud and isolation, but would be compensated handsomely ensuring a strong financial future for their children, and personal security during their retirement years.

Most importantly, Fort McMurray had successfully absorbed five thousand new residents and this translated to an explosion of additional businesses and services, churches, sports clubs and community organizations. By working together to build GCOS, overcoming its monumental challenges, camaraderie had developed between both old and new residents.

While some newcomers had initially adopted the phrase "two and out," referring to an initial commitment of two years in Fort McMurray, many chose to stay, raise families and help develop an expanded community infrastructure.

While many GCOS employees had planned to come for only a few years, they became addicted to the natural beauty and sense of community which Fort McMurray offered. A review of the 2001 phone book shows that while many of these initial GCOS workers have passed on or have retired to warmer climates, many of their sons and daughters continue to live in Fort McMurray and assume important roles in the community.

Fort McMurray had succeeded in weathering the GCOS storm, and turned its sights to the 1970s, and the eventual arrival of Syncrude Canada Ltd.

Chapter Seven:
Syncrude and beyond

As Fort McMurray moved past the frantic days of GCOS startup, many residents breathed a sigh of relief. But as local history consistently reveals, relaxing in Fort McMurray is a luxury.

During the 1960s Fort McMurray weathered a four-fold population increase, and anticipated the same during the 1970s. But with Syncrude, the anticipated numbers were staggering. The New Town hired managers, and assembled a team of planners. The community looked ahead to developing new subdivisions such as Beacon Hill, Abasand Heights and Thickwood Heights. Radio, newspaper and television outlets brought Fort McMurray in touch with the outside world. Fort McMurray had little time to play or pause before moving to fast-forward.

As the 1970s began, Fort McMurray was of two minds. While its back foot was planted in northern tradition; its body clearly faced forward. For decades, its isolation and northern solitude kept it stable and predictable. But now, recruiters trying to fill the jobs at GCOS promoted the community's modern amenities such as shopping centres, a college and hospital, and ample recreational and cultural opportunities.

In the fall of 1989, Fort McMurray business person, Al Burry invited me to take a day trip to Yellowknife. As the pilot landed our small airplane and we made our way downtown, I was immediately struck by the northerness of it all; parkas, mukluks, cool and uncompromising air. It occurred to me how much effort Fort McMurray expends denying its own northernness during periods of significant growth. This was, after all, a community built on fur, lumber and riverboats.

In many ways, the 1970s was the decade where Fort McMurray turned its back on its founding tradition, and entered the future. The community still boasted a few old-timers who remembered the past, but for the most part, Fort McMurray relished its role as an attractive northern community. Some of the community's "bona fide" characters like Dim Silin and Tin Can Charlie had passed on. Pioneers like Walter Hill, Hugh Stroud, Katie Sanderson and Real Martin carried the torch. In their place came the urban people and a tidal wave of arrivals from Newfoundland.

The 1970s was a breakthrough decade, culminating in 1980 with Fort McMurray's move to city status. During this decade, Fort McMurray's fate was handed to a group of outsiders who did not stay in the community long, but envisioned a modern future for the town. And when their work was complete, Fort McMurray's services and facilities were second to none for a community of its size. The days of trappers, riverboats and the railroad had slipped through the hourglass of time.

The death of John. A. McDonald

A bizarre discovery at the start of the 1970s caused many longtime residents to reflect about a tragedy which occurred nearly thirty years before.

One morning, in May 1970, two boys raced into RCMP headquarters reporting they had seen a pair of boots sticking up from the old Snye well. Sergeant Don Rumpel and local social services manager Don Fleming rushed to the scene and quickly concluded someone had fallen in. The side of the well had collapsed and a victim had fallen in headfirst and drowned. The deceased was John A. McDonald, the former Captain of the Slave, a tugboat which cruised the Athabasca River between Fort McMurray and Fort Chipewyan thirty years earlier.

An event during the 1940s forever changed McDonald's life. While he was piloting the Slave from Fort McMurray to Fort Chipewyan the weather turned harsh. The Slave stalled in heavy ice and with few provisions McDonald ventured north towards Fort Chipewyan for help.

As the weather continued to worsen, those on board climbed out of the riverboat and began walking north. As the group approached Fort Chipewyan, they realized that one of its members, Evelyn (Waniandy) Street, had fallen behind. A member of the group backtracked and was told by Street that she just needed time to rest. When a rescue party eventually reached Street, she was found dead of frostbite.

McDonald was never the same. He blamed himself for Street's death and became an eccentric figure, fond of alcohol, who was treated with some degree of compassion and empathy. McDonald played the fiddle and would often set fire to abandoned buildings claiming they were being used by "loose women" to lure men. He termed these shacks "houses of evil." Often, when fire chief Roy Hawkins and crew would arrive on the scene, they would see McDonald playing the fiddle a few yards from the burning building claiming he was Nero.

In spite of his drunkenness and occasional passion for arson, most members of the community, including the RCMP, pitied McDonald. As Sergeant Rumpel recalled, "Every time he saw my wife he'd sing, 'beautiful, beautiful brown eyes.' He'd walk around with a bottle of Bright's Sherry and you'd hear him in the middle of the night singing 'God Save Our Gracious King.' He'd go by the police barracks and salute the flag. Only John A. could ride in a rat canoe, and stand up playing his fiddle without tipping."[1]

McDonald's death finally brought closure to the Evelyn Street tragedy. "When we pulled him out of the well, we noticed at least he had a smile on his face," said Rumpel "He belonged to another time, but his suffering was finally over."[2]

Grey Cup live

Grey Cup day, 1970, took on special significance for Fort McMurray residents as live cable television arrived. Earlier that year, Bob Lamb, president of Alberta Broadcasting Company (ABC) promised that live television would be available in time for the game. Lamb was true to his word.

Previously, residents relied on CBCs Frontier Package which consisted of CBC week old programs. Former CBC technician Jim Pauls was paid to run four hours of the programs which were shipped by bus and played on an early model VCR which weighed about three hundred pounds. Initial programs included *Sesame Street*, *Chez Helene*, *Mr. Dressup*, *I Love Lucy*, *Hogan's Heroes* and *Hockey Night in Canada*. Service began in 1969, as CBC advanced its television signal from Edmonton to Fort McMurray from tower to tower, finally reaching a transmitter on Beacon Hill.

"There was only one tiny road in and if it was snowing it took us awhile to get there," said Paul. "We hung a fifty watt transmitter there and the antenna gave a barely readable signal. I stayed there four hours a night."[3]

In 1970, ABC decided to raise television to the next level with a clearer more consistent signal. That year, Larry Biswanger and Grace Dafoe joined Bob Lamb in launching the new cable company. "I was tired of the commercial television racket," Dafoe recalled. "I didn't like the aspect of trying to please sponsors and all that, so I decided to help start up cable TV in Fort McMurray. I thought it would be relaxing, but I sure got that wrong."[4] Since it was constantly upgrading equipment and adding stations, it took many years for ABC to show a profit in Fort McMurray.

"There were some people who were really resentful of cable TV interrupting their reading time with their children, but most people were really excited by the thought of live TV," Dafoe said. "Unfortunately, what they got was really bad and often a snowy signal. Aurora Borealis really played havoc with the signal. Sometimes we'd get stuff from San Francisco, and people would say, "thanks for bringing us the Tonight Show."[5]

During the 1970s, Fort McMurray was plagued with frequent power failures and this produced a number of complaints from cable customers.

"This one lady called and she was so angry at not having cable," Dafoe recalled. "I asked her whether her lights were on. She said "No, but I don't care—I don't' watch my damn lights."[6]

Marking the centennial

It had been exactly one hundred years since John Moberly established Fort McMurray at the junction of the Athabasca and Clearwater rivers, and in 1970 residents began discussing ways to officially mark the anniversary. There were a number of options discussed, but when the debate subsided, citizens clearly stated a preference for development of an indoor swimming pool. Residents and council began planning construction of an Olympic-sized swimming pool which was to be built in a twelve-thousand-square-foot building on land next to the Peter Pond School. It would be known as Centennial Pool.

For a community of under seven thousand, raising the necessary two hundred and sixty-five thousand dollars would be difficult. Funding the facility would require government grants, some municipal borrowing, and local donations in excess of eighty thousand dollars. While confidence was high that the Alberta government would step in with existing grants, it was agreed that raising eighty thousand dollars within a small community would require numerous private donors and a major organization to take the lead. Fort McMurray found that organization in the Kinsmen Club, which had been operating for about five years. The Kinsmen focused their energies not only on fund raising, but also in organising volunteer labour, ensuring that Centennial Pool met its total budget.

"We were young and ambitious," recalled Jim Mutton who served as president of both the Kinsmen Club and the Fort McMurray Chamber of Commerce. "We were all busy but we saw the need for the pool and made it happen."[7] Proceeds from the Blueberry Festival and other fund raising projects were routed to Centennial Pool. Kinsmen and other community members also donated time and materials. Other local fund raising efforts were spearheaded by Armand Parent, manager of Catalytic Enterprises. Parent was appointed secretary of the Pool Finance Committee.

Along with the Kinsmen, a number of corporate sponsors stepped up and donated heavily including Catalytic, Mannix Ltd., Syncrude Canada, Byers, Mail Advertising Corp, Canadian Utilities, Crane Canada, Dr. Zingle, Travis Chemicals and R. Angus.

But Parent's focus was not just on large corporate donors. He developed an innovative way to raise money which involved members of the public. Local residents were encouraged to sponsor a building brick at a cost of ten dollars per brick. Even children got into the act donating money, and having their name placed on a commemorative plaque.

The Centennial Pool project boasted wide community involvement. As the facility prepared to open on April 5, 1971, more than five hundred youngsters lined up at the door. That day, pool coordinator Sheila Scrutton reported that seven hundred and eighty people swam in Centennial Pool.

The grand opening, which was held the following month, should have been a moment for unbridled community celebration, and it would have been had it not been for a small group of protestors picketing outside.

The Sam Hardin factor

Town Board Chairman, Sam Hardin, always spoke his mind. Edmonton broadcaster Alex Mair tells the story of a visit to Fort McMurray in 1974, and his reunion with his old schoolmate Hardin. It was during the municipal by-election, and his old schoolmate, Hardin, asked him to help him prepare for a CJOK interview.

Mair began by asking his opinion on plans to expand the community into Thickwood Heights. Hardin favoured shifting development across the Clearwater River in an area which would later be called Forest Heights. As Mair recalled, "I asked Sam the question and he replied that he thought that it was a "g-d damned stupid idea." I told him you can't say that on the radio. He replied, "why shouldn't I say that? It's a g-d damned stupid idea."[8]

Sam Hardin was not known as a baby-kisser. During a time when the Town Board of Administrators' Chairman was a volunteer position, Hardin put in countless hours promoting the community, often to the detriment of his business. Often, when Hardin took a stand on an issue, residents would exercise their displeasure by boycotting his business. Hardin also had a stubborn streak. In 1974, when Town Board passed a motion that all members declare their business interests and holdings, Hardin typed his on a piece of flowered toilet paper.

In August 1970, Fort McMurray Hospital's new pediatrics wing opened. Soon after, rumours of discontent began swirling. An anonymous petition circulated voicing concern over how the hospital was being managed. When Hospital Board member Betty Griffiths resigned in April 1971, Town Board named Sam Hardin to take her place. This further agitated hospital critics who complained that Hardin was in conflict of interest sitting on both hospital and town boards. The hospital controversy came at an unfortunate time for Hardin. When Centennial Pool was officially opened by government officials in early May 1971, five picketers paced outside the pool with signs reading, "Who is Sam Hardin?"[9]

Hardin originally came to Fort McMurray in 1964 to launch Fort Drugs. In 1968, he was encouraged to run for Town Board because as he was told by board member John Polonuk "he could count to one hundred."[10] But Hardin, never one to be shy or unduly humble, noted about himself and fellow businessman and councillor Ron Wolff, "that someone had to do it, and better us than someone else who didn't know what they were doing."[11] Later that year, the issue of whether Town Board members should be allowed to sit on the Hospital Board resulted in the mass resignation of existing Hospital Board members. The issue was not resolved until a new Hospital Board was voted during 1971 municipal elections. One of the hospital board members elected in 1971 was Phoebe Spice, who would later become hospital board chair.

Hardin was seen as a hard-nosed business person who was also dedicated to expanding the number of physicians in the community and to getting Highway 63 paved. However, Hardin fell out of public favour by supporting a plan to develop housing on MacDonald Island.

When it came time for elections in 1971, the once popular Hardin finished near the bottom of the polls stubbornly maintaining the view that including housing on MacDonald Island was a good idea. In his vision, Athabasca Realty Company (ARC), would finance the water and sewer services which would eventually extend across the Clearwater River to Area Four, later named Forest Heights. It could be argued that although the eventual development of Thickwood Heights moved employees' bedrooms closer to the GCOS and Syncrude plant sites, expansion to Forest Heights would have left Fort McMurray with a less spread out community, and could have reduced costs of housing and commercial lots.

Thickwood Heights was one of two locations chosen by the Province as it began mapping Fort McMurray's future development. The other was the future location of the MacKenzie Industrial Park, which from its location at the south edge of Fort McMurray seemed better suited to accommodate Edmonton businesses than to serve the oil sands plants. Some argued that the park should have been built in the Thickwood or Timberlea areas, and was developed on an abandoned gravel pit to help recover money wasted in the development of nearby Beacon Hill.

Elections which followed in 1971 had a marked anti-business flavour and launched the political careers of two new town board members, Chuck Knight and Ron Morgan. Ron Morgan squeaked on council edging Wolff by six votes for the seventh and final council spot. Wolff did not request a recount. "I had had enough,"[12] said Wolff.

Sam Hardin contested a 1974 by-election and returned to Town Board for a few months prior to the October 1974 municipal election.

Ron Wolff, Kinsmen and the wrecked car

While Sam Hardin never hesitated to state an opinion, his friend Ron Wolff approached politics with a bit more patience. Wolff arrived in Fort McMurray during the summer of 1965 to launch a mens' wear store, and immediately turned his attention to community work. Wolff began rustling young businessmen to form a Kinsmen Club and soon after became the Kinsmen Club's charter president. The Kinsmen Club was instrumental in sustaining the Blueberry Festival which earned tens of thousands of dollars annually for local causes.

One of the Kinsmen's original fundraising projects was a car raffle which was spearheaded by Jack Shields. The idea was to sell raffle tickets to plant workers. But rather than ship the Ford Galaxy by rail, Shields decided to drive it north on Highway 63 which was not yet fully paved. En route, a tirod came off the vehicle, and Shields and his raffle prize ended up in the ditch. Shields had to be towed to Fort McMurray by a group of fellow Kinsmen. Once the vehicle was repaired it was driven to the GCOS plant site where in seven days, all tickets were sold.

The Kinsmen grew to be Fort McMurray's premiere service club of the 1960s and early 1970s and was eventually replaced in prominence by the Fort McMurray Rotary Club.

MacDonald Island and the rise of Chuck Knight

In 1971, Sam Hardin and Ron Wolff found themselves at the centre of a controversy which involved MacDonald Island, a two hundred and eighty acre area which had recently become accessible via the newly built Snye dyke road.

Athabasca Realty Company (ARC) had come before Town Board requesting to develop forty-five acres of land for executive housing. The town's recreation board and a large citizens lobby demanded that the ARC rezoning request be denied and that the area be fully dedicated for development of recreational facilities.

The lines were drawn for a June 7 showdown at Town Board chambers. On the pro development side were Hardin, Wolff and ARC which stood poised to buy a total package of fifty-eight acres at two thousand dollars per acre. Since the land had originally been granted to the New Town by Municipal Affairs in 1965, the town stood to make a substantial profit, while having to give up only a portion of the island for housing development.

On June 7, council chambers were packed. As passions began to build, it soon became apparent that the debate over MacDonald Island was more than an emotional discussion over recreational land. It was about who would earn the right to control future development within the community.

For the first few minutes, a number of residents spoke against development, but many of their arguments lacked focus. Eventually, Hardin, the board chair, recognized a tall man seated in the corner. The words that followed would forever change Fort McMurray politics. Chuck Knight, a GCOS purchaser, began to speak in favour of keeping MacDonald Island as a recreational reserve. Longtime municipal councillor Ron Morgan recalled what happened next.

"Chuck got up and spoke from the gallery," Morgan recalled. "He began slowly and like a freight train began to pick up steam."[13] The words began to flow smoothly from Knight's mouth, and listening to the momentum of his own words, he began to speak with increased confidence. Knight had the audience in his hand.

The zoning application by ARC was denied, and Chuck Knight became a local celebrity. The speech jettisoned Knight to the height of public popularity, while grounding ARC and the politicians who had supported the idea.

Citizens speak their mind

The municipal election of October 13, 1971 proved to be one of the most pivotal political battles in Fort McMurray history. Since the mid-1910s, Fort McMurray's business community had played a vital role in local decision making. The Board of Trade, until 1948, was seen as the principle advisor to the Province on civic matters. Its successor, the Fort McMurray Chamber of Commerce, was a powerful lobbying force and appeared before town council on a regular basis; providing advice on spending, taxes, finances and other issues.

That all changed in 1971 with the election of a new wave of politician. Sam Hardin plunged from a first place finish in 1969, to fifteenth out of nineteen candidates. Of those elected, businessmen Claire Peden and MacLeod's Store co-owner Walter Diener were the only ones with some business experience. The remaining candidates were seen as more closely linked with recently arrived

GCOS employees. "Fort McMurray had become more of a blue collar town,"[14] Morgan later reflected. Peden and Diener were joined by Knight, Morgan, Dave McNeilly, Dr. Al Nicholson and Armand Parent.

The 1971 election marked the beginning of a significant voter trend. For the next three decades, Fort McMurray voters consistently displayed an anti-business bias rejecting in later years mayoral candidates like Neil Costello, Bruce Otterdahl and Paul Hartigan, who carried strong chamber of commerce credentials.

From skid row to mayor's chair

One night in 1953, Chuck Knight looked up from a cardboard box in an Edmonton back alley and decided something had to change. As was the case so many times before, Knight was drunk, lost and confused. He would leave his Edmonton home and emerge many days later without any recollection of where he had been.

He was often violent and constantly troubled. Knight traced his need to drink to a facial injury he sustained during his youth which caused him to be taunted mercilessly by his classmates. Knight spent a large part of the 1940s and early 1950s exorcising his pain, until he decided one day to reverse his life.

Knight told me in 1999 that the support of his wife Lu and from Alcoholics Anonymous helped end his days as an alcoholic, and turn him towards a more constructive life's path. On January 17 1957, Chuck Knight arrived in Fort McMurray to work on building the radar station south of the town.

"The caretaker had a little too much to drink that night and forgot to fuel up the heater," Knight recalled. "I was in a cot right by the tent flap. Not knowing how cold it would get I put on my pajamas. It wasn't until morning that I realized everyone else had worn their parkas to bed. I was ready to turn around and return to my home in Edmonton."[15]

By the time his first paycheque arrived, Knight had been hired by Royalite to manage supplies earmarked for the company's experimental plant in Bitumount. Captain Billy Bird, an expert in river channels and northern travel, taught Knight how to move supplies safely between Fort McMurray and Bitumount. The two became lifelong friends.

Northern Transportation eventually hired Knight where he worked as a time-keeper. He also checked supplies and supervised workers in the field. Knight was later employed by Cities Service and again by Royalite.

In 1964, Knight was invited by Canadian Bechtel to coordinate its purchasing department and eventually joined GCOS, where he remained in relative obscurity until the June 1971 public meeting.

Following his success at the MacDonald Island hearing, Knight decided to run for Town Board in the fall of 1971, and remained in politics until his retirement in 1989. Knight was elected as Town Board chair in 1974, and in 1983 became mayor.

During his time as Fort McMurray's top elected official, Knight gained a reputation as a hard worker and strong promoter. Knight however had a short temper, and could carry a grudge against those he felt did not support him. While Knight was successful in bringing concerns of the public to the attention of council, often his temper and confrontational style made him a controversial figure whose "pro" and "cons" are debated to this day.

Knight once told me that hard work and his obsession with politics helped take the place of alcohol. He became Fort McMurray's first paid, full-time Town Board chair, and gave up his GCOS/Suncor position in 1983 to become mayor. The decision came with significant sacrifice. Knight lost benefits accrued with Suncor, and lived in a modest condominium near Kelowna prior to his passing in 2000.

One area where there is little disagreement about Chuck Knight, relates to his ability as a hockey goalie. Knight was fond of donning goalie pads in the old Fort McMurray Commercial League. While his play was usually competitive, on one particular evening, his team was bombarded 30-0, earning Knight the nickname "Red Light Knight."

Constable shot

What began as a routine traffic stop for Constable Jim Fyfe, came within a whisker of ending his life. At about three-forty a.m. on October 18, 1971, Fyfe was driving down Franklin Avenue when he noticed a car with a burnt headlight proceeding east. Fyfe stopped the vehicle in front of Centennial Pool, and as he spoke with the driver, a second vehicle approached.

The driver of the second vehicle asked Fyfe "what was going on." Fyfe advised him that it was a routine traffic stop and requested him to "move on." But something didn't seem right. Out of the corner of his eye, Fyfe noticed a rifle, but since he was already busy, the constable decided to let the second vehicle proceed. Rather than continuing downtown, the driver of the second vehicle made a U-turn in front of the Peter Pond Shopping Centre and began driving east towards Fyfe's squad car.

The driver pulled up behind the RCMP cruiser, opened his car door, lifted his rifle and took aim. Three shots were fired including one which entered the right door of the police car. Shrapnel sprayed into Fyfe's back. The wounded constable freed his revolver and fired six shots, one of them hitting the gunman in the back.

Fyfe was in shock and begun to stagger west on Franklin Avenue in search of reinforcements. Fyfe thought that the bullet had seriously injured the gunman, but the shot was only a flesh wound. The gunman rose, lifted his rifle, cocked and at close range prepared to shoot Fyfe in the back.

The driver of the first vehicle, Robert Rempel, had been crouching with his two passengers on the side of the road, and when he realized that the gunman was about to shoot Fyfe, he tackled him at the precise moment the trigger was pulled. The shot was redirected, hitting Fyfe in the forearm, passing through his elbow. Rempel grabbed the rifle and knocked the gunman over the head and stood over the assailant until two RCMP constables arrived. As the *McMurray Courier* reflected in its October 20, 1971 edition, "the quick thinking and heroic action of Bob Rempel may well have saved Constable Fyfe's life."[16]

Fyfe was examined by Dr. Des Dwyer and Dr. Al Nicholson who ordered the constable transferred to Edmonton. Fyfe survived, but due to lingering pain, was limited to desk duty.

The community quickly rallied behind Fyfe and found a way to help ease the constable's pain and boredom through his long convalescence. Fort Drugs owner Sam Hardin organized a fundraising drive to buy Fyfe a television, and a total of five hundred dollars was collected through the town office, the newspaper and local schools.

1971 at a glance

The early 1970s marked a time of transition for Fort McMurray. While the GCOS boom has subsided, Fort McMurray was gearing up for renewed growth with Syncrude scheduled for original startup in 1976.

The following are a few news items gleaned from the 1971 *McMurray Courier*.

Crash Fatal for Local Pilot

Fort McMurray lost one of its prominent businessmen in February 1971, when the plane that Bob Bergeron was flying in crashed just short of Calling Lake, about thirty miles north of Athabasca. Bergeron was a popular member of the community who was actively involved in the Kinsmen Club, Knights of Columbus and the Chamber of Commerce. It was believed that Bergeron, an experienced pilot, was blinded by a white out (February 10, 1971)

Syncrude asks for production increase

Syncrude Canada Ltd. announced it would request from the Alberta Oil and Gas Conservation Board that its maximum permitted capacity be raised from 80,000 to 125,000, Syncrude president Frank Spragins announced that if the increase is approved plans could then proceed for plant engineering and construction. (March 17, 1971)

Town manager appointed

Norman C. Crawford has been appointed Town manager and will join the New Town on May 1. In announcing Crawford's appointment, Town Board Chair Sam Hardin stated that the community required a town manager in order to ensure proper planning and orderly development during the Syncrude startup. The

Courier mused that "appointment of a town manager will hopefully avoid repetition of some of the problems encountered during the last period of rapid growth experienced in the town." (March 31, 1971)

Amoco start in Anzac

Construction has begun in Anzac by Amoco Canada Petroleum Company on an experimental oil sands project which will test in-situ (underground) combustion techniques. About fifteen workers will be employed on the project which will continue for about two years.

Cosmo walk earns $8,000

Danny Law, president of the Cosmopolitan Club, says the club hopes to collect about $8,000 from Saturday's Mukluk March and thus maintain Fort McMurray's fine record of the highest dollar per mile collection in the province. About four hundred residents took part in the walk with proceeds going to a variety of charities. The walk took place on Highway 63 from GCOS into town, about twenty miles.[17]

King and Queen of the north

No one could call a moose, duck or goose like Edwin "Tiny" O'Brien, Katie Sanderson or Lenora Mulawka. From the time the Fort McMurray Winter Carnival was established in 1967, through the 1970s, the trio were consistent winners at the event held each year along the Snye.

The carnival was launched as a way to preserve some of the northern traditions, and to stimulate the local economy. The Winter Carnival met that goal, hosting dog sled competitors from as far away as Alaska, Montana and Ontario. Other competitions involved cars and snowmobiles.

Just as the one hundred metre dash is the highlight of the summer Olympics, the top event of the Fort McMurray Winter Carnival was the King and Queen of the North competition. During the 1970s, the prestige as the most natural northerner often went to Katie Sanderson, and Tiny O'Brien. Sanderson came by her skills honestly. She was raised in a village above the Grand Rapids on the Athabasca River and came to Fort McMurray in 1922.

As Sanderson aged, she became one of the most respected aboriginal elders, as were Mulawka, Alvina Strasbourg and Evelyn Webb, who served as role models for thousands of young aboriginal people.

Tiny O'Brien on the other hand was not a local boy. He was born in Cape Breton and arrived in Fort McMurray in 1968 to become a power engineer at GCOS. In 1969, O'Brien entered the King of the North competition and with minimal training, took home the top trophy. He repeated the feat in 1970, '71, '76 and '77.

Some of the key events included moose, duck and goose calling, fire building, tea boiling, bannock baking, log chopping, snowshoe racing, jigging and wrestling. But the biggest event of all was the flour packing. Contestants were required to lift huge sacks of flour and walk forward six feet. Consistently, O'Brien could carry between eight hundred and fifty and one thousand pounds on his back, and his grimacing face was often depicted in the front photo of the *Fort McMurray Today* which followed the annual Winter Carnival.

For his trouble, O'Brien won a series of trophies and a permanent sign on his GCOS locker which read King of the North. O'Brien was also thrilled at being permitted to keep the sacks of flour he successfully carried. As for Katie Sanderson, perhaps O'Brien said it best. "Katie Sanderson was always Queen of the North even when she didn't win."[18]

The GCOS barbecue

When GCOS officially launched its Tar Island plant in 1967, there was considerable local attention paid to the five hundred visiting dignitaries and members of the media. However the following day, another party was held, ushering in an important tradition, the oil company barbecue whose popularity endures to this day.

The first GCOS employee barbecue attracted about five hundred employees and family members, and by 1971 that figure had tripled. *The McMurray Courier* reported that the July 23-25, 1971 barbecue attracted Sun Oil and GCOS President Ken Heddon. Due to rain, it was held at the Community Centre on King Street rather than at Peden's Point. Hawaiian singer Teo, along with a hypnotist named Hanale provided entertainment.

The tradition of the oil company barbecue evolved by the late 1970s into Fort McMurray's largest and most prolonged social gathering. By the late 1970s, Suncor and Syncrude rented MacDonald Island, and it sometimes it took a week of evenings to feed all of the company employees and their families.

Highway 63 paving begins

The rocky road for Fort McMurray began to improve in mid 1971. An initial three hundred thousand dollar contract was let in April to Wells Construction Ltd. to pave Highway 63 from Fort McMurray to the Hangingstone River past the Anzac turnoff. Paving would continue until mid-1970s when the total length of Highway 63 from Wandering River to Fort McMurray was completed.

Old boys club no more

The Fort McMurray Chamber of Commerce had one swinely blemish as it entered the 1970s. Women were not allowed.

The Chamber, like its predecessor the Fort McMurray Board of Trade, was seen as the community's primary networking organization. Former Town Board Chair Sam Hardin recalled that businessmen, town administrators, bankers, developers and others would meet on a regular basis and informally solve problems and broker deals without having to endure long open meetings.

However, in 1972, women began to fight back. Frances Jean, editor of the *McMurray Courier* and co-owner of Jean's Gifts and Stationery, was called by the Chamber to the Peter Pond Hotel to photograph pharmacist Walter Hill as he received a lifetime achievement award. To her amazement, she was asked to leave following the presentation.

"It was very chauvinistic," Jean recalled. "I was good enough for them to take the photo, but not to stay."[19] A second business person, Alice Haxton provided sandwiches for Chamber meetings, and, like Jean, was not permitted to stay.

In early fall 1972, Jean wrote a scathing editorial in the *Courier* lambasting the Chamber for being a good old boys club. She noted there were both good and bad businesspersons of each gender. Soon after, a vote was held, and Jean, along with Haxton, Alma Vogel and ABC accounting manager Grace Dafoe were voted in.

The next week, the *Courier* noted: "A segment of our society has come out of the Middle Ages to become part of the rest of the country."[20]

First supermarket

Although Fort McMurray has been previously served by a series of small grocery stores including the Red and White, Solo and the Hudson's Bay, it was not until 1972 that its first modern supermarket opened.

Syd Thompson had been eyeing Fort McMurray since 1968, and four years later decided to cash in on the coming of Syncrude. He opened Thompson's Super A in a new building owned by Ron and Evie Wolff and Ken and Diane Hill, just west of Hill Drugs.

Customers stampeded the new store snapping up fresh meat, fruit and vegetables minutes after they were placed on store shelves. One of those consumers, Betty Collicott recalled how during the early 1970s, customers were required to approach grocery shopping with skill and cunning. "After awhile, you'd get to know when the trucks showed up," Collicott recalled. "Then you'd study the flyer and be there ready when the truck pulled in."

Competition was fierce between Thompson's and Harry's Food Mart located in Plaza One. Often, items on special were snatched up before they ever made it on the shelves. "If you didn't get it, someone else would,"[21] recalled Collicott. It was widely recognized that Harry's had the best meat in town. Thompson's Super A's gained a reputation for good produce. As Fort McMurray continued to grow, so did Thompson's business. At one point in 1975, a typical convoy consisted of six tractor-trailers loaded with food.

Dora Thompson recalled that her husband always stressed good service. "The basis of our success was that Syd wanted to serve customers the best we could. He watched the bottom line and took care of our customers," she said. "That's how we succeeded."[22]

By 1975, Thompson's had four checkout counters. A can of tomato soup went for ten cents while pink salmon sold two for seventy-nine cents. Kraft dinner on special was priced at three for forty-three cents, and Jell-O sold for at a dime a package.

In 1976, construction was underway on a Safeway store which was to open adjacent to the Peter Pond Shopping Centre. It became obvious that major competitive forces were about to come into play. Thompson worked hard to support local community organizations, keep prices down and reinforce customer loyalty, but in 1975, when the Co-op approached with a buyout offer, the Thompsons accepted.

"I wasn't that fond of the cold weather and we felt it was time to take things a little slower,"[23] recalled Thompson. The Co-op took over in 1976 and lasted one year before going out of business. The space was later rented to the Brick, McLeod's and a video store.

Canada Safeway had been on the books since 1969 when Alarco's local manager Neil Costello announced to the Chamber of Commerce that an eighty-thousand -square-foot Safeway store would be built in the near future. Plans eventually called for Allard's company to develop the space occupied by the Sunoco station thus extending the Peter Pond Shopping Centre and forming one complex. However negotiations with Sunoco were never completed. The food chain opted to occupy a new building on the corner of the shopping centre at Franklin and Hardin.

The Courier, CJOK and The Today

Within any community, the media is more than a business. It plays a vital role in connecting newcomers, residents, businesses, and organizations. Through the first sixty years of the twentieth century, demand for a Fort McMurray newspaper or any other communication vehicle was limited.

The most effective medium around town was the *moccasin telegrah,* a system of word of mouth which carried news across McMurray and Waterways faster than any newspaper or radio station could. Coffee shops in McMurray and Waterways served as information hotbeds. There, residents would learn who arrived or departed on the train, or glean the latest gossip or local business information. During a period where Fort McMurray's population remained under fifteen hundred residents, these informal communication methods met residents' needs.

There were a few short lived attempts to launch weekly newspapers, but the combination of long hours, low profits, and transportation costs caused most to fold. During the 1950s, McMurray was served by a series of flysheets, student newspapers and add-on editions from Uranium City, Edmonton and even Grande Prairie. Then, in the 1960s, the newspapers began to roll in.

In the early 1960s, Art Playford launched the short-lived *Fort McMurray Banner* which proclaimed that it served the "Port of the North, the Doorway to the Arctic...Where Steel meets Keel, situated in the unspoiled (sic) historical wonderland of the great North West and the world's greatest oil deposit."[24] The Banner carried verbatim town council minutes, Chamber of Commerce doings and a sprinkling of community news and events.

The *Northern Star* was launched in 1967 as were both the *News and Advertiser* and the McMurray Sun. The *News and Advertiser* became the most popular and outlasted its competitors. Its content included a sprinkling of gossip and community news. The *News and Advertiser* folded in 1970 leaving a gap which was soon filled by Bernard and Frances Jean and the *McMurray Courier*. The Jeans opened a gift shop in 1968, and when the *News and Advertiser* ceased operations, decided to launch their own publication.

Former editor Frances Jean took pride in the fact that during the Courier's four year run, the newspaper never had to print a retraction. Its editorials were gutsy and its news coverage extended beyond town council highlights. Through their printing company and their church and community affiliations, the Jeans kept their fingers on the community pulse and the Courier's pages teamed with news, opinions and historical articles. One of the Jeans' special memories was of election night, 1971, when results were received at four a.m. and within two hours a special edition was available for workers to read on the buses going to the plant.

The Jeans, like so many before, saw newspaper publishing as a sacred responsibility, and often wrestled, particularly during the heated MacDonald Island debate, with how to fairly portray all sides of the issue without showing a blatant bias. But although the *Courier* provided a vital public service, it only published weekly.

During the early 1970s, broadcasting entrepreneur Roger Charest became intrigued by reports he was hearing about Fort McMurray's spectacular population growth. He recognized an opportunity to launch a radio station to serve northeastern Alberta. But there was risk.

While a great population boom was anticipated later in the decade, at the time the CRTC granted CJOK's license in 1972, there were barely eight thousand people in the community. Initial revenues would be low and startup costs would be high. Edmonton broadcaster Stu Morton was approached to head up the McMurray operation in the Hill building on Franklin Avenue.

"It was the most inexpensive installation in the history of radio," recalled Morton. "This was 1973 and the total capital cost was about seventy-thousand dollars. We were everything. We had five people and my wife was the receptionist. We worked from about five-thirty a.m. until about nine at night. Sometimes I attended the Council meeting and for the first six months or so all we did was sleep and work, living on adrenaline and caffeine."[25]

The station began with Charest, Morton and two Edmonton staff members. Then one day, Charest received a resume from a cocky eighteen-year-old whose father owned the A&W Restaurant a few feet from the station. John Shields was a local boy who had dreams of entering broadcasting. Soon after Shields applied, Morton appeared at the restaurant with a pile of albums and told Shields he would be starting immediately.

Shields hosted the evening show, offering middle of the road favourites such as Nat King Cole and Tony Bennett. The radio station eventually allowed him to try a rock program which aired long after adults were tucked into bed. Charest and Morton wanted to ensure that the station had a community feel and attempted to serve a wide audience. During the early days, the station sold space to evangelists. There was an aboriginal language program and along with Helga Williams' International House of Music.

Probably the station's most important contribution was in uniting the community. While the *moccasin telegraph* and the *Courier* were vital local media, CJOK offered residents the chance to immediately publicize events. During the mid -1970s, scores of new cultural, religious, recreational, political, occupational and leisure groups formed. Clubs could announce their plans or receive news coverage with little delay, and this factor contributed greatly to the meteoric growth of the number and success of community groups during the 1970s.

"All of a sudden you could have a meeting or hold an event and it would be on the radio station the next day,"[26] recalled longtime resident Bunny Philpott. Local sports scores and game accounts would be aired the same evening or the following morning. People heard their names or the names of friends and neighbours on the air each day, and this helped reinforce Fort McMurray's growing sense of community. CJOK also helped to orient newcomers to their new community.

"Everyone had CJOK on," recalled longtime resident Ron Morgan. "You'd get up to speed pretty quickly about news and sports if you just listened for awhile."[27]

Programs such as *Ches Dicks' sports reports*, or the *Trading Post* served to unite Fort McMurray and make superstars out of everyday residents. "I think we had a role in bringing people together," reflected Dicks. "It was an exciting time. I couldn't believe how many people listened to sports. I made one mistake and a thousand people reminded me."[28] For eight years, Dicks' gravel-voiced sports commentary "That's the way I see it," was a mainstay of the station's morning programming.

The *Trading Post* offered new and departing residents the chance to buy and sell furniture, motor vehicle parts, work clothing and other key items. "You had to host it almost as a talk show," recalled Shields, one of the *Trading Post's* first hosts. "Some people want to buy and sell, others just wanted to talk."[29]

CJOK first aired on New Year's Eve 1972, and began broadcasting on Jan 1, 1973. As Morton recalled:

We put together this tape of bits of the last year and we played that from six p.m. to midnight. We cut in about halfway through this song and the control room was full of people, staff, friends, and people we'd met. Everyone screamed Happy New Year at midnight and then we started going[30].

Throughout Fort McMurray, at parties everywhere, residents remained glued to their radios, to hear the CJOKs first song played as Fort McMurray's official radio station. It was *I Can See Clearly Now, by Johnny Nash*.

In October 1974, a new media player arrived in Fort McMurray. Based on its longtime success publishing a daily newspaper in Grande Prairie, Bowes Publishers was eager to establish a ground level presence in Fort McMurray prior to the launch of Syncrude.

But there was a problem. Bowes could not proceed in a community already supporting the popular *McMurray Courier*. On two occasions, Bowes offered to buy the Courier, and each time the Jeans refused. However, by mid 1974, the Jeans had become tired of the long hours and family sacrifices. In July, a deal was struck for Bowes to buy the Courier for one hundred thousand dollars.

Bowes took ownership in mid-September and published the Courier for three weeks before launching the *Fort McMurray Today* during the first week of October. *The Today* attempted to be many things to McMurray. It felt a responsibility to keep McMurrayites abreast of developments within the oil industry. It also attempted to be a community voice.

Peter Duffy was brought in from Bowes' newspaper in Truro, Nova Scotia to act as editor and publisher. Duffy was an expert photographer and newsman who quickly acquired accounting and management skills.

From the outset, Duffy knew he had to promote the newspaper, not just in Fort McMurray but beyond. He and wife Dawna ordered a pile of oil sand and from their small apartment began sending samples stapled to a small promotional card to businesses throughout Canada.

Sending oil sands samples outside of Fort McMurray boosted subscriptions to *the Today* and to the *Oilsands Review* which *The Today* published for one year. Day by day, Duffy watched *the Today* rise from eight pages to more than forty pages on Fridays by the close of the 1970s.

Duffy eventually moved to Halifax where he became the *Halifax Chronicle's* featured columnist. He recalled his time in Fort McMurray with fondness.

"I wouldn't be the person that I am if I hadn't lived in Fort McMurray," he said. "It was such a daunting task and an exciting opportunity to launch a daily newspaper. Here were fourteen thousand people just like me, all here from somewhere else, all with a passion to show what they could do individually and collectively. It was magic."[31]

Eddie Engstom's three mysteries

To those who remember him, Eddie Engstrom was a person of kindness and perfection, who was surrounded by mystery and suspicion.

Engstrom came to Fort McMurray after World War II where he lived on Fraser Avenue west of Hardin Street in a peaceful pink house surrounded by a pink fence, with flowers blooming throughout the summer. During the winter, he would live on his trapline about fifty miles up the Clearwater River.

After Engstrom's death in 1973, his home and lot were turned over to the Fort McMurray Scouts and Guides who used rent revenues received to partially fund development of Engstrom Lake, a youth camp located along Highway 881. During his lifetime, Engstrom took an interest in young people, teaching them to fish, build boats and survive in the bush. He was known as a perfectionist who would not tolerate trespassers or those who upset his natural surroundings. Specifically, he would become incensed if someone trampled through the perfect snow outside his home or cabin.

His memory would have remained unblemished if not had it not been for one incident which occurred in June 1973. Engstrom's siste,Greta, arrived from Sweden to visit her brother. Engstrom took his canoe, along with supplies and his two large dogs, and guided his sister up the Clearwater River to see his summer cabin. On the trip, the canoe tipped and Engstrom's dogs drowned. Engstrom told police that his sister had made it to shore but had refused to get back into the canoe. Engstrom travelled downstream to Elmer Cree's cabin where he remained that night.

Greta was never heard from again and her body was never found. The accident took place on a Wednesday afternoon, but police were only notified on Friday at five p.m. A dozen searchers combed a ten-mile area amidst thick bush, swamp and swarms of mosquitoes and black flies. Rescue attempts were hampered by heavy rain.

Many questions surrounded the tragedy. Why did the canoe tip while an expert river navigator was at the helm? Why were Engstrom's dogs tied into the boat? Why did Greta Engstrom refuse to return to her brother's canoe? Why was a body never found? Why didn't Engstrom tell Elmer Cree about the accident until the next day, and why did it take so long to report the tragedy to the RCMP?

No charges were ever laid. After his sister's death, Engstrom began to drink heavily. In early September 1973, his body was found half out of his canoe, face in the water, drifting in the Clearwater River. Engstrom had suffered a heart attack.

McMurrayites puzzled whether Greta's death had been linked to an earlier mystery: Why did Eddie Engstrom leave his wife and child in Sweden in 1923 and why did he never send for them? Did Greta hold some secret?

Upon his death, Engstrom left his money and property to the Scouts and Guides, and his canoe to his good friend and river neighbour, D.D. Williams. Williams was a longtime trapper and worker with Imperial Oil who after Engstom's death scattered his ashes, and took over his cabin. The camp used as a base by the RCMP to search for Greta Engstrom was preserved and now serves as a public campsite.

Engstrom also left behind a manuscript which spoke of a mysterious silver deposit near the southern slope of Muskeg Mountain, about halfway to the Saskatchewan border. His manuscript speaks of many nearby creeks but does not give an exact location.

Engstrom wrote: "It was easy to visualize the whole big mountain was just one huge pile of silver and I was the only man with any knowledge of it."[32] One day, while prospecting the silver deposit, small rocks began to roll. The small slide turned into an avalanche which pinned Engstrom's legs. Contact Airways pilot-owner Milt McDougall spotted him, landed and transferred him to hospital where Engstrom spent two weeks recuperating. The exact spot was never located, and Engstrom gave up his mining efforts. In his manuscript which was published in 1984, Engstrom teased his readers about the mysterious silver deposit with the following challenge.

I am too old now, so what would I do with it? So why take the thrill away from someone else finding it. It is there. I know. I found it...and you can if you want to -and good luck to you[33].

The seventh game

Some call it the best hockey game ever played in Fort McMurray. It occurred on March 24, 1973 at the Townsite Arena as GCOS and Redwood battled in the seventh and deciding game of the Fort McMurray Men's Senior Hockey League championships.

GCOS was the underdog team. Down three games to one, GCOS had battled back and set up the final game to establish hockey supremacy in Fort McMurray. Fans began camping outside the arena late in the afternoon, and minutes after the doors opened at six p.m., the seats were full.

No one remembers the final score, but what they do recall is that the game was tied after regulation time. The teams remained deadlocked after twenty minutes of overtime and through another eighteen minutes of a second overtime period.

"CJOK was broadcasting the game and as people heard that the game was in overtime, they began wandering over to the arena,"[34] recalled town councillor and sportsman Ron Morgan. "Before you knew it the place was packed with nine hundred people."

And then came the goal. Redwood forward Paul Loutit gathered the puck just inside the red line and streaked down right wing. Loutit blasted a low shot which found the net, and it was over. Redwood had recovered to win the Fort McMurray championship.

"Not only was the game great because of the tension but also because of the intensity," recalled former league official Wayne Jones. "It was end to end action for almost five periods."[35] Those who remember the game recall that it was pure hockey, played by local heroes in a cold arena which had a low ceiling and no glass separating the players and the fans.

As Jones recalled the March 24, 1973 game, he also remembered the second most important sports event of the 1970s. In 1978, Tarsands Machine and Welding won the Alberta Senior A Fastball championships and competed in the national tournament held in New Brunswick.

Although Tarsands Machine and Welding did not win top honours, it provided hope that the small community of Fort McMurray could provide homegrown champions at the national level. These heroes would eventually include NHL hockey players Chris Philips and Danny Hodgson.

Business that never closed

The Sunoco station on Franklin Avenue may have been the only building in Fort McMurray which had no front door key. From the time it opened in 1967 to its closure in 1991, the front door was never locked. During that period Sunoco often served as the port of entry for motorists who had successfully negotiated Highway 63 north from Wandering River.

The station opened in 1967 on orders from J. Howard Pew to operate on a break-even basis. This, Pew felt, would help keep gasoline and labour costs in check throughout Fort McMurray. Sunoco was the flagship retail outlet for Sun Oil, and the Fort McMurray station was the only one of its kind west of Ontario. During late 1960s and early 1970s, the station earned the distinction of selling more gas than any other Sunoco station in Canada. During the late 1970s, a twin station opened in Thickwood Heights.

The station's first manager, Keith MacLeod remained with Sunoco until 1977, succeeded by Glen Ellert who joined Sunoco in 1973. From the beginning, the Sunoco station served as a twenty-four hour a day repair shop for vehicles which had just wobbled off Highway 63. Vehicles often suffered punctured gas tanks and a variety of other rips and tears while travelling along Highway 63 which was not completely paved until the mid '70s. Undercarriage problems were so common that Sunoco purchased large rolls of industrial rubber and installed them on the undersides of many Edmonton-bound vehicles. This protected most cars and trucks from the unexpected potholes and jagged rocks which lay in waiting.

Sunoco crews were on duty twenty-four hours a day to fix flat tires. The Sunoco station also served as a pickup point and a phone outlet for new arrivals. Sometimes a half dozen people would crowd the customer area of the station in the middle of the night, some with pets and suitcases in tow, waiting for family and friends to pick them up.

"We felt we had a responsibility to keep people safe and out of the cold," said Ellert. "For many years it was the official community pick up and drop off point."[36]

When it became time for the Sunoco to finally close in 1991, a key was finally located, however because the lock had never been used, it had seized due to rust. A new lock was installed and the station was finally closed.

Father Beau

Father Maurice Beauregard once compared himself to a cat with nine lives. On at least four occasions he came perilously close to death, and each time survived.

He would frequently say that his survival was a matter of faith and that he had more of God's work to do.

Father Beauregard, known to those of all denominations as Father Beau, came to Fort McMurray in 1969 to oversee construction of the St. John's Catholic Church. He is credited with completing the project on time and on budget.

From the mid-1960s to the 1980s, Father Beau's popularity took on cult like status after surviving four close calls with death. During the 1960s, Father Beau was wounded in a hostage-taking incident in the Northwest Territories when he successfully grabbed a weapon from a gunman. On March 28, 1971, Father Beauregard was inside the Anzac Roman Catholic Church when a propane tank exploded. He recalled that the force of the explosion was so strong that a small refrigerator was lifted into the air and remained suspended for a few moments before falling. Father Beauregard suffered cracked ribs. He also survived a near fatal blood clot, and in 1982 was mugged in Florida while on vacation. Beauregard 69, at the time suffered a shattered jaw and broken ribs.

"I keep getting close, but the Lord doesn't want me yet,"[37] he said in a 1983 interview. Father Beauregard was also active in forming the Fort McMurray Ministerial Association.

Father Beau died in1998 and his name was preserved by the Fort McMurray Catholic School Board in the naming of Fort McMurray's first community school, the Father Beauregard Edu-Com Centre.

La connection francaise

You won't hear complaints from anyone within the local French community that during the 1960s and 70s there was nothing to do in Fort McMurray.

Every Saturday night, someone hosted a party, and the entire community was invited. Although French Canadians had been living in Fort McMurray since the early 1900s, the community began to gel during the GCOS and Syncrude construction booms. Community leaders such as Andy Gaudet, George Caouette and Armand Parent ensured that any new arrivals, whether they were from nearby Plamondon or from eastern Canada, found a job.

Gaudet's Esso station on Franklin Avenue often served as an landing spot for new French Canadian arrivals. In many cases, newcomers from Plamondon, Atmore and Lac La Biche lacked English proficiency. By working at Gaudet's Esso, many acquired English skills and were quickly able to integrate into the community.

And on Saturday nights, in particular during the 1970s, French clans which included the Gauthiers, Gaudets, Caoeuttes, Laroses, and Theriaults partied with only a record player and a deck of cards.

Joe Gauthier was twenty-one years old when in 1965 he first arrived in Fort McMurray. He came to town looking for an improvement over the stale life he was living in Plamondon. He was invited by Johnny Sandulac and uncle Ovilla "Slim"

Gauthier to drive cab. From there, Gauthier became a truck driver and volunteer fireman. In 1975, Gauthier was hired as Fort McMurray's third paid fireman, behind Chief Roy Hawkins and Deputy Chief Archie Goodwin. Gauthier recalled how close the Fort McMurray French community was.

"People like Andy Gaudet took us all in," he said. "Andy has a heart the size of a barn. He's the man who put us on our feet. He signed loans to help you out. We were all close, and it all came out on Saturday night."[38]

As Yvette Gaudet recalled, "There wasn't really that much recreation so we made our own parties and went down to the river together. A bunch of us got together with our kids, on a big boat down the Clearwater River. Joe Gauthier played the piano and we sang until all hours of the morning. We had a ball. Those are very good memories."[39]

Fires to remember

Prior to the 1970s, fires were a way of life in Fort McMurray. Extreme cold required local residents to pump coal and wood into dirty stoves, and often sparks would ignite and destroy the town's dry wooden buildings.

Through improved construction, heating and fire prevention, the situation improved into the 1970s with only seven fires of more than one hundred thousand dollars in damage reported. One of the most talked about was the November 1973 blaze which gutted the Islander Restaurant and surrounding businesses. The fire began in a motorcycle shop located in Plaza One and spread across to the Islander, also destroying an adjacent butcher shop.

Total damage was three hundred thousand dollars. Other serious fires during the 1970s included Redwood Redi-Mix (April 1974, one hundred seventy thousand dollars), Swanson Lumber (August 1974, four hundred thousand dollars), Black Gold Exchange (April 1976, one hundred and fifteen thousand dollars), Abasand Recreation Centre (July 1977, one hundred thousand dollars), Abasand Hangingstone Place, (October 1977, two hundred and fifty thousand dollars) and Haxton's General Store (December 1979, two hundred and fifty thousand dollars).

Heroism avoids catastrophe

One of Fort McMurray closest brushes with disaster occurred in 1960s as fire-fighters were summoned to Canadian Propane to extinguish a propane fire which had the potential to destroy a large portion of the Prairie area

While filling a propane truck, the line which carried fuel ignited, sending flames back to the station's main tank. Had the tank blown, fire chief Roy Hawkins believed that the explosion could have wiped out an entire block.

While dozens of firefighters and residents stood back at about an eighty-foot distance, Hawkins and Deputy Fire Chief Archie Goodwin heroically crept up to the tank. Hawkins covered the flames with three overcoats; Goodwin shut off the valve.

"It could have very well exploded," Hawkins recalled. "Funny thing is that everyone stood back behind the fence, but had it blown, they would have gone too."[40]

Rumours, and Election 74

The biggest issue of the 1974 election was one that was never discussed in the newspaper, radio or television. It was a rumour which raged on the street, in the bars, in living rooms and behind closed doors.

The rumours circled around businessman Sigi Lucas who until 1969 ran an establishment known as The Place which was frequented by Fort McMurray's late night crowd. Rumours began filling the community that the establishment was a popular drug haven.

It is hard for the purposes of this historical text to offer opinions on these rumours, however, there are some facts which bear mention. Sigi Lucas was never charged with any crime. The RCMP devoted considerable attention to investigating these rumours, and in spite of suspicions, no hard evidence was uncovered.

The reason Sigi Lucas was so central to the 1974 election was in the nomination of two final candidates, Al Campbell and Neil Costello. There were seven seats open on Town Board, and it appeared on nomination day that only seven candidates would run, including Sigi Lucas. By 1974, the German-born Lucas was active in a number of successful business ventures including the Peter Pond Hotel Restaurant, The Heartbreak Hotel, and a number of new apartments buildings.

At the last minute, Costello, who was Allarco's Fort McMurray manager, and Campbell, owner of the Riviera Hotel, decided to run. On nomination day, nine candidates filed papers, but Campbell withdrew the following day leaving eight to contest the election.

On the surface, the election was fought on issues such as where new development should be located; Abasand Heights, Beacon Hill or Thickwood Heights. But under the surface the real issue was Sigi Lucas.

Matters came to a head during two open line talks shows, one aired on CJOK and other on ABC Cable. On CJOK, which at the time did not have a seven-second delay, Lucas was asked live to respond to the drug rumours. Subsequently, when he appeared on ABC Cable, the issue came up again. At first, Lucas calmly stated that he appreciated the opportunity to refute the rumours, but when a subsequent question was posed, Lucas lost his temper.

In the 1974 elections, Lucas finished last of eight candidates. Lawsuits were subsequently filed against CJOK and ABC Cable, however these lawsuits were laid to rest in 1977, when the small plane Lucas was a passenger in crashed just short of the Edmonton Municipal Airport. Lucas did not survive.

The 1974 elections produced a Town Board made up of Chuck Knight, Ron Morgan, Jean Davidson, Keith MacLeod, Dr. Al Nicholson, Bill Gendreau and Neil Costello.

Gendreau's election would launch a twenty-one year career as a Town Board member and as a city council member. Gendreau served on council while working in GCOS' top shop where heavy equipment was repaired. He often brought issues of blue-collar workers to the council table, and was instrumental in negotiating union contracts with town hall employees. Gendreau was also a driving force behind the establishment of a transit system. He recalled how in late 1974 the Province forced the Town Board to develop Abasand Heights even though it was the Board's desire to develop Thickwood Heights.

Housing Minister Bill Yurko appeared before Town Board soon after the election and threatened dire financial consequences if Abasand was not developed.

"We developed it and we're still repairing the hill at the expense of the people of Fort McMurray,"[41] said Gendreau.

Being single during the boom

During Syncrude's construction period, there were many daily pressures at the Canadian Bechtel work site. But faced with a crushing number of single men working long hard hours, the most obvious pressure point may have been the lack of women.

In 1974, Debbie Cameron decided to leave her comfortable Edmonton life and venture north to Fort McMurray. She and a friend arrived at the Peter Pond Hotel at eleven p.m. one Friday evening as Fort McMurray's night life was heating up. Cameron looked around at the sea of men and asked, "are there no other women who live here?" Within minutes, Cameron and her friend were interviewed at the bar by a number of perspective employers and were hired on the spot by a surveying company.

Soon after, Cameron found work on the Syncrude construction site while living in an Atco trailer camp. She and twenty other women were protected twenty-four hours a day from the hordes of men who surrounded them.

"Guys would get a bit drunk late at night, take their clothes off and streak down our hallway." she recalled. "First time it happened it was a bit unsettling, but after awhile you took it in stride. There were always guys around trying to ask you out. You just about had to beat them off with the stick."[42]

Norma Jean Atkinson, a teacher from Saskatchewan had similar brushes with popularity. "I remember going to the Peter Pond bar and it was like a big barn when teachers would go there for a drink after school," Atkinson recalled. "I noticed women went to the washroom in twos and I wondered why until I went by myself and couldn't believe how many times someone reached out and slapped my behind or pinched it or whatever. I didn't know these people and I wasn't dressed in a seductive way. After we left, men followed us out. We were not used to this."[43]

Cameron noted that while surrounded by aggressive men, she never felt threatened. She met future husband Leo Robert at the camp and the couple went on to

---

found L. Robert Enterprises, one of Fort McMurray's most successful and community minded businesses. Debbie also became active in the professional businesswomen's association and later served as Chair of Keyano College Board of Governors.

Worked hard, played hard

During the late 1970s, John Wilson came to Fort McMurray with his dad to provide summer paving services. That job led to another and another, and soon the Wilsons were spending more time in Fort McMurray than in Dryden, Ontario where their home and business was located. It was difficult to find a permanent crew in Fort McMurray so the Wilsons brought their own team of eight workers from Dryden. The first year, 1978, the Wilson crew stayed at the Heartbreak Hotel. The following year they rented a basement with sheets of plywood separating ten rooms.

"The town was wild and crazy then," John Wilson recalled. "There were ten guys for every girl so we had to bring in their girlfriends. It was the late seventies and there was hard drinking and hard working. Sometimes after a heavy night, I'd show up for work and I was alone. No one else got up."[44]

In 1980, Wilson graduated from university and moved to Fort McMurray where he continued to build the family business. He still has some of that original crew working with him. today. Wilson has become one of Fort McMurray's most respected community leaders.

The wave of new arrivals

For ten years beginning in 1975, Karen Saunderson had a front row seat as new arrivals pulled into Fort McMurray. People from across Canada arrived in town on speculation believing rumours of immediate jobs and prosperity. During the mid-1970s, Saunderson worked in Fort McMurray as an employment counselor.

From 1970 to 1980, Fort McMurray's population grew from about six thousand six hundred and eighty-four to about twenty-seven thousand seven hundred and eighty-four representing an increase during one decade of over four hundred per cent. The community was stretched beyond capacity. One of the first stops that new arrivals often made was to Chow's Varieties, a magazine and smoke shop on Franklin Avenue. It was usual for Chow's to open at noon. One day in 1975, Chow employed some labourers to complete renovations to his store from eight a.m. to noon, and they recorded one hundred and twenty "pulls" to the locked door before the store opened.

"The local people knew that the store opened at noon, but the new people didn't know that," said owner Wayne Chow. "These were all new people with dirty cars from the highway and with license plates from Newfoundland, Quebec and Ontario. They wanted to buy a newspaper to look for jobs."[45]

The newcomers' second stop was often the Canada Employment Centre. Karen Saunderson saw repeated cases of newcomers arriving penniless, searching for immediate jobs with quick pay. "They expected the streets to be paved with gold," Saunderson recalled. "I remember one situation where a family arrived on the bus without any money expecting to be able to start working right away and have a place to live and all."[46]

Accommodation was difficult to find and even if an apartment was available, often first and last months rent, plus a damage deposit was hard to raise. These harsh realities affected many new arrivals, including one of the receptionists working at the Canada Employment Centre. After a few weeks on the job, it became apparent that the receptionist was living in the Lion's Park campground, and would go to Centennial Pool each morning to shower. She would visit the laundromat regularly so that her outfits were tidy and clean.

Faced with problems finding accommodation, many families camped at Lion's Park located at the juncture of McMurray and Waterways, or at Centennial Park situated south of Beacon Hill.

The accommodation squeeze also created a pet crisis. Because most apartments did not allow pets, many new arrivals set their dogs and cats free. As winter temperatures plunged to minus forty degrees, town officials were forced to bring hundreds of cats and dogs to veterinarian Dr. Bob Gilbert to be destroyed. He reminded the media during the height of the crisis, that "I became a veterinarian to help animals not to destroy them."[47]

In 1977, Pauline Phibbs, Dr. Gilbert and a number of other concerned citizens including Clara Johnson and Renee Spence launched an SPCA which was eventually located in space provided by the town near the municipal landfill.

Winnipeg pact saves Syncrude

Fort McMurray's road to prosperity developed a major pothole in late 1974, when one of Syncrude's partners pulled out of the consortium.

Although Syncrude construction had begun in 1973, Syncrude's partners had set a deadline of October 1974, for receiving final construction costs. However, Atlantic Richfield, which owned a thirty per cent share in the Syncrude pie began to show signs of queasiness. It was involved in explorations in Alaska and faced with projected Syncrude construction costs which had doubled to over two billion dollars, it announced that it would not be participating.

The remaining partners began searching for new investors, however based on the new technology and seemingly high risk, few oil companies jumped at the opportunity.

It soon became clear that if Syncrude were to proceed, the public sector would have to intervene. On February 3, 1975, following months of consultation, representatives of Imperial Oil, Gulf and Cities Service met in Winnipeg with officials from the Alberta, Ontario and Canadian governments to develop a formula to save Syncrude.

"The project was so important to the future of Alberta and of Canada, that we felt something of significance had to be done," said former Premier Peter Lougheed. "The plants didn't come with an instruction manual, so someone was going to have to take the risk."[48]

By nine-thirty p.m. a deal was hand written on a loose piece of paper, which eventually evolved into four fat volumes of terms and conditions. Atlantic Richfield's thirty per cent would be replaced by the Canadian government (fifteen per cent) Alberta (ten per cent) and Ontario (five per cent). Alberta also agreed to fund a utilities plant and pipeline through the Alberta Energy Company. As well, Alberta set aside its normal royalty structure in favour of a profit sharing agreement.

After details of the agreement were released, Imperial Oil Chair Jack Armstrong admitted how close the Syncrude consortium had come to folding. "There was not a doubt the whole thing could have gone down the drain," he said. "We stood to lose everything we had invested over the years."[49] At the time of the Winnipeg Agreement, the companies had already sunk five hundred million into Syncrude.

Following the release of the landmark agreement, word went out to factories around the world to push ahead on Syncrude contracts. Syncrude was now fully funded and backed by a strong mix of governments and private companies. Fort McMurray's partnership with Syncrude Canada was cemented. The oil companies, governments and particularly the residents of Fort McMurray collectively exhaled.

As Syncrude project manager Chuck Collyer later reflected:

It was a great relief, but if you would have seen how hard the owners fought to keep it alive, you would have had to believe in the final outcome. They were so determined, it encouraged all of us to try to maintain the credibility and integrity of the project while we waited for the final decision. Happily it was the right decision.[50]

Rough times

The construction of Syncrude brought to Fort McMurray a wave of humanity which would stretch all of its resources to full capacity. Bank lineups extended from the teller to the outdoors. The lineup to the liquor store on Franklin Avenue extended one hundred yards east. As was the case during the GCOS boom, hotels like the Oilsands, the Riviera and the Peter Pond were packed with hard drinking patrons who would often take their personal disputes outdoors to various parking lots within the community.

Sergeant Don Rumpel, a solid and heavy man would often venture into hotels and find one of his officers surrounded by drunken bar patrons eager to "beat up a cop." On one occasion, Rumpel walked in and threatened to arrest an entire bar if they did not stop fighting. He also recalls on one night sending a drunken group outside the back door of the Oilsands Hotel, where a forestry van was on hand and immediately recruited them for firefighting.

"Policing was hard work but it was fun," Rumpel recalled. "You had to rely on your own resources and you had no one to back you up. You had to rely on your own wits."[51]

The story is told of how one new RCMP recruit came to town with a chip on his shoulders. Rumpel challenged him to settle their differences in the back of the police headquarters on the force's wrestling mats. After some hesitation the recruit declined. The rookie remained in McMurray for some time and in Rumpel's words became a "good cop." Rumpel was tough, but had a soft side. Many a prisoner released after a night in the cells would receive from him a five-dollar bill for breakfast and cigarettes.

Tales of boom

Many stories which occurred during the Syncrude and GCOS boom never made it to the newspapers. Some actually occurred, others are urban legends.

During both GCOS and Syncrude construction periods, card games which occurred after work shifts ended took on massive proportions. It was not unheard of for thirty thousand dollars to sit on the table at any time.

Usually, games were governed by their own system of camp justice. On one occasion, a card player was observed cheating. The player was severely beaten, thrown in a truck and dumped on Highway 63.

A second story, one which the RCMP never confirmed deals with the fate of a card shark who apparently walked away with twenty-four thousand dollars without allowing fellow players an opportunity to earn it back. As the story goes, he was found at the camp dump stuffed into a garbage bag. The incident was denied by company officials and the RCMP but during the 1970s there were many workers at the plant who swore to its authenticity. Other similar stories are told of workers who won large gambling sums ending up in the Athabasca River. There is some question whether these were "camp legends" or real incidents, but they exist as part of the tales which surround the Syncrude construction period.

Former RCMP Staff Sergeant Peter Forster said it was often hard to confirm these stories because many workers at the plants were transients who in some cases were on the run or who moved between jobs. "It's possible these things happened, but most could never be confirmed."52

Suspicious grave:

With rumours swirling of missing plant workers, RCMP took seriously news of a suspicious grave which appeared in 1971 at the Biggs Avenue cemetery.

In spite of their best investigative efforts, no one could figure out whose body was contained in the grave. Sergeant Don Rumpel asked two constables to unearth the grave's contents. As both dug nervously, they hit something solid.

As they began to lift it, they saw rubber and then metal. "It was a full-sized motor bike," recalled Rumpel. We never found out who had stolen it or buried it."53

Highway 63 shootings:

One day in 1974, RCMP received three complaints within thirty minutes of someone shooting at cars on the Syncrude camp road. Sergeant Rumpel told his constables to drive along the dangerous area while he trotted about twenty yards behind.

Three shots rang out and while the vehicle sped off, Rumpel ran into the bush in search of the shooter. Rumpel and the gunman traded shots. Rumpel remained in the area all night and with the aid of dogs and Edmonton reinforcements combed the bush near Supertest Hill.

In the morning, just as he was ready to end the search, he drove one more time around the area and saw a man wandering along the road. The man later confessed to the shootings. "There was no reason he did it," said Rumpel. "He said he was just doing it for fun." [54]

One day in 1972, a motorist stopped along Highway 63 to help a pedestrian carrying a rifle. The motorists thought he was assisting a lost hunter, and soon learned how wrong he was.

The motorist was told to "take off or be shot," according to one former RCMP. The motorists drove straight to RCMP headquarters who arrested the gunman who was fined fifty dollars in Fort McMurray court.

Bechtel raisin wine

One of the biggest problems Mounties faced during GCOS and Syncrude construction was the sale of illicit camp liquor. Workers building the plants often balked at driving twenty miles to the Fort McMurray liquor store. During the mid 1970s, an enterprising duo turned their footlocker into a manufacturing plant for raisin wine.

The RCMP eventually raided the operation and found fifteen gallons of refined moonshine. One worker swore he had no idea the other was producing the spirits.

Love for hire

It was a lonely time for men working on the Syncrude construction. Some Edmonton and Vancouver based women of the night understood those urges and parlayed them into small fortunes [55].

Bechtel camp officials told the stories during the 1970s of women being dressed as men being snuck into camps in trunks. There are also stories of boogie vans being parked outside local hotels.

Bomb scares:

Former RCMP officers recall two bomb scares; one during the GCOS construction period, and other during the building of Syncrude.

The first occurred during the late 1960s following a call to GCOS that a bomb would go off at four p.m. that day. Only critical staff remained on the job. The remainder were sent home. Each department head combed their particular areas but came up empty. As four p.m. approached everyone stood outside and held their breath. But there was no blast.

At four-thirty p.m. just as everyone was about to leave, a call came in that a bomb had been located behind a control panel in the coke plant. It appeared to be dynamite wrapped up.

"We unscrewed each screw one at a time and it felt like hours," recalled Rumpel. "I remember sweat falling down and finally when we pulled it out and opened it, it was a package of cardboard tubes."[56] The plant was back to full activity the following day.

In 1975, the Syncrude site was evacuated due to another bomb scare. A heavily accented man phoned Syncrude spewing political jargon and warning that a timepiece had been planted on site.

No device was found.

Almost bank robbery

The RCMP learned during the 1970s, that the best place to gather intelligence was in the bars. There, they learned that a number of transient workers planned to knock off the Canadian Imperial Bank of Commerce.

The RCMP prepared for the robbery with officers inside the bank, outside, in unmarked police cars and plainclothes.

The would be thieves walked back and forth in front of the bank, eventually got cold feet and walked away.

No arrests were made.

Murder at the Pond

Probably the most publicized case of violence during the Syncrude boom years came in 1975 when a jealous husband walked into the Peter Pond bar with a loaded shotgun and ordered his business partner outside to answer charges of an affair with his wife. Shots were fired outside the bar, and when the smoke cleared, the accused man lay dead in a pool of blood.

In the late 1970s, RCMP were involved in a search through the bush behind Thickwood Heights. A Ross Haven Drive resident shot his wife and took his sister-in-law hostage. She was later released, and the gunman was arrested and convicted.

Both incidents were widely publicized in the Edmonton media as examples of how rough Fort McMurray was. But as former Staff Sergeant Ted Mason reflected, "We had all the ingredients for more violence to happen."[57] Mason noted that considering the quantity of liquor and small drugs travelling through Fort McMurray during the boom period, criminal incidents were remarkably few.

Bechtel 500

God help anyone who was driving north to Fort McMurray on Friday afternoon. After a full workweek building the Syncrude site, it was common for Bechtel employees to jump into their cars and speed full bore past Fort McMurray en route to Edmonton.

As former Keyano College president Doug Schmit would remember, "they drove out from Syncrude four abreast, and God help you if you were driving in the other direction." Fort McMurray's hospital was flooded with fatal car crashes during that period. Empty beer and liquor bottles littered the highway and when the RCMP organized a check stop between Fort McMurray and Marianna Lakes, they would notice a mountain of bottles in the ditch one hundred yards in each direction.

And then there was the airplane patrol. "The first time we sent the airplane in the air to catch speeders we were up for twenty-four hours and issued twelve hundred speeding tickets," recalled Rumpel. "One guy got caught four times on one trip. He didn't learn."[58]

A typical family

Often, when we look back at the GCOS and Syncrude construction period, it's the mud, the fights and the lack of accommodation which receives much of the attention. But in reality, the Fort McMurray story of the boom period is about families and the rise of such bedroom communities as Beacon Hill, Abasand Heights and Thickwood Heights.

While the RCMP was kept busy with a moderate increase in activity, neighborhoods flourished with new homes, parks and schools. It took the commitment of families to fill these neighbourhoods. Dale and Jean Unruh is such a couple.

I first met the Unruhs on October 8, 1976 two days after arriving in Fort McMurray. I answered an ad in the *Fort McMurray Today* for accommodation, and took what I could, which happened to be space in the Unruhs' backyard, holiday trailer. Later I would move inside and room with two other boarders.

The Unruhs were a typical family drawn by the Fort McMurray dream. They had seen brochures of the community's new schools and recreational facilities and decided Fort McMurray offered a compromise between big city and small town life. At the time of their arrival in 1973, the couple had a two-year-old son, Dale, and a four-year-old daughter Kelly. The Unruhs also had job offers in Vancouver, and in Cantung, NWT but chose Fort McMurray.

"We had a family vote and decided against Vancouver as it was just too big a city," recalled Jean. "There was no road into Cantung and you had to commit to live there for two years. Our new home was going to be Fort McMurray."[59]

Like so many who chose Fort McMurray, the Unruh's extended family was shocked by the decision. "Every time we mentioned to anyone where we were moving to, they reacted with negativity; the mosquitoes, cold weather and so on," she recalled. "They had never heard of the oilsands or GCOS, but they had heard of what a terrible place Fort McMurray was."[60]

Dale was provided lodging in a duplex on Pond Crescent and two days before Christmas, 1973 the remainder of the family drove up from Edmonton in minus twenty-eight degree temperatures along a highway which seemed to go on forever.

"I remember thinking to myself what have I gotten into," Jean recalled. "But there was excitement like we were pioneers going off to a new land and a new way of life. I remember driving up Franklin Avenue and thinking how wonderful everything looked with all the Christmas decorations and lights on top of each street light."[61]

The Unruh's original next door neighbors were an aboriginal family whose children would constantly flush the toilet because they had never seen a flush toilet before. Their dogs were parked in the back yard, and Fort McMurray's raven population would often swoop down and beat the dogs to their food.

"It dawned on me next summer when we again returned to Trail, B.C. for holidays that I was actually missing Fort McMurray," Jean recalled. "I had told Dale originally that I would only stay for one or two years until the job market in Trail area got better and now I was hooked on Fort McMurray. It was now our home. It was such an exciting and challenging place to live. Everyone was young with dreams and high hopes for a great future."[62]

In 1976 ,a home became available through Athabasca Realty, and the couple settled on Hill Drive just north of Manning Avenue. ARC assisted families in moving to new homes by waiving down payments. However, they would not allow families to buy out the homes until they had worked ten years for the company. This was known in Fort McMurray as the "golden handcuffs."

To help make their payments, the Unruhs took in boarders who came from a variety of places including Edmonton, Montreal, England and the Maritimes. Most were polite and trustworthy,

"I remember we had three young fellows living in our trailer for the summer and I went in to do the weekly cleaning for them," Jean recalled. "Here in the sink, were Kelly's and Dale's frisbees. They had been using them as plates. One of the fellows was having trouble waking up in the morning for work and he was scared of being fired so he hired Kelly to pound on the door each morning at seven a.m. He would pay her fifty cents to do this, so this was Kelly's first job at eight years old."[63]

Dale's salary increased two years later, so the Unruhs were no longer required to take in boarders. Dale Unruh remained with Suncor twenty-five years. The couple has four grandchildren born in Fort McMurray and son Dale remains in the community working for Suncor.

In many ways the Unruh's story is a typical of family life in Fort McMurray. Many expected to come for one or two years but most remain linked to the community for life.

"We always tell everyone we meet what a wonderful place Fort McMurray is to live and raise a family in," Jean said. "We owe Fort McMurray a lot, and it will always be our home."[64]

Yours Mine and Ours

On May 8, 1975 Alberta Vocational Centre (AVC) officially became Keyano College. The move to a full-fledged college was a significant milestone for the school which had become a vital cog in a rapidly growing community.

From its opening day in 1965, AVC fed, clothed and housed a population of single men helping them take advantage of some of the opportunities created by GCOS.

AVC began with four Atco trailers and had just four students on opening day. By the end of the week there were thirty and by October the student population had risen to seventy. Seven instructors and the chef were housed at the Riviera Motel and later moved to Block X, also known as Alberta Drive.

In 1967, Alberta Newstart, a provincial educational project spearhead by Jack Shields broadened AVCs mandate. Newstart was a research project designed to train native people to fill available jobs. It was a challenging task which involved bridging the culture gap between aboriginal people and corporate entities such as GCOS.

In later years, Jim Carbery would fill a similar role with Syncrude Canada Ltd., as he would assist aboriginal people to take advantage of business opportunities within the oil sands.

AVC, GCOS and Syncrude had to overcome biases within the community and at the plants towards native people, while at the same time ensuring that aboriginal people who were used to a more laid back lifestyle would adapt to modern employment rules. Housing provided was often regarded as communal, filled with friends and relatives. Some men who were unable to find lodging slept in vehicles which residents left unlocked. These were the humble beginnings to Keyano College[65].

The college's first registrar, Gerry Gregg recalled that in the early days, instructors filled many roles. "I was required to teach basic academic upgrading, but I taught home economics to a group of native women on Fridays," she recalled. "I taught sewing and crafts, and women taught me beading and other native crafts."

One of her most prized students was Billy Bird the legendary river boat captain. In 1907 Bird was one of the first children to be born in Fort McMurray and went on to become a skilled river boat captain. Bird would continue to enjoy a special relationship with AVC and Keyano College.

Doug Schmit

In 1969, Doug Schmit joined the college, and endeavoured to establish a more serious atmosphere.

Schmit got busy with changes. He removed the psychological fence which separated the college from the community, and opened areas such as the cafeteria to the public and to community groups. With his team of Bill Lyon, Gerry Wills and Dave Hubert he set about to apply standards to trades, and recruit new students and staff. Jim Kassen came on as vocational counsellor. Kassen researched students who had gone through AVC and found that many were not working in the area they were trained in. Some were not working at all. Schmit made it his business to develop a curriculum standard for the trades with provincially recognized benchmarks. By 1974, apprenticeship level training was approved by the Alberta Government.

Schmit's goal of AVC becoming a community centre was realized in the mid-1970s with the building of a modern gymnasium. The ninety-one hundred square foot gym became the Fort McMurray's community hall, hosting fashion shows, GCOS Christmas parties, theatre productions, and school functions.

The Virgin Mary

Staff became closely knit during the 1970s, and many lived in an apartment building on Centennial Drive nicknamed the Virgin Mary. Rumour has it that it was named after a real Mary who often complained about the parties and pranks which were common in the building.

The women's movement

In 1975, discussions around women's liberation were common at Keyano College. The college trained many women in previously male dominated areas of trade and heavy industry. Sexist humour was common as men tried to adjust to this new situation. Following are some comments in response to the question "what does women's liberation mean to you?" posed in the 1975 Keyano College Newsletter:

Cecil Short

"I believe in equal rights and equal opportunity, provided that women have the same physical, mental and moral attributes as men. Fine, give them courses in heavy equipment operation, but can they do the work?

Jack Aspen

"I believe in equal rights but they have tried to reverse everything, taking trades employment they can't physically handle. Home lives can expect to deteriorate."

Jeanne Gwin:

"Women's liberation to me means recognition of women as people, not just being typecast as wife, mother, mistress etc. and having to live within these stereotypes. If only we could liberate men!"

Gerry Greg:

I believe in equal rights, but the woman still rocks the cradle!"

Other Keyano Highlights:

In 1977, Keyano's Mackenzie Industrial Campus opened. Plans were announced to build a six hundred seat theatre to be shared by the college and Fort McMurray Composite High School.

It was also announced in 1977 that Keyano would be transferred from the department of Advanced Education and Manpower to a Board of Governors appointed by the Lieutenant Governor. Keyano College was about to "go public."

The A.Y. Jackson debate

During the late 1970s, Keyano hired artists in residence and a new focus on art was born.

An opportunity presented itself for Keyano to acquire the original copy of a Fort McMurray scene painted Group of Seven artist A.Y. Jackson "There were strenuous debates," recalled Keyano Board member Al Nicholson. The painting was purchased for twenty thousand dollars and prints were produced and sold to support the Keyano Foundation.

New apparments

Throughout the early 1970s, new apartment buildings began to spring up. Two major developers led the charge: Norman Simons and George Brosseau.

Both were lawyers, who during the late 1960s and early 1970s traveled to Fort McMurray to provide legal services. Each quickly recognized the business opportunities which existed. Brosseau, the majority partner in McMurray Imperial Enterprises, developed apartment accommodation in the Saunderson Avenue and Nixon Street area. Six apartment buildings were built which formed a ring around the Fort McMurray cemetery. McMurray Imperial also developed the Plaza One and Plaza Two Shopping Centres.

Norm Simons built a number of apartments behind the Peter Pond Shopping Centre located on Haineault Street and Charles Avenue. Simons and partners also purchased Prairie lots along Fraser Avenue for one hundred and fifty dollars each and developed light industrial and office space.

"We bought land from people who were growing potatoes there," Simons recalled. "Land was very, very cheap, relatively speaking now. It was hard to believe that you could buy at these prices. That's what gave us our start."[66]

For many in the community, Simons served as a mysterious force who was constantly pushing council to approve new apartments or to rezone lands for multi-family dwellings. Often he was met with resistance from council and accused politicians such as Town Board Chair Chuck Knight of being anti-development. Simons also dumbfounded many longtime businessmen with his elaborate series of companies. There was a logical reason for this corporate web. As yet, major banks did not recognize Fort McMurray's economic potential. However, Simons recalled that the local Royal Bank manager did.

"The local bank manager had a credit limit of five thousand dollars so every time I needed five thousand dollars I would form a new company," Simons said. "I got my come-uppance when things got bad. I was invited to the main branch and they said, "how the hell did you get all this money and what are all these companies? I couldn't tell them."[67]

About fifteen years earlier, another business person, Claire Peden, had attempted to raise cash to buy a substantial portion of the lower townsite. As his son Torchy recalled, during the late 1950s, Claire Peden approached the Red Deer Finance Company with a plan to buy sixty per cent of the lower townsite and Waterways for fifty thousand dollars. "He couldn't talk them into it."[68] Peden recalled.

Elvis slept here

During the mid-1970s, Norm Simons provided Fort McMurray with a small hotel and bona fide tourist attraction.

Faced with a shortage of accommodation for workers building the River Lot Five Syncrude housing apartments at the west end of Franklin Avenue, Simons purchased a multi-roomed one storey building and placed it on land he owned on Fraser Avenue. He named the accommodation the Heartbreak Hotel, and developed a logo of a large heart with an arrow piercing through it.

Simons and partner Sigi Lucas also operated Riverside Accommodation located just north of Hospital Street at the rear of the Park Plaza Shopping Centre. "Heartbreak Hotel was chosen because it was the Presley era and everybody knew where it was,"[69] said Simons. When the River Lot Five project was finished, the Heartbreak Hotel became the headquarters for Katimavik, a group of federal government sponsored youth workers who came to the community during the late 1970s completing community projects which included the development of Heritage Park.

In 1977, Simons attempted to sell the hotel to the provincial government for use as a youth halfway house. Instead, the Province built the Youth Assessment Centre just south of Beacon Hill.

What about the physically challenged?

Fort McMurray experienced an unprecedented development boom during the mid 1970s. Office buildings, subdivisions, shopping malls and medical centres were springing up throughout the community. In 1977, Fort McMurray set its all time development record for permits approved. But all was not completely rosy.

In 1976, Gloria Reynolds appeared at the *Fort McMurray Today* to blow the whistle on town hall and a number of developers. Reynolds talked about her excitement with the growth of Fort McMurray, but she also delivered a double-barrelled condemnation of how inaccessible many of these new buildings and subdivisions were to the physically challenged.

Reynolds was confined to a wheelchair and found it nearly impossible to maintain an independent lifestyle within Fort McMurray, a community still plagued with mud and construction. She challenged the author, a *Today* reporter at the time, to experience Fort McMurray seated in a wheelchair. The results were stunning. Sidewalks, curbs, restaurants, shops, town hall and even the newly built Canada Post centre were inaccessible. Most had constructed ramps which were too steep, or had installed concrete lips which made it impossible to pass a wheelchair over the threshold.

"I found that wherever you went downtown people would want to lift you or to otherwise help you," Reynolds recalled. "This was even true when you tried to get into a doctor or dentists office. The gesture was fine, but when you're trying to be independent, who wants to be cared for and lifted wherever you go."[70]

Reynolds was eventually asked to work closely with planners Peter Van Belle and Terry Langis to help develop more wheelchair friendly buildings, sidewalks and curb corners. Due to Reynolds' initiative, Fort McMurray moved more quickly to become a place where families with physically challenged members could get around.

The Great Flood of 1977

Fort McMurray had experienced many floods in its history, but none affected more people than the Great Flood of 1977. At about 7 a.m. on April 17, hundreds of McMurrayites lined the Grant MacEwan Bridge to watch the incredible spectacle known as the Athabasca River breakup.

As a wall of ice turned around the Horse Creek corner, the push of approaching ice produced an incredible roar. Hundred-foot shards of ice rose and shot up into the air, then fell and were absorbed by the approaching waters.

As in previous years, a barrel stood under the bridge which was rigged with a clock designed to stop at the exact point that breakup occurred. The breakup time would determine which lucky McMurrayites had won the annual breakup pool.

On that morning everything was proceeding normally, until unforseen forces took over. The wall of ice from the Athabasca River did not proceed north to Fort Chipewyan. Instead it jammed at the mouth of the Clearwater River and that caused waters to back into the Snye and eventually into some downtown areas, the Prairie and Waterways.

The home, which sat at the corner of Hardin Street and Morimoto Drive along the Snye, was submerged. Waters extended on Franklin Avenue to Hospital Street, and the Park Plaza and Clearwater Trailer Courts were decimated.

Late that night, Town Board chair Chuck Knight declared a state of emergency. The Fort McMurray Today missed the next day's publication. Its offices on Centennial Drive were flooded.

Two days later, Canadian air force bombers blasted holes in the ice jam, and soon after, water began to flow. Once the waters subsided, it was time to assess the damage which ultimately reached two million dollars. The flood commanded front-page attention throughout the country along with coverage on national television.

For the next few months, while residents of the Clearwater and Park Plaza Trailer Courts waited, the Province and the New Town argued. Under the terms of the New Town agreement of 1964, the municipality was not permitted to develop housing north of Franklin Avenue with the exception of the Manning, Fraser and Hill Drive areas.

The province refused to provide assistance to many residents of the flooded trailer parks saying that the area should never have been developed. Knight's administration countered saying that there was no other place to locate trailers during the Syncrude construction boom.

The Province ultimately agreed to pay for damages but vowed never to cover flood damage again in the Riedel Street trailer area.

Schools weather the boom

One day in early 1977, Nelson Scott, principal of Thickwood Heights School, returned from Christmas break to find his office loaded with kids he didn't recognize. It was the height of the Syncrude hiring period, and there were forty-nine children waiting to register.

By the end of that morning, he had delivered at least one new student to each classroom, and in one Grade Three class, the number of students in the room grew from thirty-four to thirty-eight. That afternoon, Scott began to search for an additional Grade Three teacher.

The same was true for schools throughout the district. To respond to the immediate need for classroom space, both the Catholic and Public school districts placed clusters of trailers, known as portables at most schools. In some cases portables were in place before the core school was built.

In 1974, in anticipation of the huge growth, both school boards decided to build schools each using the same architect and contractor. The approach was meant to reduce costs and speed design and construction. Beacon Hill and Good Shepherd schools were built in the same area of Beacon Hill, while Thickwood and St. Paul's were built in a new reserve area of Thickwood Heights.

When school began in September, only the portables were ready at Beacon Hill. For the first two months students were on shift. Primary students and teachers who attended in the morning shared their classrooms with elementary students who attended in the afternoon. That arrangement continued until October when the core school was ready.

Thickwood Heights School began as six portable classrooms on the Dr. Clark School site. This arrangement continued until March 1976 when the Thickwood School was ready to be occupied. Through that year the student population remained stable, but in September, as Thickwood boomed, so did the school.

"I began each monthly staff meeting by introducing at least one new staff member," Scott recalled. "We began the year with no portable classrooms and had added eight before the year end and would add another four before the next school year began."[71]

Scott's story is similar to those of principals throughout Fort McMurray during a time when the community added thousands of residents each year.

One of the other challenges the school district faced was providing teacher accommodation. Teachers arriving to help weather the boom were unable to find apartments. The school boards began to become landlords as they leased apartments, mainly on Haineault Street and Charles Avenues and in turn sublet them to new teachers.

Scott and family came to Fort McMurray in September 1971 and moved into a twelve-suite apartment building which was home to sixteen teachers. At times, he said, it was like living in a staff room as teachers visited from apartment to apartment.

Hospital: What really happened

On May 6, 1977, officials from the Province and the Town gathered at the foot of Hospital Hill, dug a shovel into the ground and proclaimed a beginning to construction of a forty-two million dollar hospital. But months later, the Province came within a heartbeat of cancelling the project.

On ground breaking day, all seemed in order. The Fort McMurray Marching Band played and special hard hats were handed out. Fort McMurray was about to benefit from a state of the art regional hospital which would boast some of the most modern equipment available. Eventually, some of Canada's first medical and administrative computers would be introduced in the hospital. All seemed well.

But behind the scenes, trouble brewed. As winter 1977 approached, the Province appeared to be dallying on approving construction of the hospital. Building permits were not ready, and the weather was beginning to cool. Hospital

Board Chairman Ron Wolff and project manager Roger Bernatzki decided to act, and because of their initiative, the Province came within a hair of cancelling Fort McMurray's new hospital.

In order to speed up construction of the new hospital, Wolff and his board were given special spending privileges which allowed them to allocate construction funds without having to wait for approval from the Province. By fall, the province had yet to authorize construction, so Wolff and his board made a potentially dangerous move.

"We had an agreement with government that if they didn't say "no" within seven days, we had approval,"[72] recalled Wolff. The Board approved the contract for ground clearing, and when the Province did not respond, construction officially began.

As Bernatzki recalled, the paperwork for the ground-clearing contract got lost in Edmonton, and when the Province found out that construction of the Fort McMurray Hospital had begun without its approval, fur began to fly.

"The government did not approve," noted Bernatzki. "But we had to get construction started. Even after site preparation had been done, the deputy minister asked, "how much will it cost to fill the hole,"[73] Due to the hospital board's aggressiveness, the project was on the verge of cancellation.

Wolff happened to be in Edmonton at the time recovering from a leg injury and government officials rushed to his hospital room to chastise him for approving a start to construction without its approval. As Wolff recalled, the deputy Minister, Larry Wilson arrived and spoke of the possibility that the Board could be fired. "He said you've got to stop that, but it was too late,"[74] Wolff recalled.

Faced with the possibility of public embarrassment in Fort McMurray and throughout the province, the project was allowed to proceed, and Fort McMurray's hospital came in under budget. In fact, there was so much money left over, as Wolff recalled "all the bells and whistles" were added including state of the art operating rooms, and plush administrative offices.

The hospital boardroom was fitted with such a rich looking carpet and board table, that later, during tighter financial times, many of the hospital's news conferences were held in the more spartan Horizon Room.

Bernatzki recalled that because the hospital board had such extraordinary powers and was run by Wolff and others with business experience, the facility was built on time and under budget.

"We were allowed to fast track with a private sector mentality," said Bernatzki. "You could never build a hospital that way again, but it was an amazing project to be associated with."[75]

Knight versus Mason

The biggest battle of the October 1977 municipal election didn't come during the election campaign. It happened the day after. Fort McMurray electors chose seven candidates from those who ran, and leading the list was Chuck Knight.

Selection of Knight as Town Board Chair should have been a formality, but behind the scenes, lobby forces were at work. It was felt by many business owners that Knight was anti-business, and that his confrontational approach had irritated the Province and had lost the community support and grants. Meetings were held in offices and in coffee shops to see if Knight could be ousted in favour of another Town Board member. The field of contenders included Ron Morgan, Jack Corless, Neil Costello, Grant Howell, Ted Mason and Bill Gendreau.

Morgan and Corless were seen as the front-runners. Morgan was a popular councilor who was strongly supported within the GCOS and sports community. Corless was the former mayor of Carstairs, and a popular school principal. Both declined.

Gendreau and Howell were employed at the oil sands plants. Costello was not seen as a strong selection since he finished in seventh place and had work commitments with Allarco. Attention of the anti-Knight lobby shifted to Ted Mason who the previous February had joined council through a by-election following the resignation of Keith MacLeod.

When the Town Board convened in October, Morgan and Gendreau lined up around Knight. However, Howell, Corless and Costello backed Mason who had finished fifth in the polls. Mason was selected as Fort McMurray's new Board chair.

While Knight did his best to hide his anger, he genuinely felt disappointed and betrayed. The story in the Fort McMurray Today indicated that "the choice of the voters for mayor had not been the choice of the town board of administrators."

For the next three years, council was often split along Knight/Mason lines. There was barely an issue which did not evoke a comparison between how Knight and Mason conducted business. The entire community was divided.

Matters were made worse by the fact that Knight was seen as a flamboyant and charismatic leader, while Mason was more soft-spoken, and had difficulty speaking publicly with any degree of authority.

The jury is still out on who was actually a better town board chairman. Under Knight, the New Town was always at war with the Province. The Province had to force the New Town to develop Beacon Hill, Abasand Heights and Thickwood. It is likely that opportunities for grants and extra funding by the Province were thwarted by Knight's style.

As Gary Shantz, assistant to commissioner Vic Henning once noted, when it came time for the Province to erect town signs at the entrance to every city and town listing the services available, Fort McMurray was the only community to send the bill for drilling the holes for the sign back to the province.

Under Mason's term, the City bought land from Syd Thompson, negotiated the sale to the Province for a good price, and then leased back the Civic Tower of the provincial buildings, which eventually became known as Red Square.

Ted Mason

When Ted Mason agreed to become Chairman of the Town Board he had no idea how vicious political life would be. Each decision he made, every speech he delivered and every building which was approved under his administration would be compared to his predecessor.

For example, the Thickwood Heights Arena, approved by the Mason administration was built late, over budget, and with questions over its safety. Knight would lambaste Mason reminding the community that it took only eighty-nine days to build the Beacon Hill Arena.

In later years, Beacon Hill Arena would require substantial funds to repair some initial construction flaws, however at the time, Knight used the Thickwood fiasco as an example of how his administration could handle the project better than Mason.

The rivalry became so intense that it virtually paralyzed council, much to the detriment of the citizens of Fort McMurray.

But in his quiet way, Mason got things done. Under Mason, land was acquired from Alberta Housing, and the RCMP station was built on Gregoire Drive opposite the Mackenzie Park Inn.

Mason was a man with a temper, but there were times when he attempted to quell his feud with Knight. When it was time to break ground on Knight's beloved Macdonald Island Recreation Centre, Mason turned to Knight and said, "Chuck this has been your dream, you break the ground."[76]

Mason noted that it was his town board which brought the MacDonald Island project to completion. As he reflected a week before his passing, nearly twenty years after his departure from the community, Mason had bittersweet memories about Fort McMurray.

"I can't feel that Fort McMurray was good to me," he said. "Syncrude and Suncor were supportive and the provincial people were good. I did virtually all I could do and there were not many loose ends left."[77]

But Mason still resents being drawn into the rivalry with the wounded Chuck Knight. He believes this made his stay as Town Chair unnecessarily uncomfortable. "I'm angry that is was made so hard for me," he recalled. "It didn't need to be so difficult."[78]

The Great Waterways holdup

Judy Hanson had a premonition that thieves would one day target the little Waterways bank where she worked. But no one paid any attention. After all, the Tarsands Savings and Credit Union was a small locally owned bank in a quiet community.

But on September 1, 1977, Hanson's prediction proved correct . At one p.m., two armed and masked men burst into the Railway Avenue bank and ordered everyone to the floor. Hanson, the head teller, was busy counting cash, and at first didn't notice the men.

"It was pretty scary," she recalled. "I wasn't paying attention until they yelled "you too," telling me to hit the floor."[79] The thieves had originally considered robbing the Canadian Imperial Bank of Commerce (CIBC), but decided the Waterways branch was further from the RCMP station. Thieves gathered about twenty-five hundred dollars in bills and cash, and fled in a stolen Syncrude truck behind the Legion and up the old airport road. Their spoils could have been much larger. The branch's loans officer had just left the branch to pick up twenty thousand dollars from the CIBC, the bank which supplied the credit union with its cash. And inside, a locked drawer contained thousands of dollars. The thieves parked the stolen vehicle at the base of Gregoire Park, and fled.

Although the RCMP recovered the vehicle and the rifle, it took a few weeks before they arrested the suspects. As often is the case with robberies and other crimes, the RCMP used good "bar intelligence." As former Staff Sergeant Peter Forster recalled, "they bragged about it, we got wind of it through informants and that led us to them."[80]

One day after the robbery, a suspicious finding under RCMP headquarters raised some question about whether the holdup could have carried more serious consequences. RCMP and town office employees complained that their phones were not operating properly. When an Alberta Government Telephones employee climbed under the building, he found a pail full of flammable material, a fuse and a lighter.

Police and town residents began speculating that the bomb was intended as a diversion to limit RCMP response time during the robbery.

"It was just a rumour but it seems suspicious that the two would happen virtually on the same day," said Forster. "Whether the two were connected has always been a source of speculation."[81]

Weiss and Lougheed

In 1979, Fort McMurray finally gained the opportunity to elect a hometown MLA to the Alberta Legislature. That year, Norm Weiss defeated his primary rival, NDP candidate Clare Williscroft to become MLA for the provincial Fort McMurray riding.

The election of a McMurray MLA brought a sigh of relief to local residents. Previously, Fort McMurray had been grouped with the town of Lac La Biche, and often due to the structure of the local riding association, candidates were generated from the southern part of the constituency. Prior to the 1979 election, Ron Tesolin had represented Fort McMurray, and often local residents complained that although hard working, Tesolin did not fully understand oil sands development and the social changes that it would create.

Clearly, Norm Weiss did. Weiss initially came to Fort McMurray during the late 1950s, and moved to Fort McMurray in the mid-1960s to become a partner in the Shell bulk station.

Although Weiss was involved in the Progressive Conservative riding association, his local star began to rise during the mid 1970s when he was elected citizens' representative at a number of public meetings. In particular, in 1977, Fort McMurray town administration called a public meeting to answer questions of various aspects of finance and town operations. Only two residents showed up: Weiss, and town day care co-ordinator Caterina Pizanias.

Weiss was pictured on the front page the following day asking questions on behalf of the thousands of residents who didn't bother to attend.

Following Weiss' election, Fort McMurray enjoyed one of the most aggressive government building booms in Alberta history. During the subsequent decade, a new Keyano College, City Hall and Provincial Building, Court House, Interpretive Centre and other projects were all approved.

"Premier Peter Lougheed was key and was very much on the pulse of McMurray at all times," Weiss recalled. "Because we were in a period of growth and high income and revenue we were in a position to do all sorts of things. Because of his commitment and his strong belief in the energy sector, certain things happened like the investment in Syncrude, it was the Premier's call and it was a good investment."[82]

Peter Lougheed and the NEP

Peter Lougheed was premier of Alberta during Fort McMurray largest growth spurt. And to this day, Lougheed believes that Fort McMurray and the oil sands could have been even greater had the federal government not instituted in the mid-1970s the National Energy Policy (NEP), which in effect shut down oil investment in western Canada.

The NEP slammed substantial taxes on oil developers including those considering development in the oil sands, and during the late 1970s and early 1980s projects such as Alsands, OSLO and Sandalta were shelved.

Lougheed never saw the NEP coming. Had he, perhaps Alberta would have played a more proactive role. "I didn't think anyone would be that stupid," Lougheed said, noting that it took decades before Alberta recovered the confidence of investors. "It was quite a period of time before companies participating in the oilsands would have the confidence to make major investments."[83]

During the Syncrude boom, Lougheed supported the establishment of the North East Commission which overrode many provincial laws, especially those involving labour. Lougheed said that it was vital that Syncrude be built without the threat of a strike. The government gave the commission power to prevent any labour uprisings and that was one of the legislation's major motivations.

"I was always conscious of the significance of the oil sands," he said. "We had to make the project happen as it was important as a national resource and for the people of Alberta."

Under Lougheed, the Alberta government assumed a share in Syncrude Canada. That gamble provided good results. However his second gamble did not. To show Shell Canada how serious Alberta was about assisting in the construction of the Alsands plant, Lougheed's government built a twelve million dollar bridge near Fort McKay across the Athabasca River. When Alsands was shelved in 1980, the bridge sat abandoned some days used only by rabbits, moose and deer to cross the river.

"I always thought the opposition would use that "bridge to nowhere" to embarrass the government,"[84] said Lougheed. To Lougheed's great relief, the bridge, the collapse of Alsands and the twelve million dollar bridge to nowhere were never publicly noted by the NDP opposition.

Jack Shields: Defies labels

One of Fort McMurray's most complex and colourful characters during the 1960s and 1970s was business person and politician Jack Shields.

When one reviews his role in the community over twenty five years, it is evident that Shields is deeply admired by some, and questioned by others. Some will depict him as dedicated and caring. Others talk about his brashness and arrogance during Fort McMurray's period of economic growth.

Some will call him ruthless. Others describe him as boyish and naïve. For certain, Jack Shields presence in Fort McMurray had a pronounced influence in virtually every domain. At minimum, Jack Shields was a pioneers and an innovator who trailblazed the Alberta Vocational College, the Fort McMurray Public School Board, the Fort McMurray Chamber of Commerce and the Fort McMurray Kinsmen. His also played an influential role as Fort McMurray's first and only homegrown Member of Parliament.

Shields came to Fort McMurray during the mid 1960s to establish the Alberta Vocational College (AVC), which later became Keyano College. During AVC's formative years, Shields worked tirelessly developing programs to help unskilled local residents, in particular aboriginal people to seize some of the employment opportunities available at the GCOS plant.

In some cases, Shields would approach Fort McMurray businesses and tell them of a promising young person who needed an initial opportunity to prove themselves. A number of aboriginal people who own current businesses in Fort McMurray owe their start to the interest that Shields showed in them. He and AVC president Doug Schmidt presided over the growth of the college, setting the stage for it to become one of the modern and prestigious places of learning for any midsize community in Canada.

Unbeknownst to Fort McMurray residents, every Christmas, Shields would don a Santa Claus suit and land his plane in Janvier, a small native community south of Fort McMurray. There he would appear as Santa Claus and distribute presents to needy children. As president of the Chamber of Commerce, he played a major role in recruiting new physicians to Fort McMurray, often working with businessmen such as Al Burry to ensure that office space and accommodation were prepared within a short time frame.

Shields was also one of the "movers" behind the Fort McMurray Kinsmen, a group responsible for raising tens of thousands of dollars towards construction of Centennial Pool.

Often Shield's community spirit cost him financially. Soon after he acquired the A&W Restaurant, Shields agreed to participate in a town cleanup project. Businessman Sigi Lucas suggested that Shields donate a glass of root beer for every garbage bag collected by a local youth and a free hamburger for each three bags. However, no one established any limits. While children literally picked up every scrap of paper during the town's Litter Check campaign, Shields had to honour six thousand coupons.

"That just about put us under," he recalled. "But it was the cleanest I ever saw the town."[85]

As an active member of the public school board, the chamber of commerce and later as Member of Parliament there are many stories told about Shields which speak volumes about the man and the times. Here are some:

Midsummer madness

As Chamber president in 1976, Jack Shields initiated a downtown carnival known as Midsummer Madness which involved shutting down Franklin Avenue between Hardin and Main Streets and installing a midway. Unfortunately, Shields forgot to inform the Town Administration. This heightened tension between the Chamber and the Town Board.

Shields the flyer

While flying from Fort McMurray to Edmonton one day, Shields asked his friend and passenger Ches Dicks whether he wanted a cup of coffee. When Dicks nodded "yes", he expected Shields to bring out a thermos. Instead, Shields dove the plane and landed on Highway 63 just north of Wandering River. Shields entered the Wandering River Esso and bought two cups of coffee

Traffic had to be stopped along Highway 63 to allow Shields to take off and resume his journey to Edmonton.

On another occasion, Shields forgot to put his landing gear down in Vegreville while picking up Transportation Minister Don Mazinkowski. The plane belly flopped on the runway. There were no injuries.

The naked shooter

During the 1980s Jack Shields was involved in an incident which if publicized could have cost him his political career. One night, he and wife Pat were asleep in their Hill Drive home when they heard noises. Someone was attempting to enter through their patio doors.

Shields, who sleeps in the nude, grabbed his hand gun and began chasing two men down Hill Drive. As Shields told the story, "I shot over their heads, tripped and the gun went off again. I shot the fender off a neighbour's car and the cartridge landed in the trunk. My neighbour heard the gunshot and looked out the window and thought he saw me running naked down the street, but thought "no way."[86]

The RCMP questioned Shields for discharging a firearm and after a month's investigation cleared him.

Missed by that much

Jack Shields was never one to let formalities stand in his way. As Chairman of the Public School Board, in 1979, Shields wanted Frank Spragins School built in Abasand Heights with a minimum delay and became impatient over the lack of approval from local and provincial officials.

He ordered construction to begin without the proper survey documents. A few days later, after the concrete had been poured, it was revealed that the school had been built about a foot into city property.

Lawyers wrestled with the issue for months until a settlement was reached with the city.

Police and the Royal Bank

During the mid-1970s, Shields and Dr. Des Dwyer engaged in a constant tit for tat battle of practical jokes and wagers.

One of the most famous bets involved Dwyer and a cache of silver bars he had stored at the Royal Bank of Canada main branch in Edmonton. Dwyer insisted that his silver was safe in the bank and Shields bet him that with only a key and no identification, he could enter the bank and leave with all of Dwyer's silver.

The duo entered the bank, Shields showed Dwyer's key and the two entered the safety deposit area unchallenged. While Dwyer stared in amazement, Shields began loading a duffel bag with Dwyer's silver bars. Suddenly the bag broke and the silver crashed to the floor. Shields and Dwyer burst into laughter. This attracted the attention of security guards who called Edmonton Police. Dwyer and Shields were detained for hours before being allowed to leave

Shields gained a reputation during the 1960s as an innovator, and a hard working businessman during the early 1970s, but he was also known to be pushy and aggressive. Shields was one of the businessmen who in 1977 worked to dethrone Chuck Knight from the Town Board chair, replacing him with Ted Mason.

In the 1980s, as Fort McMurray's business climate tightened, Shields fell victim. His restaurants and other holdings could not support the economic downturn caused by low oil prices and the demise of Alsands, Shell Canada's ill-fated oil sands project. His business empire collapsed.

Even his MP position was not secure. Shields took considerable heat for supporting Brian Mulroney's GST, and even alienated some longtime business associates like Alberta Motor Products owner Robert Vargo by siding with the government rather than with the public.

Shields was defeated in the 1993 federal election. Shields felt he had worked hard as an MP solving the problems of individuals, businesses and community organizations and felt betrayed by the lack of support shown at the polls. He left Fort McMurray and re-established himself by operating the Nisku Truck Stop near the Edmonton International Airport.

Longtime friend and resident Ches Dicks noted about Shields," he is a very generous man, but also a practical joker. He took on the personality of the time and was always there when you needed him."[87]

Whether you loved him or hated him, Fort McMurrayites cannot deny the exceptional contribution and influence Jack Shields had on the development of the college, school system, business community and political structure.

The famous flagpole

Fort McMurray made Time magazine in mid 1978. Was it an article about Syncrude's grand opening which occurred in April? Was it a story about how the community was dealing with massive population growth? No on both counts.

Fort McMurray received Time coverage based on a prank by a group of local businesspersons which caught physician Des Dwyer with his Union Jack showing. For months leading up to the stunt, Dwyer, an obsessive practical joker, had pulled prank after prank on his friends.

For example, when an employee from Fort McMurray Excavating (FMX) visited Dwyer to apply for Worker's Compensation, Dwyer apparently wrote that his friend, FMX owner Elmer Schneider, had caused the injury by beating the employee.

About a dozen members of Fort McMurray's business community concocted an elaborate revenge scheme. Dwyer was a proud Irishman who despised England. While Dwyer was away on holidays, a crew led by Schneider, Shields, Tip Hlushak and others moved in. Dwyer's driveway and flower garden were ripped apart, and a flagpole inserted ten feet into the ground. Atop the forty-foot-high pole was a Union Jack which blew proudly in the breeze. Dwyer's driveway was repaved, and the flagpole was surrounded by a walled flower and rock garden which included the inscription "God Save the Queen". Dwyer's driveway had been turned into a shrine in honour of Mother England.

The photo, carried in the *Fort McMurray Today,* made it to the *Edmonton Journal,* the *Globe and Mail* and *Time Magazine.*

"The town eventually sued me for having an aeronautical hazard with no lights on the top,"[88] Dwyer recalled. Eventually Dwyer got the last word. A resident of an apartment across the street took photos of the entire construction project and eventually Dwyer extracted his revenge on each participant.

For the following two weeks, Dwyer's home became a tourist attraction. "People would bring visitors over to my driveway and pose for pictures beside the flag,"[89] Dwyer recalled.

The flying doctor

I would be unfair to paint Dr. Des Dwyer solely as a practical joker and owner of Fort McMurray's most famous British flag.

While in Fort McMurray, Dwyer received the Governor General's award for bringing to light a series of health problems in small native communities.

In 1969, and through the early 1970s, Dwyer launched a "flying doctor" service to assist communities such as Janvier. Dwyer became concerned that isolated native communities were not receiving proper medical attention. He alerted the *Edmonton Journal* which investigated.

"I was shocked that poverty could exist so close," said Dwyer. "Controversial facts surfaced about unsafe conditions including water and housing, and that our approach to health care in these places was all wrong."[90] Dwyer eventually received a call from Premier Lougheed's office who toured the communities with Ministers and camera crew in tow. Lougheed organized a lunch program, and at Dwyer's request ensured that a nurse practitioner was hired. Dwyer's dramatic campaign and his flying doctor program earned him national honours.

From the moment he arrived in 1969, Dwyer immersed himself in the community. He became active with Ches Dicks in organizing one of Canada's richest golf tournaments. The Fort McMurray Open was second only to the Canadian Open in prize money, and attracted some of Canada's top golfers. But his major work came in the medical field.

"Things went nuts during the mid-70s," he recalled. "I could see eighty patients a day then get called back to the hospital at night. I carried a full obstetrical load as well – twenty to twenty-five deliveries a month."[91]

Dwyer's other claim to fame occurred during the late-1970s when he was called by the RCMP to the Park Plaza Trailer Court to speak with a man who had fired a gun.

"He said he would only speak with me, so I sat down with him, we had a couple of drinks and eventually he came out with me,"[92] Dwyer recalled.

Dwyer left Fort McMurray in 1979 and moved to Vancouver where he operates a storefront clinic. "The boom was over and it was just time to make a change," said Dwyer. "It was a great opportunity to be part of something so amazing. I got to do more than I ever would have living somewhere else. I wept as I drove out of town."[93]

Other interesting people:

As Fort McMurray continued to grow and expand, a number of additional personalities came to the forefront. While it is impossible to name all those who played a role in the community's rise during the 1970s, here are a few additional names that come to mind.

Jimmy Rogers

As the town often focused on growth, technology and further oilsands development, a voice was sounded from Waterways which promoted a more basic approach. Jimmy Rogers, otherwise known as the unofficial Mayor of Waterways, remained one of Fort McMurray's bona fide personalities throughout the 1970s and beyond. Rogers ran for council in 1980 and attracted a few hundred votes.

His words and his appearance provided an alternative to the often slick styles of those who serve the community or seek public office. Dressed in a flannel shirt, suspenders, boots and loose fitting pants, Rogers often appeared before Town Board to complain about development, or to lobby for the preservation of Waterways.

Dr. Al Nicholson

Dr. Al Nicholson came to Fort McMurray in 1966, and is still practicing medicine thirty-five years later. Nicholson established a partnership with Dr. Stephen Yung and handled everything from medicine, to tooth extractions and animal care.

Nicholson recalled early one morning a patient brought to his office a dog which required immediate surgery. Nicholson was glad to assist; however during surgery the dog began to howl. Nicholson completed the operation, and opened the door to find a waiting room of panic stricken patients who had thought that the howls of pain had come from a human.

In a 1999 interview, Nicholson made note of the compassion of the Grey Nuns who operated St. Gabriel's Hospital. He recalled that sometimes medicine took a back seat to issues of compassion.

"Sister Cardinal and I fought about why she didn't want to go with disposable syringes," Nicholson recalled. "Then I realized that the sisters had been employing someone to sterilize the medical equipment and that would have put them out of work.

"The sisters saw the hospital as a mechanism to help the community. Some of the people were in housekeeping or lab assistance. They looked after a lot of people and a lot of social ills by hiring them to work at the hospital."[94]

Later, as Fort McMurray coroner and Medical Officer of Health, Nicholson

---

established himself as a person who refused to buckle to corporate or political pressure. Once as he investigated an on-site death at Suncor, officials wanted him to brush the incident under the carpet, but Nicholson issued a full report condemning the company and a contractor for poor safety practices.

Mike and Marion Horrocks

Mike Horrocks came to Fort McMurray in 1969 to set up Fort McMurray's first fulltime law practice. Horrocks quickly found himself on the front lines of a number of criminal, domestic and social issues "Some people came to give their marriages a new start," he recalled. "There was nothing for women to do and some didn't even bother to get out of their housecoats."[95] This, Horrocks recalled, led to a number of broken marriages, and in turn litigation.

Marion Horrocks also played an active community role. Aside from her work at Centennial Pool, Horrocks became Fort McMurray's official flower counter. Since 1975, Horrocks has joined counterparts from across Canada during the last weekend of May to help identify which species of flowers are growing across the country. One weekend, Horrocks recorded one hundred and thirty flowers including fifteen types of orchids. She also located one rare flower which had rarely been seen outside the Great Lakes area. Horrocks also ran a bookstore with partner Margaret Walker.

Horrocks became a judge in 1978 and also served as Chair of the Fort McMurray Public School Board.

Rev. Bruce Mateika

As Fort McMurray's Chief Returning officer during the 1970s, Rev. Bruce Mateika had to ensure that all local residents were given the opportunity to vote, in spite of population statistics which changed day to day.

During the 1974 municipal election, the town ran out of ballots and as voters tapped their pencils Mateika had to order new ones printed.

When he wasn't overseeing the town census and elections, Mateika served as Pastor for the Fellowship Baptist Church. There he had to deal with a wide variety of social problems, and a steady stream of incoming and outgoing church members. "One Sunday, we welcomed thirteen families to church, while seventeen left,"[96] he recalled.

Mateika also served as the town's truant officer working with parents, students and teachers to improve Fort McMurray school attendance. "I tried to be non judgmental and used kindness and understanding to get kids to school,"[97] he recalled.

Ernie Eakin

The oil sands plant at Bitumount may have been abandoned in the early 1960s, but that didn't stop Ernie Eakin from guarding it with his life.

Eakin was an employee of the old plant, and long after the people and machinery were removed, he decided to remain on the site. Eakin was concerned about looting and trespassing, and lived in one of the plant's abandoned buildings where he slept with his rifle by his side.

In 1978, a group of prominent McMurrayites, known as the Over the Hill Gang, decided to cross-country ski between Fort Chipewyan and Fort McMurray. After one particularly grueling day, the skiers approached Bitumount hoping to spend the night protected from the brutally cold weather.

As the group's scout, Tiny O'Brien, approached Bitumount, Eakin dashed outside with a gun and ran O'Brien off the Bitumount site. The skiers had to continue three more miles before finding a suitable cabin.

Jack Bergeron

Jack Bergeron was a bush pilot who came to Fort McMurray in the mid-1960s, and later purchased Contact Airways. In 1971, Contact had the largest fleet of float equipped planes in Alberta. He and wife Daphne launched the Namur Lake fishing lodge. In 1971, price for a return trip from Fort McMurray to Namur Lake was a hundred and fifty dollars plus twenty-five dollars per day at the lodge.

Contact Air also spread Fort McMurray's name outside North America. Bergeron was awarded a contract to provide flying services in Africa.

Hello Suncor, Goodbye GCOS

In August 1979, the name GCOS became history. Company president Ross Hennigar announced that Sun Oil, Sunoco and GCOS would be amalgamated under a single company named Suncor Inc.

Two operating entities were formed. The Resources Group consisted of four divisions including exploration, production, resources development and oil sands. Combined, the four divisions earned 68 per cent of Suncor's 1979 pre-tax income. The second operating group, the Sunoco Group, was established to manage oil trading, refining and marketing. Operations within Fort McMurray were now referred to as Suncor Inc. Oil Sands Division.

Hennigar noted in Suncor's 1979 annual report that, "the result is a much stronger and better balanced vehicle for finding and producing energy supplies in the future."[98] Although the change in corporate name made sense from a marketing perspective, it took some time before the name Suncor rolled off the tongues of longtime residents and GCOS employees.

"No" to McDonald's arches

By the close of the 1970s, Fort McMurray's town administration had made great strides in improving efficiency and service to taxpayers. Part of the credit went to town manager David Jones who arrived in January 1976 with a mandate to modernize the town's operation.

Jones envisioned Fort McMurray as one day becoming a large and influential city. During the late 1970s, Jones wrote a paper which predicted that by 2000, Fort McMurray would grow to a population of more than one hundred thousand, with a university, major hospital, agriculture, numerous oil sands plants and a diverse economy. While Jones could not have foreseen the National Energy Policy, or a drop in world oil prices, his vision for the future proved well founded.

"When I was hired in 1976, it was conveyed to me that Town Council saw a city to be built here with an astronomical growth forecast," Jones recalled. "They wanted the infrastructure put in place."[99]

In the mid-70s Fort McMurray handled more than one hundred million dollars in building permits, a figure which Jones believes was unparalleled for a medium sized community anywhere in North America.

The town also hired former bank manager Bruce Otterdahl as treasurer who scrapped Fort McMurray's archaic book keeping system and transferred records to computer. Otterdahl also set up some rules for the new town to pay its bills. Often, businesses would have to wait nine months or more to be paid.

"I wanted to know why we just couldn't pay our bills to the people we owed," recalled Otterdahl. "It was just a matter of the town being more business focused."[100] Otterdahl was continually at odds with the Town Board who wanted to underwrite public transit or purchase a new fire engine.

"I told council that it would take operating dollars to run the new fire equipment, but they didn't want to listen,"[101] said Otterdahl.

"Council felt that it would not be a bad thing if business taxes were raised". I tried to convince them otherwise but they didn't understand."[102]

When council overturned his recommendation, and purchased a new fire engine Otterdahl resigned. During the early 1980s, Otterdahl was elected to city council and later failed in a bid to become mayor.

The relationship between Fort McMurray's administration and the council was not always smooth. Jones often battled with Town Board Chair Chuck Knight. Knight preferred to be a "hands on" mayor, often calling staff directly or attempted to personally solve internal problems. As late as 1977, Town Board members at their regular meetings reviewed lists of outgoing cheques, occasionally questioning why certain ones were issued. Jones put an end to that, and often bemoaned Knight's passion for publicly bashing town office employees.

A planning department was established in cooperation with the province to help guide the rapid development of Fort McMurray's business community and of new housing subdivisions. However the planning department had its detractors, particularly at it related to signage and zoning regulations.

Fort McMurray was one of the few communities where a McDonald's Restaurant was not permitted to erect its arches. This was due to height and aesthetic restrictions. As well, when The Brick furniture store moved to Franklin Avenue, it was prohibited from installing its waving Brick icon because it was felt that the motion of the Brick man's hand could distract motorists.

"The feeling on the McDonald's arches was that it was a grating sign of capitalism and we did not have to be dictated to by people out of the community," recalled former provincial planner Terry Langis. "That may be what was really going through the department's mind and why the arches were denied."[103]

Langis agreed that Fort McMurray's signage bylaw may have been one of the most restrictive in North America, but he noted that at the time, the demand by outside businesses and corporations to locate in Fort McMurray was great and that town hall could afford to lay down some laws relating to colour, size and location which would guarantee consistency. "We didn't want to go the Las Vegas style,"[104] he recalled.

Fort McMurray's planning department often felt that outside developers failed to respect its role in building a calmly planned community. It pointed to the example of how Syncrude's housing wing, Northward Development launched construction of the River Park Glen project, otherwise known as River Lot 5, without producing a development or building permit.

Town manager David Jones recalled that because Fort McMurray was growing at such a meteoric rate, some tensions and differences of opinions were bound to occur.

Change was taking place so fast, it took its toll on people. People were working very hard and trying to get a sense of stability and comfort in their own lives. The town asked these people to plan and bankroll the future. They did it and I've always had tremendous admiration for the people who did this[105].

Despite the tensions and the stress associated with building Fort McMurray's administration, Jones says the Syncrude construction period was a remarkable time. He noted that after living through the 1970s boom period in Fort McMurray, his own work experiences since have paled.

"There was an addictive quality dealing with unbelievable growth and opportunities," said Jones. "We who worked for the municipality were in danger of burning out due to prolonged stress. I spent a lot of my time working with staff to reduce chaos and help staff come to terms with every day erratic nature of events. We established practices to create order."[106]

Former provincial planner Terry Langis remained in the community and launched a consulting practice. But he still has fond memories of "passion" associated with the Syncrude boom "Dealing with change was an incredible experience,"[107] said Langis. "People were working at levels of responsibility they'd never have the opportunity to do in other communities."

"Working here between 1979-80 felt like being back in university. There was one great huge event after another going on. We were trying to get ahead and were always behind."[108]

By 1978 the town administration had been molded into a team of individuals who provided services to Fort McMurray residents in a more efficient and dependable manner.

In April 1978, Syncrude officially launched operations. As the decade closed, Fort McMurray began to exhale, and develop a sense of permanency. Within only one decade, true to prediction, Fort McMurray had quadrupled in size.

The National Energy Program, announced by the federal government in the October 1980, coupled with low oil prices, contributed to the cancellation of Alsands and other proposed oilsands projects. While many officials and residents publicly voiced disappointment, privately there was some degree of relief. Fort McMurray began to slow its pace, and solidify as a community.

As Town Board surveyed the massive community which had developed, it began to review its overall status and the Province's ongoing role as its chief care-taker. The time had come for Fort McMurray to become a city.

The question was posed by Town Board members. Was the Province ready to lift New Town status which had covered Fort McMurray since 1964.

The quiet Czar

On a daily basis, it appeared to most Fort McMurray residents that the Town Board, led by chairs Chuck Knight and later Ted Mason, controlled the community's destiny. However, that perception was not accurate.

In 1974, the Province under Bill 55 appointed a Northeastern Alberta Regional Commission which was granted extraordinary powers to monitor and manage Fort McMurray's growth during Syncrude's construction period. One day, Premier Peter Lougheed called in a retired navy officer Vic Henning and offered him a challenge. Under Bill 55, Henning would become a type of Deputy Minister with special powers to "fast track" development of schools, roads, water, sewer and other services without having to follow traditional government procedures.

Bill 55 gave full control of Fort McMurray and surrounding region to the Regional Commissioner who had special powers to usurp the Hospitals Act, the Schools Act and the Highway Act, among other legislation.

"The idea was to speed up development of some of these essential services and have them ready for the population to come,"[109] recalled Henning. Each Thursday morning, Henning and his staff traveled to Edmonton and met with Lougheed's cabinet where decisions on how and when to build schools, highways and other important services were discussed.

At a time when Fort McMurray's limited tax base could not support expansion of services to new subdivisions, the Regional Commissioner ensured that Syncrude, Alberta Housing Corporation and others anted their share to develop areas such as Thickwood Heights with a minimum of delay.

Schools now

One of Henning's assistants, Gary Shantz recalled that while it was government policy to refrain from building a school until enough students gathered in a given area, Henning could meet with cabinet and recommend an immediate go ahead.

Sometimes Henning would become involved in issues which appeared trivial to government officials, but were important to local residents. For example, while driving south to Edmonton on Highway 63, Shantz noticed seriously deteriorating pavement near Wandering River. When Shantz called the Alberta Transportation's manager in St. Paul to ask if the area could be resurfaced, he was told that it would take two to three years of budget approvals before the problem could be addressed.

"At the Cabinet meeting that same Thursday, we were asked how everything was and Vic mentioned that there was this problem about the pavement near Wandering River which would require three years to fix," Shantz recalled. "Transportation Minister Boomer Adair got up and picked up the phone, and by the time we returned back to Fort McMurray there were crews already working on the road."[110]

Knight versus Mason: Unvisited

While Vic Henning had ultimate power over Fort McMurray from 1974-80, he was often reluctant to use it. Henning left strict orders to his staff that at no time should the commissioner's office be seen to be interfering with Fort McMurray's elected process.

The closest Henning ever came was in 1977 following the Fort McMurray municipal election as controversy raged over who should become Town Board Chair. When it became apparent that Mason, despite finishing lower in the polls, would defeat Chuck Knight in a vote among town board members, a delegation came to Henning asking him to intervene.

"The discussion centred around whether Chuck Knight despite having led the polls was entitled to be the Town Board Chairman," recalled Henning. "I had the power to change things, but it also was clear that if I did so, three or four members of council who supported Mason would resign and I would be left to run the town."[111]

Henning stayed clear of the debate.

City or not?

In 1979, Town Board began discussing a move to city status. There were pros and cons associated with the decision. Under city status, Fort McMurray would benefit from provincial support in maintaining Highway 63 as it ran through the community. There were also some special grants which were available under city status which Fort McMurray could not access as a town.

On the other hand, moving from New Town status meant that McMurray tax-payers would potentially be responsible for the servicing of new subdivisions, and would not have direct access to the Alberta cabinet.

In the end, city status amounted to just that – status. It was felt that with a population which was approaching thirty thousand, it was time for Fort McMurray to take its place among other Alberta communities. Fort McMurray also wanted the support of other municipalities to help steer some of Suncor and Syncrude's royalties into its revenue base. City status would give Fort McMurray increased clout.

"I felt it was a good idea," said Henning. "Fort McMurray was just as big as Saskatoon in 1937 where I grew up and Saskatoon was a city. Aside from that, services had already been installed to support employees of a third oil sands plant, so the burden to taxpayers would not be huge."[112]

In late 1979, the Alberta cabinet, based partly on Henning's recommendations approved city status for Fort McMurray. The date set for final transfer was September 1, 1980, barely six weeks shy of the next municipal election. Ted Mason became the City of Fort McMurray's first mayor.

During celebrations marking Fort McMurray's shift to city status, Mayor Mason voiced a phrase which would serve as a vision statement for the community during the early 1980s., "Our city will be what we make it," he said.

From fort to city

A city? Could Peter Pond or John Moberly have envisioned it?

Could John Macoun have pictured gargantuan oil sands machines in the 1880s when he scooped his first handful of oil sand? Could Count Von Hammerstein have ever conceived that the mysterious black ground which almost drove him to madness would one day yield a million barrels a day?

The rise of the oil sands has been nothing short of a modern miracle. It has taken the efforts of dedicated scientists, researchers, workers and dreamers.

A few days after my arrival in Fort McMurray in 1976, I was sent by my editor to cover the Nistawoyou Friendship Centre's annual Oldtimer's Dinner. Aboriginal elders, surrounded by loved ones, spoke of rivers, berries, fish and birds. Meanwhile, a mile away, heavy oil sands machinery rumbled along Highway 63.

The history of Fort McMurray is one of parallel and often competing realities; oil and the outsiders versus those residents who call Fort McMurray home. Since the time of Peter Pond, Fort McMurray has been viewed by many as a place to exploit, and it would have been easy for this history to have dealt solely with commodities, such as furs, salt, fish and oil. But this would not have been true to history.

The real story of Fort McMurray will always be its people. Why is it that residents who lived in Fort McMurray up to fifty years ago still regard Fort McMurray as home? Perhaps it is because no other community challenges its residents as much.

When I co-launched the Fort McMurray Express newspaper in 1979, I had a dream of building the business up, selling it and retiring by my mid 40s. Like most people who come to Fort McMurray, the dream you seek is rarely the dream you achieve. I haven't made my million yet, but I have gained more. I learned about community and about the value of friends. I have learned about love and children and about my strengths and limitations. Aren't you the same?

In 1900, there were only twenty-six residents in Fort McMurray. We could probably name each one, and recount their stories. In 2001, there are more than forty-five thousand people in the area. They all left families. They all left communities. They all arrived with apprehension. They all came in search of a job, a dream or a better life.

While the numbers and magnitude increase each year, Fort McMurray, and the Great Spirit which guides it remain constant.

Fort McMurray booms today with shopping malls, concert halls, super stores and four lane highways, but if you listen closely, you can still hear the voices of a small community which carried on its business in isolation from the world. Each year, hundreds of former residents return to McMurray to reclaim a remnant of their past, or recapture the magic they knew. They hear the sounds and relive the feelings.

Ruth Schiltroth, daughter of Dim Silin now lives in Consort, Alberta but she travels to Fort McMurray every few years to retrieve a part of her soul. She remembers train porter Len Williams selling chocolate milk from the steps of Muskeg Express. She remembers standing along the banks of the Athabasca River on Christmas Eve, under the northern lights, hearing the approaching bells of the sled dogs, watching as the people of Fort McKay rippled closer along the river to attend midnight mass.

"I see McMurray the way it was, not the way it is now," she said. "When I'm back, it becomes what it was and I'm right back there. Maybe that's why I love to go back. I feel a very strong connection and it would be sad not to have that. I need to go back, stand in those places and feel it again."

Wherever they live now, the Spirit endures, and its people remember.

Epilogue

In June 1979, a newspaper was launched in Fort McMurray which focused on local issues and personalities. The first edition of the *Fort McMurray Express* appeared on June 21.

One of the most popular *EXPRESS* features was a column penned by the author titled *On the Street*. In the spirit of the *On the Street* column, here are some scattered facts, stories and observations about the 1970s which due to time and space were not included in the previous chapter.

Which one were you?

There were all kinds of people who rode the Diversified buses to GCOS and Syncrude. One day over the coffee machine at the Diversified bus barn, drivers categorized their passengers. Which one were you; the sleeper, the reader, the thinker, the talker, the walkman, or the most despised of all —- the snorer?

Be honest department:

During the early days of Highway 63, the left hand turn east of Grassland towards Fort McMurray was poorly marked. All those who missed the turnoff and landed up in Atmore or Lac La Biche, please raise your hand.

Bright idea department:

Whose bright idea was it to install payphones in Fort McMurray which required you to insert your dime only after the party you called answered. And how many dimes did you lose before you figured that one out?

They don't make them like that any more:

One of the most memorable moments at Town Board came in 1977 when outgoing councillor Claire Peden became incensed over the administration's plan to spend twenty thousand dollars tearing down an old boathouse along the Snye. The town was prepared to hire consultants, which Peden termed "insultants." Peden rented a "cat" and the next day mowed down the boathouse. Total cost was three hundred dollars. Of course, Peden got to keep the lumber.

How to boost movie sales:

The arrival of the Exorcist at the Fort Theatre produced a massive public outcry. Members of a number of religious groups picketed outside the theatre protesting the theatre's decision to host the movie. What was the end result? For many years, the Exorcist held the Fort Theatre's all time attendance record.

Trivia Department:

When it was complete, the Gregoire Mobile Home Park became Canada's largest mobile home park.... From the time it opened in 1970, to the mid 1980s, the water fountain at the Islander Inn had raised more than fifteen thousand dollars for local charity...The record for longest service by a municipal employee in one position was set by Jerry Bussieres who joined the town in 1959 as secretary treasurer, and remained until 1994....It has often been said that Fort McMurray is Newfoundland's third largest city. The wave of newcomers from The Rock hit full force in the 1980s, but began during the late part of the 1970s.

The great chicken story:

The late Jerry Jason was a skilled business person and great supporter of community organizations, but every now and then, he found himself in bizarre situations. In the spring of 1977, I received a call from a town employee to rush to the municipal landfill. Earlier in the day, the freezer in Jason's restaurant had broken down, and staff was told to place boxes of chickens in the nearby alley. Unfortunately, a municipal garbage truck loaded the hundreds of chickens and transported them to the land fill. Minutes later, Jason realized what had happened and raced to the dump. Jason began negotiating to retrieve his chickens. A major argument ensued. Jason lost.

Nice guys finish last department:

When you're a doctor in a small community, there's no end to the strange requests you receive. There was the time in the early-1970s when Dr. Al Nicholson took a seriously-injured dog to Fort McMurray hospital. Nicholson operated on the dog on the hospital board table. Although he saved the dog's life, Nicholson temporarily lost his privileges.

They were wrong department:

When Abasand Heights was first built there were those who predicted that within twenty-five years it would become a slum. It's been twenty-five years, and Abasand remains one of Fort McMurray's cleanest and most vibrant subdivisions.

Urban legend department:

The Riviera Motel during the early-1970s was lost and won in a poker game…One Fort McMurray resident made a mint during 1970 by betting money on Hockey Night in Canada games. Unfortunately, those he bet against in the local bar didn't realize they were betting on one week old hockey games being aired through CBC's Frontier package….Following a major win at the Bechtel camp poker table, one employee went missing and was never heard from again.

Humble beginning department:

Each one of us has a story of how we first arrived in Fort McMurray. Lawyers Bob Campbell and Adam Germain came and opened their business with no front door. They cooked wieners on the balcony of their apartment before they could afford restaurants. One night in 1974 eleven local men were taken into custody on drug charges. Germain, who had been "schmoozing" local RCMP, got the call, and their law firm moved to Fort McMurray's main stage. One of the clients gave them a $100 dollar bill as a retainer. They had no safe so the lawyers placed the cash in a law book. To this day no one can remember which book it was.

Famous people:

Actor Tantoo Cardinal who starred in Hollywood films such as *Dances with Wolves* is an Anzac native….Bob Parks, formerly of the *Beachcombers* was a cab driver and frequent resident…The famous professional wrestler, Little Beaver, was also a Fort McMurray resident. He was killed by a passing car in the late-1970s as he walked along Highway 63 near Morrison Street.

First recollections:

Everyone has a first recollection of Fort McMurray. Mine occurred on October 5, 1976 about sixty miles south of town as my 1968 Dodge Monaco came into CJOK range. As I tuned my radio to 1260 I heard an odd program called The Trading Post. A fellow named John Shields listed items and would utter four numbers at the end of each call. Later I realized that these were phone numbers. All numbers at the time began with 743…Other CJOK memories of the mid-1970s include the Bay Country Request Line, J.C Travel Time and late night evangelists Pastor Harry F. Rockwood and J.D. Carlson.

Can you name them:

During the late 1960s, planners divided Fort McMurray into areas. Can you name areas one through seven? (and don't forget Area 5A). They are in order 1)

Abasand Heights, 2) Beacon Hill, 3) unnamed 4) Forest Heights, 5)Thickwood Heights 5A) Timberlea, and 6) Gregoire Park. Area 7 remains unnamed.

Lost memories:

Beef and Brew, Café Boreal, Peter Pond Hotel, Haxton's Store, Beacon Hill Sports, MacLeods, The Tarsands Savings and Credit Union, Hill Drugs, the Townsite Arena, the Community Centre, Peter Pond School, St. John's School, Wolff's Men's Wear, Offereins, O'Reilly's Restaurant, Black Tower, Cattle Company, Pier 7, Harry's Food Market, Frontier Streak House, Mrs. Jewitt's Dress Shop, Jasper Pizza, Cote's Car Wash, Twilight Drive In, Cascade Pizza, the twice weekly NAR train.

Where have all the motels gone?

During the early-1970s, a number of motels and inns sprouted on the east end of Franklin Avenue. Hats off in memory of the Executive Inn, Caravan Motel, Prairie View, Heartbreak Hotel, Cedar Crest Lodge and Aero Motel.

McMurray Raspberry Department:

Flyers advertising lots in the Okanogan which flooded Fort McMurray mail-boxes....Lifesavers which were so old by the time they got to Fort McMurray, you needed to chew off the coating before getting to the candy...Fireworks on July 1 which no one could see....Speed bumps and dips on Alberta Drive...the McKinnon Street speed traps...Getting the last shriveled green pepper at Thompson's Super A...Nightly power failures and waking up to flashing VCR and alarm clock displays...The name "Fort Mac" coined by Edmonton media, and despised by McMurrayites.

Television oddities:

Choosing between the CBC nightly news in three times zones.....Watching Johnny Carson at 9:30 p.m......The day an errant ABC Cable employee pressed the wrong button, and replaced Sesame Street with a movie whose title began with Debbie Does...

Enduring memories:

Canadian Heavyweight boxing champion Danny Lindstrom....Ches Dicks reading the British soccer scores on CJOK...Aluminum foil covering windows during summer months....Fur coats, jeans and cowboy boots....Stereos and Camaros paid for with cash...Fireman Joe Gauthier walking on King Street each morning on his way to work...Ravens so large that they forced cars to detour...Tim Melvin singing "You Ain't Going Nowhere" on Canada Day...Waterways Pride....Sudden blizzards of dandelion fuzz or mysterious insects...Santa's helpers, Dave Golding and Tiny O'Brien....the government rite line "Clare speaking"....

Nick DeHoog:

One of Fort McMurray's unsung heroes for the last thirty-five years has been Canadian Regional Airlines manager Nick DeHoog. DeHoog has added a degree of heart and compassion into the often cold business of air travel. His contribution to the community's sports scene, in particular to the Fort McMurray Oil Barons, makes him a local legend.

DeHoog recalls during GCOS and Syncrude construction days, Pacific Western Airline (PWA) jets arriving on the hour, packed with construction workers, and leaving with burned-out, often-intoxicated labourers. On more than one occasion, when the PWA jet was delayed, DeHoog would appease his disgruntled flyers with a beer until he could find a way to get everyone home.....DeHoog also recalled an attempt by a worker who had robbed a local vending machine company to load a two hundred pound hockey bag on one of his flights. DeHoog alerted the RCMP and an arrest was made.....What are your favourite names for PWA. Do they include Please Wait Awhile, Piggly Wiggly Airlines and Peter's Wandering Airlines?

During the last two years, I have travelled throughout Canada and parts of the United States piecing together Fort McMurray's story.

At times writing this book seemed like a mission. Scattered throughout North America were former residents who clutched a small piece of Fort McMurray nestled in a period of time.

As I walk through Fort McMurray in 2001, I see so many residents with a look of bewilderment and excitement; perhaps the same look that James Cornwall, Walter Hill, Hugh Stroud, Frank O'Coffey or Mac McCormick wore.

Fort McMurray remains one of the world's best keep secrets, not just because of its oil industry, but also because of the tenacity of its people.

We remain bound by similar stories, similar frustrations and similar joys. It is said that oil and water never mix. In spite of the booms and busts associated with the oil industry, it is the people of Fort McMurray who remain the water. We flow freely and we remain forever tied to Fort McMurray.

In Fort McMurray I know who I am. Chances are, you do too.

Have a good one.

Index
of Fort McMurray Personalities

Footnotes

Chapter One

1. Saxburg & Reeves Report, Syncrude Canada Limited 1996.
2. Ibid
3. Ibid
4. Bumsted, J.M. Fur Trade Wars. Great Plains Publications, Winnipeg, Manitoba. Copyright 1999.
5. Francis, Daniel. Battle for the West: Fur Traders and the Birth of Western Canada. Hurtig Publishers, Edmonton, Alberta. Copyright 1982.
6. Bumsted
7. The Diary of Peter Pond
8. Ibid
9. Francis
10. Comfort, Darlene. Meeting Place of Many Waters: A History of Fort McMurray. Comfort Enterprises, Canada. Copyright 1973.
11. Francis
12. Gough, Barry. First Across the Continent: Sir Alexander Mackenzie. University of Oklahoma Press, Norman, McLelland & Stewart, Inc. Toronto, Ontario. Copyright 1997.
13. Francis
14. Francis
15. Gough
16. Francis
17. The Diary of Peter Pond
18. Gough
19. Gough
20. Comfort
21. Gough
22. Gough
23. Comfort
24. Gough
25. Francis
26. Comfort
27. Comfort
28. Moberly, Henry 'John'. When Fur Was King. H.J. & Cameron, W.B. London 1929. Courtesy of the University of Alberta Book & Record Depository, Edmonton, Alberta
29. Moberly
30. Moberly
31. Moberly
32. Moberly
33. Comfort
34. Moberly
35. Ibid
36. Moberly
37. Moberly
38. Ibid
39. Ibid
40. Ibid
41. Macoun, John. Manitoba and the great North-West: the field for investment; the home of the emigrant, being a full and complete history of the country...to which has been added the educational and religious history of Manitoba & the north-west, by George M. Grant: A history of the Roman Catholic missions in St. Boniface, contributed by his Grace the Archbishop Taché's secretary; also, Montana and the Bow River District compared for grazing purposes, by Alexandre Begg...; also sketches of the rise and progress of Winnipeg, by J.C. McLagan. Guelph, World Publications, Co. Copyright 1882.
42. Macoun
43. Macoun
44. Macoun
45. Macoun
46. Macoun
47. Macoun
48. Reports of Dr. Robert Bell, courtesy of the Fort McMurray Historical Society

49. Dr. G. Christian Hoffman, Geological Survey of Canada - Reports. Courtesy of the Fort McMurray Historical Society.

50. Bell, Dr. Robert. 'Report on Part of the Basin of the Athabasca River.' Courtesy of the Fort McMurray Historical Society.

51. Comfort

52. History of Athabasca Landing, courtesy of the Fort McMurray Historical Society

53. Memoirs of Lawrence Rye, courtesy of the Fort McMurray Historical Society

54. Reports of R.G. McConnell, 1890-91, courtesy of the Fort McMurray Historical Society

55. Dahlgren, Dorothy. Tales of the Tarsands. Bernard Jean Publishing, Fort McMurray, Alberta. Copyright 1975.

56. Dawson, Dr. George M. Reports to the Geological Survey of Canada, courtesy of the Fort McMurray Historical Society.

57. Northwest Mounted Police, reports - Routledge, January 5, 1898. Courtesy of the Fort McMurray Historical Society.

58. Royal Canadian Mounted Police, reports - D.M. Howard, 1898. Courtesy of the Fort McMurray Historical Society.

59. MacGregor, J.G. Paddle Wheels to Bucket Wheels on the Athabasca. McLelland & Stewart, Toronto, Ontario. Copyright 1974.

60. Dahlgren

61. Treaty 8, 1899. Courtesy of the University of Alberta Archives.

62. Treaty 8, 1899. Courtesy of the University of Alberta Archives.

63. Irwin Huberman Interviews

64. Ibid

Chapter Two

1. Irwin Huberman Interviews

2. Keele, J. - Correspondence courtesy of the University of Alberta Archives, Edmonton, Alberta.

3. Irwin Huberman Interviews

4. Ibid

5. Ibid

6. Laffont, Father Adophe - Journal courtesy of the Fort McMurray Historical Society.

7. Laffont

8. Laffont

9. Irwin Huberman Interviews

10. Ells, Sydney - Journal courtesy of the Fort McMurray Historical Society

11. Ells

12. Irwin Huberman Interviews

13. Ibid

14. Andrews, Guy R. From the Vancouver Sun, June 24, 1913.

15. Ibid

16. The Vancouver Sun, June 24, 1913

17. Irwin Huberman Interviews

18. Ibid

19. Government of Canada, correspondence - courtesy of the University of Alberta Archives.

20. The Edmonton Journal, September 23, 1913.

21. Irwin Huberman Interviews

22. Official documents, Roman Catholic Church - courtesy of the Provincial Archives of Alberta, Edmonton, Alberta.

23. Comfort, Darlene. Pass the McMurray Salt, Please: The Alberta Salt Company as Remembered by Three Fort McMurray Pioneers. First Edition, Fort McMurray, Alberta. Copyright 1975.

Chapter Three

1. Karl A. Clark Correspondence, courtesy of University of Alberta Archives, Edmonton, Alberta

2. Ibid

3. Cecil Swanson

4. Irwin Huberman Interviews

5. Irwin Huberman Interviews

6. Irwin Huberman Interviews

7. Irwin Huberman Interviews

8. Irwin Huberman Interviews

9. Parsons, E.G. McMurray Royal Bank branch opening, September 25, 1921

10. Irwin Huberman Interviews

11. Irwin Huberman Interviews

12. McMurray Courier, July 1970

13. Irwin Huberman Interviews

14. Ibid

15. Diary of Ellen McDermott

16. Irwin Huberman Interviews

17. Irwin Huberman Interviews

18. Irwin Huberman Interviews

19. Comfort, Darlene. Pass the McMurray Salt, Please.
20. Irwin Huberman Interviews
21. Irwin Huberman Interviews
22. Diary of Ellen McDermott
23. Ibid
24. Irwin Huberman Interviews
25. Irwin Huberman Interviews
26. Irwin Huberman Interviews
27. Irwin Huberman Interviews
28. Irwin Huberman Interviews
29. Irwin Huberman Interviews
30. Irwin Huberman Interviews
31. Irwin Huberman Interviews
32. Irwin Huberman Interviews
33. Ball, Max W. This Fascinating Oil Business.
34. Ells Report.
35. Irwin Huberman Interviews
36. Irwin Huberman Interviews
37. Irwin Huberman Interviews
38. Irwin Huberman Interviews
39. Irwin Huberman Interviews
40. Gwen Iris Spearman family biography, courtesy of the Fort McMurray Historical Society.
41. Ibid
42. Irwin Huberman Interviews
43. Irwin Huberman Interviews
44. Hudson's Bay Company Promotional Brochures
45. Irwin Huberman Interviews
46. Irwin Huberman Interviews
47. Irwin Huberman Interviews
48. Irwin Huberman Interviews
49. Irwin Huberman Interviews
50. Irwin Huberman Interviews
51. Irwin Huberman Interviews
52. Irwin Huberman Interviews
53. Irwin Huberman Interviews
54. Irwin Huberman Interviews
55. Irwin Huberman Interviews
56. Irwin Huberman Interviews
57. Irwin Huberman Interviews
58. Irwin Huberman Interviews
59. Irwin Huberman Interviews
60. Calgary Herald.
61. Irwin Huberman Interviews
62. Irwin Huberman Interviews
63. Irwin Huberman Interviews
64. Irwin Huberman Interviews
65. Irwin Huberman Interviews
66. Irwin Huberman Interviews
67. Irwin Huberman Interviews
68. Irwin Huberman Interviews
69. The Karl Clark Diaries, courtesy of the University of Alberta Archives, Edmonton, Alberta
70. The Truth About Alberta Tar Sands: Why they were kept out of production, 1953
71. Ibid
72. Irwin Huberman Interviews
73. Irwin Huberman Interviews
74. Irwin Huberman Interviews
75. Irwin Huberman Interviews
76. Irwin Huberman Interviews
77. Irwin Huberman Interviews
78. Irwin Huberman Interviews
79. Northwest Review, May 15; May 22, 1939.
80. Ibid
81. Ibid
82. Ibid
83. Ibid
84. Ibid
85. Ibid
86. Ibid
87. Ibid
88. Ibid
89. Irwin Huberman Interviews

Chapter Four

1. Irwin Huberman Interviews
2. Irwin Huberman Interviews
3. Irwin Huberman Interviews
4. Irwin Huberman Interviews
5. Valhalla Star, April 4, 1939.
6. Ibid
7. Ibid
8. Ibid
9. Ibid
10. Irwin Huberman Interviews
11. Irwin Huberman Interviews

12. Irwin Huberman Interviews
13. Irwin Huberman Interviews
14. Irwin Huberman Interviews
15. Irwin Huberman Interviews
16. Government correspondence, 1942, courtesy of the Fort McMurray Historical Society.
17. Irwin Huberman Interviews
18. Irwin Huberman Interviews
19. Irwin Huberman Interviews
20. Irwin Huberman Interviews
21. Irwin Huberman Interviews
22. Irwin Huberman Interviews
23. Irwin Huberman Interviews
24. Irwin Huberman Interviews
25. Irwin Huberman Interviews
26. Irwin Huberman Interviews
27. Irwin Huberman Interviews
28. Irwin Huberman Interviews
29. Irwin Huberman Interviews
30. Irwin Huberman Interviews
31. Irwin Huberman Interviews
32. Irwin Huberman Interviews
33. Irwin Huberman Interviews
34. Irwin Huberman Interviews
35. Irwin Huberman Interviews

Chapter Five

All sources marked in this chapter were taken from interviews performed by the author.

Chapter Six

1. Irwin Huberman Interviews
2. Irwin Huberman Interviews
3. Irwin Huberman Interviews
4. Irwin Huberman Interviews
5. Irwin Huberman Interviews
6. Irwin Huberman Interviews
7. Irwin Huberman Interviews
8. Fort McMurray Chamber of Commerce, courtesy of the Fort McMurray Historical Society.
9. Irwin Huberman Interviews
10. Irwin Huberman Interviews
11. Irwin Huberman Interviews
12. Irwin Huberman Interviews
13. Irwin Huberman Interviews
14. Irwin Huberman Interviews
15. Irwin Huberman Interviews
16. Irwin Huberman Interviews
17. Irwin Huberman Interviews
18. Irwin Huberman Interviews
19. Irwin Huberman Interviews
20. Irwin Huberman Interviews
21. Irwin Huberman Interviews
22. Irwin Huberman Interviews
23. Irwin Huberman Interviews
24. Irwin Huberman Interviews
25. Irwin Huberman Interviews
26. Irwin Huberman Interviews
27. Irwin Huberman Interviews
28. Irwin Huberman Interviews
29. Irwin Huberman Interviews
30. Irwin Huberman Interviews
31. Irwin Huberman Interviews
32. Irwin Huberman Interviews
33. Irwin Huberman Interviews
34. Irwin Huberman Interviews
35. Irwin Huberman Interviews
36. Irwin Huberman Interviews
37. Irwin Huberman Interviews
38. Irwin Huberman Interviews
39. Irwin Huberman Interviews
40. Irwin Huberman Interviews
41. Irwin Huberman Interviews
42. Irwin Huberman Interviews
43. The Edmonton Journal, October 2, 1964
44. Irwin Huberman Interviews
45. Irwin Huberman Interviews
46. Irwin Huberman Interviews
47. Irwin Huberman Interviews
48. Irwin Huberman Interviews
49. Irwin Huberman Interviews
50. Irwin Huberman Interviews
51. Irwin Huberman Interviews
52. Irwin Huberman Interviews
53. Irwin Huberman Interviews
54. Irwin Huberman Interviews
55. Irwin Huberman Interviews

56. Irwin Huberman Interviews
57. Irwin Huberman Interviews
58. Irwin Huberman Interviews
59. Irwin Huberman Interviews
60. Irwin Huberman Interviews
61. Irwin Huberman Interviews
62. Irwin Huberman Interviews
63. Irwin Huberman Interviews
64. Irwin Huberman Interviews
65. Irwin Huberman Interviews
66. Irwin Huberman Interviews
67. Irwin Huberman Interviews
68. Irwin Huberman Interviews
69. Fitzgerald, Joseph J. Black Gold With Grit.
70. Irwin Huberman Interviews

Chapter Seven

All sources marked in this chapter, apart from that noted 11, were taken from interviews performed by the author.

11. NB: All information on Keyano College and its history was taken from: Kelly, Patricia. Take A Look At Us Now! Keyano College: Twenty-Five Years. Copyright May 1991.

Patrons

The research and publication of this book, has been made possible through the support and generous donations by the following individuals and companies. The Historical Book Society gratefully acknowledges their contributions.

Patrons

Alberta Heritage Resources Foundation
Alberta Lottery Commission
Albian Sands - Shell Canada Ltd.
Alcor Group of Companies
Atco Electric
Bob Barrett Men's Apparel
Fred & Esther Borger
Norm and Diane Briscoe
Steve and Shirley Brooks
Byers Transport Ltd.
Campbell Germain Cooper & Jean
Canadian Airlines
The Castiglione Family
Cedar's Steak House
CEP Union
CJOK Radio
Dr. Joel Clark
Clearwater Mechanical Ltd.
Jack and Roberta Cross
Grace Dafoe
Nick De Hoog
Steve and Barb Dewar
Norm and Jeanine Dube
Duke's Transport Ltd.
Everall Construction Ltd.
Roy and Bev Ewashko
Finning Ltd.
First North Catering
Fort McMurray Visitors Bureau

Fort McMurray Plumbing & Heating
Fort McMurray Refrigeration
Fraser Milner Casgrain
Garry Shantz Real Estate
Doug and Carol Golosky
Golosky Trucking and Contracting
Sam and Selma Hardin
Ken and Sandra Hart
Alice Haxton
Heritage Park
Diane and Ken Hill
Imperial Oil Charitable Foundation
Japan Canada Oil Sands Limited
Bernard and Frances Jean
Brian and Barb Jean
Jean Family Enterprises Ltd.
Klemke Construction
Luella Knight
KYX 98 Radio
Betty Lamb
Lemax Machine & Welding
McDonald's Restaurants
Manchester Chivers & Associates
McMurray Glass
McMurray Serv-U Expediting
Dave and Vivian McNeilly
Mills Law Office
Charlotte Mitchell
Larry and Sharon Nelson

Northland Forest Products Ltd.
Oilsands Discovery Centre
Oil Sands Hotel
Oil Sands Pioneers Club
Jack and Mary-Jane Peden
Fred and Bunny Philpott
Regional Municipality of Wood Buffalo
Victoria Rivers
Leo and Debbie Robert
Roy Solbak & Walsh
Royal Bank of Canada
Emile and Louise Royer
Don and Yvette Rumpel
Doug and Inez Schmit
Charlie Somers
Sterling Crane
Suncor Energy Foundation
Syncrude Canada Limited
Dora Thompson
Hank and Lila Thompson
Tom and Dawn Weber
The Print Shop Etc.
Tridon Communications
True North Energy
Unisource Canada Inc.
Walsh Real Estate
Dave Watson
John and Leslie Wilson and family
Glen and Marilyn Young
Shirley Young
Tim and Lesa Young
Ron & Evy Wolff

Champions

Every project needs champions to set direction and drive the course. Driven by their collective passion for Fort McMurray and history, the following are the Champions of A Place Called Home....

Art Avery
Joan Barrett
David and Fern Brooks
Jerry and Elva Bussieres
Bev Ewashko
Fort McMurray Visitor's Bureau
Alice Haxton
Diane and Ken Hill
Bernard and Frances Jean
Brian Jean
Evelyn Jean-Clewes
Bert MacKay
Ron Morgan
Anne Young
Jean Woodhouse

Highway
63

Thickwood
Road

Schmidt
Creek

Grant Island

The Forks

Rocke Island

MacDonald Island

Snye

Clearwater River

Timberlea

Dickensfield   Thickwood

Heights

Moberly Rapids

Fort
McMurray

Athabasca River

Horse River

Hangingstone River

Waterways

Keyano
College
MacKenzie
Campus

Old Waterways
(Draper)

Saline Creek

Truck
Trail

63

Athabasca
River

Old HBC

Horse R
* Salt Pla